Ada® in use

Proceedings of the
Ada International Conference 1985

The Ada Companion Series

There are currently no better candidates for a co-ordinated low-risk, and synergetic approach to software development than the Ada programming language. Integrated into a support environment, Ada promises to give a solid standards-orientated foundation for higher professionalism in software engineering.

This definitive series aims to be the guide to the Ada software industry for managers, implementors, software producers and users. It deals with all aspects of the emerging industry: adopting an Ada strategy, conversion issues, style and portability issues, and management. To assist the organised development of an Ada-orientated software components industry, equal emphasis is placed on all phases of life cycle support.

Some current titles:

Life cycle support in the Ada environment
Ed. J. McDermid and K. Ripken

Portability and style in Ada
Ed. J.C.D. Nissen and P.J.L. Wallis

Ada: Language, compilers and bibliography
Ed. M.W. Rogers

Ada for multi-microprocessors
Ed. M. Tedd, S. Crespi-Reghizzi and A. Natali

Proceedings of the Third Joint Ada Europe/Ada TEC Conference
Ed. J. Teller

Concurrent programming in Ada
A. Burns

Ada for specification: possibilities and limitations
Ed. S.J. Goldsack

Proceedings of the Ada International Conference 1985
Ed. J.G.P. Barnes and G.A. Fisher

Ada in use

Proceedings of the
Ada International Conference 1985

Edited by

JOHN G.P. BARNES
ALSYS Ltd

GERALD A. FISHER, Jr
IBM Research

The right of the
University of Cambridge
to print and sell
all manner of books
was granted by
Henry VIII in 1534.
The University has printed
and published continuously
since 1584.

Published on behalf of
the Association for Computing Machinery and
Ada Europe by
CAMBRIDGE UNIVERSITY PRESS
Cambridge
London New York New Rochelle
Melbourne Sydney

Published by the Press Syndicate of the University of Cambridge
The Pitt Building, Trumpington Street, Cambridge CB2 1RP
32 East 57th Street, New York, NY 10022, USA
10 Stamford Road, Oakleigh, Melbourne 3166, Australia

First published 1985

Printed in Great Britain at the University Press, Cambridge

British Library and Library of Congress Cataloguing
in Publication data available

ISBN 0 521 309689

Contents

CHAIRMEN'S REMARKS

This conference marked a historical turning point in the development of the Ada program, in that it was ten years ago that David Fisher of the Institute for Defense Analyses in Washington DC proposed that an effort be undertaken to produce a programming language for embedded computer systems. Originally fostered by the High Order Language Working Group (HOLWG), the extension of Ada from the early stages of implementation into the era of usage, has largely been overseen by SIGAda (previously the Ada Implementers Group, and then AdaTEC). The period of uncertainty about the language as an implementable, validatible system is now over and we are entering a period when the faith which we had in Ada is confirmed by its usage. This conference marks the entry into that stage, the papers which have been collected representing only the "camel's nose" of the burgeoning acceptance of Ada into the tent of software engineering. There is no longer a concern about the respectability of being associated either with the language or its initial sponsor, the US Department of Defense.

Just twenty-five years ago another product of the DoD's initiative was taking its first steps into the commercial world of computing - COBOL. A comparison of the histories of these two languages is fascinating in their similarity. Like Ada, the COBOL community was concerned with transportability and even organised a demonstration of the ability of the language to be supported on two different computers - the precursor of Ada validation activities. Like Ada, COBOL was subjected to scrutiny by its competitors and come out a winner because of good implementations and the acceptance of the language by users. The well-known maxim of software engineering that suggests that the second implementation is a vast improvement over the first, is surely true in the case - some people are even suggesting that Ada will replace COBOL!

The organization of this conference has been a test of international cooperation which we believe has been successful. Elsewhere you will find a listing of the organizing committee and their assistants. Our thanks goes to them all, but especially we must thank Mike Rogers of the EEC, whose ignomineous title of "Secretary" belies his real contributions. Without Mike none of us would have been able to survive the ordeal of organization - he has been everywhere all the time; our special thanks to him. Our thanks also to the Program Co-chairmen Gerry Fisher and John Barnes; they have selected a set of papers which prove that the Ada community is truly worthy of membership in the scientific, technical societies of the world of information processing. They have every reason to be proud of their accomplishments.

We hope that this conference will mean as much to you following your attendance as it has meant for us to organise it. We know that Ada Augusta, Lady Lovelace, did visit Paris on occasion; we hope that this later visit of her namesake will be remembered also.

Horst Huenke
Jan Lee

Conference Co-chairmen

PROGRAM CO-CHAIRMEN'S FOREWORD

This was the first truly International Conference on Ada. It was organised and sponsored by ACM SIGAda in collaboration with Ada-Europe (Commission of the European Communities) and AFCET. It was also the third Ada conference organised by the ACM, the previous ones being in 1980 (Boston) and 1982 (Washington).

The conference theme was "Ada in Use"; 1985 is notable as being the year in which production quality Ada compilers really became widely available and so at last Ada can be considered as a tool for NOW rather than something for the future. We would like to thank the authors of the 94 papers which were submitted; unfortunately timing considerations allowed us to accept only 29 for presentation.

The quality of papers was high and the selection process was thus rather frustrating since many good papers had to be rejected. We would like to acknowledge the efforts of the two program committees (US and Europe) for their work; they were:

EUROPE	USA
Jacques Andre	Bryce Bardin
Bjarne Dacker	Ron Brender
Leif Ibsen	Gary Dismukes
Ole Oest	Larry Druffel
Michael Pickett	Robert Firth
Knut Ripken	Paul Hilfinger
Olivier Roubine	Thomas Probert
Vic Stenning	Edmond Schonberg
Joachim Teller	Tim Standish
Brian Wichmann	Douglas Waugh

We offer particular thanks to those of the program committee who also acted as session chairmen.

The conference began with illuminating opening addresses by M Hubert Curian, the French Minister of Research and Mr Christopher Layton, formerly Director of Industrial Affairs of the Commission of the European Communities. We are very grateful for the sign of the importance of Ada accorded by these addresses. Next was the keynote address from Jean Ichbiah who is known to us all. The written papers then followed and were grouped into ten sessions covering various aspects of the application of Ada, related tools, methods and training.

Finally our thanks to the cooperating organizations and their chairmen:

- ACM/SIGAda — Anthony Gargaro, Chairman
- Ada Europe — Knut Ripken, Chairman
- AFCET — Jean-Francois Omnes

Such a large and successful conference required much organisation; we offer our thanks to our colleagues on the organising committee who were Ben Brosgol, David Emery, Katie Gaines, Tony Gargaro, Garth Glynn, Horst Huenke, Jean Ichbiah, Phillipe Kruchten, Jan Lee, Eric de Massas, Knut Ripken, Mike Rogers and Ray Young.

We finally offer our thanks to Cambridge University Press and are pleased to see the publication of these proceedings in the important and growing Ada Companion Series.

John Barnes
Gerry Fisher

Program Co-Chairmen

IT Companies' Acceptance of and Attitudes Towards Ada

Mike W. Rogers at
Commission of the European Communities
200 Rue de la Loi
B-1049 Brussels Belgium

Abstract

A survey was carried out to establish the Ada countries' knowledge about itself and the market potential of the work they were engaged in. Some 62 organisations responses were received (25%) from 10 countries. Though many are well informed, the effect of distance in such a dispersed effort weakens actions. Ada Europe plays a crucial role in this, outside of the large SIG Ada organisation. The delay in validated compilers of up to two years should be removed largely by the end of 1985, with Europe notifying a higher proportion of proposed validations than to date. Average budget overruns over 50% indicate severe difficulties in implementations, but a wider range of problems were noted than just tasking and generics and highly correlated with lack of comprehension. The early indications of the adoption of SE methodology by the Ada implementors indicate a desire to have a realistic set of functionalities in an APSE. Until some of these are provided, state of the art in SEM will not advance via Ada. The markets for Ada are impossible to assess accurately. Companies who have market studies do not release them, many more feel the word "military" is sufficient. Figures available show that relative to expectations of 1982/83, Ada penetration in 1985 is far below expectations. A sizeable public and private sector is emerging, not hampered by the side issue of validation and clamouring for more intelligence from what is seen as a "closed" military activity.

1. AWARENESS OF THE ADA COMMUNITY

Few doubt that one of Ada's strengths is the underlying collaboration that provides an essential forum for exchanging information and building support for the standardisation process. The voluntary nature of this effort adds to a sense of momentum and belonging in a technically challenging environment that has often not reached leading edge users or implementors. Yet SIG Ada of ACM, Ada-Europe and Ada-UK, suffer from a lack of awareness by individuals of the depth of their activities. Ada TEC/SIGAda have held some 15 conferences in the U.S. and produce a definitive newsletter, Ada-Letters, the CEC have invested some 0.75M$ into funding Ada-Europe for 5 years and Ada UK produce a professional newsletter and hold annual conferences.

Furthermore, as the survey sample population were all members of one of the organisations, or had attended at least one major conference in the last 12 months , it was to be expected that awareness would be higher. Between 35% and 45% of responses offered no estimates of the working groups of these three principal organisations. For SIG Ada, estimates of active working groups ranged from 1 to 30, though one third of those who responded were correct and another one third were quite close. In Ada-Europe there are a number of currently inactive groups, so a wider variation may be expected. 60% of replies fell within this range out of the enumerated responses (only 40% of all replies), though a range of 1 to 20 was encountered. Ada UK has 6 working Groups, but as it is a national body only, some 40% of replies could not estimate any response. Of those who did reply (36 replies), 80% were close to the correct answer.

It seems that size/distance effects the nature of collaboration - the bigger the organisation, the less precise details are known about it internally and externally. Also, there is very little interaction between the groups, relative to their size of membership. Though Ada Europe is numerically small, it occupies a central position in fostering interchange between the groups, informally and through supporting official delegates to the ADA Board and KIT/KITIA meetings. Of the 53 responses which attempted to estimate the total membership of the three organisations, only 15% were correct. The median value (25% of all replies) estimated 2000 as opposed to actual numbers of slightly over 5500.

Implementations are evolving in 13 countries, although two thirds of replies estimated a higher number. Bearing in mind the heavy response to the implementation and comprehension difficulties elsewhere, it is perhaps no surprise to find that 85% of replies correctly identified the number of Ada Books on the market at 25+. In fact, the actual number is over 40, so the question could have been phrased more precisely. Coupled with the retraining demand described, it seems text books are a major source of material.

2. Language Features Comprehension

Respondents were asked to give an indication of which sections of the language they found hardest to understand. 36 respondents listed 108 topics, a number of references to the "sheer complexity" suggest that the named topics represented significant difficulties. Four topics were found to cause most problems: Types, Visibility, Tasks and Generics. The common high level of difficulties encountered with the first three topics is rather surprising, relative to Generics (see table 1).

Users had less difficulties than implementors in the chapters on Statements, Subprograms, Program Structure and Compilation Issues, Exceptions, Generics, Representation Clauses and I/O, either because the features were largely familiar, well conceptualised or pure implementation issues. On occasions, more detailed descriptions of problems were offered:

Table 1

Ch.	Impl. %	Comp. %	Subject
3	11.1	16.6	Declarations and Types
	6.4	2.8	Derived Types
		2.8	Types and Subtypes
		7.4	Scalar Types
7		2.8	Packages
		2.8	Private Types
8	11.1	17.5	Visibility Rules
	6.4	9.0	Visibility
9	17.4	22.3	Tasks
		3.7	Shared Variables
	3.2		Bodies and Specifications
12	19.0		Generics
	3.2		Generic Formulae Declarations
	4.7		Instantiation
13	8.0	6.5	Representation Clauses/IDF
	3.2	2.7	Representation Clauses

Comparison indicates overall a high correlation between comprehension and implementation difficulties (r=0.82) - surprising as only one half of the respondents were implementors!

3. Implementation Difficulties

Some 22 implementors responded to the invitation to list the difficulties encountered in writing an Ada compiler. Up to three topics were invited, and a listing of 63 replies shows that most implementers took full advantage of the space provided! The breakdown per LRM (ANSI 1983) chapter is shown in Table 1. Also notable is the occasional mention of the interdependency of these effects. From the replies, it seems surprising that Generics and Tasking, usually publicly hailed as the "problem area", account for less than one half of all the difficulties encountered. As nearly 12% had difficulties with Declarations and Types, it is expected that similar difficulties are encountered mapping these to the underlying machine representation (LRM Chapter 13). Nineteen organisations qualified the budget overrun on their compiler implementation. One actually claimed to be exactly on budget and seven were within 30% of their estimate. In a project of that magnitude it seems quite acceptable, five repondents who indicated an overrun of 100% or more are of more concern. The mean was a 54% overrun on budget estimates. The sample is biased to early implementors so this should reduce as more experience accumulates.

4. Validation - The Prospects

In September of 1979, the DoD awarded the first contract to study the requirements for validation to Softech, leading to the Implementators Guide document (Goodenough) to aid the construction of correct compilers. A study was also commenced by the CEC (CEC, 1983) for the need for satellite centres for the anticipated "rush" of validations. The first definitive report (Probert) set the organisational process for validation. The procedure appeared to strain when, during early validations, up to 15% of tests were challenged at some time or another. Confidence reached an all time low when the AJPO representative did not challenge a floor speaker at the Dallas Ada TEC Conference in October 1983 when he said "currently, validation is only a political statement". Successive versions of the ACVS software have clarified many of these challenges and appears to have stabilised, down to where challenges are in simple figures.

The date of attempted validation is usually one of the most closely guarded commercial secrets of any organisation. In early 1982, the following expected validations were to take place (excluding RE validations):

	US	Non US	Total	Actual (8)
1982	3	2	5	0
1983	7	3	10	3

A purely speculative estimate for 1987 suggested 100 validations per year would be a lower bound. From the Arpanet file (Arpanet, 1985), 2 of the 3 of the 1983 validations have revalidated and there are 10 organisations who validated various host/target pairs in 1984. This was still well below expectations based on the survey:

Year	ACVS	Expected Validations	Assumed Re-Validations	Total
84	1.4	29	3	32
85	1.5/6	33	32	65 *
86	?	23	55	78

* 8 validations were expected on V1.5, and these would be expected in 1985.

Over one half of all expected 106 validations in the four operational centres in the U.S., France (BNI) and West Germany (IABG) were anticipated by end 1985, indicating that the "dam" has been breached. Of the 34 organisations who responded, 20 intended to use cross compiling techniques and 14 did not.

65 validations have been notified by European organisations up to the beginning of 1987, but nearly three quarters were foreseen by the end of 1985. This may be as a direct result of the diversity of machines covering the market sectors. Of the first 8 validations, 3 were from Europe. Based on these expectations, European organisations would be responsible for slightly over 50% of all validated Ada compilers by the end of 1985. This does not map into military market-sector coverage directly.

5. Generating Resources for an Ada Capability

Though the respondents represented companies employing 0.25M people by the end of 1985 the expectation was for a modest 1800 Ada programmers. Companies had only been able to hire 8% of those with some Ada experience. The (re-)training need is thus very high. No doubt the advent of video courses (average US$ 5,000 each (Arpanet, 1985), or about 200-500 US $/hour) has eased the strain on attended courses which were frequently overflowing. Educational discounts on compilers (eg. York, Karlsruhe, Telesoft) also no doubt helped. 80% of respondents felt more resources should go into education for the use of Ada - a view often reflected by conference BOFS. It is predicted that a shortfall of 1M software professionals by 1990 (NTIS, 1982) (DoD, 1982) will occur in the U.S. alone. Indications are that although Ada could easily raise productivity in the long term, resource shortages in the short term are likely to accentuate the problem. The CEC MAP programme allocates less than 5% of its funds to this aspect, but generated quite disproportionate interest through its major study presented in Washington in November 1984. One can only hope that CAI/CAE will snowball to automate the educational process. Currently, text books are a major source of know-how.

6. USING ADA TO FURTHER SOFTWARE ENGINEERING (SE)

The survey asked if the advent of Ada would cause SE principles to be implemented. "Principle" (Shorter Oxford English Dictionary, 1968) is the ultimate basis of the existance of something - no principle, no implementation! Principles are known to be capital intensive (Wegner, 1983) and to be "lip" served. 97 replies were recorded (table 2) - again indicating that for those willing to break into prose, available space was used, hinting that those who saw, saw much.

However, who questions the intention to use Ada to optimise features for fostering the adoption of more rigorous engineering practices - if for no other reason than to control the complexity of the paint-box of functionalities available? It was most surprising to find that ONLY 50% of respondents felt that Ada either did, or enabled, anything in SE that may be labelled "important".

Table 2 Recurring Concepts Considered Important

Concept	Frequency
Abstract Data Types/Abstraction	15
APSE	4
Configuration Control	3
Generics	3
Information Hiding	6
Modularity	7
Packages	3
Project Control	6
Reusability	5
Specification	4
Structured Programming	5
Tasking	4

Surprising by only receiving one or two mentions were: Exceptions, Libraries, Life Cycle, Pragmas, OOD, Portability, Rapid Prototyping, Separate Compilation, Static Checks, Strong Typing, Validation. There are no concepts expected that have not been theoretical conventional wisdoms for some time; so expectations are modest. Perhaps most disappointing are the absence of PORTABILITY and VALIDATION. Portability may not be a concept the reality of which has been wholly economically grasped.

VALIDATION has suffered from early set backs, but with stability and the impending increase of validations, the benefits of this activity will be seen. "PAR (Boehm, 83)" - Productivity, Adaptability and Reliability did not appear. Issues related to APSE's do not figure prominently, due to the current pressing preoccupation with implementing the language.

The analysis of the 166 keywords occurring in responses showed that CONTROL was mentioned embedded most often (Configuration/Project/Life Cycle/Version) - a hope that large projects can be controlled using Ada and APSE tools. Typing and Types were mentioned a similar number of times. The strong typing of Ada is clearly seen to be an asset. Coupled with the ambitions of the AI paradigm PSE's, one could regard these aims as rather pedestrian in their nature, yet they appear fundamental to underpinning an industry.

Ada will surely be "the last of its line". It should therefore be acknowledged that the rise of the STARS programme is a major visionary step. Today, the hopes of closing the "software gap" by 1993 must appear to be receding, though not as pessimistically as one year ago. In one year from now, when the availability of Ada tools gathers momentum, perhaps the target date will be stationary at last.

7. Ada Markets - Perceptions and Commercial Reality

Table 3 - Perceived Market Values in M US$ (at 1985 Prices) Worldwide

	1985	1987	1989	Sector
Low	10	30	60	
Medium	123	258	761	Military
High	400	800	1500	
Low	0	1	3	
Medium	32	97	214	Public
High	100	300	500	
Low	0	2	5	
Medium	67	173	462	Private
High	400	1000	2000	

The expectations (Table 3) vary widely amongst the respondents to the survey. The military market is always thought to be dominating the public plus private sector in relative terms. The majority offered no estimates and a 20% follow-up failed to elicit any more details, even from marketing departments! The pessimists virtually dismiss any public or private sector impact, but do tend to come from military oriented companies. The expectation of growth rates of optimists and pessimists alike - in the military sector 50% p.a., public and private sectors 50-100% p.a. (which are well in excess of any IT sector growth rate), point to an expected deeper penetration of Ada in established areas. Growth rates 1985-1987 were expected to be twice that of 1987-1989.

Actual markets are notoriously difficult to estimate. Experts agree that the SW market for DoD and Europe are comparable in size. In 1974 the DoD software cake was attributed to Embedded Systems 56%, DP 19%, Scientific DP 5% and "other" 20% (Ripken, 1982) and once Ada became a MIL Standard, a 20% DoD market penetration was forecast by 1985 (Mitchell, 1983). The DoD SW budget has grown from US$ 3B in 1984 (Ripken, 1982) to US$ 10B in 1985, the U.S. Department of Energy exceeding US$ 1B since 1979 and the NASA Space Station Project US$ 8B (1984-1994). DoD's own data (Kopp) shows Ada expenditure rising from US$ 350M to 1.3B in 1990.

Since the birth of Ada in 1975, weapon systems have become more complex and 56% embedded category has maintained its dominance. Ada represents only about 7% of DoD SW expenditure and in 1990 this would be expected to have risen to not more that 15%. However, most companies only expect the first Ada products revenue late 1985/1986. These will contain tool sets that will aid the penetration of Ada in this market niche to match expectations (Arthur, 1984) and indeed, 75% of vendors intend to use Ada "special" features to help the process. The UK MOD may encounter problems (Vaux, 1985) in implementing to "mandatory" level within two years, in a market estimated to be in excess of US$ 1B in 1985/1986 (Table 4).

A recent call for proposals by the CEC in Ada (Fall of '84) in line with the industrial/academic consultation with Ada-Europe (CEC, 1982) showed that although the advantages of Ada were well recognised, commercial companies were still in need of funding for potential product development. Excluding the "Ada Formal Definition", 22 proposals were received from 9 of the 10 member states of the EC (with 39 participants, mainly: UK-12, Germany-9, France-7). Funding was over subscribed about four times, with "industry" representing well over one half of participants. Some points that were evident in the CFP were:

- there was some hesitancy to commit to policy in advance of compilers becoming generally available

- full scale APSE development was premature at that time
- there seemed to be a lack of awareness of activities by others and the momentum that had gathered

Work that has commenced under this CFP can be grouped into a number of categories:

1. The Formal Definition of Ada by a very strong team with, it is hoped, useful input from others also.
2. Distributing a MAPSE, including management and configuration control, leading to a requirements analysis and outline design for a DAPSE.
3. Evolution of a MAPSE, tools, utilities, comparative designs, CAIS issues, syntax oriented-program handling and instrumentation for Ada.
4. Pilot Implementation of Numerical Libraries.

The timescale of these projects is 2 years, and attention is paid to the means of dissemination of the results once work is completed. The CEC's support of AdaKom (Patel), the European answer to Arpanet, is being extended to the end of 1985, on a 50% basis of costs of connect time only.

Table 4 - 1986 Ada Market

M$	Expectations
375+	US DoD
390	Commercial - N. America
80	Support of various sorts - N. America
65	Internal R&D, US
5	UK MoD
5	FRG MoD
150	European Commercial (CEC+EFTA)
5	Institutional Finance for R&D - Europe
1075	: Total Market size in M$ (N. America/Europe)

In Europe, in contrast to expectation, sales and firm orders for non military applications (including Ada specific architectures) are estimated to have exceeded US$ 150M in 1985.

Overall, it seems that military penetration may not be as deep as initially hoped for and nowhere as rapid as planned at the start of the HOL initiative. Also, private and public sector markets performed quite well, given the low exposure and should blossom given commercially useable APSE's to control costs of production.

8. Ada in leading IT Companies

An assembly of press statements, discussions and Arpanet information was compiled into a table to summarise the actions of some of the larger companies in the field:

Table of Principle IT Companies and Ada Activity

Company	Country	WR	ER	USM	
IBM	USA	1	1	43.7	Rights to compiler for 370 - IBM PC coming
DEC	USA	2	4	6.4	VAX Implemented
CDC	USA	3	8	5.2	"Expect to move to Ada shortly" (Press Release)
NCR	USA	4			
Burroughs	USA	5	10	4.8	Implementing on Large Systems
Sperry	USA	6	7	5.0	1100 Series Implementation
Fujitsu	J	7		4	Access via joint venture
Honeywell IS	USA	8	15	3.2	DPS-6
HP	USA	9		3.2	Purchased for porting
ICL	UK	10	5		PERQ
CM Bull	F	11	2		Committed to full implementation
Olivetti	I	12	6		Committed via joint venture
Hitachi	J	13			)
Toshiba	J	14			)=Interest declared,
NEC	J	15			) nothing concrete
Siemens	D	16	3		Committed to full product
Nixdorf	D	17	12		Intention to implement
Data General	USA			1.4	Implementing with Rolm
Amdahl	USA			0.7	470's
ATT/Bell	USA			0.9	VAX implementation
TRW				1.5	Full implementation
Nippon TT	J				Firmly committed implement
				> 80%	

Note: For other companies implementing, refer to Ada IC Implementors Matrix

USM - % share of US DP market in 1983

WR - World ranking in 1981

ER - European ranking in 1981

Even at an early stage in Ada, interested companies committing significant resources to investigating the language for adoption or implementation amount to 80% of the

U.S. market. 11 of the top 17 including the leading three companies in the world will implement. 9 of the top 10 European companies will follow and it should be noted that the vast majority of these companies have very significant markets outside the military sphere.

The next 1-2 years will see compilers moving from R&D to make way for APSE work and into marketing organisation. That will mark the commercial DP watershed for Ada. Apart from a skills shortage, all other indicators are positive, and strong.

BIBLIOGRAPHY

01 Informatique, "Principaux Constructeurs", 15 Feb. 1982
ANSI/MIL Std 1815A, Reference Manual for the Ada Programming Language January 1983 US Govt. Printing Office
Arpanet, directory VALIDATED-COMPILERS, 10 Feb. 1985
Arpanet, File: Courses in Ada-Implementation Status 15.02.85
Arthur, C., Witty,R. "Ada will be last of its line", Computer Weekly, 10 January 1984
Arthur, C., Computing Europe, "US Ada Market - $1 B by 1986" Article, 26 April 1984
Boehm, B.W., Standish, T.A., Software Technology in the 1990's : using an evolutionary paradigm, Computer, November 83.
CEC, Ada Europe Consultation Meeting, Brussels, 29 July 1982 Doc MWR 009127-16.08.82
CEC, Study on Ada Compiler Validation in Europe, MAP, Final Report Jan. 1983
Dept. of Commerce, A Competitive Assessment of the US Software Industry, Dec. 1984
DoD, Jt Services TF on SW Problems, for DUS of Defense for Research and Advanced Technology 7/82
Druffel, L., Redwine, S.T., Riddle W.E., The DoD STARS Program, Computer November 1983
Goodenough, J.B., The Ada Compiler Validation Implementors Guide DARPA, Arlington VA
Infotran : World Markets for Information Processing Products to 1993, A.D. Little Resources, April 1984, R840402
Kopp, A, "World of Ada" Vol III, USAF, AJPO
Mitchell,M., "Market Penetration, Query" Private Telex to K. Ripken TECSI 10:12:06/27/83
NTIS, Strategy for a DoD Software Initiative Vol 1/2, AD A 121-737, 121-738, October 1982
OCBE, "A Competitive Assessement of the US Software Industry", Secr. Trade Dev. December 1984
OECD, Software, A new Industry. ICCP (84)4, 17 Feb.1984
Patel, A., Rogers, M.W., "AdaKom", Proceedings of the Third Joint Ada E/Ada TEC Conf. Brussels, ed. Teller, CUP
Probert, T.H., Ada Validation Organisation : Policies and Procedures, MTR-82W00103, June 1982
Ripken, K., "US DoD Motivation - Engineered Language Design", TECSI, EFDPMA, London, 20-21 September 1982
Rogers, M.W., ed Ada : Languages, Compilers and Bibliography, CUP,1984
Shorter Oxford English Dictionary, 3rd edition, Oxford, 1968
Syms, T., The NATO Requirements for Ada, MoD Central Staff, Ada UK Conference, January 1984
Vaux, J., MoD Centre Boosts Ada, New Technology, 25.02.85
Wegner,P., Towards Capital Intensive Information Engineering, Ada-Europe Annual Conference, 16-17 March 1983, CEC, Brussels

NOTES ON BUILDING A RELATIONAL DATABASE MANAGEMENT SYSTEM IN ADA

Olavi Poutanen, Kari-Matti Varanki, Tapio Välimäki
Oy Softplan Ab, Box 209, SF-33101 Tampere, FINLAND

Abstract. It seems, at the moment, that although there have been papers published that deal with database management in an Ada environment there is still very little practical experience in that field.

Using Ada we have developed an Ada compatible relational database management system, called DMS/MPS10. In this paper we discuss some of its basic implementation ideas as well as some Ada specific issues that have arisen in the course of the work. Mostly we concentrate on describing how database design and documentation can take place using Ada concepts. That is, defining database domains as Ada types, defining table rows as Ada records etc. At the end of this paper there are some notes on the DMS/MPS10 runtime arrangements.

1 INTRODUCTION

The DMS/MPS10 (Nokia 1984; Poutanen & Varanki 1984), henceforth referred to as the DMS ,is a relational database management system (DBMS). It manages tabular data structures and supports a high level SQL-like data definition language. It can be used from Ada applications and later interactively by means of a query language.

The DMS is a full scale DBMS (Codd 1982)/ designed for use in demanding production applications. It features:

- data storage, retrieval and update
- a data dictionary
- transaction support
- recovery services
- concurrency control
- support for user defined domains

The DMS is available for the Nokia MPS10 (Nokia 1983), a 32-bit supermini computer developed by Nokia Electronics, Finland. The MPS10 is an Ada machine and it has an object oriented system architecture and a capability-based addressing scheme which provide for good data abstraction and encapsulation. An object in the system (including databases) is accessible only through an object type manager (OTM) of the type, using the operations that the OTM provides.

2 THE DMS/MPS10 SYSTEM, AN OVERVIEW

The main components of the DMS system are illustrated in fig. 1 below.

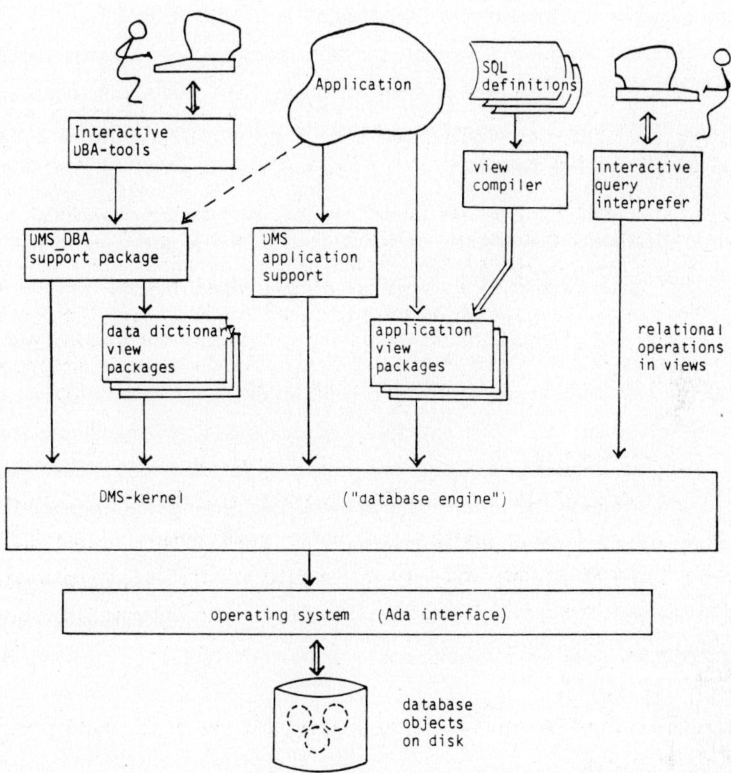

Figure 1. Overview of the DMS/MPS10 system

The application program gets from the package DMS_application_support general operations for the database, such as opening and closing, transaction delimeters, etc.. The views are first defined in SQL form according to the specific needs of the application. Then they are compiled with a view compiler to Ada packages, which are then compiled with the Ada compiler. The view packages provide operations for manipulating the view rows. Their bodies implement the relational algebra expressions contained in the SQL definitions and let an application manipulate, with simple-to-use operations, the virtual tables they thus derive row by row from the stored tables.

The application program may also use the services of the DMS_DBA_SUPPORT package. It contains maintenance-like operations for the database, such as table and index creation, taking database backup, performing recovery actions, etc.

The system component 'Interactive DBA-tools' is a collection of utility programs which can be used from a terminal for the purposes of database design and maintenance. The view compiler is one of these DBA tools but because of its importance in the system it is shown as a separate utility. The query language/report writer is a sketch for the future.

The DMS kernel performs a multitude of functions ranging from handling the physical tables to concurrency control and recovery. These topics are discussed further in chapter 4.

A person (or role) of central importance, the database administrator (DBA) supports application development by, for example, generating view packages from SQL definitions, defining domains, defining and creating tables and indices. He is also responsible for maintaining the data dictionary and performing maintenance activities such as making backup copies and recovery.

As an object in the virtual memory of the MPS10, a DMS database consists of two sets of tables, the user tables and the system tables comprising the data dictionary, cf. fig. 2.

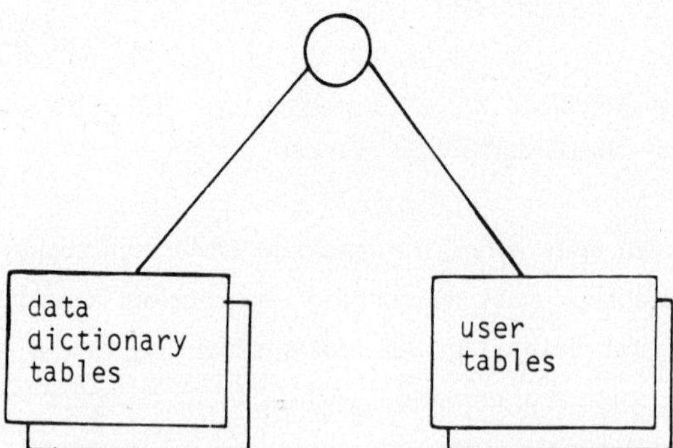

Figure 2. The DMS database object in the virtual storage of the MPS10.

3 APPLICATION DEVELOPMENT

Domains are an essential concept in both the relational model and the DMS. They allow modelling reality with a database using concepts of the application rather than the DBMS or the machine. In database tables, those columns that describe some common feature of the real world are defined over the same domain. On the other hand domains enable the system to enforce sensibility checking to the comparison of values (preventing, e.g. the comparison between prices and weights).

The use of Ada types to represent domains was a natural way of expressing them in our environment. This enables an application to take full advantage of the possibilities Ada typing has to offer.

In principle all different type classes of Ada (with some exceptions, like access types) can be used in defining domains. Data defined over these domains can directly be stored in a database and retrieved from it. No conversions by applications are necessary.

To make domains available to an application they are defined in so called domain packages. These are Ada packages having type (or subtype) definitions and they may be any packages that the application uses. For example, the personnel register of a company might be defined over domains such as the following:

```
package PERSONNEL_DOMAINS is

    subtype CHRISTIAN_NAME is STRING (1..20);
    subtype FAMILY_NAME is STRING (1..30);
    type EMPLOYEE_ID is new INTEGER range 1000..9999;
    type SALARY is new FLOAT;

end PERSONNEL_DOMAINS;
```

To an application using the package PERSONNEL_DOMAINS all the above types are available. They can be used in a normal way and deposited as such into the database the application is using.

To enable the DMS system to manipulate domains defined within packages that are out of control of the DMS system (packages are "controlled" and "interpreted" by the compilation system) information must be given to the DMS about how to deal with each domain. This information is given by the DBA and it is fed into the data dictionary of the system. What the DBA must tell the DMS about each domain includes a unique domain name (package name and type name), the Ada base type (integer, float, character etc.) of the domain, whether the domain is scalar, whether it is composite or whether it is something of which the DMS system needs to know only the allocated storage size.

It is the responsibility of the DBA to make sure that this "interpretation" of domains to the DMS is valid. To certain extent the DMS system could at run time check the validity of these definitions. These checks can be based on Ada´s attributes, like SIZE and FIRST_BIT.

Once the domains have been defined to the DMS system the tables of the database can be defined. Also these definitions are given by the DBA, using a DBA tool, and they are fed into the data dictionary. This defining can take place in terms of Ada. That is, the row structure of a table is defined as an Ada record, see below

```
type PERSONNELL_TABLE_REC is
   record
      EMP_ID       : PERSONNEL_DOMAINS.EMPLOYEE_ID;
      NAME         : PERSONNEL_DOMAINS.FAMILY_NAME;
      IS_MARRIED   : BOOLEAN;
      DEPT_NO      : DEPARTMENT_DOMAINS.DEPT_NUMBER;
 end record;
```

Application development using the DMS can begin once the database design phase has ended (or at least produced a sufficiently stable conceptual schema of the database). What is required for application development is that the database has been created (as a "skeleton", containing only the data dictionary tables) and that user tables have been described in the data dictionary.

The next step is to define the needs of the application in terms of the database tables. This is done by defining views in SQL, for example:

```
DEFINE    VIEW MARRIED_PEOPLE_OF_DEPT AS
SELECT    NAME, EMP_ID
FROM      PERSONNEL_TABLE
WHERE     IS_MARRIED    =    TRUE  AND
          DEPT_NO       =    $1
```

(The notation DEPT_NO = $1 means that the value of the field DEPT_NO is compared with a parameter given to the view at runtime by the application.)

The specification parts of the corresponding view packages are then generated from the SQL language view definitions using the view compiler, cf. fig. 3.

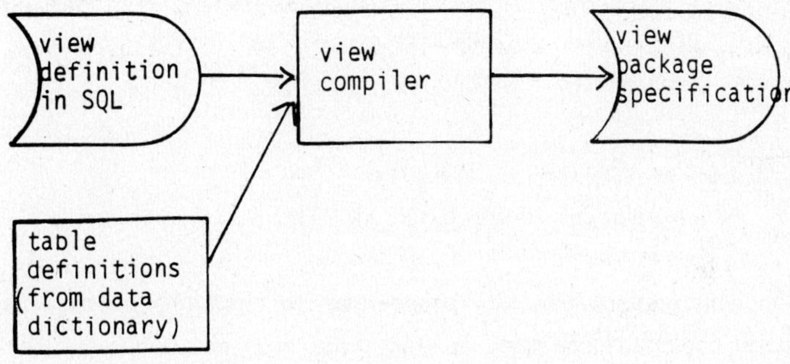

Figure 3: The view compiler

The specification of the generated view package looks as follows (those parameters that are not essential to this presentation have been omitted):

```
with PERSONNEL_DOMAINS, DEPARTMENT_DOMAINS;
package MARRIED_PEOPLE_OF_DEPT is
  type VIEW_ROW is
     record
        NAME    :  PERSONNEL_DOMAINS.FAMILY_NAME;
        EMP_ID  :  PERSONNEL_DOMAINS.EMPLOYEE_ID;
     end record;


  procedure     OPEN ( ... );
  procedure     CLOSE;
  procedure     PARAMETERIZE
                ( ...; PAR1: DEPARTMENT_DOMAINS.DEPT_NUMBE
  procedure     FETCH  ( ...; ROW: out VIEW_ROW; ...);
  procedure     UPDATE  ( ...; ROW: in VIEW_ROW; ...);
  procedure     INSERT  ( ...; ROW: in VIEW_ROW; ...);
  procedure     REMOVE  ( ... );
  ...

end MARRIED_PEOPLE_OF_DEPT;
```

Application development can now proceed up to compilation phase using the view package specifications. Note that at this stage it is not necessary that user tables have been created in the database. The compilation time arrangements for an application using the DMS are given in fig. 4. The arrows represent with relations between compilation units.

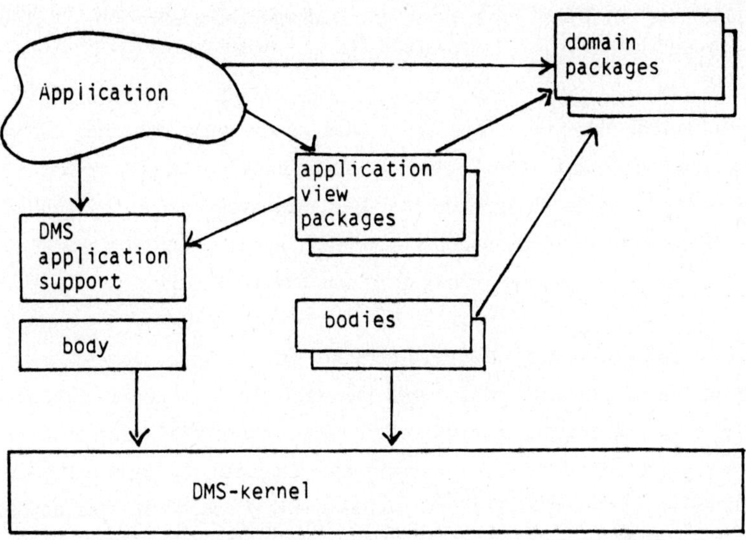

Figure 4: Compilation time arrangements.

At this point, both database design at the conceptual level and external modelling of the database to the needs of the application have been completed. What remains is physical database design. This includes definition of indices to be utilized as access paths and definition of storage allocation for tables.

The DBA can define the storage allocation for tables into the data dictionary. Within the DMS system, this means using the record representation clause of Ada, for example:

```
for PERSONNEL_TABLE_REC use
   record
         EMP_ID        at 0 range 0..14;
         DEPT_NO       at 0 range 15..29;
         IS_MARRIED    at 0 range 30..30;
         NAME          at 1 range 0..239;
   end record;
```

The DMS system itself determines the storage representation, if it is not given by the DBA.

After physical database design the bodies of the view packages can be generated by the view compiler. The bodies utilize indices but the information needed for generation can be obtained from the data dictionary. Thus, the application can be linked (after compiling the bodies of view packages) and the physical user tables must be created only when starting to use the application.

As shown above, application development can flexibly proceed in parallel with database design. On the other hand, the fact that views are implemented as Ada packages means that it is relatively easy to tune the implementation later, e.g. on the basis of experience from using the database, by generating new bodies to the desired view packages. The new bodies possibly use a new strategy for accessing data, e.g. utilize a new index, thus giving better performance. Only those regenerated bodies need then to be compiled and, once linked, the application is again ready for use.

The new bodies possibly use a new strategy for accessing data, e.g. utilize a new index, thus giving better performance.

4 THE RUNTIME ENVIRONMENT

The application interfaces are the DMS_application_support package and the view packages (cf. fig. 1.). The view packages show the database data with user defined Ada types . The view packages also implement the relational algebra using the lower level primitives of the DMS kernel.

The DMS kernel manages the stored database, maintains indices to tables, provides services for transaction processing, enforces concurrency control and provides services for recovery.

The DMS uses two phase locking (Date 1981). Within a transaction, all data that an application reads or writes, will be locked. Locks will be collected until the end of the transaction and released only then. There are two locking granules, namely a view row and a view. The locking is directly reflected in the stored tables as row and table locks.

In cases of lock conflicts the DMS schedules the execution of concurrent transactions. Concurrency control in the DMS allows serialization of concurrent access to common data from different Ada programs. Concurrency control between tasks of a program is left to the application.

If a DMS operation fails, it raises an exception. The choice between the use of an exception and an out-parameter in each procedure of the DMS was not an obvious one. In earlier versions of the DMS the status parameter approach was adopted instead of exceptions. This was, however, abondoned later. Some reasons are given below.

With the use of exceptions we hope to gain better clarity and readability in applications using the DMS, since checking the status parameter after every procedure call clearly makes the program logic in source form more difficult. Many error situations are also by nature such that there is no sensible way for an application to recover and retry. In this case it seems suitable that control is transferred out of that part of the application where the error occurred and exceptions are an Ada way of doing that.

The DMS raises only one exception in all error cases (that arise within the DMS). This is to assure that exception handlers in applications won't grow too large (an application will probably have to handle a wealth of other exceptions in any case). An application can, e.g. in the exception handler, call a subroutine of its own that pinpoints the failure and the exact reason for it by using services the DMS offers and, finally, performs the necessary closing actions. On the other hand, to make sure an application can recover and retry in cases where it is conceived possible means adding block statements and exception handlers to appropriate places.

5 SUMMARY AND FUTURE DIRECTIONS

In this paper we have highlighted some of the implementation ideas of our relational database management system DMS/MPS10. It has been implemented using Ada in an environment that also was rapidly evolving (the hardware, operating system, programming environment). This has caused some additional challenge.

The system supports database design in terms of both Ada and the relational model. We can provide the conceptual and operational power of both to application designers and programmers. In managing domains the DMS is not dependent on the compilation library.

The DMS has been operational since September 1983. Some major demonstrative and prototyping systems have been built on it. Currently there are many projects in progress whose purpose is to produce production applications where the DMS will be used.

The acceptance of the DMS in the user community has been promising. Currently we are working especially on implementing the view compiler (now the views are edited upon "skeletons") and extending the DBA tools for manipulating the data dictionary tables. We estimate to have a release with these features in the coming months.

References

Codd, E.F. (1982). Relational Database: A Practical Foundation for Productivity. Communications of the ACM, Feb, vol 25, No. 2.

Date, C.J. (1981). An Introduction to Database Systems, Volume II. Addison-Wesley Publishing Company, Inc., pp 102-107.

Nokia (1983). MNS 10 Dokumentation series, vol. 1 & vol. 2. Nokia Data, Terminal Systems, Finland.

Nokia (1984). MPS10 Database Management System, User´s Manual vol. I & vol. II. Nokia Electronics, Finland.

Poutanen, O. & Varanki, K-M. (1984). An Ada Implementation of a Relational DBMS. Third Scandinavian Research Seminar on I Information Modelling and Data Base Management, Edited by Hannu Kangassalo. Acta Universitatis Tamperensis ser B vol. 22, pp 503-513.

Extending the Scope of the Program Library

Kjell-Hakan Narfelt
Dick Schefstrom

University of Lulea & TeleLogic AB

ABSTRACT

The idea of a database as a central facility of a programming environment is explored, taking the Ada program library as a starting point. The database used is based on a node model similar to the one proposed in the CAIS standard (KIT/KITIA 1984). The paper suggests an expansion of the scope of the program library into the area of configuration and version management in an environment with several ungoing projects sharing software objects. The authors furthermore present a technique for the manipulation of the relationships in a relational algebra inspired way - providing some of the powerful capabilities of the relational approach within the context of node models.

1. Introduction

Increased automation of software production require that the automating tools have access to a lot of reliable input in a form suitable for mechanic manipulation - which is generally not the case today.

It has been proposed, (Us DoD 1983; Osterweil 1981), that a more rigourous management of the many objects, and relations between objects, that occur during software development and maintenance, could be a way of improving the situation: the term "programming environment database" was coined. This database could be a very central facility of the environment, acting as a vehicle to make explicit the many relationships between objects that today often exist only in the head of some programmers. It could act as a standardizing element, to avoid having different tools invent their own ways of representing information, and as a media of communication between different tools/users.

Programming languages like Modula-2 and Ada already requires some support from the environment to implement their separate compilation scheme. In Ada, if a module need some facilities provided by another module, it "imports" that module by naming it in a "with-clause"...

```
with B;
package A is
    ... -- declarations using B's
    ..  -- facilities
end;
```

But from where is B imported? What determines what B is when the compiler is not explicitly provided with the source of B? A very reasonable answer to this is "B is retrieved from the programming environment database".

But, people generally do not take that view today. Instead separate "program libraries", (Digital Equipment Corporation 1984; Dansk Datamatik Center 1984), are built, primarily aimed at efficient support of the compilers need when implementing separate compilation. However, the effort described here, the Library Manager, investigates the possibilities of expanding the scope of the program library towards a programming environment database.

2. Advantages and drawbacks of the approach

A program library for Ada must at least contain information on which different parts a system consists of: which modules are imported, and what subunits there are. A programming environment database would probably contain such information too, leading to an unnecessary redundancy. This is avoided if the program library and the environment database are the same thing.

And how does the information find its way to the database? If we, as suggested here, integrate the compiler and the database, a high level of automation is achieved. Other approaches to programming environment databases, (Lampson & Schmidt 1983; Leblang & Chase 1984), often relies on a "system model": a separate user provided description of the module interconnections. In our case the basis for the "system model" is generated implicitly by compiling Ada source text.

A programming environment database must be able to manage more than just code and versions thereof. It should reflect a project organization, and the status and responsibilities of different parts of the product. It must manage different kinds of documents, and their relationships to different parts of the software product. If most of these needs could be fulfilled within the same framework, we would achieve a highly integrated system, providing a seemless path from programmer concerns to project/product organization.

There are two main objections to this approach. First, the needs of the compiler may be so special that it pollutes the design of the database. Second, compilation speed may suffer if the tailored/highly efficient program library is generalized. Since compilation speed often seems to be a problem of Ada compilers, it is easy to reject the approach just because of this risk.

So, the design of a program library is a tradeoff between the user and tool needs for generality and abstraction, and the special requirements and efficiency concerns imposed by a particular implementation of, in our case, an Ada compiler.

3. On Datamodels

The word "open-ended" has been used to mean systems which are easy to expand with new facilities, taking advantage of what is already there. This is a desireable property of a programming environment, since it means that we doesn't have to pin down all the detailed needs of the software production process right from the start: they can be added when felt appropriate, giving the possibility to adapt to changes and new requirements.

One way of achieving this is to provide basic mechanisms, specialized enough to be directly useful, but general enough to adapt to new usages and changing requirements. In the context of data management this leads to the introduction of a data model: a framework known and accepted by the software tools, within which more specialized functions can be provided.

A natural datamodel to consider in this context is the directed graph, since languages like Ada encourage people to think about software as a network of modules, with an arc from module A to module B if A uses resources provided by B. This view of software also harmonizes with design methods like "object-oriented design", (Booch 1984). Finally, the usage of graphs is not restricted to pure software, other objects can be included within the same framework.

The problem of plain graphs is that they are too simple to be really useful here: describing software by just giving nodes and edges is not very helpful since we know too little about their meaning.

So, these simple graphs must be extended, and there are a number of ways to do that...

(1) One could partition the edges, letting each partition represent a different type of edge. Different types of edges could then be given different semantics.

(2) One could associate attributes with the nodes, as a way of introducing more semantics.

(3) One could introduce a "third dimension", or several layers, of the graph. Each layer could then be used to represent different versions, or different parts of the full graph.

The datamodel used here introduces all these extensions to graphs, resulting in an attributed directed graph with typed edges, possibly distributed over several layers.

The idea of using "layered graphs" in programming environments seems to have been pioneered by Bobrow and Goldstein (1984), in a version of the Smalltalk programming environment. In this paper we show how some of these ideas can be moved over to a "compiler-oriented" environment like the one for Ada.

Bobrow and Goldstein use the graph to describe the software to a finer granularity than the "module", they use the graph down to a declaration part/procedure level. The Library Manager stays at a module level, and infact, simplifies even more, nodes representing software will correspond to Ada separately compiled units: procedures, packages, or subunits. This decision may be critisized on the basis that the Ada separate compilation scheme is an implementation technique used to achieve effiecient recompilation, and may have little to do with software system structure. It is true that this may be the case if the programmer doesn't make it that way: but he can with little effort if he wants to.

4. Using Layered Graphs in an Ada Environment

Let us now examplify some potential usages of layered graphs in some typical programming situations. To do that we first need to introduce a typing of edges: assigning special meaning to edges of certain kinds. Since an edge of type "X" from a module A to a module B also can be treated as if A stands in an "X"-relation to B, we call this typing a "relation scheme", and sometimes say that an edge belong to a certain "relation" instead of to a certain type.

To connect together the different separately compiled parts of an Ada program, the following categorization of edges can be used...

Definitions:

Let CU1 and CU2 be two compilation units, then

(*) CU1 IMPORTS CU2 iff
(i) CU2 is mentioned in the context clause of CU1

(*) CU2 is PARENT of CU1 iff
(i) CU2 contains the specification part of CU1 or
(ii) CU2 contains the body stub of CU1

(*) CU1 is BODY of CU2 iff
(i) CU2 contains the specification part of CU1

(*) CU1 is SUBUNIT of CU2 iff
(i) CU2 contains the body stub of CU1

Now, assume we have the following Ada-program...

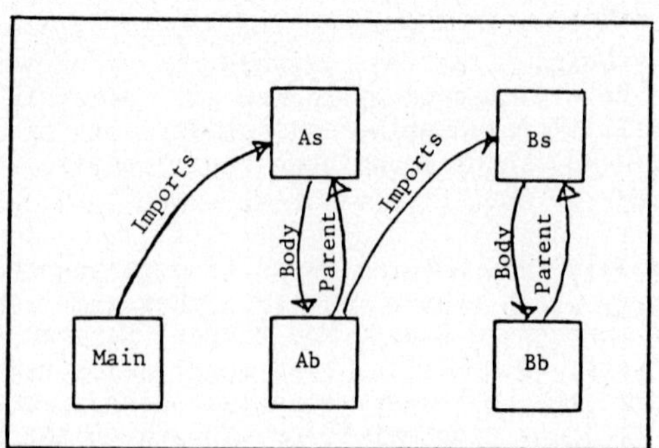

The graph above consists of a single layer, and was generated by compiling a corresponding Ada source code. Assume now that we are not satisfied with the body of A, (called Ab in the figure), or that we just want to try a new version. We then put a new, maybe empty, layer on top of the old one, and compiles the new version of Abody. This new version will then belong to this new layer as shown below...

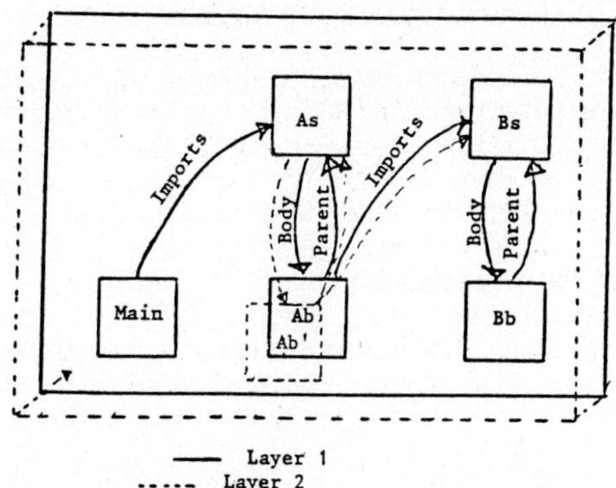

The new version of Abody will hide the old one, but will inherit the rest of the context. So if we now ask for execution of "Main", the new version of Abody will be used. If this turned out to be a dead end the newly created layer may be removed, returning us to the original situation.

If we allow free combination of layers, this basic idea can be used not only as a means to manipulate with different versions of a single module, but to a number of other things...

- <u>Different design alternatives</u> may be represented by different layers. If changes that belong together are put together in the same layer, we also see very clear what differs between the alternatives.

- Layers may be used as a <u>media of communication between users</u>. Different parts of a large system are almost always constructed by different programmers. Putting these parts together can then be done by putting together the corresponding layers.

- <u>Reuse of existing software</u> is done by composing graphs out of layers that contain commonly used modules. Putting layers together may be used as a way of composing configurations.

To connect back to Ada program libraries we also use the word <u>sublibrary</u> for a single isolated layer, and use the term <u>library</u> for the combination of one or more layers/sublibraries into a full graph.

Each sublibrary has an owner, and read- or read-write locks may be put on sublibraries. Libraries are constructed by giving the names and ordering of the sublibraries one want to put together. When running the compiler the user now has to provide two things: the source code to be compiled, and the library in which context compilation is to be done. A successful compilation results in a corresponding modification of the top layer/sublibrary.

Finally, it turned out to be useful put a little more internal structure inside a layer: the nodes of a single layer are organized into a hierarchy, so the resulting model might be called "a sequence of attributed hierarchies, with a superimposed directed graph with typed edges".

5. High-level operations and further extensions

The full graph of a library can be quite complex, with many different types of edges between the nodes, corresponding to the different "relations". But both tools and the user might want to use a special "view", containing a subset of the information of the full graph, and have powerful operations for its manipulation.

As a solution to this we define a way of retriving a subset of the full graph, and a set of relational algebra inspired operations for the manipulation of this subset. This "activation" of a subset of the full database also provides for simple and efficient implementation, since the data structures used are small and temporary, and can therefore be kept in main memory.

One obvious subset of the full graph is the graph containing all the nodes reachable by following one or more relations starting at a given set of nodes. We call such a graph a reachability graph...

```
function REACHABILITY_GRAPH(LIB_NAME: STRING;
                            STARTNODES: SET_OF_NODES;
                            RELATIONS: STRING) return GRAPH;
```

...where LIB_NAME is the name of the library to use, STARTNODES is the set of nodes to start with, and RELATIONS describe the set of relation names to follow when computing this reachability graph. The result of this operation is of the abstract datatype GRAPH.

The "Graph" is represented as a set of typed edges...

```
type GRAPH is limited private; -- representing a set of EDGE's

type EDGE is
      record
        TAIL,
        HEAD: NODE;
        RELATION: RELATION_NAME;
        STATUS  : STATUS_TYPE;
      end record;

type STATUS_TYPE is (OK, VERSION_MISMATCH, DANGLING);
type RELATION_NAME is ...
type NODE is ...
```

The record (a, b, rel, stat), for example, is in a graph if there is an arc from a to b.

Because of the special needs of this context, (programming environments), we introduce an attribute called the status of an edge. The status value is assigned when retrieving the graph in the first place, and is meaningful when treating the edge (a, b,,) as directed from a to b. The meaning of the status values are appearent from their names: VERSION_MISMATCH means that we are now referring to a different version compared to the moment when the corresponding edge was introduced in the graph, DANGLING means that the referred node is now not there at all, while OK tells us that the referred to node is there and the same as before.

This acts as a basic mechanism for consistency control: if edges are introduced by trusted tools, (like the compiler), which checks the consistency at that occation, consistency control can be treated as a problem of detecting changes, and this may now be done by checking the "status" attribute of the edges.

To enable tools to manipulate this graph in a convenient manner, there is a set of relational algebra operations: select, project, union, difference and so on. It turned out to be convenient to have some special graph oriented operations defined too: toplogical sort of a graph, and the reachability graph, starting at some set of nodes following some set of types of edges.

6. Why Not Use A Relational Database ?

Relational database technology, e.g. (Ullman 1982), appears to be potentially useful in many fields, so even in programming environments, (Snodgrass 1984; Linton 1984). A natural idea would be to use it for the tasks addressed by the Library Manager, thereby avoiding implementation work and providing the generality inherent in the relational approach. Moreover, relational database managers often provide for the protection of data integrity, handling of concurrent accessess, crash recovery, and query languages of a very high level.

Very aware of all this, we have chosen not to use a relational database, and will now try to explain why.

Commercially available relational databases are often very general, providing much more than we have need for. This generality gives birth to very large systems, heavy to use, and with poor performance compared with tailored solutions. As an example, RCS, (Tichy 1984a), was reimplemented using INGRES, (Stonebraker, Wong, Kreps & Held 1976), giving a 20 times slower system than the original, tailored, implementation, (Tichy 1984b). The implementation work was also reported very awkward and the lack of structured types in domains seems to result in a lot of parsing-unparsing into strings. Also, data can't always be stored in the database because the data is too large: instead one has to store in the database the name of files where the data actually is stored. This is an important point where the requirements for an engineering database differ from that of traditional databases. Here we have two kinds of data: representations of objects, like program texts, documents, intermediate and code files, and attributes summarizing aspects of these data. The attributes may be subject for traditional database treatment, (comparing, searching, indexing), but in the case of the representations we are probably only interested in storing them in a convenient way.

The database approach to concurrency control and crash recovery, leads to the introduction of transaction management: imposing even more generality and overhead even though a simple approach would suffice in our case. Also, the amount of work invested in the implementation of the Library Manager is felt to be less or equal to the work neccessary to adapt a relational database to our needs.

7. The Ada Library: An Implementation Using The Library Manager

The tools of an Ada Programming Support Environment will view the data base information in terms of the Ada program structure. The Library Manager, however, does not directly provide any scheme suitable for these tools. In order to make it useful in an Ada environment, some naming conventions or typing of data must be enforced. A simple, Ada-specific, relation scheme was introduced earlier, and we will now develop this Ada specialization further.

7.1. Basic Requirements

The most abstract view of an Ada program is as a collection of one or more compilation units submitted to the compiler in one or more compilations, where each compilation unit defines either a library unit or a secondary unit. According the the LRM, each secondary unit has exactly one library unit as its "ancestor". Every Ada program can therefore be looked upon as a "forest", where each library unit acts as a root of a "tree". Thus, an Ada Library should contain a representation of this forest structure.

In order to describe the compilation and recompilation rules enforced by the language semantics, a binary relation DEPENDS_ON has to be defined:

Def: A DEPENDS_ON B iff
A is "potentially affected" by a change in B.
change in B. (Potentially affected as described
in US DoD 1983, ch. 10.3).

The order of compilation can now informally be stated by:

i) A compilatin unit must be compiled after all compilation units it depends on. (The Compilation Rule).

ii) If a compilation unit B is successfully recompiled, then all compilation units depending on B must also be recompiled. (The Recompilation Rule).

In terms of the language requirements, the relation DEPENDS_ON, must be retrievable from the information collected in an Ada Library.

7.2. Structuring the Ada Library.

Each compilation unit is either a secondary unit or a library unit, and the two kinds are separated within a layer/sublibrary by being in separate subhierarchies. Compilation units furthermore exist in several "incarnations", lets assume TEXT, SYMBOL_TABLE, and CODE. The figure below illustrates this...

The structure of the Ada library

* **A forest of compilation unit trees...**

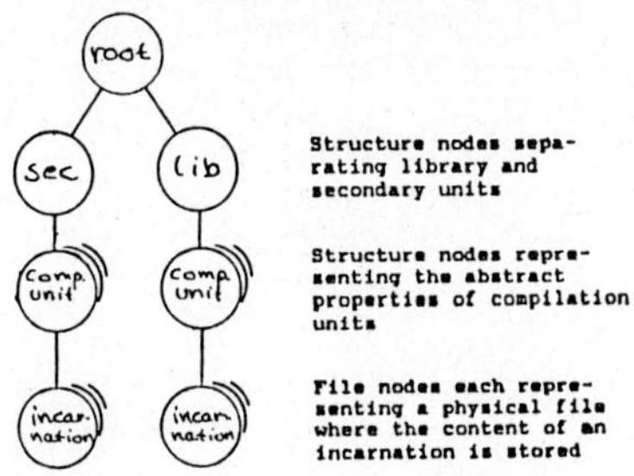

Organization of nodes within a single sublibrary/layer

The middle-level nodes represent the abstract properties of compilation units, and it is between these, maybe crossing layers, that we currently have edges.

In order to satisfy the requirements stated above, at least two kinds of relations have to be maintained by the Ada Library: a relation(s) describing the structure of an Ada program and the relation DEPENDS_ON. As presented earlier, we chose to represent the connection between a compilation unit and its secondary units by means of two relations: BODY and SUBUNIT. By having these two relations, we also get a convenient way of categorizing secondary units: instead of defining and interrogating attribute information during e.g graph traversal, we now use the operations provided for manipulating and selecting certain kinds of edges. This makes the manipulation of the Ada program structure much more efficient than if attributes had to be inspected.

The Ada Library should furthermore be able to easily distinguish between with'ed compilation units and a compilation unit being a parent unit, (a compilation unit having the specification part or the body stub of a secondary unit). We therefore chose not to maintain DEPENDS_ON explicitly. Instead, we introduced the two relations PARENT and IMPORTS.

In terms of these relations, DEPENDS_ON is the union of the relations PARENT and IMPORTS. Since the operations provided by the Library Manager for manipulation of graphs supports unions of relations, there is no inconvenience.

There are also other types of relations maintained by the Ada Library, introduced to determine special elaboration ordering, suspended compilations due to missing generic template bodies etc. To avoid being to detailed, we leave them out here.

7.3. The Operations provided by the Ada Library

The Ada Library constitutes an essential part of an Ada programming environment, by acting as a repository for software associated data, collected at least during the development phase. The Ada Library Interface should therefore be carefully designed, in order to meet the needs of cooperating tools using the library as the basis for information exchange.

The operations of the Ada Library allow tools to introduce and retrieve library information in terms of the syntactic categories of the Ada programming language.

7.3.1. Detecting and introducing compilaton units in general.

The introduction of compilation units are done by means of procedures like...

```
procedure SUBPROGRAM_DECLARATION(NAME: STRING;
                                 C   : out POSITION );

procedure SUBPROGRAM_BODY(SPEC: POSITION;
                                 C   : out POSITION );
      ...
```

...which are called by the compiler when it discovers which syntactical construct is applicable.

The POSITION returned is an abstract address to the, maybe just created, node representing this compilation unit. The NAME parameter always denotes the name of the corresponding library unit. When bodies or subunits are introduced, the user has to provide a POSITION to the parent unit.

Besides creating compilation units, these operations also update or define an edge of type "PARENT" between a body and its specification.

After compiling the context clause of a compilation unit, the compiler knows which library units the compilation unit is directly dependent on. This dependency is represented via the relation IMPORTS as defined above. The compiler can instruct the Ada Library to define an instance of this relation by calling the following procedure...

```
procedure IMPORTS(DEPENDING,
                  IMPORTED   : POSITION );
```

The procedure creates an arc of type IMPORTS to the unit identified by the position IMPORTED. The arc is associated to the compilation unit denoted by the POSITION "DEPENDING".

7.3.2. Context Analysis

Separate compilation issues must be considered at two stages of the compilation process, namely: during semantic analysis and at binding time. Before semantic analysis, at least the correct order of compilation has to be ensured. At binding time all the object codes of the separetely compiled units belonging to a Ada program have to be linked and elaborated according to the partial order defined by the language rules.

Consistency control in general is provided by the procedure...

```
type REQUIRED_CONSISTENCY is
      (COMPILABLE, EXECUTABLE, UP_TO_DATE);

procedure CONSISTENCY_CONTROL(C : LM.POSITION;
                              T : REQUIRED_CONSISTENCY;
                              G : out GRAPH;
                              OK: out BOOLEAN);
```

The procedure determines if the required consistency "T" is satisfied. If this is the case, then the parameter "OK" becomes TRUE. When doing this checking, a reachability graph is computed starting at the given node, containing all the nodes depended upon given a level of consistency. This graph is useful for other purposes, (e.g. computing recompilation orders), and is therefore returned.

Among several types of consistencies a user may want to have satisfied by the context of a compilaton unit "C", we have decided to identify four...

(1) A compilation unit is CONSISTENT <u>iff</u>

```
TEXT'TIME_STAMP <=
     SYMBOL_TABLE'TIME_STAMP <=
          CODE'TIME_STAMP
```

We assume that if a compilation unit has some of these incarnations, then the above relation must hold between the incarnations. (TIME_STAMP refers to the attribute every component has associated with it). In general, the incarnations are derived from each other and what is really required here is that each incarnation is younger than the one it is derived from. The assumptions about these "micro-dependencies" are hard coded into the code of the checking procedures. The node representing the abstract unit, (which has the incarnations as childs), has the time stamp of the last time the TEXT incarnation was successfully compiled.

(2) A compilation unit A is COMPILABLE <u>iff</u> every edge of the reachability graph starting at A of the relation DEPENDS_ON has the status 'ok'.

(3) A compilation unit A is UP_TO_DATE <u>iff</u> the unit is <u>compilable</u> and <u>consistent</u>, and if every compilation unit in the reachability graph of the relation DEPENDS_ON starting at A is <u>consistent</u>.

(4) A compilation unit A is EXECUTABLE <u>iff</u> every edge of the reachability graph of the relations DEPENDS_ON, BODY, and SUBUNIT, starting at A, has the status not equal to 'dangling', and further that all edges of type DEPENDS_ON has the status 'ok'.

The relation DEPENDS_ON is actually not represented explicitly in the database, but is computed using the union of some other relations. The returned graph "G" is used to evaluate a recompilation order that restores the required type of consistency. The recompilation order is retrieved by calling the function...

```
function TO_BE_RECOMPILED(G: GRAPH)
                               return NODELIST;
```

The function returns a list of compilation units to be recompiled. The returned order is consistent with the partial order implied by the Recompilation Rule.

The control of the Compilation Rule is for an arbitrary unit, here denoted by the name X, controlled by calling the following procedure...

```
CONSISTENCY_CONTROL(X, COMPILABLE, DEP_ON, OK);
```

Returned in the parameter DEP_ON, is the reachability graph of the relation DEPENDS_ON, starting with the component "X". Using the definition above, this graph must have the status of all edges OK for "X" to be compilable. If such is not the case we can use the returned graph to compute a recompilation order...

```
if not IS_EMPTY(
        SELECT(DEP_ON, STATUS, NOT_EQUAL, OK)) then
  INCONSISTENT_UNITS:= TO_BE_RECOMPLIED(DEP_ON);
end if;
```

The list INCONSISTENT_UNITS can then be traversed by means of the nodelist operations...

```
while not EMPTY(INCONSISTENT_UNITS) loop
   HEAD_OF(INCONSISTENT_UNITS, NEXT);
   COMPILE(NEXT);
end loop;
```

7.3.3. Implementing the consistency control.

This consistency control is easily implemeneted using the graph manipulating operations: A graph is retrieved from the library by means of the operation "Reachability_Graph" given a start node and a list of relation names. For example computing the graph corresponding to the consistency level COMPILABLE...

```
function COMPILABILTY_GRAPH(C: COMPILATION_UNIT)
                               return GRAPH is
begin
  return REACHABILITY_GRAPH(C,
                "parent | imports | spec_dep_on");
end;
```

The graph is retrieved by transitively follow each edge either within the "parent", "imports" or "spec_dep_on" relations, (spec_dep_on keeps track of compiler introduced dependencies maybe caused by in_line or generics).

The graphs retrieved by the procedure CONSISTENCY_CONTROL may then be used by the function TO_BE_RECOMPILED in order to obtain a consistent recompilation order...

```
function TO_BE_RECOMPILED(G: GRAPH) return NODE_LIST is
  ROOTS: NODE_LIST;
  TARGETS,
  PROPAGATED: GRAPH;
begin
  TARGETS:= SELECT(G, STATUS, NOT_EQUAL, OK);
  ROOTS  := PROJECT(TARGETS, TAIL);     -- 2
  PROPAGATED:=
      REACHABILITY_GRAPH(G, ROOTS, CONVERSE); -- 3
  return TOPOLOGICAL_SORT(PROPAGATED, CONVERSE);
end;
```

The list is retrieved by selecting all inconsistent edges from the given graph, then retrieving the tail nodes from this set, (2nd statement). These (the "roots") are the units directly dependent on a modified unit. Every unit reached from the "roots" in the converse direction (i.e. depending on some of the "roots") (3rd statement), are then subjected to a topological sort with respect to the converse relation (last statement). This gives a partial order consistent with the language rules.

8. Configuration Management using the Library Manager

It would be a waste not to build a configuration management tool on top of the Ada program library. Since it is recorded, for every unit, which units are imported and which body and subunits there are, we have the skeleton describing the structure of a configuration. This gives us a high degree of automation: the user never has to tell the system about the structure of his programs - this information is collected as he runs the Ada compiler.

As a consequence of this we also have the mechanisms to support a notion of configurations, and can provide users and tools with a way to refer to them without mentioning all its constituating parts. Using this idea, a configuration is defined given a main program and a sublibrary list. Since we now have a convenient way to refer to configurations, we can manipulate them as a whole.

If we choose to be slightly more formal...

(1) A <u>configuration graph</u> is the reachability graph of the relations DEPENDS_ON, BODY, and SUBUNIT starting at a given set of units, called the <u>root</u> of the configuration, together with the list of sublibraries in which context this reachability graph was computed.

(2) A <u>configuration</u> is the set of units in a configuration graph.

(3) A configuration is called <u>complete</u> if its roots are EXECUTABLE, (see definition above).

A user can compose different configurations by manipulating the context in which the configuration graph is computed, in other words: constructing a sublibrary list.

To name a configuration, we only have to provide the root, ("start units"), and the context, (list of sublibraries), in which the configuration graph is computed...

```
Configuration_id = (Root Context)
Root    = (Cid)-set
Context = LibName
```

Since all these concepts are directly supported by the basic mechanisms of the library manager, it is easy to write tools which uses them.

8.1. Tools

Besides basic services like copying and moving of compilation units between sublibraries, merging, creating, and deleting sublibraries, tools for the manipulation of configurations are under construction. The need for configuration management occur at least at two levels:

(1) At the programmer level there is a need for frequent creation of rather short lived configurations. The programmer often has a private baseline from which he explores different structuring ideas. Sometimes the new idea turns out to be a failure, and he wants to return to the baseline and try some other way. To achieve this, the programmer just constructs a new sublibrary list, often identical to the previous except for the first sublibrary of the list, (where modifications take place). The old configuration can be restored at any time by using the old sublibrary list.

(2) At the project level there is a need for more stringent management of rather long lived configurations. We have chosen to support a concept of released sublibraries and released configurations.

A sublibrary is released by submitting its name to a tool which copies it, (and the corresponding files), to a safe place. A released sublibrary should not be modified.

A configuration is released by submitting a 'Configuration_id', to the configuration manager. The library units of the first sublibrary of the context are assumed to define the root. A configuration is accepted iff...

i) its context sublibraries are released, and
ii) the configuration is complete.

In other words: an accepted 'Configuration_id' is just a library having the property that its sublibraries have been released, and that the configuration it describes is complete.

9. Implementation status

Except for the configuration control tools, (which are under implementation), the system is currently running as described in this paper, and is under integration with the TeleSoft Ada compiler. All of the software is written in Ada, using the TeleSoft Ada Compiler on a Unix/VAX computer.

10. Acknowledgements

Richard Kaufmann at TeleSoft, San Diego, USA, trigged some of the basic ideas, from which the current system has developed. Stefan Bjornsson at TeleLogic, Nynashamn, Sweden, has reviewed and given valuable comments on the design.

11. References

Barstow, D.R. Sandewall, E. & Shrode H.E. (1984).
eds. Interactive Programming Environments, New York: McGraw-Hill.

Bobrow, D.G., & Goldstein, I.P. (1984).
A Layered Approach to Software Design. In (Barstow, Sandewall & Shrode 1984).

Booch, G. (1984).
Software Engineering with Ada, Menlo Park, CA: Benjamin/Cummings Publishing Company.

Dansk Datamatik Center (1984).
DDC Ada Compiler System Separate Compilation Handler, Functional Specification, Lyngby, Denmark: Dansk Datamatik Center.

Department of Defense (1980).
Requirements for the Programming Environment for the Common High Order Language, STONEMAN. Washington: US Department of Defense. Febr 1980.

Digital Equipment Corporation (1984).
VAX Ada Technical Summary, Cambridge, Mass.: Digital Equipment Corporation.

KIT/KITIA (1984).
Common Apse Interface Set, (CAIS),version 1.4. Ada Joint Program Office.

Lampson, B.W. & Schmidt, E.E. (1983).
Organizing Software in a Distributed Environment. ACM SIGPLAN, June 1983.

Leblang, D. & Chase, R. (1984).
Computer-Aided Software Engineering in a Distributed Workstation Environment. In ACM SIGSOFT/SIGPLAN conference on Practical Software Engineering Environments, Pittsburgh, April 23-25 1984.

Linton, M. (1984).
Implementing Relational Views of Programs. In ACM SIGSOFT/SIGPLAN conference on Practical Software Engineering Environments, Pittsburgh, April 23-25 1984.

Osterweil, L. (1981).
Software Environment Research: Directions fore the Next Five Years. In IEEE Computer Magazine, April 1981.

Snodgrass, R. (1984).
Monitoring in Software Development Environment: A Relational Approach. In ACM SIGSOFT/SIGPLAN conference on Practical Software Engineering Environments, Pittsburgh, April 23-25 1984.

Stonebraker, M.E., Wong, E., Kreps, P. & Held, G. (1976).
The Design and Implementation of INGRES. In ACM Transactions on Database Systems, 1:3 1976.

Tichy, W.F. (1984a).
RCS - A System for Version Control. West Lafayette, Indiana 47907: Dep of Computer Sciences, Purdue University,

Tichy, W.F. (1984b).
private communication. West Lafayette, Indiana 47907: Dep of Computer Sciences, Purdue University,

Ullman, J.D. (1982).
Principles of Database Systems. Rockville, Maryland: Computer Science Press.

US DoD (1983).
Reference Manual for the Ada Programming Language. Washington DC: US Department of Defense.

A TOOL KIT FOR DATABASE PROGRAMMING IN ADA

John M. Smith
Arvola Chan
Sy Danberg
Stephen Fox
Anil Nori

Computer Corporation of America
Four Cambridge Center
Cambridge, Massachusetts 02142

Abstract. This paper describes an Ada-compatible database application development environment being designed and prototyped at Computer Corporation of America. This environment is intended to provide uniform access to centralized, homogeneously distributed, and heterogeneously distributed databases. There are two key interfaces: an interactive interface called Daplex which is based on a semantically rich data model and a powerful access language, and an application program interface called Adaplex which consists of an expression level integration of Daplex with Ada. The objective of this paper is to explain our rationale for designing Adaplex and to describe its support environment.

1 INTRODUCTION

Computer Corporation of America has been engaged in a research project that investigates the major issues of providing an advanced database management capability to support development of database application programs written in Ada. The key deliverables of this project are three closely related prototype database systems implemented in Ada:

1. LDM (Chan, et al., 1981; Chan, et al., 1982 a,b; Ries, et al., 1982) -- an advanced, centralized database system that also is specially designed to support distributed database operations.
2. DDM (Chan, et al., 1983 a,b; Chan & Gray 1985; Goodman, et al., 1983) -- a homogeneous distributed database system that interconnects multiple LDMs in a computer network and that hides the distribution and replication of data on these LDMs from end users and applications.
3. Multibase (Landers & Rosenberg 1982; Dayal 1984; Dayal & Hwang 1984) -- a heterogeneous distributed database system that provides integrated retrieval access to a collection of databases stored in existing DBMSs.

All three systems support a new, semantically rich data model that is intended to capture more application semantics than conventional hierarchical, network, and relational data models. Each system has been designed to support both interactive users and database access from Ada application programs. The interactive language for defining and manipulation databases is called Daplex. The application programming language is called Adaplex. It consists of an expression level integration of the Daplex data manipulation constructs and Ada.

In (Chan, et al., 1985), we gave an overview of the capabilities of our three prototype DBMSs and explained how they were designed to satisfy a wide-range of Ada database management requirements. This paper describes a tool set that supports the development of database application programs in Ada. It explains our rationale for the design of Adaplex and gives an overview of the language.

Section 2 examines several approaches for coupling Ada programs with a DBMS. Section 3 highlights the Daplex data model and gives an overview of the Adaplex language. Section 4 describes the Adaplex support environment. Section 5 summarizes our conclusions on Ada/DBMS interface issues and gives the status of our implementation effort.

2 ADA/DBMS INTERFACE APPROACHES

The problem of providing DBMS functions within a general purpose programming language previously has been addressed in the context of popular languages like COBOL, PL/1, C, and Pascal. The earlier interfaces based on the hierarchical and network data models tend to be access path dependent and not amenable to automatic access path optimization or physical schema optimization. Since the advent of relational database systems, which emphasize data independence and automatic optimization, several widely used programming languages have been coupled with relational database sublanguages. Notable examples include the embedding of QUEL in C, the embedding of SQL in PL/1, and the design of integrated database programming languages like Pascal/R, PLAIN, and RIGEL.

It is not coincidental that the development of database environments for contemporary programming languages has resulted in extensions to the host programming language. This is true because the specifications of typical database transactions can involve a lot of closely interdependent details that can get very complex unless expressed in an appropriately structured language. On the other hand, since Ada contains important new features not found in previous widely-used languages, it is not immediately obvious whether Ada would have to be extended to accommodate database applications. In particular, Ada's package construct offers the potential for defining database extensions within Ada itself.

2.1 Problems with a Generic Package Approach

At first sight, an attractive approach for developing an Ada database environment is through a generic package. This package would provide subprograms for retrieving and updating data in a database. In effect, such a package encapsulates the DBMS. The generic package would then be instantiated for a particular database using the schema type definitions as generic parameters. Transactions against the database could then be written in Ada by making subprogram calls on the instantiated package. Unfortunately, this approach to developing a DBMS has three overwhelming problems.

First, the DBMS is effectively a single-user system. When independent application programs access a shared package, some form of synchronization protocol is required. The only protocol provided through Ada is individual locking of external files (Note that Ada tasking is program relative and cannot be used to synchronize independent Ada programs). Since a DBMS typically references multiple large external files in processing a database transaction, this protocol is both very dangerous and extremely inefficient. For all practical purposes, the database transactions have to be executed sequentially without interleaving.

Second, a separate version of the DBMS must be compiled and linked for each database. Since a full-function DBMS typically contains hundreds of thousands of lines of code, the compilation and linkage of DBMS modules can take many hours to complete. This is required not only when a new database is created, but also when the database schema or its physical representation needs to be modified. The proliferation of distinct DBMS versions, which cannot be shared, will have a major impact on storage efficiency and execution time performance. All-in-all, the administration of such a database environment becomes a problematic undertaking.

Third, the DBMS does not have enough scope to perform effective transaction optimization. Using the generic package approach, the DBMS is only aware of record-at-a-time data accesses to retrieve or update the fields of particular database records. The loop structures that enclose these data accesses are contained in the Ada application program and are not visible to the DBMS. As a result, the DBMS is unable to invoke multiple loop optimization strategies. This can lead to orders of magnitude degradation in transaction performance.

In order to overcome the above three problems, the following steps must be taken. First, for the DBMS to support multiple application programs simultaneously, it must provide its own synchronization protocol which would have to be written outside Ada. Second, to avoid separate DBMS versions for each database, the DBMS must be a general-purpose system driven by database schema descriptions. The DBMS must interpret these descriptions at execution time. Finally, to provide effective transaction optimization, the DBMS must be given specifications of complete transactions, which must include the loop structure as well as individual record accesses. These three steps lead to the database module approach discussed in the next subsection.

2.2 Database Module Approach

There have been a number of proposals for coupling database management capabilities to Ada through the package construct (Holland, et al., 1981; Nokia Data Terminal Systems 1983; Vine 1983). All of these are based on the relational data model and they achieve database definition outside Ada. Their architecture is characterized in Figure 1.

Figure 1. Database Module Approach to Ada/DBMS Coupling

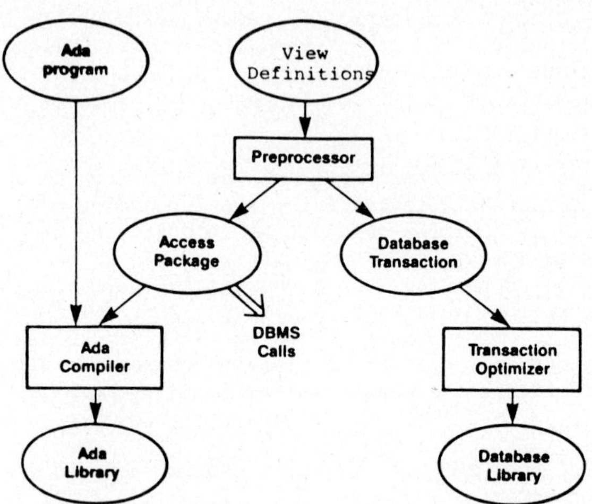

One major component in this approach is an external view preprocessor. For each user view definition, the external view preprocessor is responsible for compiling the definition and generating Ada type definitions that correspond to relations and tuples in the view definition. The Ada type definitions are embedded in a skeleton package to form an external view access package. This is compiled using the Ada compiler and stored in the Ada program library. Ada application programs requiring access to a particular external database view must include the corresponding access package using a "with" statement. The schema compiler is responsible for compiling the initial database definition and for selecting an optimized plan for materializing each external view. The optimized access plans are stored in the database library. An access package invokes the DBMS by identifying the particular access plan that corresponds to the external view it provides. Typically, an access package provides subprograms for iterating through tuples of a relation for retrieval and update.

The external view may in general contain one (Nokia Data Terminal Systems 1983) or more (Holland, et al., 1981; Vine 1983) relations. In the latter case, the access package will include the definition of an abstract data type called relation, and abstract objects of that type, one corresponding to each relation in the external view. The access package also will provide subprograms that implement high level operations on view relations and on temporary relations that result from these operations.

A number of drawbacks of the database module approach can be identified:

1. Two distinct languages with potentially incompatible syntax and semantics are used. Either the DBA must be burdened with defining appropriate views for individual application programs or application programmers must deal with the distinct languages.
2. There may be complicated conventions for invoking subprograms in the access package. The Ada compiler will not be able to ascertain that an application program is invoking subprograms in the access package in the correct sequence. Sequencing errors can be detected only at execution time.
3. If high level relational operations are permitted from within an access package (in order to allow multiple applications to share the same external view), local optimization with limited scope must be performed at execution time. This results in increased overhead and reduced optimality. In general, the danger of not tailoring the views to suit individual application program/subprogram is that unnecessary data transfer from the DBMS may result.

2.3 Adaplex Approach

In order to overcome the drawbacks of the database module approach, we decided to embed our database sublanguage in Ada. This leads to the architecture shown in Figure 2.

Figure 2. Adaplex Approach to Ada/DBMS Coupling

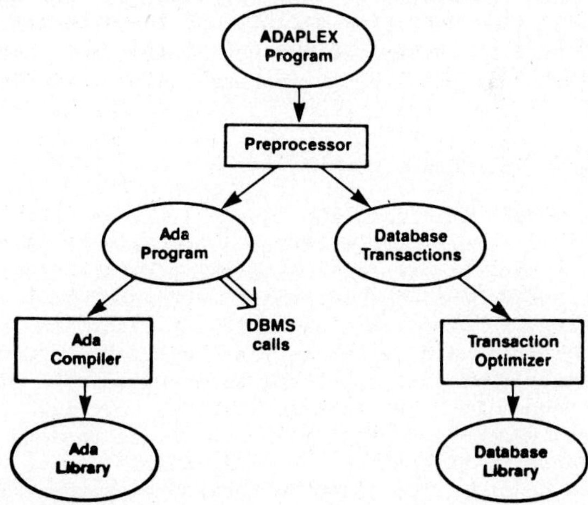

This architecture is very similar to the architecture shown in Figure 1. The only difference is that the preprocessor is now in a position to carry out more correctness checking and to facilitate more global optimization. The external view desired by each application subprogram (transaction in DBMS parlance) is exactly specified such that the database access subprograms generated by the preprocessor can be tailored. At the same time, since the preprocessor is responsible for modifying the source program with embedded calls on the access subprograms, complicated calling conventions can be completely invisible to application programmers.

So far as portability is concerned, both the database module approach and the embedded approach pose identical requirements. As long as the target system has an Ada compiler, and the preprocessor, transaction optimizer, and DBMS are all written in Ada, database applications and their support environment will be portable.

It is our thesis that if the database sublanguage is carefully designed, an embedded approach like Adaplex is more conducive to ease of use and gives the programmer more freedom to mix Ada constructs with those of the database sublanguage.

3 THE ADAPLEX LANGUAGE

The basic goal of the Adaplex effort was to design the best language environment for developing database applications in Ada. Subsidiary goals included:

- Incorporating recent advances in data model and database languages
- Expressing the environment within Ada, except where this would significantly impair database capabilities
- Ensuring that any introduced non-Ada constructs were compatible with Ada in syntax and semantics
- Leaving unchanged the existing syntax and semantics of Ada itself

This section summarizes the novel aspects of the data model that underlies the Adaplex language and gives an overview of the language itself.

3.1 Daplex Data Model

Data models and associated query languages have evolved significantly over the past two decades. The early hierarchical models were superseded by the network and relational models. The latter are in turn being superseded by so-called semantic data models. The design of the Adaplex language is based on a semantically rich data model called Daplex which combines and extends the key features of earlier data models. For example, Daplex's modelling constructs are a strict superset of those found in the relational model. Daplex is designed to enhance the effectiveness and usability of database systems by capturing more of the meaning of an application environment than is possible with conventional data models. The semantic knowledge captured in Daplex is not only meaningful to end users, but also is usable by the database system and database administrator for the purposes of query and physical schema optimization.

The basic modelling constructs in Daplex are entities and functions. Entities correspond to conceptual objects. Entities are classified into entity types, based on the generic properties they possess. Functions represent properties of conceptual objects. Each function, when applied to an entity of appropriate type, yields a single property associated with that entity. Such a property is represented by either a single value or a set of values. These values can be simple, being drawn from Ada supported scalar types and character strings, or composite, consisting of references to entities stored in the database. We illustrate these constructs with an example. Consider a university database modelling students, instructors, departments, and courses. Figure 3 is a graphical representation of the definition of such a database.

Figure 3. A Daplex Database

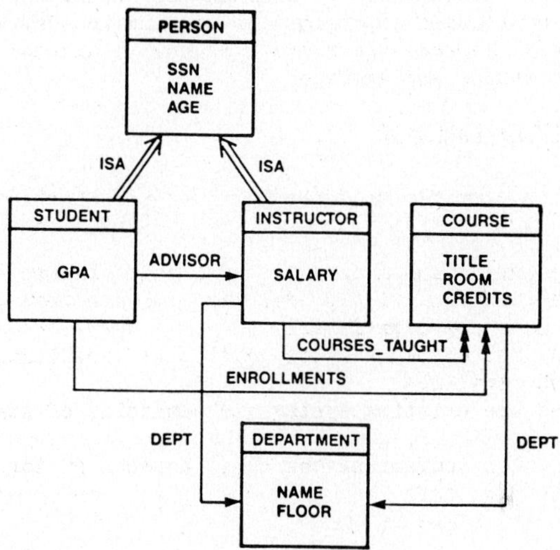

The rectangles depict entity types. The labels within the rectangles depict functions that range over Ada scalar and string types. The single-headed and double-headed arrows represent single-valued and set-valued functions that map argument entity types to result types. The double-edged arrows indicate isa (subtype) relationships.

One major difference between Daplex and the relational model is that referential integrity constraints (Date 1981), which are extremely fundamental in database applications but not easily specifiable in a relational environment, are directly captured. For example, when a student is inserted into the database, the database system will ensure that it has been assigned a valid instructor (i.e., one that is existent in the database). Likewise, when an instructor is to be removed from the database, the database system will see to it that no dangling references result (i.e., there are no more students in the database who have the instructor in question as advisor).

Another important semantic notion captured in Daplex is that of a hierarchy of overlapping entity types. In relational systems, a real-world entity that plays several roles in an application environment typically is represented by tuples in a number of relations. In the university application environment, we might have an instructor entity named John Doe and also a student entity named John Doe. In this case, it might be desirable to impose the constraint that the age of John Doe as an instructor should agree with the age of John Doe as a student. One possible strategy in a relational system is to represent this information only once by having a relation person that stores the age information, and rely on joining operations to determine the age information for students and instructors. In Daplex, we can specify that student and instructor are subtypes of person whereby we can utilize Daplex's function inheritance semantics to simplify the formulation of queries and updates. Figure 4 shows a relational equivalent of the university database.

Figure 4. An Equivalent Relational Schema

PERSON (SSN, NAME, AGE)

STUDENT (SSN, ADV-SSN)

INSTRUCTOR (SSN, DEPT)

COURSE (ROOM, CREDITS)

ENROLLMENTS (SSN, TITLE)

COURSES_TAUGHT (SSN, TITLE)

Figures 5 and 6 show a Daplex query and its equivalent in SQL (Date 1984 a).

Figure 5. A Daplex Query

```
for each S in STUDENT where
    "F320" is in ROOM(ENROLLMENTS(S))
      and
    DEPT(ADVISOR(S)) = CS
loop
    PRINT(NAME(S));
end loop;
```

Figure 6. An Equivalent SQL Query

```
SELECT PERSON.NAME
  FROM  PERSON, STUDENT, ENROLLMENTS, COURSE, INSTRUCTOR
  WHERE PERSON.SSN = STUDENT.SSN
        AND PERSON.SSN = ENROLLMENTS.SSN
        AND ENROLLMENTS.TITLE = COURSE.TITLE
        AND COURSE.ROOM = "F320"
        AND STUDENT.ADV-SSN = INSTRUCTOR.SSN
        AND INSTRUCTOR.DEPT = CS
```

The intent of this query is to print the names of all students taking a class held at room "F320" and taught by an instructor in the "CS" department. Notice how explicit join terms have to be introduced in the SQL query, which tend to obscure readability. On the other hand, the absence of such constructs from the Daplex query allows the query to be read in a more or less English-like manner. A complete description of the Daplex data model and access language can be found in (Fox, et al., 1984).

3.2 Adaplex Overview

Adaplex consists of the integration of the Daplex database sublanguage and Ada. The first step in the design process was to revise the Daplex language to be compatible with Ada. Although Daplex originally had been designed for use in conjunction with a modern programming language, it had to undergo substantial revision before its syntax and semantics were made consistent with Ada. In the data definition area, Daplex was extended to support Ada derived types and subtypes. In the data manipulation area, Daplex was extended to support all of the Ada operators, string slices, short circuit control forms, and many of the Ada type attributes. The major part of the design effort was to embed the adapted Daplex language into Ada.

Adaplex programs provide a clear separation in the program text between schema definition, transaction definition, and Ada computations. Figure 7 shows the principal new constructs added to Ada to form Adaplex and their structural relationships.

Figure 7. The Principal Constructs Added to Ada

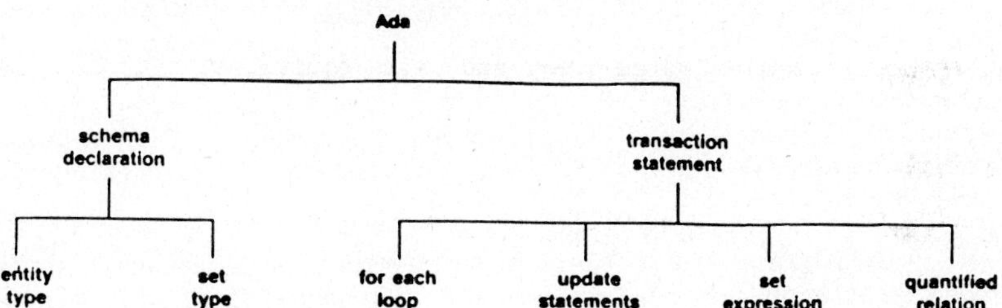

Fundamentally, Adaplex adds two constructs to Ada, the <u>database declaration</u> and the <u>atomic statement</u>. These constructs provide for schema definition and transaction definition respectively. A database declaration specifies the data objects in a database, the types of those data objects, and their consistency/integrity requirements. An atomic statement specifies a compound operation that must be indivisibly executed with respect to a database.

A database is similar to a package since it is a related collection of data and type declarations. However, a database differs from a package in three principal ways. First, there are explicit protocols within Adaplex for several independent main programs to share the use of a database. Second, a strong discipline is imposed on the specifications allowed in a database declaration. Third, as we shall explain in Section 4, database declarations are developed interactively via the database compiler, and they are stored for future reference in the database library.

An atomic statement is similar to a block in the sense that it is a compound statement that has associated declarations and exception handlers. However, an atomic statement differs from a block in three ways. First, atomic statements are executed indivisibly with respect to databases. Second, strong disciplines are imposed on the contents, nesting, parallel execution, and exception handling of atomic statements. Third, atomic statements are transformed by the preprocessor to extract database transactions.

Within a database declaration, new constructs are introduced that specify data types and their consistency/integrity requirements. These constructs are _set types_, _entity types_, _consistency rules_, and _integrity declarations_. A set type encapsulates the mathematical notion of a set. An entity type is a composite type whose instances may be created dynamically by allocators. Consistency rules specify properties of entity types that must be left invariant by individual update statements. Integrity constraints, on the other hand, specify properties of entity types that must be left invariant by atomic statements as a whole.

An entity type is similar to an access-to-record type since it has named components and may be created dynamically. However, an entity type has three key differences from access-to-record types. First, each entity type is associated _explicitly_ with the collection of dynamically created objects of the type. This collection is called the _extent_ of the type. Second, entity types have a much richer subtype structure than access-to-record types. Third, a strong discipline is imposed on the components that entity types may contain. Figure 8 shows the database declaration for the university database depicted graphically in Figure 3.

In addition to the type and subtype declarations, several constraint statements have been specified. The specification:

```
overlap INSTRUCTOR with STUDENT;
```

indicates that it is legal for a PERSON entity to be both a STUDENT and INSTRUCTOR simultaneously. The specification:

```
unique TITLE within COURSE;
```

indicates that all COURSE entities must have unique TITLEs.

Within atomic statements, extensions have been made to both the statement level and the expression level of Ada. The statement level extensions will be discussed first.

Figure 8. An Adaplex Database Declaration

```
database UNIVERSITY is

  type DEPT_NAME is (CS, EE, MA);
  type YEARS is new INTEGER range 0 .. 120;
  UNKNOWN_AGE : constant YEARS := 0;

  type COURSE is
    entity
      TITLE      : STRING (1 .. 6)
      ROOM       : STRING (1 .. 5);
      CREDITS    : INTEGER range 1 .. 4;
    end entity

  type PERSON is
    entity
      NAME       : STRING (1 .. 30);
      AGE        : YEARS := UNKNOWN_AGE;
      SSN        : INTEGER;
    end entity;

  subtype INSTRUCTOR is PERSON
    entity
      DEPT             : DEPT_NAME;
      COURSES_TAUGHT : set of COURSE;
    end entity;

  subtype STUDENT is PERSON
    entity
      DORM          : STRING (1 .. 10);
      ADVISOR       : INSTRUCTOR withnull;
      ENROLLMENTS : set of COURSE;
    end entity;

  overlap INSTRUCTOR with STUDENT;

  unique TITLE within COURSE;

end UNIVERSITY;
```

The <u>for each loop</u> is similar to a for loop, except that iteration is over the extents of entity types rather than over discrete ranges. Each iteration of a for each loop allows one entity to be processed for purposes of update or retrieval.

The <u>create</u> and <u>destroy statements</u> are used for allocating and deallocating entities respectively. Entities must be explicitly deallocated since they are always accessible through the extent of their type. In contrast, objects of an access type can be automatically deallocated when they are no longer designated by an access value.

The <u>move statement</u> is used to dynamically change the subtypes to which an entity belongs, and thus the components that it possesses. In general, an entity can be removed from several subtypes and added to several other subtypes in one indivisible operation. A strong discipline is imposed on the specification of move statements to ensure that consistency rules will be satisfied. In simple cases, a move operation on an entity is analogous to an assignment on a record discriminant.

Entity types may have set valued components. Include statements and exclude statements are introduced as special forms of assignment to set valued objects. Include adds new members to a set, while exclude removes existing members from a set.

Within atomic statements, two principal extensions were made to expressions, namely set constructors and quantified relations. Set constructors allow sets to be constructed from other sets by selecting either some of their members or some component of their members. Quantified relations allow variables within relations to be existentially or universally quantified. In this way, Adaplex expressions provide a predicate logic of relations, as opposed to the boolean logic of Ada expressions.

Figure 9 shows an Ada code fragment that contains an atomic statement.

Figure 9. An Adaplex Database Transaction

```
with UNIVERSITY; use UNIVERSITY;
  .
  .
  .
ADD_COURSE:
  declare
    NEW_COURSE : COURSE;
  atomic
    NEW_COURSE := new COURSE (TITLE    => "CS-101",
                              ROOM     => GET_ROOM(CS),
                              CREDITS  => 3);
    include NEW_COURSE into
      COURSES_TAUGHT
        (I in INSTRUCTOR where NAME (I) = "Adam Jones");
  exception
    when UNIQUENESS_CONSTRAINT =>
      PUT_LINE("Duplicate course name");
  end atomic;
```

This transaction creates a new COURSE entity and indicates that the course will be taught by the INSTRUCTOR named Adam Jones. Notice that the database type declarations are made visible by the with and use statements. The expression level integration of Daplex and Ada is illustrated by calling an Ada subprogram GET_ROOM to generate a value to assign to the ROOM function. Since COURSEs are constrained to have unique TITLEs, it is possible that the create statement may fail. An exception handler is included to cleanly handle this failure.

Interested readers are referred to (Smith, et al., 1983) for a complete description of the Adaplex language.

4 ADAPLEX SUPPORT ENVIRONMENT

This section describes facilities that do not belong to the Adaplex language itself, but to the environment in which Adaplex application programs will be developed and executed. It provides a set of database-related tools that, in conjunction with Ada tools, support the development and execution of database application programs.

In addition to an Ada environment, Adaplex requires the following minimum facilities to support applications programming.

Schema Compiler

The schema compiler accepts database specifications and translates them into an internal form. This internal form is used in the processing of atomic statements. A database specification includes the following components:

- Database declaration
- Authorization declaration
- Statistics declaration
- Representation/view declaration

The source and target forms of database specifications are stored in the database library.

Authorization information describes the permitted use of a database by potential users. Statistics declarations specify the distribution and correlation of component values across entity types. This information is used for optimization purposes. If the database is physically realized, a representation declaration defines its representation at a physical level. If the database is logically derived, a view declaration defines the derivation of its schema from some other database schema.

Databases in the database library are made visible to Adaplex programs by use of "with" clauses. In this respect, the database library is indistinguishable from the Ada program library. Only the database declaration part of a database specification is visible to an Adaplex program.

Adaplex Preprocessor

The preprocessor accepts an Adaplex program and generates a pure Ada program that contains subprogram calls to a database management system. In essence, each atomic statement in the Adaplex program must be transformed into a transaction executable by the DBMS. Further, the atomic statement must be replaced in the Adaplex program by Ada statements to invoke the database transaction and to buffer the data it returns. The preprocessor is a very powerful tool. It provides the same integrity checking across the application program/DBMS interface that the Ada compiler provides for an Ada program.

Transaction Optimizer

Optimization of database transactions is a practical necessity, particularly if the database is geographically distributed. Orders of magnitude improvement in transaction execution time and database throughput often can be achieved. Since such optimization is itself a time-consuming activity, it is important for optimization to be accomplished before execution time.

For these reasons, the preprocessor should invoke the transaction optimizer. Optimization involves the translation of the transactions into efficient sequences of low level database operations. To perform this translation, the relevant database specifications (as produced by the schema compiler) are required. The transactions in optimized form are stored in the database library. At execution time, the pure Ada program need only initiate execution of each optimized transaction and synchronize buffering as data is returned by the DBMS.

Database Management System

The database management system (DBMS) is responsible for executing database transactions while maintaining database integrity standards. The DBMS must provide at least the following capabilities:

- User authentication and data access validation
- Statistics collection and maintenance
- Database library management
- Storage management for data records and auxiliary structures used to represent the database
- Concurrency control to ensure concurrently executing transactions do not interfere with each other
- Recovery management to maintain the integrity of the database in the face of failures such as fatal transaction errors, "soft" system crashes and "hard" memory losses
- Integrity Control to efficiently check integrity conditions prior to transaction termination

The four tools described above (schema compiler, preprocessor, transaction optimizer, DBMS) form the minimum set of tools for database applications programming in Adaplex. These tools must be invoked via a special interactive command language that lies outside of the Adaplex language itself. The combined configuration of these tools is shown in Figure 10. Any one of the Multibase, LDM, DDM systems can be substituted in place of the box labelled DBMS.

Figure 10. Configuration of Adaplex Programming Tools

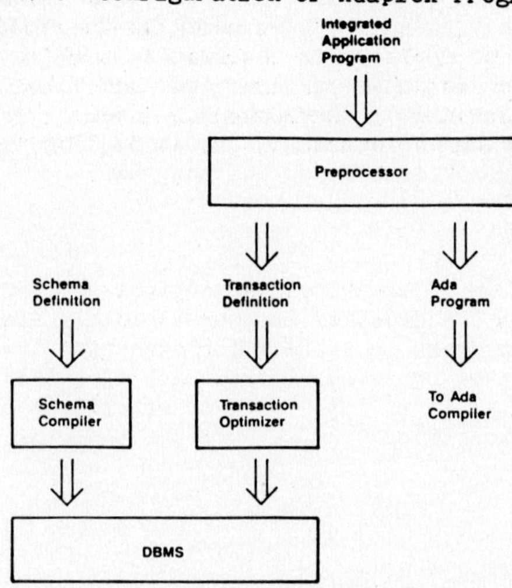

5 CONCLUSIONS

We have examined various approaches for Ada/DBMS coupling, including those that do not embed transaction definitions in Ada (Holland, et al., 1981; Nokia Data Terminal Systems 1983; Vine 1983). and those that do (Horowitz & Kemper 1982; Smith, et al., 1983). It is our conclusion that:

1. All approaches make use of some form of a preprocessor to handle the view definition/data selection, regardless of whether such specification is done inline or physically separate from the application program.
2. The embedded (inline) approach along with the use of a preprocessor on the integrated language provides a higher degree of integrity checking across the Ada/DBMS interface than the nonembedded approach. In fact, the embedded approach can provide the same degree of integrity checking as the Ada compiler.
3. An integrated language is easier to use, more compatible with Ada compile time type-checking, and more conducive to improved data integrity.

As of the writing of this paper, designs of the Daplex and Adaplex languages are complete. Prototype versions of Multibase and LDM have been in existence since 1984. Implementation of DDM is also well underway. To date, the systems contain approximately 500,000 lines of Ada source code. Because of the unavailability of an Ada compiler for our development efforts in earlier years, the systems were initially implemented in the Pascal subset of Ada and were restricted to support only the interactive Daplex interface. Conversion of all three systems to full Ada is in progress using the DEC VAX Ada compiler. The initial target environment is VAX/VMS. An intensive evaluation and tuning phase will commence once the conversion process is complete. Implementation of the Adaplex preprocessor is expected to begin in the near future.

6 ACKNOWLEDGEMENTS

This project is supported jointly by the Advanced Research Projects Agency of the Department of Defense (DARPA) and the Naval Electronics Systems Command (NAVELEX) under contract N00039-82-C-0226. The views and conclusions contained in this paper are those of the authors and should not be interpreted as necessarily representing the official policies, either expressed or implied, of DARPA, NAVELEX, or the U.S. Government.

7 REFERENCES

Chan, A., et al., (1981). "The Design of an Ada Compatible Local Database Manager." Technical Report CCA-81-09, Computer Corporation of America.

Chan, A., et al., (1982 a). "Storage and Access Structures to Support a Semantic Data Model." VLDB Conference Proceedings.

Chan, A., et al., (1982 b). "The Implementation of an Integrated Concurrency Control and Recovery Scheme." ACM SIGMOD Conference Proceeding.

Chan, A., et al., (1983 a). "Overview of an Ada Compatible Distributed Database Manager." ACM SIGMOD Conference Proceedings.

Chan, A., et al., (1983 b). "Supporting a Semantic Data Model in a Distributed Database System." VLDB Conference Proceedings.

Chan, A., et al., (1985). "A Database Management Capability for Ada." ACM Washington Ada Symposium Proceedings.

Chan, A. & Gray, R. (1985). "Implementing Distributed Read-only Transactions." IEEE Transactions on Software Engineering, Vol. SE-11, No. 2, February.

Date, C. (1981). "Referential Integrity." VLDB Conference Proceedings.

Date, C. (1984 a). A Guide to DB2, Addison Wesley.

Date, C. (1984 b). "A Critique of the SQL Database Language." ACM SIGMOD Record, Vol. 14, No. 3, November.

Dayal, U. (1984). "Query Processing in a Multidatabase System." in Query Processing in Database Systems, (W. Kim, D. Batory, D. Reiner, editors), Springer Verlag.

Dayal, U. & Hwang, H. (1984). Database Integration in Multibase: A System for Heterogeneous Distributed Databases." IEEE Transactions on Software Engineering, Vol. SE-10, No. 4, November.

Fox, S., et al., (1984). "Daplex User's Manual." Technical Report CCA-84-01, Computer Corporation of America, March.

Goodman, N., et al., (1983). "A Recovery Algorithm for a Distributed Database Management System." ACM PODS Conference Proceedings.

Holland, J., et al., (1981). "An Ada Relational Database Interface Using Abstract Data Types." TR 81-07, North Carolina State University.

Horowitz, E. & Kemper, A. (1982). "Extending Ada to Include Relations and Non-Procedural Language Constructs." Computer Science Department, University of Southern California.

Landers, T. & Rosenberg, R. (1982). "An Overview of Multibase." in Distributed Databases, (H. Schneider, editor), North Holland Publishing Company.

Nokia Data Terminal Systems (1983). "MPS 10 Database Management System Functional Description." Version 1.0, June.

Ries, D., et al., (1982). "Decompilation and Optimization of Adaplex: A Procedural Database Language." Technical Report, Computer Corporation of America.

Smith, J., et al., (1983). "Adaplex: Rationale and Reference Manual." Technical Report, Computer Corporation of America.

Vines, D. Jr. (1983). "An Interface to an Existing DBMS from Ada (IDA)." GTE Network Systems.

HIGHLY PARALLEL ADA - ADA ON AN ULTRACOMPUTER

Edith Schonberg[1]
Edmond Schonberg[2]

Courant Institute of Mathematical Sciences
251 Mercer St.
New York, N.Y. 10012

ABSTRACT. We examine the suitability of Ada to a specific multiprocessor architecture, the NYU Ultracomputer. The Ultracomputer is an MIMD machine with shared memory, and a special hardware primitive, the *fetch-and-add* operation, with which non-blocking versions of well-known synchronization primitives can be implemented. We show that fetch-and-add can be used to implement some common Ada tasking idioms, and that well-known algorithms for MIMD machines find a natural description in Ada. Furthermore, Ada solutions implemented with fetch-and-add have fewer and smaller critical sections than previously presented versions. The fetch-and-add primitive also provides an efficient solution to the problem of initializing a number of identical tasks, and to the potentially expensive implementation of termination for large numbers of tasks. We conclude that the Ada tasking model "fits" well an MIMD architecture such as the Ultracomputer.

1. Introduction

Programming language features supporting concurrency serve several functions. Certain algorithms, such as operating system algorithms, are inherently concurrent, and are therefore written more clearly in concurrent languages. The advent of multiprocessor architectures has led to an explosive growth in the study of the complexity of parallel algorithms, and provided further motivation for devising ways to specify parallel execution of program components. In this paper we show how Ada can be used to exploit the potential for parallelism provided by a particular multiprocessor computer, the NYU Ultracomputer ([3], [4]). That Ada can be used in this fashion is not obvious a priori, given that the architecture of the Ultracomputer lies far from the embedded systems that underlie (at least in part) the Ada view of tasking.

---

1) This work has been supported in part by Office of Naval Research Grant N00014-82-K-0381, and by grants from the Digital Equipment Corporation, the Sloan Foundation, the System Development Foundation, the IBM Corporation, and by National Science Foundation CER Grant No. NSF-DCR-83-20085.

2) This work has been supported in part by U.S. Army Contract no. DAAB027-82-K-J196 (CORADCOM - Fort Monmouth, N.J.) and by the Ada Joint Program Office.

The Ultracomputer is a MIMD (Multiple Instruction Stream-Multiple Data Stream) computer with a large number of processors, shared memory, and a special synchronization primitive, called *fetch-and-add,* which allows a high degree of parallelism. We show how the fetch-and-add primitive can be incorporated into Ada without extending the language. More precisely, we show that a common kind of monitor task can be implemented in a distributed fashion by means of fetch-and-add. This task can be recognized and special-cased by a compiler on the Ultracomputer. The type of program transformation used has been described in [6] and [7].

While the use of Ada tasking for operating system concurrency problems has been widely discussed, and the unsuitability of Ada for some multiprocessor applications and architectures has been observed ([2], [11]), it is worth noting that certain features of the Ada tasking model are quite naturally suited to an MIMD shared memory architecture. Globally shared variables can be allocated in shared memory. Furthermore, Ada provides the facilities, typically required by MIMD algorithms, to spawn large numbers of both identical and non-identical tasks in parallel and to wait for all simultaneously spawned tasks to terminate. A shortcoming of Ada, observed in [11], is that tasks themselves cannot have parameters, and therefore data must be distributed serially to identical tasks created in parallel. The availability of the fetch-and-add within Ada programs alleviates this serial bottleneck.

In Section 2, we describe the Ultracomputer and the fetch-and-add primitive. Section 3 presents a special task type called *beacon,* and shows how any code that invokes entries of such a task can be replaced in transparent fashion by code containing fetch-and-add instructions. We show that the transformation is correct in the presence of abort statements. In Section 4, a large example using tasks of type *beacon* is described. Section 5 presents some tentative conclusions on the use of Ada for Non-Von Neumann architectures.

2. The NYU Ultracomputer

The NYU Ultracomputer is a MIMD machine. The design of the Ultracomputer is based on an ideal model of parallel computation called the *paracomputer* in [9]. A paracomputer consists of many processing elements (PEs) that share a common, or *public,* memory. Each PE also has a local memory for private computations. A PE can access the public memory in a single memory cycle. Moreover, if several PEs update the same memory location simultaneously, the effect is *as if* these several operations occurred serially. This property of serializing simultaneous updates is called the *serialization principle*.

The Paracomputer is useful as a characterization of the maximum speed-up achievable through parallelization; it is of course not realizable physically, because single cycle memory access cannot be obtained in actuality (if nothing else due to fan-in problems). The Ultracomputer uses a switching network, called an Ω-network, which enforces the serialization principle, to access public memory. In this network, a memory access travels a path of length log n, where n is the number of processing elements.

2.1. The Fetch-and-Add

Critical regions, necessary for synchronization and communication, introduce serialization into otherwise parallel algorithms. The negative impact of critical regions becomes increasingly significant when the number of processors is large, as with the Ultracomputer. To address the critical region problem, the Ultracomputer has a special operation called *fetch-and-add* that also obeys the serialization principle. A simple, low-level primitive, fetch-and-add is the basis of communication among PEs. A collection of techniques and "Ultracomputer idioms" have evolved to implement critical sections in a non-blocking fashion.

The fetch-and-add operation is described as follows. Let V be a public integer variable with initial value V_0, e_1 an integer valued expression, and l_1 a variable local to PE_1. If a fetch-and-add instruction of the form

$$l_1 := F\&A(V,e_1); \tag{1}$$

is executed by PE_1, then e_1 is added to V. The value of V before the addition is performed is returned to PE_1 as the value of the function, and assigned to l_1. If at the *same time* another processor PE_2 executes

$$l_2 := F\&A(V,e_2); \tag{2}$$

then, again, e_2 is added to V, and the value of V before the addition is returned to PE_2. Thus, after (1) and (2), V has the value $V_0 + e_1 + e_2$. Since (1) and (2) are simultaneous, either $l_1 = V_0$ and $l_2 = V_0 + e_1$, or $l_1 = V_0 + e_2$ and $l_2 = V_0$. That is, the effect of the two fetch-and-add operations that occur simultaneously is as if they occurred in some unspecified serial order.

The fetch-and-add operation is implemented directly in the switching components of the network. This allows concurrent fetch-and-adds directed at the same location in memory to be accepted in the time required for a single load or store. It is important to note that reads, writes, and fetch-and-adds can all occur in parallel on an Ultracomputer, and the serialization principle holds for any combination of them.

2.2. Uses of the Fetch-and-Add

The fetch-and-add primitive has been used to implement synchronization procedures for a variety of Ultracomputer applications ([4]). The Dijkstra semaphore can be implemented with fetch-and-adds, as well as a counting semaphore that can be used to solve the many readers/one writer problem. The Ultracomputer fetch-and-add solution to readers/writers has the interesting unique property that if there are no writers, readers are never blocked nor serialized, even when accessing the generalized semaphore.

A very important Ultracomputer structure is a highly parallel queue manager that uses fetch-and-adds. The manager allows simultaneous insertions into and deletions from a FIFO queue provided it is not full (resp. empty). Any number of processors can insert objects into the queue without being serialized. There is also a non-blocking queue manager for objects with priorities and multiplicities, which is the core of a distributed Ultracomputer operating system.

3. Implementing Ada On The Ultracomputer

For reasons mentioned in Section 1, the multi-tasking facilities of Ada appear to make it suitable for describing algorithms on architectures like the Ultracomputer. However, to take full advantage of the parallelism available, the fetch-and-add needs to be accessible to the programmer in some fashion. For example, the applications described in Section 2.2 can then be implemented directly in Ada. The challenge is to use this primitive without extending Ada, and thus retain the portability of Ada programs even when written with the Ultracomputer in mind. This is the focus of the following section.

3.1. The Fetch-and-Add in Ada

We incorporate the fetch-and-add into Ada without any actual extension to the language by defining a task type called ***beacon***, which can be treated in a special way by the Ultracomputer Ada compiler. A program using the ***beacon*** task type will execute correctly on any conforming Ada system and produce the same result as on the Ultracomputer, (provided the program is not erroneous by the definition of RM.9.11(6)). The ***beacon*** is defined as follows:

```
task type beacon is
   entry init(e: in integer);
   entry read(l: out integer);
   entry write(e: in integer);
   entry F_and_A(l: out integer, e: in integer);
end beacon;
```

It is a monitor that synchronizes reads, writes, and updates of a protected variable *v*. As such, it subsumes many familiar synchronization mechanisms. In normal usage, a master task MT in which a ***beacon*** task T is created initializes the shared variable *v* by calling the entry T.***init***. After initialization, other subtasks of MT synchronize among themselves by performing rendezvous with entries of the beacon. The body of the beacon is given in figure 3.1.1.

Calls to beacon entries are of course serialization points. The interest of the fetch-and-add operation consists precisely in providing the needed synchronization, without blocking any of the callers. A beacon can be implemented in terms of read, write, and fetch-and-add operations, by "distributing" it over all tasks that invoke its entries. A beacon thus disappears as a separate task entity, and leaves behind a simple data structure and code fragments to access it. This is an example of the kinds of

```
task body beacon is
   v: integer;
begin
   accept init(e: in integer) do
      v := e;
   end init;

   loop
      select
         accept read(l: out integer) do
            l := v;
         end read;
      or
         accept write(e: in integer) do
            v := e;
         end write;
      or
         accept F_and_A(l: out integer, e: in integer) do
            l := v;
            v := v + e;
         end F_and_A;
      or
         terminate;
      end select;
   end loop;
end beacon;
```

Figure 3.1.1. Definition of *beacon*

transformations proposed in [6] and [7].

The precise transformation is as follows. A task Tb of type *beacon* becomes a record T with four fields allocated in public memory:

```
type beacon_struct is record
   value:   integer ;
   initialized: boolean := false ;
   completed:  boolean := false ;
   initsync: integer := 0 ;
end record ;

T: beacon_struct ;
```

The field *value* stores the integer value of the task variable *v*, the flags *initialized* and *completed* store information on the callability of the task, and the field *initsync* is used to guarantee that only one task is allowed to initialize *v*. Tasks can read, write, and fetch-and-add the value field only if it is *initialized* and not *completed*. The task Tb becomes *completed* when either it is aborted or the master task and all its descendents terminate. If a task tries to access the value when it is *completed* then TASKING_ERROR is raised in the caller.

More specifically, entry calls to Tb are transformed into accesses to the record T as follows:

```
(1) Tb.init(e)  ==>     if T.completed  then
                                   raise TASKING_ERROR;
                        end if;

                        num := F&A(T.initsync, 1);
                        if num /= 0 then
                        -- task Tb is already initialized.
                        -- if this is a timed entry call, wait for the
                        -- stated time and then goto exitini.
                        -- if a conditional entry call, goto exitini.
                        -- else block until aborted or Tb is completed.
                        ...
                        end if;

                        T.value := e;
                        T.initialized := true;

                 <<exitini>>
```

Note that the fetch-and-add operation on *T.initsync* is necessary to avoid race conditions among various tasks trying to initialize *T.value*. (We assume that there is no 'uninitialized' value that could be used in *T.value* to play this synchronization role).

Below, we give the transformations for calls to the *read, write,* and *F_and_A* entries of a *beacon* task. As before, the code obtained depends on whether the call is an ordinary call, a timed entry call, or a conditional entry call. In these transformations, *call* means either *(i) read(l), (ii) write(e),* or *(iii) F_and_A(l, e).* The clause *code_for_call* used in the transformations below stands for: *(i') l := T.value;* , *(ii') T.value := e;* , or *(iii') l := F&A(T.value, e);* for (i), (ii), and (iii) respectively.

```
(2) Tb.call       ==>          while not T.initialized or T.completed
                               loop
                                  if T.completed then
                                     raise TASKING_ERROR;
                                  end if;
                               end loop;
                               code_for_call;
```

```
(3)  select         ==>        if T.completed then
        Tb.call;                  raise TASKING_ERROR;
        [statements-1]         end if;
     else                      if T.initialized then
        [statements-2]            code_for_call;
      end select;              [statements-1]
                               else
                                  [statements-2]
                               end if;
```

```
(4)   select        ==>        DT := CLOCK + D;
         T.call;               while not T.initialized or T.completed
         [statements-1]        loop
      or                          if T.completed then
         delay D;                    raise TASKING_ERROR;
         [statements-2]           end if;
      end select;              exit when CLOCK > DT ;
                               end loop;

                               if CLOCK < DT then
                                  code_for_call;
                                  [statements-1]
                               else
                                  [statements-2]
                               end if;
```

While at first glance it may seem that we have traded a rendezvous for a busy wait in (2) and (4), in fact there should be very little busy waiting. In normal circumstances, T.*value* will be initialized soon after master task activation, after which the while loop bodies of (2) and (4) will never be executed.

An informal proof of the correctness of these transformations can be found in [8].

3.2. Handling of Abort

We now examine what happens if either a called *beacon* task Tb or the caller task is aborted. If the *beacon* task Tb is aborted, then its status becomes *completed*, and any calling task (which has not already entered the rendezvous code) will detect completion before accessing the value.

More complications arise if the caller is aborted. We must first of all ensure that the integrity of Tb is maintained if the caller is aborted during a rendezvous. Secondly, since the start and end of the rendezvous are synchronization points, we must be able to detect calls to abort that occurred both before and during the rendezvous.

Note first that while the proposed transformation makes the *beacon* task itself disappear, the data structure that replaces it is in shared memory and independent of the tasks that call the beacon. Therefore, if any particular caller gets aborted, the other tasks that call the beacon still have access to it. We must also ensure that if the caller is aborted in the middle of executing the code for Tb (e.g. a F&A), then this execution is completed before the caller is actually aborted. This is guaranteed by the fact that the F&A, once initiated, is executed by the network and not actually by the caller.

If the calling task is aborted before the rendezvous is entered, then the code accessing *T.value* must not be executed. Therefore, a condition testing abortion must be included before the rendezvous code, which allows the calling task to disappear gracefully if aborted by someone else. This test simply interrogates a location in shared memory that holds the status of the calling task. This location is also accessed by the task that performs an abort. A similar test must be performed after the rendezvous code, to detect whether the caller was aborted during the rendezvous. In this fashion each task monitors its own status and recognizes when it has been aborted. The economy of this solution on the Ultracomputer also follows from the existence of fetch-and-add.

4. An Example - Solution of Laplace's Equation

In this section, we discuss an example of a numeric application which is presented in full detail in [5] (This example is also used in [11]). We first describe it in its original form as given in [5], and then in Section 4.1 show how we can modify it to use *beacons*. By using *beacons*, we are able to cut in half the number of required tasks, and remove almost all blocking caused by synchronization.

The algorithm belongs to a family of so-called asynchronous iteration algorithms [1] which are particularly suitable for multiprocessor systems because they require fewer synchronization points than other iteration methods.

The technique is generally applicable to various elliptic boundary value problems (the Laplace equation in the case of [5]) on a rectangular domain D. The discrete representation of D is an (m x n) matrix of points. D is subdivided into a grid of rectangular regions, and one task of type *region_task* is assigned to the solution of the boundary value problem on each region. A region task R iteratively computes new values for its region, until its local values converge. However, this local convergence does not mean that R may complete. A neighbor task R' may change a value of a point of D that lies on the boundary of R and R', forcing R to begin iterating again. Global convergence is achieved only when all tasks have converged locally. Thus it is necessary for a task that has not converged locally to notify an idle neighbor that it should restart its processing. This communication among near neighbors is the crux of the algorithm, and a potential source of serialization (as well as race conditions and deadlocks!). This communication is accomplished as follows:

Each region task has an associated coordinator task to handle communication with neighboring region tasks. This coordinator receives notifications from neighboring region tasks that further iterations are required, and awakens its corresponding region task when it becomes idle. A coordinator task also receives notification from the region task that detects final convergence, and awakens its region task in this case also.

To determine final convergence, a global counter is used to store the number of regions that have not converged locally. When the counter, initially equal to the number of region tasks, becomes 0, convergence is achieved. This counter is updated by all region and coordinator tasks. Therefore a separate monitor task called *Unfinished_Counter* synchronizes updates to the counter.

The procedure *ParRelax_Inner_Proc,* the outline of which is given in Figure 4.1, is the main procedure of the algorithm. The variable *NumRegions,* global to *ParRelax_Inner_Proc,* stores the number of regions. In this procedure, *NumRegions* * 2 + 1 tasks are created, corresponding to the region tasks, coordinator tasks, and counter monitor. The program then executes as follows.

Initialization. *ParRelax_Inner_Proc* initializes the global counter to *NumRegions* by calling *Unfinished_Counter.Initialize.* It then passes parameters to the region tasks via *Region_Task* entry *SetParameter.* Since all region tasks are identical, this initialization is necessary for each task to know the region to which it is assigned.

It has been observed in [11] that this initialization of identical tasks introduces a serial bottleneck into an otherwise parallel execution. Furthermore, task identification procedures like this are typical of multiprocessor applications, indicating a real shortcoming of Ada. We return to this issue in the next section.

Region Task Execution. At each loop iteration of a region task R, all values of its region of D are updated and local convergence is tested. If there is no convergence, R notifies its four neighbors to continue, by calling the *KeepOnGoing* entry of each of its neighbor's coordinator task. The *KeepOnGoing* entry is responsible for incrementing the *Unfinished_Counter*

```
procedure ParRelax_Inner_proc is

   task type Region_Task is
      entry SetParameter(SetMyRowRegion, SetMyColRegion: in Integer);
   end Region_Task;

   task type Coordinator_Task is
      entry Wait;
      entry KeepOnGoing;
      entry Finish;
   end Coordinator_Task;

   Regions: array(1..RowRegions, 1..ColRegions) of Region_Task;
   Coordinators: array(1..RowRegions, 1..ColRegions) of Coordinator_Task;

   Unfinished_Counter: ... ; -- global counter monitor task


begin

   Unfinished_Counter.Initialize(NumRegions);

   -- Set the parameters of the regions tasks:

   for I in Regions'RANGE(1) loop
      for J in Regions'RANGE(2) loop
         Regions(I,J).SetParameter(I,J);
      end loop;
   end loop;

   -- Now wait for all tasks to terminate.
end ParRelax_Inner_Proc;
```

Figure 4.1. ParRelax_Inner_Proc Outline

for its region task via a nested entry call. This is necessary to avoid a race condition, as described in Section 4.1.

If R has converged locally, it decrements *Unfinished_Counter*. When this counter becomes 0, the program has converged globally. The region task that decrements the counter to 0 notifies all other region tasks (via their coordinators) to terminate. If the counter is not 0, R goes to sleep, waiting for notification either to continue to iterate or to terminate. R waits by calling the *Wait* entry of its coordinator task.

Thus each iteration that does not converge requires the overhead of up to four rendezvous. While the length of any queue for a coordinator

KeeponGoing accept statement is at most four (there are four neighbors), there is still substantial system/communication overhead associated with each rendezvous.

Termination. The last region task R to converge locally decrements the global counter to 0. R then notifies all region tasks that they may terminate. This notification is performed by calling the *Finish* entry of all coordinator tasks. All other region tasks will then rendezvous with the *Wait* entry of their coordinators, and subsequently terminate. Therefore, as with initialization, termination is a serial process.

4.1. Adaptations for the Ultracomputer

In this section, we show how to modify the Ada implementation outlined above to take advantage of the Ultracomputer. We use *beacon* tasks to eliminate serial bottlenecks during initialization, execution, and termination. After activation the region tasks rendezvous only with tasks of type *beacon*, so that on an Ultracomputer they will run until termination without ever being blocked or serialized. The most profitable transformation is obtained by making the coordinator tasks into *beacons*. This is not a mechanical transformation because as written (see [5]) the coordinator tasks contain critical regions that are not immediately reducible to fetch-and-add operations. In particular, a coordinator task has an entry call to the *Unfinished_Counter* task, which is nested within an accept statement. We shall see that a modification of the algorithm can simplify the structure of a coordinator task to that of a *beacon*, at which point the total number of bona-fide tasks required is halved. We modify the original algorithm as follows.

Initialization. To solve the problem of region task parameter distribution, we transfer the responsibility of initializing region tasks from the master *ParRelax_Inner_Proc* to the region tasks themselves. A *beacon* task, *SetParm* is declared in *ParRelax_Inner_Proc*. The accept statement at the beginning of the region task body that initializes parameters is then replaced by the calls:

```
SetParm.F_and_A(MyNum, 1);
MyRowRegion := MyNum / RowRegions + 1;
MyColRegion := MyNum mod RowRegions + 1;
```

Each region task thereby obtains distinct values for *MyRowRegion* and *MyColRegion*. Note that there is no relation between the position of a region task in the array *Regions*, and the region of the domain on which this task computes. Each task can nevertheless communicate with the tasks in charge of neighboring regions, because the coordinator tasks (and later beacons) serve to establish the needed mapping between regions and their assigned tasks. The initialization code in *ParRelax_Inner_Proc* is replaced by code to initialize the *SetParm* shared variable:

```
SetParm.init(0);
```

With the implementation of *beacons* given in Section 3.1, the region tasks are then able to initialize themselves in parallel, and the serial bottleneck is removed.

Removal Of Coordinator Tasks. In order to transform coordinator tasks into *beacons*, we must remove the entry calls that each such task performs on *Unfinished_Counter*. It is instructive to examine why this call is actually needed: a region task will discover that termination is possible if the *Unfinished_Counter* is zero *and* if it is idle and there are no pending notifications from its neighbors that it should iterate. When a neighbor notifies a region task to keep on going, the program must ensure that *Unfinished_Counter* does not become zero before the region task has a chance to find out that it should keep on going. Otherwise, there is a race condition, and the possibility of premature termination. In order to remove this critical section, we modify the meaning of *Unfinished_Counter* to reflect the total number of pending notifications that all tasks have received from their neighbors while performing their iteration cycle. Each region task R has in turn its own counter to store the number of pending notifications that it has received from neighbors to keep on iterating. The coordinator task for R now only serves to monitor this counter, and has thus become a *beacon*.

These modifications are reflected in the following code:

When a region task determines that its neighbors must iterate again, it performs:

```
Unfinished_Counter.F_and_A(c, 1) ;   -- total global count
Coordinators(k, l).F_and_A(c, 1) ;   -- and local neighbor count.
```

for the four neighboring values of (k, l). (The value returned in c is not used further).

Each region task reads the value of its counter into a local variable *pending* before each iteration cycle. (This variable is initialized to 1 for the first iteration.)

When a region task converges locally, it performs:

```
Coordinators(MyRowRegion, MyColRegion).F_and_A(c, -pending) ;
Unfinished_Counter.F_and_A(c, -pending) ;
```

to indicate that this many pending calls were taken care of. The region task then executes the following polling code:

```
loop
   Unfinished_Counter.read(tot_pending);
   exit OuterLoop when tot_pending = 0 ;
   -- and turn off the lights. Otherwise...
   Coordinators(MyRowRegion, MyColRegion).read(pending) ;
   exit when  pending /= 0 ;
   -- and restart iteration.
end loop;
```

The invariant: *Unfinished_Counter* ≥ pending_msgs(R) for all regions R, where pending_msgs(R) is the pending message counter for R, is maintained by the preceding code. This invariant guarantees that when *Unfinished_Counter* reaches zero, the system is totally quiescent and termination can take place.

The solution does not come completely for free. A region task which is not actively computing is polling. While polling is not as expensive on a multiprocessor computer as on a single processor computer, there is a price paid in terms of increased network traffic, as well as in processor monopolization. We note, however, that the situation is somewhat better on the Ultracomputer because the switching elements are implemented in such a way that there is no additional cost for accessing the same memory location by many processors.

Termination. Finally, the serial bottleneck at termination has also been eliminated. As indicated in the preceding code, each task detects termination directly by reading *Unfinished_Counter*.

5. Conclusions

The final version is satisfyingly efficient, and 'fits' the Ultracomputer architecture well. The region tasks run until termination without any blocking, there are 50% fewer tasks for a given partition of the initial domain, and the Ada code is portable and free from machine-dependent idioms.

This indicates that Ada may be well-suited for programming MIMD machines and for describing algorithms that require moderate amounts of synchronization between tasks. The method which we have used, to transform the tasks bodies into special instances of *beacon* tasks, should be regarded as a useful programming discipline when writing Ada for the Ultracomputer. There are also indications that those aspects of Ada implementation that on other architectures seem to require large amounts of message passing, (e.g. termination) can be realized very efficiently on the Ultracomputer. This bodes well both for the Ultracomputer and for Ada.

Acknowledgements.

We want to thank Norman Shulman for a critical reading of the manuscript and many valuable comments.

REFERENCES

[1] G.M. Baudet, "Asynchronous Iterative Methods for Multiprocessors," *Journal of the ACM*, Vol. 25, No. 2, pp. 226-244, Apr. 1978.

[2] N. Gehani, "Concurrency in Ada and Multicomputers," *Computer Languages*, Vol. 7, No. 1, pp. 21-23, 1982.

[3] A. Gottlieb, R. Grishman, C. Kruskal, K. McAuliffe, L. Rudolph, and M. Snir, "The Ultracomputer - Designing an MIMD Shared Memory Parallel Computer," *IEEE Trans. Comput.*, Vol. C-32, No. 2, pp. 175-189, Feb. 1983.

[4] A. Gottlieb, B. Lubachevsky, and L. Rudolph, "Basic Techniques for the Efficient Coordination of Very Large Numbers of Cooperating Sequential Processes," *ACM TOPLAS*, Jan. 1983.

[5] P.A. Hibbard, A. Higen, J. Rosenberg, M. Shaw, M. Sherman, *Studies in Ada Style*, Springer-Verlag, 1981.

[6] P.N. Hilfinger, *Abstraction Mechanisms and Language Design*, MIT Press, 1982.

[7] P.N. Hilfinger, "Implementation Strategies for Ada Tasking Idioms," *Proc. AdaTec Conf. on Ada*, pp. 26-30, Oct. 1982.

[8] E. Schonberg, E. Schonberg, "Highly Parallel Ada - Ada on an Ultracomputer," N.Y.U. Ultracomputer Note #81, 1985.

[9] J.T. Schwartz, "Ultracomputers," *ACM TOPLAS*, Vol. 2, pp. 484-581, 1980.

[10] U. S. Department of Defense, *Reference Manual for the Ada Programming Language*, 1983.

[11] S. Yemini, "On the Suitability of Ada Multitasking for Expressing Parallel Algorithms," *Proc. AdaTec Conf. on Ada*, pp. 91-97, Oct. 1982.

SOME PROBLEMS IN DISTRIBUTING REAL-TIME ADA PROGRAMS ACROSS MACHINES[1]

Richard A. Volz[2] Trevor N. Mudge
Arch W. Naylor John H. Mayer

Abstract

The Ada Research Group of the Robotics Research Laboratory at The University of Michigan is currently developing a real-time distributed computing capability based upon the premises that real-time distributed *languages* provide the best approach to real-time distributed computing and, given the focus on the language level, that Ada offers an excellent candidate language. The first phase of the group's work was on analysis of real-time distributed computing. The second, and current, phase is the development of a pre-translator which translates an Ada program into *n* Ada programs, each being targeted for one of a group of processors and each having required communication support software automatically created and attached by the pre-translator. This paper describes the pre-translator being developed and a number of issues which have arisen with regard to the distributed execution of a single Ada program, including language semantics, objects of distribution and their mutual access, network timing, and execution environments.

1. Introduction

"Ada" is the result of a collective effort to design a common language for programming large scale and real-time systems." So states the foreword to the Ada Language Reference Manual [DoD83]. This statement has often been elaborated to mean that Ada is intended for large, embedded, real-time systems executing in a coordinated fashion on a number of machines. Yet, to date, while tremendous effort has gone into the design of the language, the development of compilers for it, and the development of the Ada Programming System Environment, relatively little emphasis has been placed on the distributed and real-time issues. This paper addresses there latter two issues through the vehicle of distributed language, that is, one in which a single program may be executed on a distributed set of processors.

There are, nevertheless, a number of advantages to the use of a real-time distributed language capability, including:

- Real-time distributed systems are typically large and complex, and, consequently, difficult for a programmer or programming team to mentally encompass. The conceptual advantages associated with viewing the system as one large, highly-structured, program in one language are enormous.
- Interprocessor communication has been found to be one of most difficult and time consuming aspects of building complex distributed systems [VMG84], [VoM84], [Car84]. If this could be made implicit, the programmer could be spared a great amount of onerous detail. Fortunately, this is usually possible because the compiler can "see" the entire program at one time.
- Modern software concepts such as data and program abstractions [Sha80], and compile time error checking intended for the language level can be applied over the entire system as opposed to just over each of several individual parts with no checking between them.

---

[1]This work is supported by Land Systems Division of General Dynamics under contract #DEY-600483

[2]The Ada Research Group of the Robotics Research Laboratory, Department of Electrical Engineering and Computer Science, The University of Michigan, Ann Arbor, Michigan 48109.

- Synchronization and timing is, on the one hand, more straightforward for the programmer, while, on the other, the tedious details, as in the case of communication and conversion, are suppressed.

Once the need for a real-time distributed language is accepted, there are three choices: create a new language, modify an existing language, or, if feasible, use an existing one. Ada is an excellent candidate for the latter approach for a number of reasons. The Ada concept was designed to provide modern software tools for programming large, complex systems, to be highly portable, to provide closely monitored standards, to have an excellent support environment, and to provide programming mechanisms for real-time systems. Moreover, it provides mechanisms, e.g. pragmas, which can be implementation defined and are suitable for managing the distribution of a program in situations where the distribution is possible, while remaining consistent with the Ada language definition, even when distribution is not possible.

One approach to the distributed execution of a single Ada program would be to write an entirely new compiler and run-time system to manage the translation, and it may eventually be shown that this is the correct approach. However, it is not clear that enough is yet known about the ramifications arising from distributed execution to make the large investment necessary for this approach worth while. Instead, our group is taking a simpler approach. An experimental pre-translator is being developed which will translate a single Ada program into a set of inter-communicating Ada source programs, one for each node of the target network. Each of the Ada source programs created: (1) realizes part of the original Ada source program (typically this is close to a copy of a portion of the source); and (2) adds Ada packages to support the harmonious distributed execution of the resultant Ada programs. Each object Ada program is subsequently compiled by an existing Ada compiler for the processor for which the program is targeted, as illustrated in Figure 1.

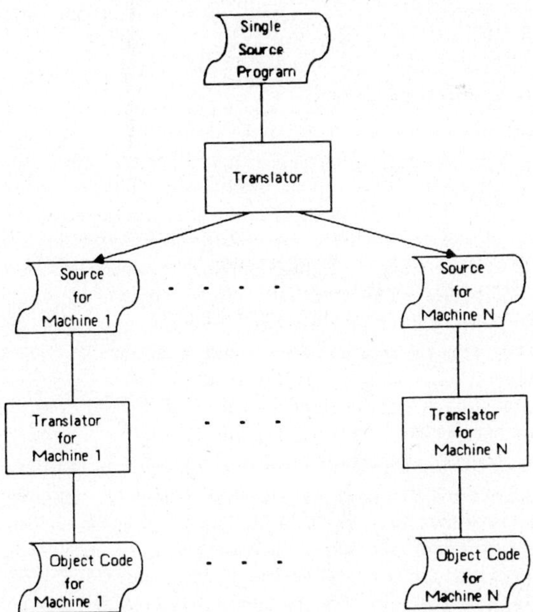

Figure 1

The development of the pre-translator is intended not only to provide an experimental tool for exploring many aspects of distributed real-time systems, but to expose language and implementation difficulties as well [VMN84]. Work to date has, indeed, revealed a number of problems in the distribution of Ada programs across heterogeneous processors. This paper discusses the more important part of these problems, organizing them under the headings of Definitional Issues, Object Access, Network Timing, and Execution Environments. This is followed by an introduction to the strategy being used to develop the pre-translator. Armitage and Chelini [ArC85] describe somewhat similar issues but in less detail.

2. Definitional Issues

Understanding the legal behavior of an Ada program which executes in a distributed manner requires extended study of the Language Reference Manual (LRM). Some issues which seem clear in the uniprocessor case are less so when distributed execution is considered. This section identifies some of these issues and discusses possible interpretations.

2.1. Objects of Distribution

The first question facing anyone who wishes to build a system allowing distributed execution of Ada is "What can be distributed?" The Language Reference Manual does not give an answer to this. Nor does it say how the distribution is to be specified. All that can be said is that the distributed execution of the program must be in accordance with the LRM. There are many levels of granularity at which one could define a set of entities to be distributed.

A rather coarse degree of granularity, which could be convenient from the perspective creating machine load units, is the use of packages as the objects of distribution. Through items declared in their visible part they can provide considerable flexibility in the items made available on remote machines. The distribution of most units smaller than packages creates a problem in building load units, as it becomes necessary to embed them within a library unit of some kind. For example, if a task or data item alone is to be distributed how is it to be stored and loaded on the remote machine? Tasks and data items alone can not be compilation units.

Nevertheless, in our experimental system we opted for a fine degree of granularity and allow the distribution of any object that can be created. Any object which can be allocated, data or execution, is allowed to be distributed. This choice was made for two reasons. First, it will allow us to explore the implementation strategies needed for all kinds of objects. Second, taking what are essentially the smallest meaningful distribution objects permits a study of distributed programming styles which is uninhibited by restrictive implementation decisions. The flexibility made possible by these two choices is important because systems that allow distributed execution are new and techniques for writing distributed programs (as opposed to writing collections of cooperating programs) have yet to be created.

2.2. Conditional Entry Calls

Conditional entry calls are a source of possible confusion in the distributed execution of a program due to network delays in calling across machines and the meaning of the word "immediate" in the semantic description of the call. The LRM states that "A conditional entry call issues an entry call that is then cancelled if a rendezvous is not immediately possible." The possible difficulty is in the word "immediate". At least one group [DGC83] has determined that due to network delays, conditional entry calls should always fail when the call is to a remote machine. However, the LRM also suggests a different interpretation when it restates the conditions for cancellation of the call, "The entry call is cancelled if the execution of the called task has not reached a point where it is ready to accept the call, .., or if there are prior queued entry calls for this entry".

If one adds the interpretation "when the call reaches the called task" to the second LRM statement given above, a clear interpretation results. This interpretation is independent of the time required to initiate the rendezvous. It depends only upon the readiness of the called task. This is appropriate. If a sense of time is required, timed entry calls should be used.

2.3. Timed Entry Calls

The timed entry call is the one place in the LRM where an upper bound on the time duration for some action to take place is stated. There are several questions to be considered with respect to timed entry calls. The LRM says both that the entry call ".... is cancelled if a rendezvous **is not started** within a given delay," and that if the "..rendezvous **can be started** within the specified duration ..., it is performed ...". (emphases added). The former implies that execution of the rendezvous must be started within the delay, while the latter implies only that it be able to be started within the given delay.

In most distributed situations the problem will be complicated, not only by a network delay, but also by an uncertainty in the consistency of the sense of time maintained on two or more processors (see section 4 for a detailed discussion of this point). Since there is likely to be an uncertainty in the difference in the sense of time available on two different processors, it may not be possible to make a precise determination of whether a rendezvous can or cannot be started within a given time interval. However, in many implementations it will be possible to provide bounds on the difference in the sense of time between two processors. This will make it possible to guarantee that if the rendezvous can be started within a calculable bound (as measured on the processor on which the called task resides), the called task can also be started within the given delay as measured on the processor from which the call was made. In these cases, there will be an uncertainty interval in which it will not be possible to determine whether or not the call can be started within the given time delay as measured on the processor from which the call is made.

An interpretation of timed entry calls for the distributed environment which would reflect these considerations would be that "if the call can be guaranteed to be able to start within the given delay it is started, and is cancelled otherwise". For the uncertainty interval, during which it might or might not be possible to start the called task, the timed entry call would be cancelled.

A second issues arises from the statement that timed entry calls with zero or negative delays are to be treated as conditional entry calls. Under the condition that the called task is ready to accept a call, an inconsistency arises with respect to whether the rendezvous is completed or cancelled. Due to delays in network transmission, there will be a set of small delays for which the rendezvous fails, while for delay values either above or below those in the set the rendezvous would succeed. This situation is illustrated in Figure 2 below. To be consistent, there should be a single dividing line, above which the calls succeed (if the called task is ready) and below which they fail. A more consistent statement would result if the LRM did not contain the phrase about treating the case with zero or negative delay as conditional entry calls. Nevertheless, though unfortunate, the LRM does state quite clearly that the situation is as shown in Figure 2.

The implementation aspects of timed entry calls will be discussed further in conjunction with network timing in section 4.

3. Object Access

3.1. Modes of Access

The structure of Ada permits two different modes of access among execution objects (subprogram units or tasks). One is by passing parameters in subprogram calls or task entries. The other is by shared variables that exist in the common scope of the execution

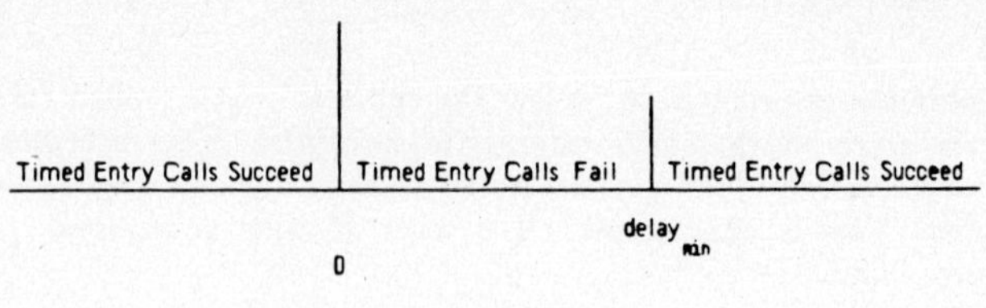

Figure 2 Time entry call success vs. delay time, assuming called task read to accept the call.

objects.

Ada requires that parameters be passed by copy. To avoid possible inefficiencies parameters that are arrays, records or task types may be passed by reference provided the effect is by copy. In the case of execution objects on tightly coupled machines[3] passing by reference, while keeping the appearance of by copy, can be efficient and makes sense. However, in the case of loosely coupled machines[4], passing by reference will lead to cross machine communication on each reference to the object passed. It thus seems natural to pass all parameters by copy. When the execution objects communicate over a Local Area Network (LAN), such communications are normally thought of as messages. This leads us to refer to access by copying parameters as message passing.

On the other hand communication between two execution objects through shared variables can be most naturally implemented with a shared logical memory. In the case where the shared logical memory is implemented as a shared physical memory this presents few problems. However, in the case where there is no underlying shared physical memory the run-time system must create the illusion. This leads us to refer to communication through shared variables as shared memory communication. If we return to the case of execution objects communicating over a LAN, but now consider shared variable access, the potential for inefficient communication becomes clear.

3.2. Addressing

The assumption that the objects of distribution may be any object that can be created in the language results in a large set of object access situations which must be explored. Objects may be created in three distinct ways: by declaration statement, by the **new** allocator, and, in the case of blocks, by their occurrence in the instruction stream. The types of objects which can be created by declaration statements are:

- scalars
- arrays
- records
- subprograms
- tasks
- packages
- access variables

The complications in object referencing arise primarily when one is implementing shared

[3] Machines that share physical memory.

[4] Machines that do not share physical memory.

memory access on loosely coupled machines. The Ada scoping rules make it convenient, though not necessarily well-advised, to write programs in this manner. Comparison with the tightly couple case will clarify this point.

3.2.1. Object Access in Tightly Coupled Machines

In the case of tightly coupled machines, shared data object references can be implemented as in a uniprocessor case. This requires that the underlying hardware memory protection system allow user processes on multiple machines to access the same regions of physical memory, but otherwise creates no problems for handling variables or pointers not already present in the language. Access to remote execution objects requires a signalling mechanism among the processors involved to permit the receipt of a remote call, but requires no special mechanisms for handling the actual parameters of the call. The tradeoffs between communication by shared variables or message passing are the same as for a uniprocessor implementation.

The principal difficulties that accrue to the translation system in the tightly coupled case lie in the recognition that a reference to a remote execution object has occurred. This recognition is straightforward if the distribution specification is done statically. However, if it is to be done dynamically, e.g. by placing a "site" pragma immediately preceding a **new** allocator for a task instantiation, an implicitly declared and assigned data structure is required to hold an identifier for the processor on which the execution object is to be placed. All references to execution objects via access variables must then reference this implicitly declared variable to determine the residency of the called object.

3.2.2. Object Access in Loosely Coupled Machines

In a loosely coupled architecture, the situation is considerably more involved, some of the solutions considerably less efficient and there are significant differences between shared variable and message passing communication. Each shared variable reference to a remote data object must be translated into a remote procedure call to a server of some kind on the processor holding the object. This server must then perform the required operation, and, if necessary, return a message containing the value of the object. On the other hand, if the variables are communicated via message passing references to them will be to the local copies and communication overhead will be substantially less.

The question of address representation is also immediately raised. The address of an object must include the address of the machine of residence. In the case of static distribution and direct references, this does not necessarily require any change to the local methods of address representation because the machine of residence can be identified in the pre-translator's symbol table and the pre-translator can place the code so that only local references are necessary, with messages sent between processors as needed.

Additional complications arise with either static or dynamic allocation when access variables are used because the pointer held in an access variable may reference an object on another processor, and the representation of that access variable might be different than the representation of access variables on the machine holding the object. The address of an object may be modeled, though not necessarily implemented, as a record with variant parts; the first component would contain a processor designation, and the variant part would contain the address of the object on the processor on which it resides. Note that this generalized view of addresses is required for pointer variables, though not for direct references, even in the static distribution case because assignments to access variables can change the machine containing the object referenced.

The referencing of remote execution objects requires, as in the shared memory situation, a signalling mechanism to permit the remote machine to receive the call. In this case, however, the actual parameters of the call must be sent to the remote processor, presumably via some type of message passing system. As noted above, for scalar variables the message passing is quite natural, since Ada requires call by copy. Although in the case of arrays and records, the LRM allows call by reference to be used under certain conditions, it would seems more appropriate to use call by copy since otherwise, each reference to the argument will involve the same kind of cross machine communication that occurs in the use of shared variables. The programmer always has the option of using access variables if it really is desired to access the arguments by reference. The problem can be further complicated by the fact that the actual arguments might not reside on the processor from which the call is made. In particular, if they should happen to reside on the same processor as the execution object being called, then in the case of records and arrays, the use of pointers might still be the most efficient method of parameter passing.

4. Network Timing

The Language Reference Manual does not absolutely require that an implementation provide delay timing; it is legal for an implementation to go away and never return on a **delay** statement. However, for many applications the language would be significantly reduced in utility without this capability. As the principal applications of interest here are real-time systems, all of the discussion in this section is pertinent to the situation in which an implementation does provide timing capabilities.

4.1. Network Sense of Time

The package CALENDAR provides functions which return values of type TIME. The implication is that there is a single sense of TIME throughout at least the execution of the program, if not between different executions of the program. That is, if CLOCK is called twice, with an intervening interval of one second, the calculated difference in the times should be one second. This poses an implementation problem when multiple processors are used for the execution of the program. How is a consistent sense of time maintained across the network? There are at least two possibilities, maintain a network time server to which all processors go when they need a value for time, or maintain separate but synchronized clocks on each processor. Combinations, of course, are also possible. Each has its own set of problems and limitations.

In the case of the network time server, the principal difficulty occurs because of the time required to access the time server. Two subproblems must be considered, the propagation delay, and interfering access requests. It might be possible to compensate for the first by subtracting the response time from the time returned, if the response time were reliably known. However, the second problem usually injects an uncertainty in the response time from the server. For some timer server configurations, however, it may be possible to bound the uncertainty in the time value returned.

The maintenance of perfectly synchronized local clocks is not possible. The best that can be done is to choose one as a master an update the others from it periodically. Between clock update points, there is an uncertainty of the difference between values of TIME read on different processors. The purpose of updating the clocks is to bound this uncertainty. One might, for example, try to keep this uncertainty less than one half of DURATION'SMALL. One experiment in maintaining synchronization among system clocks has been reported by Gusella and Zatti [GuZ84]. They found that to keep a network of VAX computers and SUN workstations synchronized to within 20 ms required updates once every 173 seconds. Scaling this to 25 microseconds (half of the 50 microsecond DURATION'SMALL recommended in the LRM) is moderately discouraging. Major improvements might be possible, though, by using a more stable clock in each of the processors.

4.2. Timed Entry Call Implementation

Most of the Ada constructs which reference time only require a local sense of time at each processor. For example, a delay statement within a task is simply a local delay with respect to processor on which the task resides. Similarly, the use of a delay alternative in a **select** statement with an **accept** statement is strictly local. There is one Ada construct, however, which if implemented in a nontrivial manner requires both an **upper** bound on the time within which a given action must take place (all other constructs just place lower bounds on time intervals) and a consistent sense of time among the distributed processors. This construct is the timed entry call.

The trivial implementation of the timed entry call would be to say that there is no sense of time (across the network) and therefore that the rendezvous never takes place and the calling unit executes the alternative reference of code. If a nontrivial implementation is to be accomplished, then the timing of the action to be taken on the called unit must be determined with respect to the time scale of the calling unit. Otherwise, the language specification of the LRM cannot be guaranteed.

Consider a timed entry call made at time t_1, with a delay d, from a processor A to an entry on processor B. The time $t_2 = t_1 + d$ is the time by which the called task must be able to accept the call. Figure 3 illustrates the timing involved for non-negligible network delays. Two cases are shown. For case 1, the called entry is able to accept the call at time $t_2 - \epsilon$ and the rendezvous is accepted. For case 2, time t_2 is reached without the entry call being accepted and the timed entry fails. Note that is both cases processor A cannot know whether or not the call was accepted until some time after t_2. This requires a liberal interpretation of paragraph 9.6 of the LRM which states that "..the entry call is canceled **when the specified duration is expired** and the optional sequence of statements of the delay alternative is executed" (emphasis added). Taking the alternative sequence (if present) at time $t_1 + d + n_d$ on processor A is consistent with the LRM if one takes the view that taking the alternative sequence only means making it ready at some time after t_2. The network delay, n_d, might or might not be known, or even bounded. It might well be different on the two transmissions. If $n_d > d$, then the rendezvous must fail.

4.2.1. Network Time Server

With a network time server, the scenario would be as follows:

- The processor containing the calling process will obtain the time from the network server and include both it and the specified delay in the timed entry call message

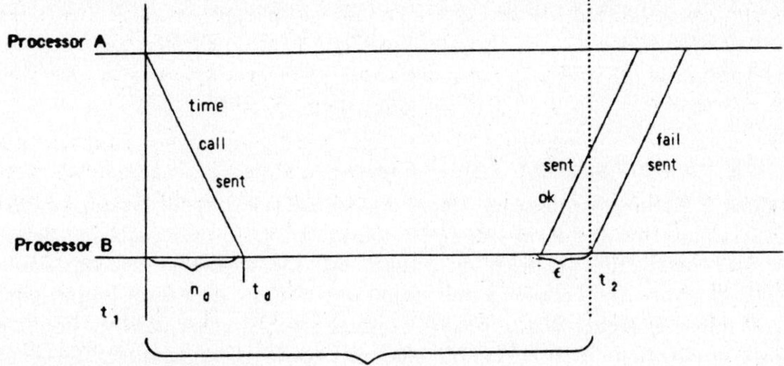

$t_1 =$ time of time entry call
$d =$ delay in timed entry call
$n_d =$ network delay
$t_2 = t_1 + d =$ time by which called task must be able to accept.

Figure 3

sent to the processor holding the called task.

- The processor having the called task will call the network time server to obtain the time at the time the call is received.
- The processor containing the called task will compute the remaining time delay with which the called task is requested to start.
- Local management of the timed entry call will proceed as usual.

In this case the network delay used above must include the two timer server access times in addition to the call transmission time.

In order to obtain an expression for the local delay to be used on processor B in implementing this call, let t_1' be the value returned from the network timer server corresponding to time t_1 at which the call was made and t_a' be the value returned corresponding to t_a, the time at which the call message is received at processor B. Then, if the error in the times returned is bounded by d_B, then the local delay d_l satisfies the following inequality:

$$\begin{aligned} d_l &= d - (t_a - t_1) \\ &> d + t_1' - t_a' - 2d_B \end{aligned}$$

and the right had side of the inequality may be used to calculate the local delay on processor B.

4.2.2. Maintain Synchronism Among Local Clocks

An alternative method of providing timing is to maintain synchronism among the local clocks of the processors. Similar to the situation in the previous section, there will be an uncertainty interval in the difference between the measured values of the same instant of time between any pair of processors. For purposes of analysis, take the time measured on processor A as the reference and let t^A, t^B be the values for time t as measured on A and B respectively. Let $| t^A - t^B | \leq d_B$. Then the delay time from t_a to the upper bound for t_2 can be bounded as follows.

$$\begin{aligned} d_l &= d - (t_a^A - t_1^A) = d + t_1^A - t_a^A \\ &> d + t_1^A - t_a^B - d_B \end{aligned}$$

The RHS of the inequality can safely be used as a bound on the local delay time from the receipt of the request until the maximum value of t_2. Similarly, there is a minimum of delay time that can succeed.

$$d > n_d + d_B$$

4.2.3. Rely on the Exported Value of Delay

A third mechanism to manage timed entry calls is to export the time from the calling unit and use only this and local timing to manage things on the receiving processor. This requires knowledge, or at least a bound on the network transmission times. If $| n_d | \leq d_B$, then the receiving unit could use $d - d_B$ as a local bound on delay until t_2. The required existence of the bound d_B in the purest sense imposes limits on the type of network connection. Ethernets, for example, could not guarantee this bound; on the other hand, they might be acceptable in a practical sense.

4.2.4. Uniprocessor Considerations

Considerations such as those described above can be carried out in a uniprocessor situation as well. For example, the delay n_d corresponds to the overhead associated with implementing the checking and rendezvous. Indeed, these times should be included in n_d

in the distributed situation as well. Depending upon the granularity of delay interval implemented, n_d may be significant. This is likely to be the case for most processors at the 50 μsecond granularity recommended in the LRM and even more likely for the 10 μsecond granularity discussed for some implementations. Strictly speaking, in these cases a timed entry call for small delays should fail even though a conditional entry call should succeed. This conformance is likely to be very difficult to measure, however.

5. Execution Environment

Implementations of Ada are to provide several predefined packages as part of the environment available to the user. These include STANDARD, CALENDAR and TEXT_IO, and in general, must be available on more than one processor. The questions which arise are the consistency of data objects contained in or generated by subprograms in the package and the need to reference an object in one of these packages on a different processor, e.g. for I/O. These questions do not necessarily create a problem, but do require an awareness on the part of the programmer of the semantics associated with multiple occurrences of these packages.

In package STANDARD, the values for objects like SYSTEM.MIN_INT or SYSTEM.MAX_DIGITS may be different for the different occurrences of the package. Likewise, INTEGER, LONG_INTEGER, SHORT_INTEGER, etc. may have different meanings. The meanings, however, will be correct for the processor on which the package resides, and this is exactly what the programmer will need. As a matter of programming discipline, the programmer may find it useful to make greater use of some of the system descriptive objects to help in writing correct programs which can operate in the distributed environment. The distributed translator, however, must be aware of the possible differences in representation and supply the necessary translations. Also, it will be necessary to check values and, when necessary, raise exceptions, during the translation process.

Particularly in the case of I/O, it may be desired to reference an object supplied by TEXT_I/O from a processor other than the one on which the object resides. By embedding such requests in a block which is placed on the same processor as the referenced TEXT_I/O object, one can avoid the need to invent new naming conventions which might cause difficulties with the current definition of Ada.

Finally, since a fine degree of granularity is used, the implementation must provide a suitable shell (probably a package) to house distributed objects such as data items or tasks.

6. Experimental Translator Implementation

An Ada translator is being implemented which will convert a single Ada program into a set of inter-communicating Ada source programs, one to run on each node of the target network. The individual Ada programs will subsequently be compiled by existing Ada compilers, as illustrated in Figure 1. The mapping of objects to network nodes will be indicated by a pragma named SITE(.). When placed immediately before an object declaration, a **new** allocator or the occurrence of a block in the instruction stream this pragma will cause the following object to placed on the machine designator given as the parameter to the pragma. Any object created without a SITE pragma preceding it is assigned to the same node as the program unit in which the creation occurs. An alternative mapping scheme would use a distribution language which allows the same mapping information to be specified separately from the program itself as a sort of postscript [Cor84].

6.1. Translator Strategy

The global strategy for handling cross-machine references is based on the static construction of one or more special executable objects called agents. Each agent is designed to serve one particular executable object of the original program which makes an off-machine reference. The original executable object is called the master, to distinguish it from its agents. The agents will typically be of the same type as their masters. If during execution a master should need to access data or code located on a remote machine, it will order its agent on that machine to access the data or code for it. One master task may thus have several agents and in the extreme case, may need an agent on each of the other machines in the network.

To illustrate the general translation scheme, Figure 4 shows the source program and the translations of a distributed program for an autonomous vehicle. The example system has three interacting tasks: a planner, a vision system, and a drive control . The tasks are labeled PLANNER, CAMERA, and WHEELS, respectively. In the source program they are targeted for three different nodes. The translator will produce the three output programs shown. Note how PLANNER, itself residing on M3, has indirect access to both CAMERA through AGENT OF PLANNER ON M1, and WHEELS via AGENT OF PLANNER ON M2. For example, if the original PLANNER calls a procedure P within CAMERA, PLANNER will be modified so that instead making the reference directly, which is not possible, it will place the parameters of the call in a message which in then sends to its agent residing on M1. PLANNER's agent will receive the message, decode it, and discover that its master is attempting to call procedure P and, using the parameters that were included in the message, the agent will make the procedure call on its master's

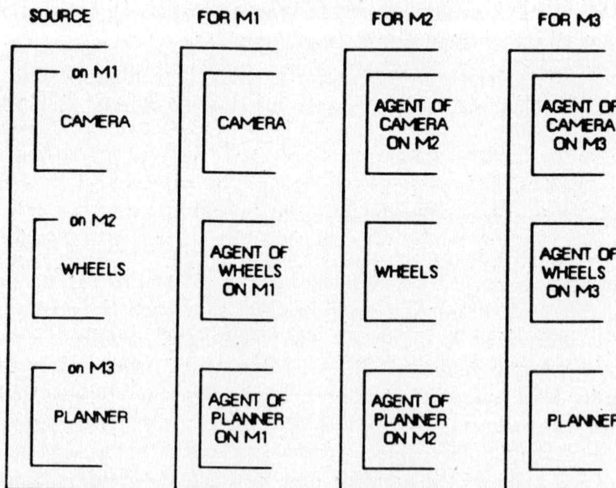

Figure 4 Distribution of source program to separate machine with agents inserted to represent task on remote machines.

behalf. After the call is done the agent will copy any **out** parameters into a message which is then sent back to the master PLANNER. The master copies these parameter values from the returned message into its local variables and, having completed the call to the remote procedure P, it continues execution.

The translator can be constructed in two distinct passes. The first pass produces an agent structure for each processor which is copy of the original program structure. Each executable object will have an agent on each processor which it (or an object it contains) references. The agents will be of the same type and will be nested in exactly the same manner as their masters, thus preserving the proper scope of objects created within them. This scheme, while generally applicable, can produce unnecessary messages among the processors (see further discussion below). The second pass is an optimization pass which removes these unnecessary messages.

More specifically, the first pass involves three basic operations, one on overall program structure, one on object declarations or blocks, and one on executable statements. The first operation forms the distributed structure of the output code, maps the input program into the appropriate parts and creates the necessary agents. It begins by extracting the skeleton of frames of executable objects, where the skeleton consists of the following parts:

- an opening line which marks the beginning of the frame, e.g. "declare" for a block or "procedure main is" for a procedure,
- the keyword "begin" which separates the declarative region of the frame from its executable code,
- the "end" statement which closes the frame.

These frame skeletons, reflect the nesting of the frames of the program. On the one node to which a frame is mapped, the skeleton encloses master version of the frame. On all others, an agent is created from the skeleton by adding an infinite loop which begins each iteration waiting for a command (message) from the master. After receiving a message, it executes a case statement which contains one choice for each of the remote operations required by the master. The agent uses the command to index into the case statement.

An agent is able to respond to any remote request it may receive from its master as long as both master and agent are in corresponding nesting levels in the program structure. To ensure that this correspondence exists, each agent will enter and exit its version of a frame in synchronism with its master. To illustrate, suppose that PLANNER is about to call procedure P, also located on M3. PLANNER's agents will have been executing server loops enclosed in their versions of the task PLANNER frame. Just before calling procedure P, PLANNER notifies its agents of the impending procedure call allowing them to switch frames as well. One of the advantages of this scheme is that any remote objects which have been declared in P will be allocated automatically as the agents enter their P frames.

The operation on data object declarations is fairly straightforward. An object resides only on the node to which it is mapped. There are multiple output streams, one for each machine in the network, and all streams are in synchronism with respect to the code being emitted. The declaration is simply placed in the skeleton of the agent for the machine on which the object is to be located.

The situation for remote object creation via allocators is slightly more complex, as it is both a run-time activity and involves pointers. The allocation expression is placed in the appropriate agent in a manner similar to the way declarations are handled, and the statement in original program is replaced by a remote procedure call to the agent, as described below. The pointer variable is placed in a record structure as described earlier.

Within an execution object, off-machine subprogram or task entry calls are replaced by remote subprogram calls to the appropriate agent which makes the call on behalf of the master and returns whatever results are required. Each reference to an off-machine data object, e.g. remote shared variables, is replaced by a remote subprogram call to the agent on the machine holding the referenced object, with an appropriate command code and any parameters required encoded into the call. If required, values are returned as function results, and used as normal in executing the statement in which the reference occurs.

7. Summary and Conclusions

A number of important issues which occur in the distributed execution of a single Ada program have been raised, and an experimental implementation of a translator which allows distributed execution described. The issues raised include the interpretation of the LRM in the context of distributed execution (e.g. constructs such as conditional and timed entry calls), the need for a consistent network view of time, and a number of implementation problems such as remote object access, network time management, data and address representations, and execution environments.

The experimental translator allows any data or named execution object to be distributed. It recognizes a pragma type named SITE as specifying the distribution. The translator takes a single Ada program as input and produces a set of Ada programs, one for each processor in the distributed computer network, as output. The general strategy for the implementation has been developed, and at the time of this writing, the translator is functional, but only partially complete, handling only simple distribution of tasks with no entry parameters.

References

[ArC85] Armitage, J.W. and J.V. Chelini, "Ada software on distributed targets: a survey of approaches," *Ada Letters,* vol. 4, no. 4, pp. 32-37, January-February 1985.

[Car84] Carlisle, B., "Sensor-based control: robot programming issues," *Workshop on Intelligent Robots: Achievements and Issues,* SRI International, Menlo Park, CA, Nov. 13-14, 1984.

[Cor84] Cornhill, D., "Partitioning Ada programs for execution on distributed systems," *1984 Computer Data Engrg. Conf.,* 1984.

[DGC83] Darpa, A., S. Gatti, S. Crespi-Reghizzi, F. Maderna, D. Belcredi, Natali, R. A. Stammers, and M.D. Tedd, *Using Ada and APSE to support distributed multimicroprocessor targets,* Commission of the European Communities, July 1982 - March 1983.

[DoD83] *Ada programming language (ANSI/MIL-STD-1815A).* Washington, D.C. 20301: Ada Joint Program Office, Department of Defense, OUSD(R&D), Jan. 1983.

[GuZ84] Gusella, R. and S. Zatti, "TEMPO - A network time controller for a distributed Berkeley UNIX system," *Distributed Processing Technical Committee Newsletter,* informal publication of *IEEE Computer Society Committee on Computer Processing,* vol. 6, no. SI2-2, pp. 7-14, June 1984.

[Sha80] Shaw, M., "The impact of abstraction concerns on modern programming languages," *Proc. of the IEEE,* vol. 68, no. 9, pp. 1119-1130, Sept. 1980.

[VoM84] Volz, R.A. and T.N. Mudge, "Robots are (nothing more than) abstract data types," *Proc. of the Robotics Research Conference: The Next 5 Years and Beyond,* Aug. 14-16, 1984.

[VMG84] Volz, R.A. , T.N. Mudge and D.A. Gal, "Using Ada as a programming language for robot-based manufacturing cells," *IEEE Trans. on Systems, Man and Cybernetics,* December, 1984.

[VMM84] Volz, R.A., T.N. Mudge, A.W. and J.H. Mayer "Some Problems in Distributing Real-Time Ada Programs Across Heterogeneous Processers," *IEEE Workshop on Real-Time Operating Systems,* Wakefield, Mass., November 1984.

THE USE OF ADA IN THE DESIGN OF DISTRIBUTED SYSTEMS

P. Inverardi
IEI - CNR Via S. Maria 46, PISA-ITALY

F. Mazzanti
external collaborator c/o IEI - CNR

C. Montangero
Department of Computer Science, University of Pisa - ITALY

Work supported by CNR-PFI-P1-Cnet

1 INTRODUCTION

Background and aims

The paper addresses the issues related to the use of Ada in the design of large distributed software systems (DSS) such as office automation systems and distributed embedded applications.

The work is part of the research activities of Cnet, a project funded by a special Program in Computer Science of the Italian National Research Council. Cnet aims at implementing a distributed system on a large bandwidth LAN, using Ada as system and application language (Lijtmaer 1984).

We want to build on the interesting features of Ada from the standpoint of software engineering, to deal with some relevant facets of DSS e.g. commonality of environment and separation of memories. We aim at maintaining the advantages that Ada provides to the process of software design and development by its advanced linguistic constructs (packages, generics, tasks, etc) and separate compilation features (program libraries, subunits, etc). Our approach relies essentially on a suitable structuring of the, usually flat, Ada program library. It allows to develop a component of a DSS as a collection of modules which satisfy the same constraints about the visibility of the rest of the system and/or about their internal structure. Such a structuring and constraining are obtained by suitable pragmas, so that the resulting program is still a valid Ada program.

As a result, the overall logical structure of the distributed system may be specified at the very first step of design, at the same time allowing its refinement by successive steps.

The issue of the mapping of the logical structure onto a physical one is out of the scope of this paper. However, we expect to deal with them in a totally orthogonal way.

Related works

With respect to the design of DSS using high level languages there are at least two schools: the former strives for an explicit model of the distribution of the system in the language itself, the latter defers the issues of distribution to linking/loading time. Typical examples of the latter are the use of Remote Procedure Call (Nelson 1981) and that of a distinct configuration language, such as APPL for Ada programs (Cornhill 1983). One of the most interesting examples of the former school is Argus (Liskov et al. 1983) that shows how the explicit visibility of distribution may help to deal with important issues such as resiliency and robustness. An example of the approach that deals with distribution explicitely is shown in (Dapra *et al.* 1984), in the framework of Ada. The last section of this paper shows (as an example) in which way that schema can be expressed in our approach.

We belong to the former school since we believe that it should be possible to start specifying the distributed architecture of the system at the logical level as soon as possible, because of the design consequences that such a structure may have.

2 ADA VS DSS

One of the main features of Ada is that it makes the idea of incremental program development precise by its notion of program library and compilation. Moreover the idea of a program library allows one to distinguish between compile time and run time configuration, the latter being that particular subset of library units elaborated because of the activation of a specific main program. As a consequence, Ada provides the designer and the user with great flexibility and some kind of dynamicity, that must not be lost when implementing distributed systems. On the contrary, we aim at maintaining such a flexibility even at the level of single components of a DSS which might be large enough to be treated like systems by themselves.

Therefore, what must be added to the facilities already provided by Ada are ways to collect library units in clusters, to express structural constraints, and to check that all the compilation units composing each cluster satisfy their constraints.

A prototypal implementation of the facilities described in the next chapters is available for SubAda (Barbacci *et al*. 1981), written in SubAda. It is going to be ported to full Ada on Unix system V for the Olivetti - AT&T 3B2 machines to be used as hosts in Cnet.

3 A SOLUTION

A bubble is a collection of library units sharing the same constraints about the visibility of the other units included in the Program Library (PL) and the same constraints on their structure. In Ada a compilation unit can make use of any other library unit in the PL by means of with clauses. The first purpose of bubbles is precisely that of limiting the set of library units that a unit can name in its with clauses, thereby making it possible to express accessibility constraints related to the distribution of resources as well as the logic structure of the design.

Creating and refining bubbles

```
pragma MK_BUBBLE (NAME => path_name_string_literal,
                  KIND => bubble_kind_enumeration_literal);
```

provides for the creation of a new bubble.

A library unit can be added to an existing bubble by the

```
pragma INTO_BUBBLE (PARENT => path_name_string_literal);
```

all its secondary units (if any) will be implicitly inserted into the same bubble.

Structural constraints

The second argument of MK_BUBBLE addresses the other purpose of introducing bubbles; namely that of constraining the structure of the compilation units which might be inserted into a bubble.

It is assumed that an implementation dependent enumeration

type BUBBLE_KIND is predefined naming all the possible constraints.

Each one of the elements in BUBBLE_KIND defines a statically checkable subset of Ada: examples of sensible sublanguages are presented in Section 4.

A bubble may contain only units that satisfy the KIND constraints. A compilation unit that does not satisfy these constraints is still inserted in the PL but it is included in a special (top level) implicit "ERRORS" bubble. In this way the legality of an Ada program is not influenced by the presence of the pragma.

Visibility constraints

Two contexts are associated to a bubble: its visible context and its full context. A context is a set of bubbles initially (i.e. upon bubble creation) containing only the single bubble itself. Moreover, the visible context is a subset of the full context.

The with clauses of a compilation unit inserted into a bubble "B" are legal (with respect to the bubble structure) only if the library units named in them are included (at any level) in a bubble of one of the contexts of "B", namely in the visible context if the compilation unit is a library unit, in the full context if the compilation unit is a secondary unit. In other words, the visible context is accessible from the "specification part" of a unit, while the full context is accessible from its body. In this way the separation between specification and implementation is retained at the bubble level.

If a compilation unit does not satisfy the above constraints it is inserted in the PL but it is included in the already mentioned "ERRORS" bubble.

Any context of a bubble may be extended incrementally with the visible context of another bubble:

```
pragma EXTEND_FULL_CONTEXT (NAME => path_name_string_literal,
                              BY => path_name_string_literal);
```

allows the extension of the full context of a bubble;

```
pragma EXTEND_VISIBLE_CONTEXT (NAME => path_name_string_literal,
                                 BY => path_name_string_literal);
```

allows the extension of the visible and full context of a bubble. The full context of a bubble (as well as its visible context) is closed under the transitivity of the pragmas EXTEND_VISIBLE_CONTEXT, and evolves in time together with the evolutions of the context of the bubbles used to extend it.

In order to control the evolution of full and visible contexts of a bubble better, two pragmas are introduced allowing to "freeze" the contexts of a bubble and to "hide" an existing bubble, respectively. After the elaboration of the

pragma FREEZE (NAME => *path_name_* string_literal);

the visible and full contexts of the named bubble are considered "frozen" and cannot be further extended using the EXTEND___..._CONTEXT pragmas. Moreover, subsequent extensions of the visible context of any bubble in the context of the frozen one will not propagate.

We believe that it is important to be able to "freeze" the set of bubbles belonging to the context of a bubble "B" because only in this way we can ensure that all the visibility constraints specified until now will be respected by all the units that will be later defined and included in "B". We can observe that freezing the bubbles belonging to a context neither prevents subsequent inclusions of units in these bubbles nor their use.

Bubbles in fact are not used to model the functionalities of a system but its overall structure.

pragma HIDE (NAME => *path_name_*string_literal);

After the elaboration of this pragmas the named bubble cannot be used to extend any other context directly. Nevertheless this pragma does not prevent the named bubble to extend other contexts indirectly because of the transitivity of the pragma EXTEND_VISIBLE _CONTEXT. This pragma is useful for "hiding" a bubble belonging only to the full context of other bubbles, therefore realizing a sort of "implementation environment".

We can observe that these pragmas allow structuring a component of a system like a package construct allows (see fig. 1) but with many important advantages:

- The interface and the implementation of such a component can be developed incrementally in the same way the whole system is.
- Structural constraints can be defined and checked about the definitions to be included in both parts of a system component.
- Visibility constraints towards other components of the system can be imposed and checked during the construction of the component itself.
- Visibility constraints from other components can be stated and verified.

```
pragma MK_BUBBLE (NAME => "INTERFACE",...);
pragma MK_BUBBLE (NAME => "IMPLEMENTATION",...);
pragma EXTEND_FULL_CONTEXT (NAME => "INTERFACE",
                            BY => "IMPLEMENTATION");
pragma HIDE (NAME => "IMPLEMENTATION",...);
pragma EXTEND_VISIBLE_CONTEXT (NAME => "IMPLEMENTATION",
                               BY => "INTERFACE");
```

fig. 1

Hierarchical structure

Bubbles can be nested hierarchically. A bubble may be created inside another one, giving it as a name an extension of its parent's. The KIND of the inner bubble must be "compatible" with that of the parent, in the sense that it must define a stronger structural constraint.

There is a predefined top level bubble "SYSTEM" in which any user defined bubble is inserted. (For the user's convenience the prefix "SYSTEM" may be omitted). Any context of a bubble may only be extended with bubbles already included (at any level) in a bubble belonging to the context of its parent.

If this rule is not verified (i.e. one or both the arguments of a pragma extending a context do not identify existing bubbles or the second argument does not identify a suitable bubble) the effect of the pragma is null.

This hierarchical structure allows complex schemas of distributed systems to be defined and subsequently refined.

4 EXAMPLES

As first example of utilization of these constructs we propose the description of the Cnet system. Initial requirements on this application were:

i) Existence of a unique functional (i.e. without store) global environment.

ii) Existence of a finite set of nodes, each one having visibility of the global environment only.

Relying on these requirements we are already able to specify our system structure, e.g. with two nodes:

```
pragma MK_BUBBLE (NAME => "global_env",KIND => NO_STORE);
pragma MK_BUBBLE (NAME => "node1",KIND => FULL_Ada);
pragma MK_BUBBLE (NAME => "node2",KIND => FULL_Ada);
pragma EXTEND_VISIBLE_CONTEXT (NAME => "node1",
                               BY => "global_env");
pragma EXTEND_VISIBLE_CONTEXT (NAME => "node2",
                               BY   => "global_env");
pragma FREEZE (NAME => "node1");
pragma FREEZE (NAME => "node2");
pragma FREEZE (NAME => "global_env");
```

In Cnet, kind "NO_STORE" specifies that the only library units allowed to be included in the "global_env" bubble are only generic units and packages whose declarative part contains only type declarations (but no access types declarations) and generic units declarations, and whose body does not contains statements. No structural constraints are instead imposed on nodes. The visibility relations between components are defined and fixed at the initial stage of development because they reflect some "a priori" requirements on the system structure.

Since nodes have no visibility of each other, it is evident

that they can neither cooperate via rendezvous nor by memory sharing, because of the structural constraints imposed to the global environment. Therefore a suitable communication mechanism is needed allowing nodes to interact. In Cnet this is provided by a generic package shared in the global environment having one instance per node:

```
pragma INTO_BUBBLE (PARENT => "global_env");
 generic
 package NET_COMMUNICATIONS is
   ...
 end NET_COMMUNICATIONS;
```

The predefined package "SYSTEM" should belong to the bubble "global_env", defining the abstract distributed machine correspondidg to the whole system and allowing to define rigorously the internal representation of the values exchanged between nodes (whose type declarations must be global).

This structure can be subsequently refined either defining the needed library units for each system component or structuring a node in a deeper way. A graphical representation of Cnet structure is shown below.

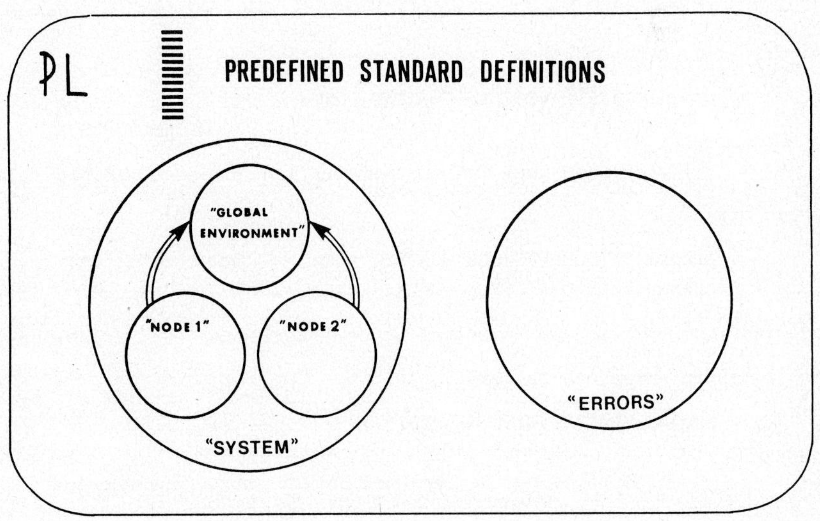

fig. 2

A second example: The Virtual Nodes approach

As a second example we illustrate how the "virtual nodes" approach proposed in (Dapra et al. 1984) could be modelled. In the proposal, tasks are partitioned by the system designer into task groups (called virtual nodes) so that the sharing of data between virtual nodes is banned. This design schema can be modelled by the following sequence of pragmas.

```
pragma MK_BUBBLE (NAME => "GLOBAL_ENVIRONMENT",
                  KIND => NO_STORE);
```

The existence of particular structural constraints over the global environment is shared with the Cnet example.

```
pragma MK_BUBBLE (NAME => "VN1", KIND => TASK_ONLY);
```

A structural constraint is imposed on program units belonging to the interface of a virtual node, namely that only packages defining only tasks are accepted.

```
pragma MK_BUBBLE (NAME => "VNI_IMPL", KIND => FULL_ADA);
```

No structural contraints are imposed on program units belonging to the implementation of a virtual node.

```
pragma EXTEND_FULL_CONTEXT (NAME => "VN1", BY => "VN1_IMPL");
pragma HIDE (NAME => "VN1_IMPL");
```

The implementation of a virtual node has to be accessed by its interface but not by the users of its interface:

```
pragma EXTEND_VISIBLE_CONTEXT (NAME => "VN1,
                               BY => "GLOBAL_ENVIRONMENT");
```

Interfaces and implementations can access obviously all the shared definitions;

```
pragma EXTEND_VISIBLE_CONTEXT (NAME => "VN1", BY => "VN2");
pragma EXTEND_VISIBLE_CONTEXT (NAME => "VN1"_IMPL, BY => "VN1");
```

and they can access other virtual nodes interfaces, VN2, following some static schema which can be fixed:

```
pragma FREEZE (NAME => "VN1");
```

Definitions can be included in the shared environment

```
pragma INTO_BUBBLE (PARENT => "GLOBAL_ENVIRONMENT");
generic
package INTERNODE_COMMUNICATIONS IS
... end;
pragma INTO_BUBBLE (PARENT => "VN1");
package ELEMENT1 is
    task T1 is
      entry E1;
    end T1;
    task T2 is
      entry E2;
    end T2;
end ELEMENT1;
```

and/or in the interfaces, in a statically checkable, consistent way.

Single components will be refined, after this top level design specification. For example, coming back to the previous Cnet example, we could model each Cnet node as a collection of "virtual nodes", modelling in an easy way clusters of processes connected through a local area network.

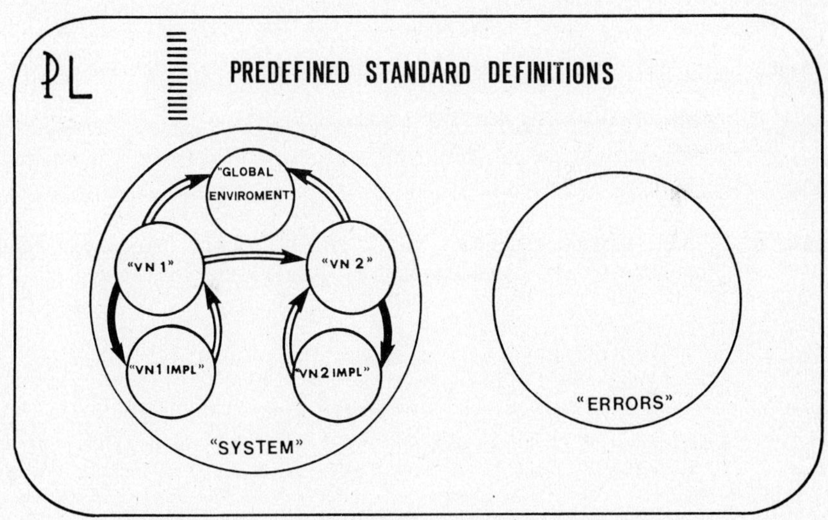

The visible context of a bubble is grafically represented by the set of bubbles reachable with ⟹ in one or more steps. The full context is represented by the union of the visible context of the bubbles reachable in one step with ➡ or ⟹.

References

Barbacci, M. & Harbison, S. (1981). Spice Ada (Subset) Compiler. Technical Report, Department of Comp. Science, Carnegie Mellon University, Pittsburgh.

Cornhill, D. (1983). Survivable Distributed Computing Systems for Embedded Applications Programs Written in Ada. AdaLetters vol. IV, n. 3.

Dapra, *et al*. (1984). Using Ada and APSE to Support Distributed Multimicroprocessor Targets. AdaLetters vol. III, n. 6.

Lijtmaer, N. (1984). The first one hundred Cnet reports. Cnet report 101.

Liskov, B. *et al*. (1983). Preliminary Argus reference manual. Programming Methodology Group Memo 39, M.I.T., Laboratory for Computer Science.

Nelson, B. (1981). Remote Procedure Call. PH. D. thesis, Technical report CMU-CS-81-119, Carnegie Mellon University, Pittsburgh.

SAVING TRACES FOR ADA* DEBUGGING

Carol H. LeDoux
D. Stott Parker, Jr.

Computer Science Department
University of California, Los Angeles

Abstract. A trace database model for debugging concurrent Ada programs is presented. In this approach, trace information is captured in an historical database and queried using Prolog. This model was used to build a prototype debugger, called Your Own Debugger for Ada (YODA). The design of YODA is described and a trace analysis of a sample program exhibiting misuse of shared data is presented. Because the trace database model is flexible and general, it can aid diagnosis of a variety of runtime errors.

1 INTRODUCTION

Debugging is a trial-and-error process that does not easily lend itself to automation. One facet of debugging that can be automated is capturing a knowledge base of a program's structure and past behavior.

In this paper we present a model for collecting and organizing trace data (information about the dynamic activity of a program) into an historical database to aid in debugging Ada programs. We describe a prototype debugger, called Your Own Debugger for Ada (YODA), that has been implemented in Prolog and runs on the Digital Equipment Corporation (DEC) VAX 11/780 computer under UNIX**. An example is given of a trace analysis to illustrate the diagnostic features of YODA.

Previous approaches to debugging concurrent Ada software have focused on reporting "deadness" errors, such as deadlock. Static program analysis has been used (Taylor, 1983) to detect deadness errors but was constrained to debugging simple programs since every possible state must be examined. Another approach (Luckham et al., 1981; German et al., 1982; Helmbold & Luckham, 1984)

---

*Ada is a registered trademark of the U.S. Government -- Ada Joint Program Office

**UNIX is a registered trademark of AT&T Bell Labs

used runtime monitoring of current task state information and simple diagnostic descriptions of deadness errors. This work demonstrated that current task state information is inadequate for diagnosing many runtime tasking errors.

YODA provides a more comprehensive approach to debugging. It supports diagnosis of a wider class of errors because its runtime monitor records a history of program events. It supports effective diagnostic features because the event history can be queried. The programmer can abstract appropriate information from the event history to aid in formulating hypotheses about program errors. In addition, the programmer can express constraints to be checked against past program behavior to aid in evaluating hypotheses about program errors.

One problem in collecting trace data is the difficulty in selecting events to monitor. We capitalize on Ada features that eliminate some classes of runtime errors, such as strong typing for preventing undefined variables. We focus on Ada features that alter the runtime behavior, such as concurrency, exception handling, and dynamic storage allocation.

Collecting trace data from concurrent Ada software raises many interesting problems. For example, the timing and sequencing of events that caused an error may be difficult to reproduce. Also, the overhead of monitoring real time software will perturb its behavior, as noted previously (Fairley, 1980).

In producing traces for debugging there is a "Heisenberg uncertainty principle": whatever mechanisms are introduced to elicit trace information will interfere with program performance and may ultimately modify the behavior of the program. In a non-deterministic programming environment, collecting trace data may be acceptable only when debugging occurs in simulated time. An interesting research area is how to design mechanisms that refrain from interfering with race conditions and other timing dependent behavior.

2 PREVIOUS WORK

One approach to viewing debugging as a database application is the OMEGA debugger (Powell & Linton, 1983; Linton, 1984) for Berkeley Pascal programs. This debugger uses the relational database management system, INGRES, with the query language, Quel, to process queries and updates about the runtime state and history of a running program. Only static program information is stored in the database; current program state information is accessed in real time.

An approach similar to OMEGA represents dynamic program information in a relational database (Snodgrass, 1984). This approach uses INGRES with TQuel, a query language that extends Quel with temporal relations. No static information is stored in the database. Dynamic information is stored either as states (two timestamps) or as events (one timestamp). Temporal relations are limited to those recognized by the TQuel compiler.

3 THE TRACE DATABASE MODEL

The trace database model improves on previous work in debugging because it is more general and more flexible. Some important aspects of this model are the use of Prolog, temporal logic, and a uniform representation of program states and events. Both static and dynamic program information are included in the database.

We have chosen to use Prolog because it is more general, concise, and powerful than a conventional relational database management system, such as INGRES. Prolog is a programming language based on symbolic logic. It was developed around 1972 in Marseille (Colmerauer, 1978; Kowalski, 1979; Gallaire, 1981). Its suitability for database systems has been described previously (Kowalski, 1978; Warren, 1981).

To maintain information in a dynamic environment we have adopted an interval-based temporal logic approach (Rescher & Urquhart, 1971; Allen, 1983). The trace database model supports queries with temporal constraints. Prolog provides the mechanics for declaring any temporal relation between time intervals, e.g. *during*, *before*, and *after*.

We have chosen to capture execution history as an event stream, unlike the TQuel monitor where both states and events are recorded. Events are program actions that appear to occur instantaneously, whereas states are conditions that span a time interval. Most of the work in debugging is state-based; however, we view events as primitive entities that delineate a state.

Proponents of the event-based debugging model (Smith, 1981; Bates & Wileden, 1983) argue that an event stream provides a higher level abstraction of program activity than states and that ordering of events is crucial to debugging.

Storing all program activity as events reduces storage overhead since only a single timestamp is associated with each database entry. We assume a global clock such that distinct times are always comparable on their relative position in an ordering of earlier/later.

States can be described (characterized declaratively) as sets of constraints on events. For example, an Ada task is "callable" after task activation and before task completion or termination. This representation of states fits Prolog well.

4 IMPLEMENTATION

The prototype debugger, YODA, is a stand-alone system, although the trace database model can serve as the basis for a debugger that is integrated with a specific translator and runtime system. YODA parses an Ada program, generates a symbol table, and embeds diagnostic output statements into a copy of the source program. When the annotated program is compiled and executed, the diagnostic statements invoke a program monitor to capture trace data.

4.1 Major Components

All components of YODA are written in "standard" Prolog, (Clocksin & Mellish, 1981), except for the program monitor, which is written in ANSI Ada (ANSI, 1983). YODA consists of the following components:

- A lexical scanner.
- A top-down parser to produce an abstract syntax tree.
- A semantic analyzer to build a symbol table.
- An annotator to augment the source code with diagnostic output statements.
- A pretty-printer that outputs the annotated source.
- A program monitor to build the trace database.
- A trace query processor that supports references to time.

Semantic analysis, annotations, and pretty-printing are performed while traversing the abstract syntax tree. The parser fails if the input program has syntactic errors; thus, we assume that the program to be debugged has been successfully compiled.

4.2 *Symbol Table*

The symbol table contains the name, base type, and "declarative context" of each identifier in the program. By declarative context we mean the hierarchy of an identifier's enclosing declarative region(s), as opposed to its scope. Declarative context is represented as a Prolog list, such that the most deeply nested declarative region is at the head of the list. YODA generates names for loops and blocks when they are not explicitly declared. Since our focus is on showing feasibility of this debugging model, we chose not to support overloading. Separate compilation is supported by saving symbol tables of parent program units (in particular, the predefined library package SYSTEM). Appendix B shows a symbol table for the program example in Appendix A.

4.3 *Annotations and the Trace Database*

YODA monitors variable definition and use, task synchronization, and changes in task status. Table 4-1 shows the structures representing these events in Prolog notation. Each name in a trace database entry is qualified by its declarative context. Each variable definition and use includes the program unit and block in which it occurs (in lieu of a statement number).

Table 4-1: *Trace Database Events*

```
entry_called(Caller,Callee,Entry,Time).
call_canceled(Caller,Callee,Entry,Time).
entry_queue_lengthened(Caller,Callee,Entry,Time).
entry_queue_shortened(Caller,Callee,Entry,Time).
rendezvous_started(Caller,Callee,Entry,Time).
rendezvous_completed(Caller,Callee,Entry,Time).
var_read(Variable,Location,Value,Time).
var_updated(Variable,Location,Value,Time).
entry_parm_set(Caller,Callee,Entry,Parm,Mode,Value,Time).
task_activated(Task,Time).
task_completed(Task,Time).
ready_to_terminate(Task,Time).
abnormally_terminated(Task,Time).
program_ended(Program,Time).
```

To generate trace database entries, YODA embeds calls to the program monitor wherever they are syntactically and semantically appropriate. Entry calls are detected before their execution. Rendezvous start and completion are detected in the accept statement of the called task. The formal part of each entry declaration and accept statement is annotated to capture the name of the calling task. An annotation for variable use precedes its occurrence, whereas an annotation for variable definition follows its occurrence. Initializations in object declarations cannot be annotated with a monitor call, owing to the separation of body and declarative region in Ada.

In keeping with our emphasis on showing only feasibility, monitoring of variables is restricted to scalars. Monitoring can be further restricted, e.g. according to type, variable usage or declarative region, by adding a few simple rules to the annotator. We limit tracing of formal parameters to the beginning and end of an accept statement or subprogram body. If a parameter is of mode **in**, then its value is captured on entering a program unit. The value of an **in out** parameter is captured just before exiting a program unit. Tracing of **out** parameters is not supported in YODA since reading them is illegal in Ada.

Monitoring the status of each task object requires tracing task activation, task completion, and task termination. Annotating an Ada program to record a task termination event is difficult. Tracing of normal task termination can be replaced by recording the time at which a task is "ready to terminate," e.g., on the execution of a select statement with a terminate alternative. Abnormal task termination can be detected by annotating each task body with an exception handler for the exception choice **others** (where there is no explicit others exception).

Task types are only partially supported in that the type, not the name, of the task is captured in trace database entries. One naming strategy that has been suggested relies on adding an entry to each task such that it receives its identity from its parent program unit (Booch, 1982). Entry families are not supported but can be added by adopting a naming strategy similar to the one used for generating names of loops and blocks. Conditional and timed entry calls are supported with annotations for detecting a canceled entry call.

4.4 *Program Monitor*

The Ada program monitor converts trace data into Prolog clauses and updates the trace database. Also, the monitor controls the global clock. The clock is implemented as an Ada task with one entry, such that each recorded event triggers one "tick". This approach guarantees a FIFO ordering of the event trace. Thus the timestamps reflect the order in which events occur in the system. Updating the length of an entry queue, however, does not advance the clock but is synchronized with an entry call, rendezvous start, or cancellation of an entry call. Appendix C shows some of the events recorded in a sample trace.

4.5 *Trace Queries*

The trace query processor uses definitions of temporal relations and inferential knowledge about program behavior to answer queries about data not explicitly stored in the symbol table or trace database. All queries are expressed in Prolog, which is well-suited as a general query language (Futo et al., 1978; Dahl, 1982). In Prolog the user can add new queries and definitions, unlike in OMEGA and TQuel. User views are easily defined, for example, the user can qualify a query with temporal constraints to simulate a breakpoint retroactively. To give the flavor of trace queries, we present some examples paraphrased in English:

"List all tasks in procedure P."

"Which tasks updated X?"

"Did task T2 update X during a rendezvous?"

5 TRACE ANALYSIS SHOWING MISUSE OF SHARED DATA

Both the syntax and semantics of a programming language determine the program errors that can occur (Eggert, 1981). For example, Ada prevents activating the same task object more than once. On the other hand, Ada does not guarantee avoidance from deadness errors. Also the order of statement execution can affect the integrity of data accessed in shared variables. Examples of timing dependent errors that can occur in the misuse of shared variables have been described previously (Taylor & Osterweil, 1980).

The sample program in Appendix A shows a simple example of a *serializability* error caused by the misuse of shared data. That is, there is no sequential execution of the tasks in this program that could produce the same effect as the interleaved execution. (This program was translated and executed by the New York University ANSI Ada/Ed Version 1.1 translator/interpreter.) In this example, a shared variable, X, is assigned an incorrect final value because task T1 reads X at the start of a rendezvous, although X is updated by task T2 before T1 updates X and completes its rendezvous. If tasks T1 and T2 were executed in sequence (e.g., both called from a single task) this error would not occur.

We have chosen to diagnose this error by applying concurrency control concepts from the database field (Ullman, 1980; Bernstein & Goodman, 1981; Date, 1983). The trace database is checked against constraints on the sequence of events. If we make the assumption that whenever a task updates a shared variable, X_i, it has previously read X_i, then the following query detects a serializability error:

"Is there a cycle of tasks $T_0..T_{n-1}$ such that
for each i
T_i accesses (either reads or writes) some shared variable X_i
before $T_{i+1(mod\ n)}$ writes on X_i."

6 CONCLUSIONS

We have introduced a trace database model that supports a high-level abstraction of program behavior based on an event stream. We have argued that Prolog provides a more appropriate formalism for trace information than the relational database model. The flexibility of the trace database model has been demonstrated with a stand-alone, prototype debugger for Ada, called YODA, that captures trace data by embedding the source with diagnostic output statements to aid in debugging a restricted class of runtime errors associated with concurrency.

This work opens many other avenues for research, for example, integrating a trace database model with a specific Ada programming support environment. Other issues that can be investigated include generalizing to distributed clocks and to distributed databases. The approach we have described rests on the use of Prolog for expressing queries; however, natural language question-answering systems have been designed in Prolog (Warren, 1981). Another area for future research is to use the trace database as a resource for animation of program execution.

APPENDIX A. SAMPLE PROGRAM: MISUSE OF SHARED DATA

```
with TEXT_IO; use TEXT_IO;
procedure MAIN is
  X : INTEGER:= 0;
  task T1 is
    entry E(A_WHILE: DURATION);
  end T1;
  task T2  is
    entry E;
  end T2;
  task C1;  task C2;
  task body T1 is
  begin
    loop
      select
        accept E (A_WHILE: DURATION) do
            if X < 1 then
              delay A_WHILE;
              X := X + 1;
              put_line("X = " & INTEGER'IMAGE(X));
            end if;
        end E;
      or
        terminate;
      end select;
    end loop;
  end T1;
  task body T2 is
  begin
    accept E do
      if X < 1 then
        X := X + 1;
        put_line("X = " & INTEGER'IMAGE(X));
      end if;
    end E;
  end T2;
  task body C1 is
  begin
    T1.E(50.0);
  end C1;
  task body C2 is
  begin
    T2.E;
  end C2;
begin
  null;
end MAIN;
-------------------------------------------------------
  Begin Ada execution

X =  1
X =  2
  Execution complete
```

APPENDIX B. SYMBOL TABLE FOR SAMPLE ADA PROGRAM

symbol (Name, Declarative_Context, Usage).

```
symbol(main,[],subprogram_name).
symbol(e,[t1,main],entry_name).
symbol(c1,[main],object_name(task_type,anonymous,[main])).
symbol(a_while,[e,loop_name1,t1,main],
        object_name(real_type_definition,duration,[])).
symbol(c2,[main],object_name(task_type,anonymous,[main])).
symbol(e,[t2,main],entry_name).
symbol(loop_name1,[t1,main],loop_name).
symbol(t1,[main],object_name(task_type,anonymous,[main])).
symbol(t2,[main],object_name(task_type,anonymous,[main])).
symbol(x,[main],
        object_name(integer_type_definition,integer,[])).
```

APPENDIX C. SAMPLE TRACE DATABASE

<event> (<Description> , Timestamp).

```
task_activated(task(c2,[main]),1).
task_activated(task(t2,[main]),2).
task_activated(task(t1,[main]),3).
task_activated(task(c1,[main]),4).
entry_called(caller(c2,[main]),callee(t2,[main]),e,5).
ready_to_terminate(task(t1,[main]),6).
entry_queue_lengthened(caller(c2,[main]),callee(t2,[main]),e,5).
entry_called(caller(c1,[main]),callee(t1,[main]),e,7).
entry_queue_lengthened(caller(c1,[main]),callee(t1,[main]),e,7).
rendezvous_started(caller(c2,[main]),callee(t2,[main]),e,8).
entry_queue_shortened(caller(c2,[main]),callee(t2,[main]),e,8).
rendezvous_started(caller(c1,[main]),callee(t1,[main]),e,9).
entry_queue_shortened(caller(c1,[main]),callee(t1,[main]),e,9).
var_read(variable(x,[main]),[e,t2,main],0,10).
var_read(variable(x,[main]),[e,loop_name1,t1,main],0,11).
var_read(variable(x,[main]),[e,t2,main],0,12).
var_updated(variable(x,[main]),[e,t2,main],1,13).
rendezvous_completed(caller(c2,[main]),callee(t2,[main]),e,14).
var_read(variable(x,[main]),[e,loop_name1,t1,main],1,15).
task_completed(task(c2,[main]),16).
task_completed(task(t2,[main]),17).
var_updated(variable(x,[main]),[e,loop_name1,t1,main],2,18).
rendezvous_completed(caller(c1,[main]),callee(t1,[main]),e,19).
task_completed(task(c1,[main]),20).
ready_to_terminate(task(t1,[main]),21).
program_ended(main,22).
```

REFERENCES

Allen, J.F. Maintaining Knowledge About Temporal Intervals. *Communications of the ACM*, November 1983, *26*(11), 832-843.

ANSI/MIL-STD 1815A. *Reference Manual for the Ada Programming Language*. U.S. Department of Defense, 1983.

Bates, P. & Wileden, J.C. An Approach to High-Level Debugging of Distributed Systems. In *Proceedings of the Symposium on High-Level Debugging*. ACM SIGSOFT/SIGPLAN1983.

Bernstein, P.A. & Goodman, N. Concurrency Control in Distributed Database Sytems. *ACM Computing Surveys*, June 1981, *13*(2), 185-222.

Booch, G. Dear Ada. *Ada Letters*, November, December 1982, *2*(3), 10..13.

Clocksin, W.F. & Mellish, C.S. *Programming in Prolog*. Springer-Verlag, 1981.

Colmerauer, A. Metamorphosis Grammars. In L. Bloc (Ed.), *Lecture Notes in Computer Science*. Vol. 63: *Natural Language Communication with Computers*. Springer-Verlag, 1978.

Dahl, V. On Database Systems Development Through Logic. *ACM Trans. Database Syst.*, March 1982, *7*(1), 102-123.

Date, C.J. *The Systems Programming Series*. Vol. II: *An Introduction to Database Systems*. Reading, Massachusetts and Menlo Park, California: Addison-Wesley Publishing Company, 1983.

Eggert, P.H. *Detecting Software Errors Before Execution* (Tech. Rep. CSD-810402). Univ. of Calif., Los Angeles, Computer Science Department, April 1981. (Ph.D. Thesis).

Fairley, R.E. Debugging and Testing Support Environments. *SIGPLAN Notices*, November 1980, *8*, 16-25.

Futo, I. et al. The Application of PROLOG to the Development of QA and DBM Systems. In H. Gallaire and J. Minker (Ed.), *Logic and Databases*. New York: Plenum Press, 1978. (Symposium on Logic and Data Bases, Centre d'Etudes et de Recherches de Toulouse, 1977).

Gallaire, H. Impacts of Logic on Databases. In *Proceedings of the 7th VLDB Conference*. Cannes, France: VLDB 1981.

German, S.M. et al. Monitoring for Deadlocks in Ada Tasking. In *Proceedings of the AdaTEC Conference on Ada*. ACM SIGPLAN 1982.

Helmbold, D. & Luckham, D. Debugging Ada Tasking Programs. In *Proc. of the 1984 Conf. on Ada Applications and Environments*. IEEE Computer Society 1984.

Kowalski, R. Logic for Data Description. In H. Gallaire and J. Minker (Ed.), *Logic and*

Databases. New York: Plenum Press, 1978. (Symposium on Logic and Data Bases, Centre d'Etudes et de Recherches de Toulouse, 1977).

Kowalski, R. *Logic for Problem Solving*. New York: North Holland, 1979.

Linton, M.A. Implementing Relational Views of Programs. In *Proceedings of the Software Engineering Symposium on Practical Software Development Environments*. ACM SIGSOFT/SIGPLAN 1984.

Luckham, D.C. et al. *ADAM - An Ada based Language for Multi-Processing* (Tech. Rep. STAN-CS-81-867). Stanford University Department of Computer Science, July 1981.

Powell, M.L. & Linton, M.A. A Database Model of Debugging. In *Proceedings of the Symposium on High-Level Debugging*. ACM SIGSOFT/SIGPLAN 1983.

Rescher, N. & Urquhart, A. *Temporal Logic*. New York: Springer-Verlag, 1971.

Smith, E.T. *Debugging Techniques for Communicating, Loosely-Coupled Processes* (Tech. Rep. 100). University of Rochester, Dept. of Computer Science, December 1981. Ph.D. Thesis.

Snodgrass, R. Monitoring in a Software Development Environment: A Relational Approach. In *Proceedings of the Software Engineering Symposium on Practical Software Development Environments*. ACM SIGSOFT/SIGPLAN 1984.

Taylor, R.N. A General Purpose Algorithm for Analyzing Concurrent Programs. *Communications of the ACM*, May 1983, *26*(5), 362-376.

Taylor, R.N. & Osterweil, L.J. Anomaly Detection in Concurrent Software by Static Data Flow Analysis. *IEEE Trans. on Software Engineering*, May 1980, *SE-6*(3), 265-277.

Ullman, J.D. *Principles of Database Systems*. Potomac, Maryland: Computer Science Press, 1980.

Warren, D.H.D. Efficient Processing of Interactive Relational Database Queries Expressed in Logic. In *Proceedings of the 7th VLDB Conference*. Cannes, France: VLDB 1981.

EXECUTION MONITORING AND DEBUGGING TOOL FOR ADA USING RELATIONAL ALGEBRA

A. Di Maio

S. Ceri and S. Crespi Reghizzi

Dipartimento di Elettronica, Politecnico di Milano
Pza Leonardo da Vinci, 32, 20133 Milano, Italy

Abstract. This symbolic run-time debugger for Ada provides facilities for observing and manipulating the execution of a monitored program, also for concurrent aspects. The debugger can be used interactively, and also as a monitoring program to control the application. A feature of this project is the use of relational algebra for defining compiler and kernel interfaces and for handling debugger information. The implementation is based on an Ada task to interface with the debugging operator and a set of user-defined Ada monitoring tasks. A prototype of the debugger was completed as a part of ART, a relational translator and interpreter for Ada.

1. INTRODUCTION

Run-time debugging of software is very important in order to properly evaluate the effectiveness and efficiency of an application, which is essential for acceptance and validation. Execution monitoring (a more general term than debugging) allows to verify if a monitored application satisfies functional and performance requirements. This is particularly critical in concurrent and real-time applications, where certain hard to discover errors and faults (starvation, deadlock, time-dependent errors) can be traced by accurate monitoring.

While proper software tools have been developed for sequential applications (where methodologies and techniques are well understood), debugging of concurrent and real-time applications is still subject of research [Glass 1980], [Gross & Zwaenepoel 1983] , [Seidner & Tindall 1983].

Ada has several challenging features for a symbolic debugger, such as tasks, generic units and overloading, which raise new problems for designers and implementors: furthermore, conflicting requirements should be satisfied such as completeness, ease, minimal environmental support and bounded intrusivity.

The debugger described here is a part of ART (Ada Relational Translator) compiler-interpreter project, a 3 years on going research on the experimental application of a relation-based approach to the design and implementation of compilers [Ceri & Crespi Reghizzi 1983]. HARD (High-level Ada Relational Debugger) main targets are:

- use of Ada features to debug Ada programs so as to provide an homogeneous tool which should be easily learned by an Ada programmer;
- two usage modes: interactive debugging and unmanned execution monitoring and analysis;
- use of relational model and relational algebra to describe and manipulate data (interfaces, execution environment);

- bounding of delays and real-time artifacts due to debugger intervention.

HARD is a completely symbolic debugger: every displayed or required information refers to the Ada source program. No reference to internal representation is visible to the user.

In Sect. 2 we present an overview to the problem of debugging; in Sect. 3 the architecture of HARD is described; Sect. 4 provides a descriptions of functionalitiesof HARD; Sect. 5 investigates some executive problems; Sect. 6 concerns the relational organization of interfaces and execution environment.

2. THE PREDICATE-ACTION APPROACH TO DEBUGGING

For the purpose of debugging, a concurrent application program can be modeled as a system of processes, each one going through a sequence of states. Let us define a process state [Plattner & Nievergelt 1981] as a triple:

1) process source code,

2) control point, which consists of pointers to static and dynamic chains, program counter and "status" (waiting entry call, ready, etc. [Ada RM 1983]),

3) data set, where "data" refers to user-defined variables.

A system state can be defined as an ordered set (cartesian product) of process states: in a non-distributed environment the execution of a concurrent program is a sequence of system states. A transition between states is called an event: process and system events respectively refer to changes of process and system states (e.g.: an assignment is a process event, while the end of a certain rendezvous is a system event).

The essence of debugging is to identify and detect certain events (or sequences of events) and to intervene when such events happen. The so-called predicate-action is the basic mechanism. Predicates (i.e. boolean functions) are defined for each event to be detected; the truth of a predicate triggers the action.

In order to organize debugging functionalities and to compare various proposals for concurrent debuggers, predicates can be classified according to their domain. We can distinguish four kinds of predicates:

- state predicates [Johnson 1981a] [Fairley 1979], which are obtained through the logical product of control predicates (defined on the set of control points) and data predicates (defined on the union of variable domains);

  e.g.: (line_number = 16) and (variable ALFA = 20)

- process predicates [Johnson 1981b], defined on sequences of process states;

  e.g.: (line_number = 16 executed 3 times)

- multiprocess predicates [Curtis & Wittie 1983], defined on sequences of process states;

  e.g.: (end of rendezvous between T1 and T2)

- system predicates [Bates & Wileden 1983] [Bruegge & Hibbard 1983] [Baiardi et al. 1983], defined on sequences of system states;

  e.g.: (end of rendezvous between T1 and T2 after

start of rendezvous between T3 and T4)

All predicates, whose domain should be a set or a sequence of events, take as their arguments states, state components or sequences of states. In fact if ε is the event between σ_1, σ_2, two contiguous states in a computation, a predicate defined on ε is the same as a predicate defined on the sequence $\langle\sigma_1, \sigma_2\rangle$.

Simpler state and process predicates seem useful for a primary phase of debugging, in order to find errors in single tasks: more complex system predicates should instead allow to detect hidden errors due to synchronization between tasks and real-time features and should be used to perform an execution analysis [Power 1983] of error-free applications.

Predicates are often referred to as "breakpoints": such term emphasize the fact that the truth of a predicate cause the application to suspend execution and the debugger to perform proper actions.

Actions can be classified as neutral and non-neutral. The first ones allow to examine state components, obtaining information about control point, values of variables, execution history and so on without affecting the subsequent program execution. On the contrary, non-neutral actions cause changes in states of a single process or system states so as to affect the following evolution of program execution. Moreover, actions can be classified according to their domain or range (control point, data set, process or system state): e.g. display of variables is a neutral action on a data set, while a task queue manipulation is a non-neutral action affecting system state.

The classification of predicates and actions can be used as a design tool in order to properly meet debugging requirements through an increasing set of facilities.

3. THE ARCHITECTURE OF HARD

The debugger provides two usage modes: the interactive mode and the unmanned mode. The aim of interactive mode is to remove bugs from an application which does not fully meet design requirements. A simple concise command language is provided in order to manipulate breakpoints and perform single actions. Ambiguity solution, control on non-neutral actions and menu-driven breakpoint management should make debugging rather easy.

After the application program has passed effectiveness requirements, time-dependent errors and performance should be checked. The unmanned usage mode (i.e. execution of debugging tasks which are not directly controlled), which requires a proficiency of Ada, is a powerful tool for this kind of monitoring: programs can be profiled and statistical evaluation is feasible about loops, subprogram calls, rendezvous and so on.

HARD was specifically conceived for Ada: therefore syntactical and executive concepts typical of Ada are largely used. The main features are:

- breakpoint implementation as entry calls which are inserted in the executable code;
- action implementation through a set of procedures which are actually written in an interpreted intermediate language discussed later;
- use of Ada tasks to build predicates and actions;

- use of Ada packages to organize control tasks and procedures.

The debugger provides definition of Ada tasks to monitor execution: each task declares one or more entries where debugging actions are described. Thus a breakpoint is implemented as an entry call: when a breakpoint occurs, a previously specified entry is executed, then control returns to the debugged application, whose execution is continued.

The procedures and functions which perform debugging facilities are contained in a predefined Ada package, called DEBUGGER (fig.1).

```
package DEBUGGER is
  task I_TASK is
    entry INT;
    pragma TOP_PRIORITY;
  end I_TASK;
     -- procedures written in Ada
  procedure SETLINE (LINENUM: INTEGER);
  procedure DISFORWARD (LINENUM,RANGE: INTEGER);
     ...
     -- procedures written in E2_CODE
  procedure DISVAR (UNIT,NAME: STRING; STOP,FILE: BOOLEAN);
  procedure DISSCOPE;
  procedure TRACEBACK;
     ...
  function CALLING_SUB return STRING;
  function STATE (TASK: STRING) return INTEGER;
  procedure ANALYZE;
private
  pragma INTERFACE (E2_CODE,ANALYZE);
  pragma INTERFACE (E2_CODE,DISVAR);
          -- E2_CODE is an intermediate interpretable language
          -- extended with a set of instructions for debugging
     ...
end DEBUGGER;

package body DEBUGGER is
  ACTION,PRTY: INTEGER;
  QUIT: BOOLEAN:= FALSE;
  UNIT,NAME: STRING;
    ...  -- other variables
    ...  -- body of I_TASK
    ...  -- bodies of procedures written in Ada
 end DEBUGGER;
```

fig.1

The predefined Ada task called Interaction task (I_TASK) contains an entry (INT) performing command language interpretation. When a breakpoint calling this entry occurs, a rendezvous with I_TASK starts and the command interpreter is available for the user to execute debugging actions or breakpoint manipulation. I_TASK body is:

```
task body I_TASK is
begin
  ANALYZE;
  while not QUIT loop
    accept INT do
      ANALYZE;  -- command interpreter
    end INT;
```

```
    end loop;
  end I_TASK;
```

The command interpreter (for interactive mode only) uses a relation-based recursive descent LL(1) syntactic analyzer. The priority of I_TASK is higher than that of any other user-defined task: pragma TOP_PRIORITY gives I_TASK such priority.

Procedures listed in package specification of DEBUGGER perform debugging actions or provide useful information in order to define complex predicates (e.g.: procedure DISFORWARD displays source lines; procedure DISVAR displays the value of variables; function STATE returns a numeric code denoting the state of a task, i.e. waiting_rendezvous, delayed, etc.).

DEBUGGER is predefined and belongs to the program library of the existing APSE; therefore a reference to DEBUGGER in the context clause suffices to invoke the debugging of an application.

4. FUNCTIONS PROVIDED BY HARD

4.1. Predicates

Simple predicates are the basic features: they correspond to rather typical events such as statement execution (through line number), subprogram call/return, accept/end accept, exception raise, task activation/completion.

Breakpoint insertion is menu-driven: the user selects a simple predicate and completes it with information required to place the breakpoint (user must also provide the names of the called entry and, if desired, of the called task: if interactive mode is required when the breakpoint occurs, the called entry must be INT in I_TASK). Ambiguities, due to homonimies and overloading, are solved through a dialog.

Let us consider the application in fig.2, which is a simple example of producer-consumer buffer management. We want to insert two breakpoints: the first one on BUFFER activation and the second one on line number 16. They respectively call entries INT (owned by I_TASK) and STAT_REACHED (owned by task FREQ) and homonimy exists in the second case. The interaction is:

```
>> Command:
bi
 CODE   BREAKPOINT
   1    Statement
   2    Subprogram call
   3    Subprogram return
   4    Task activation
   5    Task completion
   6    Accept
   7    End accept
   8    Exception raise
   9    MENU
   0    esc
>> Select code:
4
>> Unit name ?
BUFFER
>> Breakpoint name ?
INT
```

```
>> Select code:
1
>> Statement number ?
16
>> Breakpoint on task BUFFER
  16:   POOL(IN_INDEX):= C;
>> Breakpoint name ?
STAT_REACHED
>> Unit name ?
FREQ
```

The possibility of inserting breakpoints in generic units or task types exists, but on all instances and objects of a certain type, because of the shared code solution which was chosen for ART implementation [Millovaz & Pipponzi 1985], [Di Maio & Paolillo 1985]: however HARD displays useful information about any breakpoint when it occurs (names of instances and objects are also displayed).

```
     ...
task body BUFFER is
     ...
begin
  loop
    select
      when COUNT < POOL_SIZE =>
        accept WRITE(C: in CHARACTER) do
          POOL(IN_INDEX):= C;                  -- line 16
        end
        IN_INDEX:= IN_INDEX mod POOL_SIZE + 1;
        COUNT:= COUNT - 1;
    or
      when COUNT > 0 =>
        accept READ(C: out CHARACTER) do
          C:= POOL(OUT_INDEX);
        end;
        OUT_INDEX:= OUT_INDEX mod POOL_SIZE + 1;
        COUNT:= COUNT + 1;
    or
      terminate;
    end select;
  end loop;
end BUFFER;
task type PRODUCER is
  CHAR: CHARACTER;
begin
  loop
       -- produce next character CHAR
    BUFFER.WRITE(CHAR);                      -- line 40
    exit when CHAR = ASCII.EOT;
  end loop;
end PRODUCER;
     ...

PROD1,PROD2: PRODUCER;
CONS1: CONSUMER;
     ...
```

fig.2

A breakpoint is active until an explicit remove command (br) is given: a numeric identifier is assigned to each breakpoint when it is inserted, in order to make its manipulation easier.

Complex predicates can be defined through unmanned usage mode. User-defined control tasks (called Debugging tasks or D_tasks) providing proper entries are inserted in the source program (preferably in a package) before compilation: these entries contain calls of procedures and functions declared in package DEBUGGER and such subprograms can be used in order to define predicates in a D_task.
The general structure of a D_task is:

```
task D_TASK is
   -- declarations of entries
  pragma TOP_PRIORITY;
end D_TASK;
task body D_TASK is
   -- declarations of variables
begin
  loop
    accept ... do
      if ...            -- predicate
        then  ...       -- action
      end if;
    end ... ;
  end loop;
end D_TASK;
```

Note that D_tasks are very often structured as loops without any exit condition: this means that they remain active until a proper command is given in interactive mode, which stops all D_tasks and removes all breakpoints.

Therefore a complex predicate is to be considered as the logical product of a breakpoint and a programmer-defined predicate. The user can insert a breakpoint calling an entry owned by a particular D_task. When such breakpoint occurs, this entry is called and the corresponding predicate is evaluated: if it is true, the corresponding action (or sequence of actions) is performed.

4.2. Actions

HARD provides neutral and non-neutral actions to survey process and system states during execution. Some neutral actions are:

a) Display variable. Every declared (also structured) variable can be displayed by giving its name and the name of the unit which declares it (access variables were not considered).

b) Display scope / backtrace. To trace procedure nesting, both static and dynamic chains can be symbolically displayed. The first action consists of displaying the names of the units which statically enclose the current one. The second action shows the path of the execution through subprogram calls and entry calls from the beginning to the currently active breakpoint. In contrast to sequential programs, a generic trace for a concurrent application contains a certain number of "subtraces", each one originated from an active rendezvous. The backtrace after breakpoint on line 16, where two subtraces refer to the rendezvous between BUFFER and PROD1, is:

```
>> Command:
trb
```

```
... entry WRITE     (at 16)
[1]
... task BUFFER     ()
... main            ()
[2]
... task PROD1      (at 40)
... main            ()
```

c) Display task/entry descriptor. Symbolic information is provided about task/entry state, priority, active unit, restart address, related queues and so on. For instance the display of a task descriptor and an entry descriptor, in which all displayed information is completely symbolic, is:

```
>> Command:
dt PROD1

 Name: PROD1
 Type: PRODUCER
 State: wait_end_RV with BUFFER on entry WRITE
 Priority: 1
 Restart Address:
  40:   BUFFER.WRITE(CHAR);

>> Command:
de BUFFER,WRITE

 Entry: WRITE
 Task: BUFFER
 Queue:
  [1] PROD1 PROD2
```

d) Editing actions. Selected parts of source program can be displayed.

Non-neutral actions are much more critical to deal with than the neutral ones, especially for concurrent and real-time applications, since an action can indirectly affect several tasks and cause a waterfall of exceptions or errors. Several bounds and controls are provided in order to minimize such inconveniences. Some non-neutral actions are the following.

a) Modify variable. Controls concern range constraints (for subtypes and indexes).

b) Modify scope. Active unit and current line can be changed but active task or entry must remain the same.

c) Modify task descriptor. Task priority and state can be altered through debugger-driven operations: the debugger only shows the allowed (i.e. not critical) transitions in order to drive the user to a safe non-neutral execution monitoring. For instance if we want to complete task PROD2, the interaction is:

```
>> Command:
mt PROD2
 Code Action
   1  esc
   2  priority
   3  state
>> Select action code:
2
>> Allowed states are:
 Code State
```

```
    0  esc
   10  completed
   11  ready
  >> Select state code:
  11
```

d) Modify queue. Task descriptor entries in any queue (on entry, ready) can be displaced.

Other actions not discussed concern displaying and raising exceptions, restarting the program after debugger intervention, etc.

For all actions, ambiguities are solved as for breakpoint manipulation. Sequences of actions can be built in the unmanned mode: in fact any sequence using procedures of package DEBUGGER can be defined in the entries of D_tasks. For instance D_task FREQ allows to display the value of variable CHAR of the application task PROD1 when a breakpoint calling entry STAT_REACHED has occurred more than five times:

```
task body FREQ is
  COUNT: INTEGER:= 0;
begin
  loop
    accept STAT_REACHED do
      COUNT:= COUNT + 1;
      if COUNT >= 5 then
        DISVAR (PROD1,CHAR,true,false);
    end STAT_REACHED;
  end loop;
end FREQ;
```

Predicates can be also defined using a different kind of breakpoint as basic mechanism. Instead of calling a D_task through an entry call, the actions can be automatically executed when a specified delay time finishes. This allows a quasi-asynchronous intervention on the monitored application which is useful to prevent or find out certain critical situations (such as starvations).
For instance D_task TIME-OUT calls the command interpreter every twenty seconds (not considering debugger interventions), in order to allow the user to investigate and manipulate the kernel situation:

```
task body TIME-OUT is
  SAMPLE: constant INTEGER:= 20;
begin
  loop
    delay SAMPLE;
    I_TASK.INT;
  end loop;
end TIME-OUT;
```

Remember that all D_tasks, as I_TASK, have a higher priority (as stated by pragma TOP_PRIORITY) with respect to any other application task. The reason is that D_tasks must run before any application task in the same condition. The "control priority" has a value which is greater than the upper bound of the predefined subtype PRIORITY (see [Ada RM 1983] , 9.8)

With respect to the described classification of predicates, it can be easily seen that interactive mode allows to define state predicates, while unmanned mode also provides process, multiprocess and system predicates.

At present D_tasks are made part of the application at compilation-time, but they could be inserted at run-time if an incremental compiler were available. Such feature should allow non-neutral actions on source code: in fact selected part of the application could be modified at source level and locally recompiled.

5. EXECUTIVE FEATURES

Debugger intervention implies delays and real-time artifacts in the monitored application. Two alternatives exist for the implementation:

1) to accept delays entirely, dealing with control tasks as if they belonged to the application (apart from priority management);

2) to stop the clock while monitoring operations take place, restarting upon their termination (the same as time management rules in basketball or football.

The most critical situations are caused by delay statements, delay alternatives and timed entry calls, where a time is given whose exhaustion implies a transition to a new state. Solution 1) causes the delay time to be logically shorter since the clock goes on during debugger intervention. With solution 2), which was adopted, the delay time is elongated, but it remains logically the same so as to preserve task synchronization as much as possible. The clock-saving mechanism consists of recording the duration of intervention and adding it to the delay times before resuming application execution.

Two solutions exist for breakpoint implementation too:

a) non-intrusive: the debugger works as an interpreter and evaluates predicates before fetching the next instruction;

b) intrusive: the interpretable code is locally altered by substituting the next instruction with a call to the debugger.

The second solution was adopted with the "call" being an entry call: the next instruction is temporarily saved until the breakpoint is removed.

6. RELATIONAL IMPLEMENTATION OF HARD

The most peculiar aspect of ART project (see fig. 3) is the use of the relational model to organize data and procedures [Ceri & Crespi Reghizzi 1983]. A special resident relational data base provides all storage facilities for ART modules. ART modules are described below.

- SIRE is the relational data base manager, which provides data base definition and manipulation;
- LEXSYN performs syntactical analysis and produces an intermediate representation in R_TCOL (a relational version of $TCOL_{Ada}$ [Brosgol et al. 1980]);
- SEM performs semantical analysis, overloading solution and translation into E_CODE, an interpretable relational language;
- GEN is concerned with management of generic units;
- EX is the E_CODE interpreter plus kernel.

All interfaces and internal data are normalized relations and algorithms use operations of relational algebra (projection, selection, join, etc.). For instance in EX module code, data and kernel are completely relation-based: activation records, descriptors, queues and so on are structured as third (or Boyce-Codd) normal form relations.

The most striking advantages of this choice concern software development and team work: interaction between designers which are responsible of different modules is rather easy and ART experience demonstrates that major projects can be conveniently managed using a relational approach. The drawback is the very poor efficiency that makes the approach suitable only for prototypes.

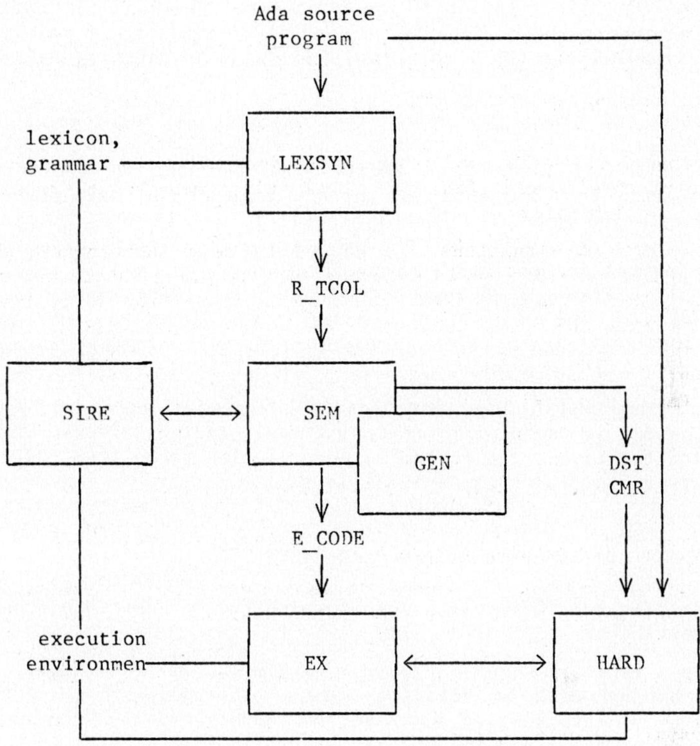

fig.3 ART project

A monitored program thus requires to translate the user program and the HARD debugging tasks using the ART translator, and then is executed by a modified run-time system (EX module) which is driven by a modified E_CODE language, called E^2_CODE. E^2_CODE incorporates some operating codes which are specific for the debugging actions. Thus only the low-level actions which affect the kernel structures of the ART run-time system are directly written in E^2_CODE, while the remainder of HARD is directly specified using the Ada language.

The later addition of HARD to the project was helped by ART relational structure. Debugger-friendly interfaces (such as debugger symbol table) are easy to build by postprocessing the compiler symbol table through operations of relational algebra. Furthermore the executive environment is completely relation-based: therefore all actions are described in terms of relational operations.

6.1. Interfaces

A rather complex issue of conventional debuggers is the definition of proper interfaces between debugger and compiler. Information from scanning, parsing and translation must be accessed by the run-time symbolic debugger in order to provide all mentioned facilities in terms of predicates and actions. Much information produced during compilation is to be held which would be otherwise thrown away after translation (i.e. symbol table, syntactic tree, etc. [Johnson 1979]).

The advantages of relational approach are obvious in building interfaces. Debugger-compiler interfaces consist of two sets of relations: the Debugger Symbol Table (DST) relations and the Code Matching Relations (CMR).

DST consists of three subsets: Type Description Relations (TDR), Variable Descriptions Relations (VDR) and Static Structure Relations (SSR). TDR provide all information about types and subtypes declared in the source program: they are obtained through projections, selections and joins on the relation-based abstract syntactical tree (R_TCOL in fig.3). VDR provide the correspondence between symbolic entities (such as variables and units) and objects (memory locations, etc.): they are built during translation from R_TCOL into E_CODE using relational operations on relations that are private of SEM module. SSR describe the static structure of the application (such as nesting, context clauses, parameter profiles, etc.).

CMR give the mapping between source program lines and E_CODE instructions, which is useful for breakpoint manipulation, display of task descriptors and backtrace. For instance, one relation taken from TDR class is (notation is taken from [Ullman 1983]):

$$D\_SUBTYPESYM \longleftarrow \pi_{T\#,NAME,PARENTTYPE,PARNSUBSYM}(SUBTYPESYM)$$

where SUBTYPESYM is a R_TCOL relation from which the debugger projects the interesting attributes.

Interfaces were designed trying to meet rather conflicting requirements between ease of building versus accessing. As with other modules of the ART translator, we have not emphasized performances or memory saving in the development of HARD. If more effective file management primitives were provided, virtual memory facilities could have been used in order to reduce average memory occupation.

6.2. An example of relational execution environment

Let us consider a typical procedure for queue manipulation. Queues are organized as follows:

QUEUE (PRTY,FIRST,LAST)

where attributes FIRST and LAST refer to numeric identifiers of the first and last queued tasks.
A task descriptor consists of four normalized relations:

TASK_ID (TASK_NAME,TASK_INDEX,MASTER_DATA_REL,MASTER_DATA_T#,ID)

SAVE_CONTEXT (ID,NEXT,TASK_DATA_REL,TASK_DATA_T#,
REST_ADD_CODE_REL, REST_ADD_CODE_T#,PRIORITY)

EXC_RAISED (ID,EXC_NAME)

TIME (ID,READY_TIME)

where -DATA_REL and -DATA_T# attributes refer to the activation tuple (see 6.1.), while -CODE_REL and -CODE_T# attributes refer to a single E_CODE instruction (in fact interpretable instructions are tuples in "code relations", one for each compilation unit). Other information concern priority, names of raised exceptions, restart time after a delay, etc. In SAVE_CONTEXT relation ID is the above-mentioned numeric identifier, NEXT is the identifier of the next task in a queue.
The specification of the basic procedure used to display a queue is:

```
procedure dis_queue(id: INTEGER) is
   -- id is the identifier of the first queued task
begin
  if id ≠ 0
    then
      tskname <-- π_taskname(σ_ID=id(TASK_ID));
      " print tskname ";
      nxt <-- π_next(σ_ID=id(SAVE_CONTEXT));
      dis_queue(nxt);
  end if;
end dis_queue;
```

In the same way any neutral or non-neutral action is implemented through a procedure containing operations of relational algebra. The only non-relational actions are the editing ones: in fact the corresponding procedures can be easily written in Ada.

7. CONCLUSIONS

HARD proposes an original approach to the problem of debugging concurrent real-time applications written in Ada. The use of Ada tasks that are made part of the monitored application means easy usage of execution analysis facilities for a typical Ada programmer. The debugger can be easily introduced in a software development environment such as an APSE since it is organized as an Ada package. Other advantages are completeness of predicates and actions, security about ambiguity resolution and modification bounds, temporal non-intrusivity.

HARD can be compared with other existing or proposed Ada debuggers such as [Giannessi & Nicodemi 1982], [Holdsworth 1983], [Elliott 1983], [Ploedereder 1984]: it is more homogeneous and provides features which are typical of dynamic analyzers [Fairley 1980], [Power 1983]. Besides that, it can be used at different levels, according to the required detail of analysis and to the previous experience of the user.

However, HARD does not provide post-mortem dumps and in-flight asynchronous activation, which means that it does not cope with uncorrect programs unless proper user-defined breakpoints are inserted.

The use of the relational model is another peculiar feature of our implementation. Interfaces are easy to obtain and access, which means advantages in the design of both compiler and debugger. Other relation-based debuggers were proposed [Powell & Linton 1983], [Snodgrass 1982], but two major differences exist with HARD. First the execution environment is traditional (and more efficient) in other proposals, whereas it is completely relational in ART. Second in HARD the debugger-user interface is via a command language or Ada language according to the chosen usage mode, while other proposals force the user to access the relational data base by using a general purpose query language.

The current implementation of HARD is complete but very inefficient, and remains a research prototype (the entire ART project was developed in Berkeley Pascal on a DEC VAX 11/780 computer under UNIX operating system). Nevertheless an efficient implementation of HARD could be made by transforming the relational data structures and algorithms of the prototype and mapping them on the actual structures of a chosen APSE and run-time support.

REFERENCES

Ada Reference Manual (1983). MIL-STD-1815A, D.o.D. U.S.A.

Baiardi, F. & Di Francesco, N. & Matteoli, E. & Stefanini, S. & Vaglini, G. (1983). Development of a debugger for a concurrent language. ACM Sigsoft/Sigplan Symposium on High-level Debugging, March, 6-23.

Bates, P.C. & Wileden, J.C. (1983). An approach to high-level debugging of distributed systems. ibid., 24-33.

Brosgol, B.M. et al. (1980). $TCOL_{Ada}$: Revised report on an intermediate representation for the preliminary Ada language. Department of Computer Science, carnagie-Mellon University.

Bruegge, B. & Hibbard, P. (1983). Generalized path expressions: a high-level debugging mechanism. ACM Sigsoft/Sigplan Symposium on High-level Debugging, March, 61-78.

Ceri, S. & Crespi Reghizzi, S. (1983). Relational data bases in the design of program construction systems. ACM Sigplan Notices, 18, no. 11, 34-44.

Curtis, R & Wittie, L. (1983). BugNet: a distributed applications debugging system. ACM Sigsoft/Sigplan Symposium on High-level Debugging, March, 138-141.

Di Maio, A. (1985). Controllo simbolico dell'esecuzione di un programma Ada nel progetto ART. submitted for publication.

Di Maio, A. & Paolillo, G. (1985). Ambiente esecutivo per l'interpretazione di Ada nel progetto ART. submitted for publication.

Elliott, J.K. (1983). The ROLM Ada Work Center. Ada Letters, 2, no. 4, 97-100A.

Fairley, R.E. (1979). ALADDIN: Assembly Language Assertion Driven Debugging Interpreter. IEEE Trans. on Software Engineering, SE-5, no. 4, 426-428.

Fairley, R.E. (1980). Ada debugging and testing support environments. ACM Sigplan Notices, 15, no. 11, 16-25.

Giannessi, F. & Nicodemi, F. (1982). Architettura e funzionalita' del sistema di debugging di programmi Ada. Olivetti DIDAU, July.

Glass, R.L. (1980). Real-time: the 'lost-world' of debugging and testing. ACM Comm., 23, no.5, 264-271.

Gross, T. & Zwaenepoel, W. (1983). System support for multiprocess debugging. ACM Sigsoft/Sigplan Symposium on High-level Debugging. March, 192-196.

Holdsworth, D. (1983). A system for analysing Ada programs at run-time. Software - Practice and Experience, 13, 407-421.

Johnson, M.S. (1979). Translator design to support run-time debugging. Software - Practice and Experience, 9, 1035-1041.

Johnson, M.S. (1981). A software debugging glossary. Hewlett-Packard Company.

Johnson, M.S. (1981). DISPEL: a run-time debugging language. Computer languages, 6, 79-94.

Millovaz, A. & Pipponzi, M. (1985). Trattamento dei packages generici di Ada nel progetto ART. submitted for publication.

Plattner, B. & Nievergelt, J. (1981). Monitoring program execution: a survey. IEEE Computer, Nov., 76-93.

Ploedereder, E. (1984). Project SPERBER: background, status, future plans. Ada Letters, 3, no. 4, 92-98.

Powell, M.L. & Linton, M.A. (1983). A database model of debugging. ACM Sigsoft/Sigplan Symposium on High-level Debugging, March, 257-263.

Power, L.R. (1983). Design and use of a program execution analyzer. IBM Systems Journal, 22, no. 3, 271-294.

Seidner,R.I. & Tindall, N. (1983). Interactive debug requirements. ACM Sigsoft/Sigplan Symposium on High-level Debugging, March, 318-320.

Snodgrass, R. (1982). Monitoring distributed systems: a relational approach. PhD dissertation, Dept. of Computer Science, Carnagie-Mellon University.

Ullman, J.D. (1983). Principles of database design. 2nd ed. Computer Science Press.

AN EVENT-DRIVEN DEBUGGER FOR ADA

Claude MAUGER

Kevin PAMMETT

Alsys
29, Avenue de Versailles
78170 La Celle Saint Cloud
France

Abstract. In this paper, we present the main concepts used in our symbolic debugger for Ada. Described also is a companion tool, the Ada Program VIEWer, which gives users full access to program source while debugging. This debugger is one of the components of the Alsys Tool set which aims at providing high-level Ada-oriented tools, incorporating state-of-the-art techniques for software design, documentation, and development.

Introduction

Ada has been developed as an answer to the increasing costs of software development. It contains a lot of advanced features such as tasking, exceptions, safe separate compilation, generics, etc.

Our debugger has been designed to cope efficiently with these features of Ada, as well as with the more traditional aspects of program development. Moreover, DEBUG co-operates with other tools to provide a comprehensive capability, state-of-the-art wrt Ada program development, within a highly productive tool-rich environment.

Co-operating Sets Of Tools

Traditionally, debuggers have been forced to co-operate in an intimate manner with numerous "environment" tools, and with Ada we are forced even more into this architecture because of the Ada Program Library notion. For DEBUG, the compiler, binder, and linker co-operate to pass on symbolic information, source file names, exception tables, etc; thus DEBUG can transparently manipulate the execution of Ada programs.

Rather than build-in a "viewing sub-system" for displaying program source, we have chosen to architect a Program VIEWer as a standalone tool which also has a mode in which it can "co-operate tightly" with DEBUG (and other tools). The VIEWer is a highly interactive tool, specialized in the dynamic presentation of Ada source. When invoked by DEBUG, the VIEWer takes its command line input from DEBUG, so the interactive user sees this as a tightly-bound VIEWing sub-system, an integral part of the debugger. In this mode you can choose to "enter the sub-system", in which case the user can input VIEWer commands directly, thereby taking full advantage of the extra power the VIEWer provides (that DEBUG doesn't directly use).

A final aspect, a feature of all tools in the Alsys Ada tool kit, is that the user interface is standard, consistent, and highly ergonometric. This is provided by a set of Ada packages, used in each of our tools, that provides "layered-on" facilities for interfacing the tool with the user in a fashion designed for high productivity, evolvability, and ease of use.

Ada DEBUG

The debugger, from the beginning, has been conceived as the implementation of a higher level language tied to Ada where every details about hardware system, and a particular compiler are intentionally hidden. All state-of-the-art language design principles have been applied.

Only 4 new concepts are introduced, all of them being regular extensions of concepts of the Ada language itself: these are **context, event, action, abbreviation.** They are combined freely using a small set of operators, each of them with a constant intuitive meaning. The interpretation of each sentence and of each component is highly contextual, removing almost all redundancies.

The **context** notion is a regular extension of the Ada concept of **Frame** [a subprogram body, a task (type) body, a package body, a block; hence every construct that can have an exception part]. It denotes a frame; by extension it can be used to designate the objects created by that frame. As a consequence of task allocators and recursivity, a frame may have several instances at runtime. A context can specify a particular instance or some consistent subset of them.

Contexts are used to set on the view on the program, thus getting a way to apply the Ada visibility rules.

Generally, a context is denoted by the name of its frame. When this one is not visible, the notation is relative to another context, using one of the following operations:

Selection: It is the Ada expanded name notation, with a disposition to overcome overloading ambiguity.

< : The right name is evaluated from the activator of the left context. If the left context was a subprogram, the activator is the caller; if the left context was a task, the activator is the master of the task.

> : This operation is inverse of "<". It denotes **the** instance(s) currently created by the left context, e.g.: all tasks of a given type dependent of a given master.

Moreover, a frame may be designated by a reference to one of its source lines; this location in the text can be given by the VIEWer facility: a context thus can be specified by showing it in the program text.

Error detection and handling: the events and actions

It is one of the main part of the debugger. The function is to detect an abnormal situation and then perform a related action. The general form, named a clause, is:

[context:] scope event [=> action]

The **scope** of a test may be either local or global. When global, the check is performed all along the execution of "context"; conversely, if local, the check is performed only within "context".

The **context** acts as a guard for the clause and defines the visibility and objects manipulated in "event" and "action". As soon as the event is produced in the context, the action is executed. This kind of clause inherits from the classical daemon concept. []

The kind of **event** that can be specified are:

(a) an **exception name.** It is the ground of the event concept. The form

when CONSTRAINT_ERROR => action

is somewhat reminiscent of Ada itself, and may be interpreted as a way of adding dynamically new exception handlers to the program.

(b) Any unhandled exception is an event denoted **others.** The clause "when others" is a default clause.

(c) To overcome the checking limitations of the standard Ada subtype checking, an event can be an arbitrary Ada **relation.** By this way, any explicit assertion can be specified upon one or many variable objects.

"if DATA not in SOME_SUBTYPE => raise CONSTRAINT_ERROR"

reflects typical tests issued by the compiler. In addition, checks such as: "if DATA mod 2 > 0" can be specified.

(d) In order to cope with erroneous situations, efficient expedients have been designed. A careful inspection of erroneous situations should convince that most of them are a consequence of multiple access paths to the same physical object; when **one** of the names of such a kind of object is known, the form **mod** (name) may be quite efficient. The event occurs when some updating of the object occurs, or when it is destroyed by an instance of UNCHECKED_DEALLOCATION.

(e) There is a built-in cycling check, denoted **loop** [(factor)]. Looping is a permanent problem in every sequential languages including Ada. The fact that a cycle is always locally generated is an interesting property of Ada. A cycling factor may be provided for evident efficiency reasons. This factor is proportional to the expected time complexity of the algorithm and not at all dependent of the way this algorithm is actually programmed. The event occurs in some context when the same uniform execution cycle is performed more than the predefined factor.

(f) An event can be specified when some particular action or action kind, generating visible side effect, is performed by the program. The general form is:

instruction_class [(parameter)]

Almost all imperative Ada statement can be specified as instructions:

goto, raise, call return, accept, delay, abort

The additional parameter specified on what the statement applies. Even faced with highly optimized programs, this form generally remains significant, as long as the named statements are still in the object program (i.e. not removed by an optimizer). The form has been introduced mainly for extraction of specific information related to the monitored statements, and as a way to logically synchronize other events. The extracted information is displayed as event information or can be kept for extensive external treatment.

(g) Finally, going through some particular source line is considered as an event. It can be used in conjunction with other events to localize them physically. It is denoted "**at** source reference". The source reference can be a label name, or any substitute; in particular, it can be retrieved from the VIEWer, in an interactive environment.

(h) Moreover, for user convenience, 2 asynchronous events are defined:

key-call: interrupt of the program (by the user)

task abort: when some task of the context is the target of an abort instruction.

On top of those basic events, event expressions can be built up freely, combining some other events using the following 5 operators:

and is the simultaneous conjunction of events,

or is the union of events,

then is used for sequential occurrence;

times is used for a repetition of defined length, e.g. N times mod (x),

in is used when an event must be checked in some part of the program out of the visibility area of the clause. This disposition is useful to specify events related to packages, recursive subprograms and task instances.

When the event occurs, if the related action implies an interaction, the event trace is displayed, that is, every component of the composite event is displayed. Each elementary check performed is associated with a particular kind of information.

In a global check, a skeleton of the execution path from the event context up to the clause context is given. This path may be non deterministic in case of tasking.

All the information displayed is oriented towards diagnose upon the specified event.

Actions

The main action is **display**ing. It is a mean for the user to gain further information about the actual state of the program, when the event trace information is insufficient.

The general forms are:

1. display [all] {invalid|undef} [with access] display-list [of context]
displays values of particular objects or values of attributes,

2. display [all] {invalid | undef} [with access] type-list [of context]
displays a set of objects selected by this type,

3. display [all] {invalid | undef} [with access] [of context]
displays a set of objects,

4. display [all] task [with access] task-list [of context]
gives the detailed status of a set of tasks, selected by their type,
5. display [all] task [with access] [of context]

Displaying object values, the invalid or undef option has a functional basis; it filters objects of the selected set that offends their subtype constraints or that are not representable. In Ada, this situation is possible as a consequence of undefined values.

The type selection has a similar justification; the contamination of data almost always clusters among types, as a consequence of Ada rules on assignment.

The **all** option implies consideration of all accessible objects, as opposed to visible ones; **of** context is used to further reduce this set to objects belonging to the given context.

The **with access** option implies the use of any reference to other objects and a display of the same kind on that new objects. This mechanism is used to display linked structures as a whole, or to obtain an explicit display of all tasks synchronized with a particular one. It is a consequence of combination of options that a display of local or global dead-lock situations is made explicit.

The display of any object is always in Ada symbolic form, whatever is the object's type; the display uses implicitly many attributes of the object and of its subtype and that image is totally independent of any applying representation clause.

The display of tasks is designed to show clearly the synchronization errors. The task state is synthetized in a standard uniform status and displayed along with the references of tasks in direct relationship with that one. The display is independent of the physical representation of the task: passive or not, multiplexed or not.

[There is no event specification for dead-locks. In fact, this point is dependent of a particular Run Time System. Wherever an impossible situation occurs according to its implementation, the availability of some exception name associated to those situations are sufficient].

All above combinations are available using **keep** instead of display. In that case, identical information is selected and put upon a keeping channel in a core-image format.

The command input is specified with a particular action named **accept**. In interactive environment, this is the default action of clauses. The execution of that action is merely to accept new sentences from an input channel and interpret them in the current event context. The user interaction protocol is thus defined by the used himself, not by the debugger.

The debugger also contains miscellaneous functionalities: there is a time measurement procedure, of the "**time in** context" form; there is a mechanism of I/O redirection on input, display and keeping channels; each of them can be redirected upon a file, an interprocess link, or a terminal; in the later case, windows can be specified allowing effective intermixing of several asynchronous activities.

There is a **Terminate** order to stop running clauses, or to suppress checking upon particular objects, event kind, contexts, etc. The **use** order displays all or part of the debugger state and currently running clauses.

There is an abbreviation mechanism. It has a semantics reminiscent of the Ada renaming mechanism, and applies upon everything the debugger manipulates: events, contexts, actions, display orders, objects. Moreover, there is a help facility used among others to document error messages.

The Program VIEWer

The Ada Program VIEWer is conceptualized as an environment tool that is specialized in the **presentation** of Ada program source. It is a learning tool, and a tool for understanding programs at various levels. While it, too, can function "in batch" the VIEWer is primarily intended as an interactive tool for use on terminals that permit windowing and other advanced video effects like reverse video, etc. (Because of the User Product Interface (UPI), the VIEWer, like all Alsys tools, will work on "any terminal" although we do not promise that all features will work optimally on older terminals).

From DEBUG, one sees the VIEWer more like a "viewing sub-system" than a separate tool. You do not have to know about invoking the VIEWer or, in fact, about **any** of its command language. If you simply let DEBUG operate in its normal manner, (feeding commands via PIPE to its slave child process), you see the **multi-windowing** and dynamic source display provided by the VIEWer in such a way that you think it "part of DEBUG".

This closely-coupled co-operation is not only a convenience for DEBUG users; it is a conceptual facet of our tool set that is pervasive: when tools co-operate tightly, they are not seen as separate tools at all. This is analogous to the UNIX MAKE tool; you invoke "make", but indirectly you are invoking compilers, linkers, and who knows what else. A more apt (but less common) analogy would be a powerful editor that offered a wide range of capabilities via a single "editing interface" ... by calling up specialized tools (like a real text formatter) behind the scenes without the user knowing which tool was really doing what work when.

What's in a VIEW?

The term "VIEWer" has been adopted specifically to promote the formal notion of "a **VIEW** of something" (for now, "of a program,", later, "of documents and other structured things"). That is, a **VIEW** of something has a very rigorous definition with component aspects: height, depth, width - even a density or diffusion aspect. And the user is given full control over the VIEW he has at any time.

For example, you can specify a VIEW of program P's compilation unit F, with a 6-line context (window) around source line 123, and a very diffused VIEW where deeply-nested source lines (around line 123) are omitted in the interest of stretching the "wide angle" VIEW as far as possible. You could even "freeze" this VIEW in one window, and create a new window where you want to work with a different VIEW (of the same or of a different compilation unit). Given CRT screen size limitations, both of these windows could be visible at the same time - even if you also had a glass teletype scrolling region where you were interacting with DEBUG.

At the other extreme, you might define a VIEW centered around a certain source line, specifying that all source lines in the vicinity - no matter how deeply nested - be visible. This is more the "highly magnified" VIEW where every detail of the program is visible.

The Dynamics Of Presentation

One of the most useful aspect of VIEWing comes via the numerous ways that you can alter what you see. A typical VIEW produced by the VIEWer is almost never "just like a listing"; too much information is presented in listings, and it is presented in a way that often makes it very difficult and error prone to find something very specific.

Instead, the VIEWer incorporates the notion of **Zoom Level** and **line type**, along with various commands based on these concepts. For example, when you start outlooking at a module, you are at a zoom level which lets you get a "wide angle" or "diffused" VIEW. This corresponds to all source lines at nesting level 1 (the top level) or 2, (the level where things within packages but at the top level are usually declared).

It is convenient to have a wide-angle VIEW of a program when you want to understand its structure. If you "Zoom IN" one level, you see one more level of detail - but not more. Thus, having a VIEW of some real Ada code, one might see something like:

```
22: if (MY_VARIABLE) then
39: else
47: end if;
```

displayed as consecutive lines in the source display window. There are several lines missing, above, because they are more deeply nested than the "current zoom level".

The ZOOM commands let you change the amount of source in a VIEW, but not the actual contents of what you see. To provide orthogonal ways of changing what you see, we offer several OPTIONS, and the SEE command. There are OPTIONs for changing window sizes, the use of advanced video or not, whether you want to see line numbers or not, and etc. A more useful OPTION lets you have all Ada comments (and blank lines) suppressed or displayed. Not seeing comments is useful when you are working in a small window, and when you "know" the code and are looking for details. On the other hand, it is sometimes useful to suppress the code -seeing **only** the comments.

More powerful (but less obvious) than ZOOM are the commands NEXT and SEE, which are based on the notion that every source line has a "line type". Ada keywords are used to reference these line types, as in the command NEXT LOOP which will take you in the current direction, given the current ZOOM level, leaving you repositioned to the next LOOP construct. This is **not** a searching operation; the VIEWable representation of the source contains the information fundamental to line type and zoom level.

The SEE command is more basic than NEXT; it lets you specify which line types (which source lines) you want to be **visible** or hidden. For example, if you turn off comments and then issue the VIEWer command:

```
SEE -* +fun +pro +pack
```

what you have effectively done is to change your source window into a menu from which you can select a function, procedure, or package declaration.

No matter how you scroll, search, or page through the current compilation unit, all source lines that are not of the types indicated are completely invisible. This mechanism offers an enormous reduction capability; modules of several thousand lines of Ada are reduced to just the part you are interested in. In addition, ZOOM still works as always, here. At the top zoom level, given the above SEE command, you would see only top level subprogram declarations in their respective packages. You could then Zoom IN to see nested lines of the types that are currently visible.

Akin to line numbers is the notion of **FINGERpoints.** Modeled after "book marks", a FINGERpoint is a way to put a label on a VIEW via the MARK command. A corresponding GOTO lets you return to that VIEW. Since FINGERpoints are "global", they provide a natural mechanism for working with the **whole program** at once - a major drawback of most editors.

Since MARK allows for FINGERpoints that don't have names, the VIEWer provides the notion of a "**Progression Set**", a sequence of VIEWs. That is, a sequence of GOTOs let you visit each of these VIEWs in succession, using a backwards (in time) circular model. Such Progression Set can be created by DEBUG (e.g. to "show" a cycle) and passed to the VIEWer. A VIEWer tool kit utility (mkPS) can also create a Progression Set based on a search string and a list of source files. (We will have other examples of tools like this). The PS command in the VIEWer lets the VIEWer inherit the notion of VIEWing a progression even where independent external tools determine what is meant by "the progression".

Like DEBUG, the VIEWer works in "glass teletype mode" for "dumb" terminals. More interesting, is the multi-windowing capability, where the VIEWer displays a highly-user-tailorable VIEW of Ada program source.

UPI: The (Alsys Standard) User-Product Interface

Since we are looking towards the day where bitmap terminals, mice, and other "futuristic" user-interface devices become prevalent, we made the decision early on that the user interface part of each tool would **not** be considered the domain of that tool. Rather, we decided to define each of our tools as based upon a keyword - and punctuation - oriented command language, so that we could interpose a layer of intelligence between the tool, which sees only this language, and the user, who sees a consistent interface for a host of things like:

* "non-keyword input", that is, keypad input and the ability to use function keys if they are available on the user's terminal.

* A consistent and standard abbreviation mechanism. The UPI knows nothing of the underlying-tool command language, but it can still provide abbreviations and transliterations since it is in full control of what the underlying tool gets as input.

* Command line editing and a HISTORY mechanism,

* "Escaping to the system", that is, being able to "push down" the current context to have command or a command session interpreted by the surrounding environment,

* Providing a consistent way to input command files, and to capture output in "log files", "displays" (suitable for interactive perusal), or "learning sequences" (for re-execution).

* A consistent and standard model of virtual screens and windows.

The UPI, as we call this "layer of intelligence", is critical if we are to provide DEBUG and the VIEWer as separate tools - and also in combination, as in the more traditional model. Moreover, the Alsys tool set is larger than "DEBUG plus VIEWer", and is growing rapidly. We see many more examples of tool co-operation surfacing to the user interface level, and view the UPI as an essential part of this strategy.

Interfaces With the Compiler

DEBUG operates on the exact memory image of the program, i.e. the compiler generates **exactly** the same optimized object code, regardless of whether the "debug" option has been specified or not. If "debug" is requested, the compiler simply generates additional tables for use by DEBUG. Moreover, DEBUG can be applied to highly optimized programs, the only drawback being that the way the debugger specifies than an event has occurred is less accurate.

Conclusions

We have developed a high-level, source language debugger for Ada, focussing on what will be the problems specific to the debugging of Ada programs. The debugger is event-driven, i.e. that the user is free to concentrate on what event he wants to be detected, letting the debugger take care of all the clerical problems of where to set break-points of traces (etc.) to detect the requested events.

The debugger is coupled with a source VIEWer which provides the user with access to all his Ada source code at debug time. The VIEWer can be seen as part of DEBUG, in which case you see only the source that DEBUG considers relevant ... or, you can invoke the VIEWer directly from - or outside of - DEBUG to take advantage of the VIEWer's many features for finding things or otherwise learning about the program.
The most significant aspect behind what have we achieved has been possible because of the tool-to-tool co-operation that we have described. A **Software Bus**, message-passing architecture permits tools to work standalone or in a tightly-coupled fashion.

Acknowledgements

Etienne MOREL and Pascal PLISSON have contributed greatly to the UPI and VIEWer concepts. Thanks are also due to Arra AVAKIAN, Dave BAKIN, Ben BROSGOL, Christophe CHAUMET, Frederic DURAND, Jean-Loup GAILLY, Paul-Marie GROJEAN, Jean-Claude HELIARD, Jean ICHBIAH, Dominique JEANJEAN, Francoise LE BRIS, Pascal LEROY, and Jacques SEVESTRE, for their helpful suggestions, patience, and support.

Ada® and the Graphical Kernel System

Thomas M. Leonard
Harris Corporation
Government Information Systems Division
Melbourne, FL 32901

Abstract

The Graphical Kernel System (GKS) is a general purpose, Device-Independent, two-dimensional graphics system currently in the final stages of standardization by both the International Organization for Standardization (ISO) [ISO 1982] and the American National Standards Institute (ANSI) [ANSI 1984c]. Associated with each GKS standardization effort are programming language bindings which standardize language-specific interfaces for implementations of GKS. Currently in the draft proposed phase of standardization is the Ada language binding to ANSI GKS [ANSI 1985]. This paper describes the effort to produce the Ada language binding to ANSI GKS and an implementation of GKS in Ada (GKS/Ada) which conforms to this draft proposed Ada language binding. This work will be the first standardized Ada graphics capability.

OVERVIEW OF THE GRAPHICAL KERNEL SYSTEM

The Graphical Kernel System defines a functional set of programming language independent graphical operations for providing a standard interface to a two-dimensional, colour graphics kernel system. GKS supports both device and host independence while still allowing a system to be tuned to take advantage of a particular device's capabilities. The major features of GKS include multiple graphical workstations having both output and input capabilities, a full range of graphical output primitives and input device classes, and the abstraction of World Coordinates. The output primitives include Polyline, Polymarker, Text, Fill Area, and Cell Array, each with its own attributes for controlling its appearance. There are six classes of logical input devices, Locator, Choice, Valuator, Text, Stroke and Pick, each of which may operate in any of three modes -- Request, Sample or Event. GKS also supports the concept of Segments for capturing a picture, manipulating it, and redrawing it over time, and Metafiles for storing graphical information in a Device-Independent form. Hopgood et al. [1984] provides a very good introduction to GKS, and Enderle et al. [1984] discuss in detail the features of GKS and its history.

The specification of the Grahical Kernel System is divided into several levels of increasing functionality. The ANSI version of GKS defines 12 levels of functionality while ISO GKS defines only 9 levels. These functional levels of GKS are divided into a matrix according to the output and input capabilities available at a particular level. The output levels are **m**, **0**, **1** and **2**. Level **m** supports only minimal output and control capabilities, level **0** supports an extended set of output and control capabilities, level **1** defines the concept of Workstation Dependent segment storage and Metafiles, and finally level **2** supports full output capabilities including Workstation Independent Segment Storage (WISS). In the ISO specification of GKS there is no output level **m**, instead all operations defined at level **m** of ANSI GKS are defined at level **0** of ISO GKS. Three levels of input functionality are defined by GKS. These levels are **a**, **b** and **c**, where level **a** has no input capability, level **b** supports a subset of input capabilities, and level **c** supports full input functionality. Thus, a particular level of GKS is defined by both its output and input functionality. For example, level **mc** has minimal output functionality, but has complete input functionality excluding the PICK input class. Figure 1 illustrates the martix organization of ANSI GKS.

Output level \ Input Level	**a**	**b**	**c**
m	minimal control individual attributes subset of output functions	initialize input devices input mode setting REQUEST input	SAMPLE and EVENT input
0	extended control predefined attribute bundles extended output functions	- no new operations -	- no new operations -
1	full bundle concept segments metafiles	initialize PICK input PICK mode setting REQUEST PICK input	SAMPLE and EVENT input for PICK
2	Workstation Independent Segment Storage	- no new operations -	- no new operations -

Figure 1. ANSI GKS Matrix Organization

Ada LANGUAGE BINDING TO GKS

As mentioned above, the Graphical Kernel System is specified independently of any programming language. Therefore, associated with the GKS standardization effort are language bindings which standardize the syntactic interface to GKS in various languages. The initial effort of the GKS/Ada project was to develop an Ada language binding to ANSI GKS under the guidance of the

ANSI Language Bindings and Conformance Subcommittee of the Graphics Technical Committee (X3H34). The result of this effort is now an ANSI draft proposed Ada language binding to GKS [Cuthbert 1985, ANSI 1985]. In addition, a modified Ada binding which conforms to ISO GKS is now an official work item for ISO standardization.

The task of developing an Ada binding for GKS was rather straightforward, however, there did exist concepts in GKS which were inconsistent with the philosophy of Ada. However, the guidelines for developing language bindings allows for variations from the standard where language features clearly represent better and more natural solutions and provide equivalent functionality. The effort to define an Ada language binding may be divided into 4 tasks -- Data types, Functionality, Error Handling, and Packaging [Gilroy 1984].

The GKS specification defines several simple and composite data types for the purpose of defining the interface to its operations. For the most part, the GKS types are bound to derived types visible to the application so that the predefined operations are available. In many cases these types are declared with constraints thereby precluding several error conditions defined by GKS when illegal values are used for certain types. In some cases, types are declared as private and specific operations defined for the types. In particular, the GKS data record types, used to encode information about input devices, Metafile Items, etc.; and GKS list types, used to provide lists of GKS elements, are declared as private types with specific operations. It is likely that Ada's power to provide data abstraction could have been used more extensively, however, it is unclear how to do this while remaining conformant to GKS.

Providing for the functionality of GKS operations is done nearly in a one-to-one correspondence with Ada procedures. However, in some cases parameter lists are changed when Ada language features precluded the necessity of certain parameters. For example, GKS operations frequently have a parameter which specifys the length of an accomanying array paramter. Certainly, this is not required since the Ada attribute 'LENGTH provides this information.

The Ada exception is used as a replacement to the error handling mechanism defined in the GKS standard. Rather than providing for an application defined procedure which is invoked when an error condition occurs as defined by GKS, error conditions are mapped to Ada binding defined exceptions which are raised and propogated to the application upon detection of an error. This realization of GKS error handling is significantly different from that defined by GKS, however, very faithful to Ada's philosophy of error handling and therefore consistent with the goals for defining language specific bindings to GKS.

The Ada language binding to GKS defines two packages for providing the functionality of a particular implementaiton of GKS -- GKS_TYPES and GKS_xx, where xx specifies the level of GKS functionality the application wishes to use. The GKS_TYPES package defines all of the types necessary to use GKS, and the package GKS_xx provides for at least each of the GKS operations defined by that level. The binding also defines three generic packages which provide for a Cartesian Coordinate system, List manipulation and Matrix manipulation. Internally, of course, an implementation is free to use packaging as it wishes. The section, PACKAGING GKS, later in this paper describes how our implementation uses Ada's packaging mechanism to implement GKS.

The remainder of this paper descibes our implementation of GKS/Ada with specific attention on how Ada language features are used to implement various parts of GKS functionality.

IMPLEMENTATION MODEL

The implementation described here is a complete implementation of each of the 12 levels of ANSI GKS in Ada which conforms to the draft proposed Ada language binding to ANSI GKS. The implementation achieves device independence and accomdates highly-, partially-, and non-distributed graphics environments. Currently, the implementation supports a Lexidata 3700 and Summagraphics digitizing tablet for graphical output and input. In addition, GKS Metafile workstations and a prototype Computer Graphics Metafile [ANSI 1984b] workstation are supported. Our current development environment is a Data General MV8000 running the Rolm Ada Development Environment.

The implementation model on which this implementation is based was designed with consideration of four underlying goals. First, the model must be extensible. That is, the implementation must be easily reconfigured for new and differing types of graphics devices and application environments. Second, the model must allow for distributed implementations. Although our initial implementation is not for a distributed environment, distributed graphics environments are quite common and we expect that GKS/Ada will certainly be used in such environments. Third, GKS is a large graphics system with extensive features which interact in complex ways. It is very important that the implementation model promotes the use of efficient solutions to many of GKS's features. (Only a few of the implementation strategies which lead to efficient implementations of GKS are presented here since the topic is beyond the scope of this paper. Waggoner, et al. [1984] provide some insight to some other strategies which lead to efficient implementations of GKS.)

Finally, the model must promote the use of reusable code among workstations and implementations of each level of GKS.

In consideration of these goals the system architecture illustrated in Figure 2 is that which this implementation is based upon. The architecture consists of five major components and three interfaces. These components are the Device-Independent Application Interface, the Workstation Manager, the Workstation Resources, the Workstation Driver, and the Device Driver. Responsible for communciaton between these components are three interfaces. The first interface is of course the Ada language binding to GKS which is used by application programs to gain access to the operations provided by GKS via the Device-Independent Application Interface component. The Virtual Workstation Interface (VWI) is the second interface defined in the system. The VWI is used by the Device-Independent component to interface with each of the workstations in an implementation. The last interface defined by this model is the Device Driver Interface. There are multiple Device Driver Interfaces in the system, one per device type. A Device Driver Interface provides the Workstation Driver access to each of the operations available on the device through the Device Driver.

The Device-Independent Application Interface component is the highest level component in the system. It is responsible for providing to the application program the complete functionality of a specific level of GKS through the standarized Ada language binding. The Device-Independent component then communicates with workstations in the system through the Workstation Manager via the Virtual Workstation Interface. The Workstation Manager is primarily a distribution point for VWI operations. It determines which workstations should receive an operation and, when necessary, waits for a result from a workstation to deliver it back to the Device-Independent component. Finally, the Workstation Driver together with the Device Driver are responsible for providing the functionality of a GKS workstation for a particular graphics device or metafile. The following sections address, in more detail, some components of the implementation which are more interesting with respect to Ada.

PACKAGING GKS

Ada's packaging mechanism is probably the single most important language feature employed in the implementation of GKS. Not only does it provide a natural mechanism for breaking the implementation into manageable parts, but easily provides for reusable code. As described above, the GKS/Ada project is an implementation of all 12 level of GKS where each level is composed of a combination of output and input cababilites. Across levels, certain operations change

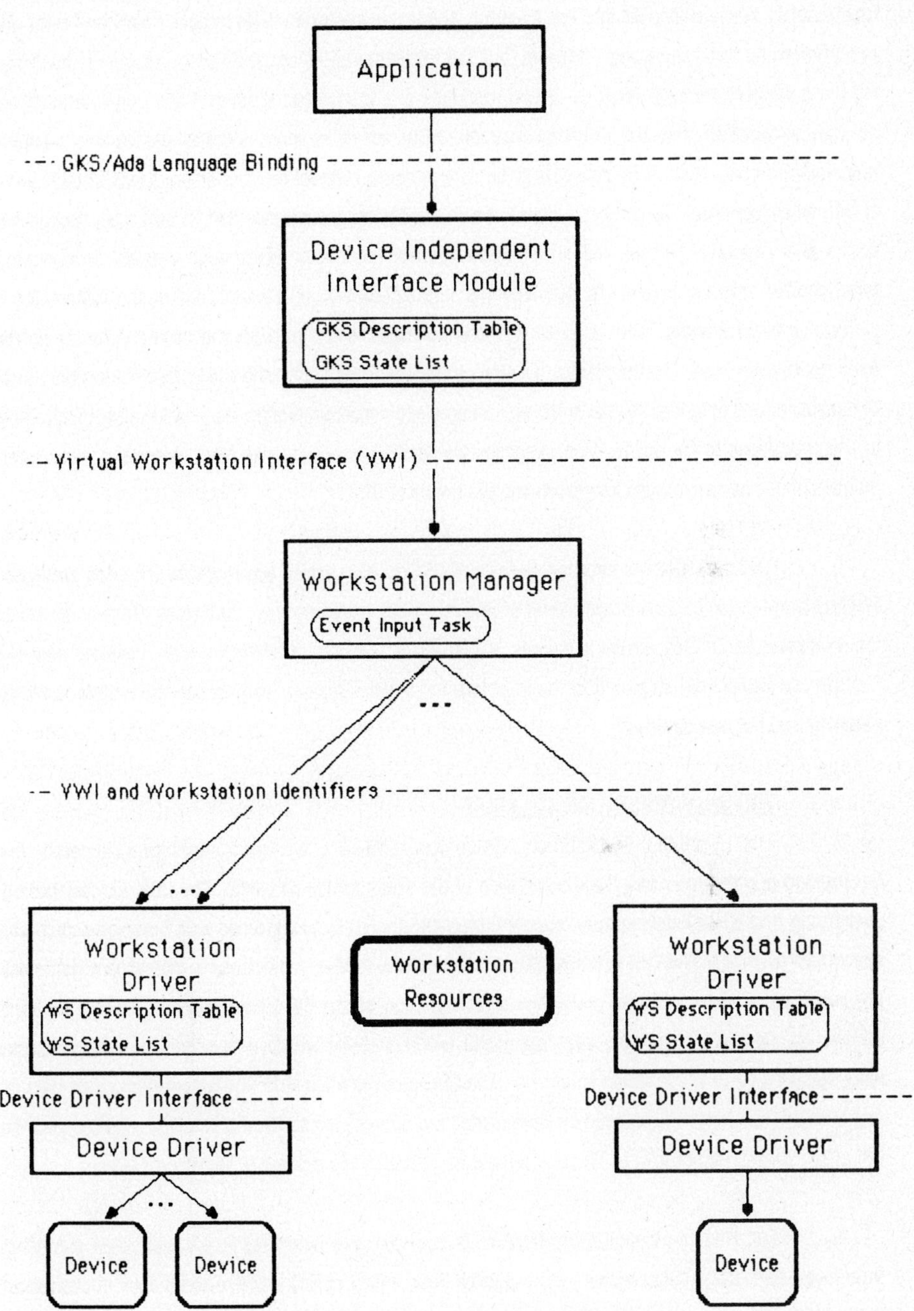

Figure 2. GKS/Ada System Architecture

functionality while others do not. For example, the implementation of an Inquire routine at level **ma** is sufficient for the remaining 11 levels, but the implementation of the Polyline routine at level **ma** is only sufficient through level **0**. When segments are introduced at level **1** the Polyline must be re-implemented so that the Polyline may be captured in segment storage and have a segment transformation applied. It is desirable to be able to reuse code across implementations of each level of GKS when possible. To achieve this our implementation groups together in packages, operations which are logically related and which have similar characteristics with respect to changing functionality between levels. In this way the implementation of a component of the system for a particular level merely "with"s together those packages which provide the required functionality for a particular level. In the case of the Device-Independent Application Interface component, each of the operations provided by the "with"ed packages are renamed in order to provide direct visibility of the operations to the application program. Using this technique, we have obtained a very large number of reusable packages for use among the levels of GKS.

The multiple workstation feature of GKS is also easily accomodated with Ada packages. The implementation of a particular level of GKS may support various workstations. To gain access to the Workstation Driver which supports a particular device, the Workstation Manager merely "with"s the package which provides the interface to the workstation. In this way the system is easily reconfigured for new devices.

VIRTUAL WORKSTATION INTERFACE

The Virtual Workstation Interface (VWI) is the interface between the Device-Independent Interface Module and each of the Workstation Drivers. The interface defines all operations that a workstation must support in order that it be considered a GKS workstation. The operations defined in the VWI are basically a subset of the operations defined in GKS except that some parameters have been changed and a few additional operations have been added. The VWI is very similar the Computer Graphics Interface (CGI) [ANSI 1984a] which is currently a draft proposed ANSI standard for a workstation interface. The CGI is not used in this implementation since the CGI provides a much larger functionality than needed for supporting a GKS workstation, and because the CGI effort is still very early in its standardization effort and is subject to significant change.

For this implementation the VWI is realized as a data interface rather than a control interface (individual subprogram calls and/or task entry calls). There exist four fundamental reasons for defining a data VWI. First, a data VWI greatly simplifies and allows for a more efficient implementation of several GKS features. For example, segment storage must store as data many of the VWI operations in order capture the appearance of a picture so that it may be redrawn. With a data VWI the implementation of segment storage need only make a copy of a VWI operation and retain it in a linked list for the currently open segment as the operation passes through the viewing pipeline. Second, the implementation of the GKS multiple workstation concept is greatly facilitated by a data VWI. Communication between the Workstation Manager and each workstation consists of only a single path for passing a VWI operation rather than a path for each operation supported by the workstation. Third, the implementation of Metafile Input workstations and the associated GKS Read_Item and Interpret_Item operations are greatly simplified by a data VWI. The data record returned from a Metafile Input workstation on a Read_Item operation merely returns an encoded VWI operation, and when the data record is interpreted using the Interpret_Item operation the encoded VWI operation is placed in the viewing pipeline as if the Device-Independent Interface module had created it. Finally, in a distributed environment the VWI must be encoded and sent across a communication line to a remote workstation. Since the VWI is already packaged as data, extending the implementation to accomodate distributed workstations is straightforward. In this implementation the system may be distributed at either the Workstation Manager or at one or more of the Workstation Drivers.

The Virtual Workstation Interface is defined as an Ada variant record. An enumeration type, VWI_OPCODES, is declared such that an enumeration literal exists for each VWI operation. The VWI is then declared as a variant record, VWI_INSTR, with a discriminant of type VWI_OPCODES. Each variant in the VWI_INSTR record corresponds to a VWI operation where the variant defines the required data necessary to implement the operation. The package VWI in Figure 3 below provides a flavor of the basic structure of the VWI.

```
package VWI is

   type VWI_OPCODES is (
      NO_OP,
      OPEN_WS,
      POLYLINE,
      SET_LINE_TYPE,
      ...);

   type VWI_INSTR(OP: VWI_OPCODES := NO_OP) is record
      EI: ERROR_INDICATOR := GKS_ERRORS.SUCCESSFUL;
      case OP is
         when NO_OP =>
            null;
         when OPEN_WS =>
            WS_TO_OPEN              : WS_ID;
```

```
                CONNECTION_OPEN        : ACCESS_CONNECTION_ID_TYPE;
                TYPE_OF_WS_OPEN        : WS_TYPE;
                ATTRIBUTES_AT_OPEN     : OUTPUT_ATTRIBUTES;
            when POLYLINE =>
                LINE_POINTS            : ACCESS_POINT_ARRAY_TYPE;
            when SET_LINE_TYPE =>
                LINE_TYPE_SET          : LINE_TYPE;
            when others =>
                null;
        end case;
    end record;

end VWI;
```

Figure 3. The Virtual Workstation Interface.

WORKSTATION MANAGER

The Workstation Manager is a relatively small, but very important component of the system. The primary responsibility of the Workstation Manager is to support the multi-workstation feature of GKS. The Workstation Manager acts as the distribution point for VWI operations. Upon receiving a VWI operation from the Device-Independent Interface module, the Workstation Manager examines it to determine which workstation(s) should receive the operation. There are four cases for handling the operation. The operation is sent to no workstations, a single workstation, all open workstations, or all active workstations. In the case that the operation is sent to no workstation, the Workstation Manager is responsible for achieving the effect of the operation. For example, the Event Queue operations discussed below are handled completely by the Workstation Manager. For those operations which are sent on to a single workstation, the VWI operation contains the Workstation type or Workstation identifier which indicates the specific workstation which must receive the operation. These are usually Inquire or Input operations. Finally, for those operations which are sent to either all open or all active workstations, the Workstation Manager uses the List of Open Workstations and the List of Active Workstations respectively to determine which workstations are to receive the operation. The Set attribute operations and Output Primitive operations are examples which are sent to all open and all active workstations respectively.

The communication to the Workstation Drivers from the Workstation Manager may be implemeted by either a procedure call to the Workstation Driver directly or by a call to a task entry which then calls the Workstation Driver. A procedure call is more desirable in implementations where only a single workstation is configured since no tasking overhead is incurred. However, in a multi-workstation environment it may be more desirable to use tasks as the communication mechanism to workstations so that execution of VWI operations which do not return information to the application program can proceed asynchronously from the rest of the system. This is especially desriable in I/O bound applications where processing can automatically switch among workstations while a workstation is waiting for access to an I/O channel. Our implementation of GKS/Ada allows both mechanisms to be used depending on the requirements of the application environment.

As discussed in the introduction, GKS defines three operating modes for each of the six classes of input devices supported by GKS. These modes are Request, Sample and Event. The implementation of Request and Sample input is rather straightforward since the operations are performed under control of an application program. However, event input occurs asynchronously with respect to the application program, and thus deserves some attention, especially with respect to how Ada's multi-tasking features provide for a very natural implementation of event input. Providing for the implementation of Event Input is the responsibility of the Workstation Manager.

GKS defines that a single Event Queue be maintained for recording input operations from all input devices in event mode on all open workstations. GKS also provides two operations to the application program for manipulating the Event Queue -- AWAIT_EVENT and FLUSH_DEVICE_EVENTS. When an application wishes to obtain an event input, it calls the AWAIT_EVENT procedure to retrieve the oldest event in the Event Queue and make it the current event input value. If the queue is empty, AWAIT_EVENT waits for an event to occur within a specified amount of time. If the timeout expires before an event occurs, the request for an event input returns indicating no input is available. FLUSH_DEVICE_EVENTS is the second operation available to the application for manipulating the Event Queue. This procedure allows the application to remove all event inputs in the Event Queue which are associated with a particular workstation and input device.

The GKS Event Queue can be implemented with the Ada task EVENT_QUEUE_MANAGER having three entries -- AWAIT_EVENT, FLUSH_DEVICE_EVENTS and RECORD_EVENT -- in a selective accept statement. Figure 4 below illustrates a skeletal example of how this task might be implemented with a fixed size queue. The AWAIT_EVENT entry is guarded so that a rendezvous can not occur when the queue is empty. Thus, the GKS procedure AWAIT_EVENT can perform a timed entry call to this entry to implement its timeout semantics since the call will not be accepted unless at least one event is in the queue. The GKS procedure FLUSH_DEVICE_EVENTS is directly implemented with the FLUSH_DEVICE_EVENTS entry. And all input devices in Event mode perform entry calls to the RECORD_EVENT entry to place event inputs in the queue.

```
task EVENT_QUEUE_MANAGER is
   entry AWAIT_EVENT ( );
   entry FLUSH_DEVICE_EVENTS ( );
   entry RECORD_EVENT ( );
end EVENT_QUEUE_MANAGER;

task body EVENT_QUEUE_MANAGER is
   MAX_EVENT_QUEUE_SIZE: constant := 500;
   type EVENT_QUEUE_RANGE is range 0..MAX_EVENT_QUEUE_SIZE;
   EVENT_QUEUE: array (EVENT_QUEUE_RANGE) of EVENT_RECORD;
   NEXT_IN,
   NEXT_OUT: EVENT_QUEUE_RANGE := EVENT_QUEUE_RANGE'FIRST;
begin
   loop
      select
         when NEXT_IN /= NEXT_OUT =>
         accept AWAIT_EVENT ( ) do
            -- Remove the event at position NEXT_OUT in the queue then increment
            -- NEXT_OUT modulo the queue size.
         end AWAIT_EVENT;
      or
         accept FLUSH_DEVICE_EVENTS ( ) do
            -- Remove all events in the Event queue associated with the specified
            -- workstation and logical input device. After removing the events,
            -- compact the Event queue so that no holes exist.
         end FLUSH_DEVICE_EVENTS;
      or
         accept RECORD_EVENT ( ) do
            -- Increment the NEXT_IN modulo the queue size. If NEXT_IN wraps
            -- around NEXT_OUT, log error 148 indicating the Event queue
            -- has overflowed.
         end RECORD_EVENT;
      end select;
   end loop;
end EVENT_QUEUE_MANAGER;
```

Figure 4. Skeletal example of the EVENT_QUEUE_MANAGER.

WORKSTATION RESOURCES

The Workstation Resources is a collection of global data and operations available to all workstations. The purpose of the workstation resources is to provide for the implementation of various operations which are common to most workstations, thereby reducing the effort required to implement workstations. The Workstation Resources help achieve our goal of reusable code among workstations. The contents of the Workstation Resources may be catatgorized as follows.

- Table Manipulation Operations
- Transformation and Clipping Operations
- Segment Storage and Segment Operations
- Database for Stroke Text Precision

The table manipulation operations implement most of the Set and Inquire operations for Workstation Description Tables and Workstation State Lists to the extent of changing or obtaining values in the data structures and performing error checking. If a workstation requires functionality beyond what is provided for by the resources, the particular workstation must implement it itself. For example, if a colour representation is changed the resource will update the colour table stored in the Workstation State List, but if the device has a hardware colour lookup table then the workstation is responsible for calling the device driver to update the device. The transformation resource provides the operations necessary to transform a point or an array of points represented in Normalized Device Coordinates to Device Coordinates by either a workstation transformation or a combined segment and workstation transformation when a segment is open or being redrawn. The clipping resource operations provide the clipping operations necessary to clip each of the output primitive types given the current clipping rectangle when clipping is not available on the device.

The segment storage and segment operation resource provide all of the operations necessary to implement segments for those devices which to not have a hardware segment capability. As mentioned above, the Workstation Manager is responsible for adding output primitives, clipping rectangles, attribute settings, etc. to the segment storage resource. At the workstation level this resource is made available to those workstations with stored segments via the segment operations. The segment operations resource allows a workstation to playback a segment for redraw purposes, to manipulate the priority ordering of the segments stored for workstation, and to change a stored segment's attributes. Again the resource may not support the full functionality of a particular operation. For example, if setting a segment visibility attribute leads to an implicit regeneration of the display surface, then the workstation must determine this itself and cause the regeneration, possibly making use of other resources.

Finally, the last major component of the Workstation Resource is the database for Stroke text precision. This resource is basically a software character generator for those devices without raster fonts or similar capability such that text strings can be transformed and clipped exactly at the clipping rectangle.

The Workstation Resource is one of the most important components of the GKS/Ada implementation. The resources remove from the workstations, the responsibility of implementing numerous operations which are common to all workstations. The resources greatly reduce the complexity of implementing a workstation and allow new workstations to be quickly added to the system.

WORKSTATON DRIVER and DEVICE DRIVER

A Workstation Driver together with a Device Driver provide for the implementation of a particular graphical device, metafile or the Workstation Independent Segment Storage (WISS) workstation. The responsibility of a Workstation Driver is to support the each of the operations defined in the Virtual Workstation Interface which is applicable to a particular workstation type, while the Device Driver supports exactly the operations which are available on the device. The Workstation Driver / Device Driver combination are implemented such that they may support multiple devices of the same type. That is, a system with two or more identical devices configured can be implemented with the same Workstation Driver / Device Driver.

A Workstation Driver is basically an instruction decoder. It receives VWI operations from the Workstation Manager as a data package and then 'cases' on its VWI operation. The Workstation Driver has a large case statement with a case alternative for each operation it supports. The case alternative then decides for this workstation whether or not the operation can take advantage of one or more of the Workstation Resources to achieve the effect of the operation, if it must implement the operation itself, or if a combination of resources and its own code can be used. Thus, the Workstation Driver consists only of code which is peculiar to supporting its device, all other operatons are achieved making use of the shared Workstation Resources.

All Workstation Drivers have a Workstation Description Table which describes the static characteristics of the workstation, and a Workstation State List for each open workstation the driver is supporting which maintains information about the current state of the workstation. These two data structures are identical for all workstations. Thus, this implementation defines a generic package which declares these objects and necessary operations to manipulate them. The package has two formal procedure parameters -- one to initialize the Description Table and the other to initialize a State List. Thus, creating a new workstation would only require writing the two initialization procedures to support the complete functionality of Description Tables and State Lists.

SUMMARY

The adoption of the Graphical Kernel System as an international graphics standard will provide implementors of graphics applications a very valuable tool. Implementors will be able to converse in common terms and be removed from the details of the multitude of varying graphics devices available today. This implementation of GKS/Ada has proved that Ada is a very natural language for implementing systems outside of the embedded systems environment. Ada's package and generic features proved most useful in creating software which was reusable both within a particular implementation of GKS, and among implementations of GKS at different levels. The multi-tasking features of the language provided very natural solutions to the GKS Event Queue and multiple open workstations. This implementation of GKS/Ada accomodates distributed graphics environments, is easily configurable, and portable to any environment supporting a validated Ada compiler.

ACKNOWLEDGEMENT

This paper is the result of work performed under contract F49642-84-C-0176, sponsored by the World Wide Military Command and Control Systems (WWMCCS) Information System (WIS) Joint Program Office (JPMO). The Ada language binding to GKS has received careful guidance from the American National Standards Insitute X3H34, the Language Bindings and Conformance Subcommittee of the Graphics Technical Committee. The author would also like to acknowledge the hard work of all those involved in implementing GKS/Ada, especially Geri Cuthbert, whose dedication to GKS has made this project a reality.

REFERENCES

International Organization for Standardization. (1982). ISO/DIS 7942 Information Processing -- Graphical Kernel System (GKS) Functional Description: GKS version 7.2. ISO/TC97/SC5/WG2 N163.

American National Standards Institute. (Mar. 1984). dpANS Computer Graphics Interface (X3H3/84-45).

American National Standards Institute. (1984). dpANS Computer Graphics Metafile (X3H3/84-122).

American National Standards Institute. (Dec. 1984). ANS Graphical Kernel System (X3H3/83-25r3).

American National Standards Institute. (Feb. 1985). dpANS GKS Binding to ANSI Ada (X3H3/83-95r2).

Cuthbert, G. (Apr. 1985). ANSI Graphic Standard and Ada Binding. In Proceedings of the 23rd Annual Conference of the Southeast Region, ACM.

Enderle, G., Kansy, K., and Pfaff G. (1984). Computer Graphics Programming: GKS -- The Graphics Standard. New York, NY: Springer-Verlag.

Gilroy, K. (Mar. 1984). Experience with Ada for the Graphical Kernel System. In Proceedings of the Second Annual Conference on Ada Technology.

Hopgood, F.R.A., Duce, D., Gallop, J.R., and Sutcliffe, D.C. (1983). Introduction to the Graphical Kernel System (GKS). New York, NY: Academic Press.

Waggoner, C.N., Tucker, C. and Nelson, C. (July 1984). NOVA*GKS, A Distributed Implementation of the Graphical Kernel System. In ACM Computer Graphics 18, no.3, 275-282.

AN APPROACH FOR EVALUATING THE PERFORMANCE EFFICIENCY OF ADA® COMPILERS

Mitchell J. Bassman
Computer Sciences Corporation

Gerald A. Fisher, Jr.*
Computer Sciences Corporation

Anthony Gargaro
Computer Sciences Corporation

BACKGROUND AND RATIONALE

There have been several studies that have reported upon the performance of the early Ada language (US DoD 1983) compilers. These studies have been oriented to quantitative performance testing relying on approaches proven useful in evaluating previous contemporary language compilers. These approaches include writing (1) a set of small well-established numerical benchmarks (Harbaugh & Forakis 1984), (2) a sample of representative programs from the application domain (Rosenberg 1984), and (3) a synthetic benchmark (Weicker 1984) in Ada and other high order languages, viz., FORTRAN and Pascal, and comparing the resulting compilation and execution times. All three approaches yield incomplete data. The quantitative measures are not refined to a level of detail at which remedial action might be suggested to the compiler implementor or user so that improved results might be obtained. Even the synthetic benchmark approach, which provides a model of the application domain based on an analysis of the most frequently used language constructs, fails to provide information sufficient for understanding the differences in results, thereby allowing diverse interpretations.

The key requirements for evaluating the performance efficiency of the code generated by an Ada compiler are:

1. To provide quantitative data on overall performance efficiency for a particular application domain.
2. To provide quantitative data on performance efficiency that promotes an informed interpretation of the above data.

Ada® is a registered trademark of the U.S. Government, Ada Joint Program Office.

*Author's present address is the IBM Thomas J. Watson Research Center.

3. To provide a qualitative assessment of the code generated by the compiler with respect to its immediate and future use.
4. To counteract any specific effects or interactions, not explicitly required, that may invalidate an evaluation of code efficiency.

APPROACH

None of the approaches reported in the literature satisfies all of the stated requirements. Quantitative performance data can be derived by testing a representative sample of programs from the application domain. This is an established reliable method for quantitatively assessing overall time and space performance characteristics of the generated object code when the intended application domain is well understood. Confidence in the results obtained from this testing methodology depends on the adequacy of the program sample. However, this method does not provide any insight into, or explanation of, the resulting performance efficiency of the object code.

Quantitative performance testing of the important language features that combine to form programs can provide an analytic model of the object code performance for an application based upon a specific combination of language features. Derivation of an accurate model requires exhaustive evaluation of the compiler-generated code for all relevant language features. Since the individual abstract features have numerous variations, and since code quality depends upon interaction of the features, overall performance evaluation may be impractical. The results obtained from this method can, however, provide the needed insight into code generation inefficiencies observed during subsequent application program testing. Since the object code efficiency may be evaluated with respect to many different application domains, test cases should be developed for all language features if possible.

Qualitative assessment of the generated code must be performed by inspection and hence is subjective. Visual inspection may be required to resolve inconsistencies raised by quantitative measurements and to confirm initially that the tests have properly compensated for any Ada-specific effects.

Establishment of an approach for developing language test cases requires consideration for the goals of the compilation process. In a compiler, code is generated from an intermediate representation of a program. In this representation the program is decomposed into fundamental language functional components, for example, units for control structures, expressions, addressing, etc. For the most part, code is generated for each functional unit independently of the others. To improve quality, information about the locality and interaction of functional units is gathered and is used to guide the generation of code. This process is called optimization or code improvement (Aho & Ullman 1978).

With a consideration for the code generation process and recognizing the potential need to compare the efficiency of the code generated by the Ada compiler with that generated by a compiler for an alternative high order language (HOL), the following approach is used:

1. Test cases for fundamental language features are programmed in Ada, the HOL, and assembly language. The space and time measurements derived from executing these programs are compared in order to diagnose possible deficiencies in the Ada or HOL basic code generation schemes.
2. Test cases for code improvement are written in Ada and the HOL. The space and time measurements derived from executing these programs are used to determine whether or not classical code improvement techniques are implemented by the compiler.
3. Representative applications are programmed in Ada, the HOL, and assembly language. The space and time measurements derived from executing these programs are compared to obtain an overall performance evaluation of code generation efficiency.

This approach provides both overall performance efficiency data and also the necessary insight into code generation and code improvement techniques required to diagnose possible inefficiencies in the object code for fundamental Ada language features. The approach is quantitative; except for an initial concept validation, there should be no need to examine the generated code. The language features tests and application tests are coded in the target computer's assembly language to provide (1) a common base for comparison and (2) the ability to compensate for language-specific effects, e.g., constraint checking. The code improvement tests are not coded in assembly language since the pertinent result is whether or not a specific optimization is performed in generating the object code. A choice may then be made between two compilers that achieve similar object code efficiency, one having excellent basic code generation and one having a sophisticated optimizer. The Ada and HOL compilers are assumed to generate correct code. Since the alternative HOL compiler could be another Ada language compiler, this approach can also be used to compare the efficiency of code generated by multiple Ada compilers for the same target. A by-product of compiling and executing the test cases and application programs is an assessment of the usability of the compilers in terms of host resource requirements.

Although an evaluation of the efficiency of Ada run-time system features, e.g., tasking, input/output, exception handling, and memory management, is an important consideration in the determination of whether or not to use Ada for a particular application, those features are typically implemented by calls to target run-time library routines rather than by the inline generation of target machine instructions. The emphasis of this approach methodology is on evaluating the time and space efficiency of the generated object code; therefore, the run-time system is specifically excluded. The evaluation of the Ada run-time system is being addressed in on-going research (Ruane 1984).

TEST CONSTRUCTION

The initial tests developed using this approach were intended to support an evaluation of the performance efficiency of the code generated by an Ada compiler being developed for use in a mission-critical system. The selected application benchmark test for overall performance analysis was characterized by complex data structures, iterative control constructs, and fixed point numeric computation. The language feature tests and code improvement tests initially developed were restricted to those that would be supported by the evolving and partially implemented Ada compiler. All tests were designed in Ada and then recoded in the alternative HOL and assembly language. Pascal (Language Resources, Inc. 1982) was the alternative HOL; however, since the tests were designed in Ada, they are not biased toward Pascal. The baseline assembly language was that for the Motorola 68000 (Motorola 1984). The remainder of this paper will report on the approach methodology in this context, concentrating upon the language features and code improvement tests.

A taxonomy of the fundamental features of the Ada language and of classical optimization techniques was used as a basis from which to construct the initial tests. The language features taxonomy includes:

1. Control flow
2. Data reference

3. Expression evaluation
4. Subprogram calls
5. Type representation.

The code improvement techniques include:

1. Local (basic block) optimizations
2. Loop optimizations
3. Global optimizations
4. Target-dependent optimizations.

Each major category is further decomposed into functional categories. The control flow categories, for example, comprise conditional statements, case statements, loop statements, and transfers of control. Similarly, local optimization categories include value propagation, constant folding, expression simplification, and common subexpression elimination.

Corresponding to each functional category within the taxonomy is a single generic package containing the test procedures for all relevant features. The generic package for loop control tests includes tests for a loop statement without an iteration scheme, a loop with a while iteration scheme, and several variants of loops with a for iteration scheme. It is important to recognize that this approach does not measure the efficiency of the Ada implementation of generics. The use of generic packages facilitates the instantiation of the Ada tests for different data types. Tests written in assembly language and in the alternative HOL are explicitly coded for the different types.

Language Features

For each Ada language feature, a quantitative measure of its space and time cost is obtained for code generated by the Ada compiler and the HOL compiler. The cost is determined by compiling and executing the test, both with and without the feature present, and computing the difference. The efficiency of the Ada implementation of a language feature can be deduced by comparing its cost with the corresponding assembly language cost. The efficiency of the HOL implementation is deduced in a similar way.

Each test comprises a pair of procedures: a test version and a control version. The test version makes use of the feature under evaluation. The control version must have exactly the same execution time and space requirements except for the use of the specific language feature.

Example 1 demonstrates the straightforward use of this approach in evaluating the cost of using a loop statement with a <u>while</u> iteration scheme.

<u>Example 1</u>:

```
procedure While_Loop is
begin
  Let(Global, Ident(Zero));
  while Global = Zero loop    -- executed only once
    Let(Global, Ident(One));
  end loop;
end While_Loop;

procedure While_Loop_Control is
begin
  Let(Global, Ident(Zero));
--while Global = Zero loop    -- executed only once
    Let(Global, Ident(One));
--end loop;
end While_Loop_Control;
```

The object of the test is to evaluate the cost of using the loop construct itself. It is essential to isolate the fundamental feature in order to prevent unexpected interactions with other features and to ensure that unwanted optimizations do not effect the measurements. The number of iterations must be known a priori to the test constructor, but not to the Ada compiler. If the number of iterations were small and could be determined by the compiler, a loop unrolling optimization might be performed. If the loop body comprised only an assignment to an otherwise unused variable, the dead variable and the dead assignment might be eliminated resulting in a loop with a null body that might also be eliminated as dead code.

In the example, the conditional expression compares the value of the global variable Global with the value of Zero, a generic formal object of mode <u>in</u>. Function Ident has the effect of an identity function, and procedure Let has the effect of an assignment statement. Those effects cannot be deduced by the compiler. The compiler must, therefore, generate code for the loop construct. Since the value of Global is reset to One within the loop, the loop will be executed exactly once. Global, Let, and Ident are defined within a generic support package, which must be instantiated for the applicable generic actual parameters.

The loop statement with the <u>while</u> iteration scheme provides a simple example of the construction methodology used to develop the language feature tests. More complex tests must be developed to evaluate the cost of using other language features, e.g., a case statement. Examples of such tests have been shown previously (Bassman et al. 1985).

Code Improvements

The purpose of investigating the code improvement techniques is to determine whether or not the Ada compiler and the HOL compiler employ classical optimization techniques (Davis et al. 1978; MacLaren et al. 1982; Goos et al. 1983).

Construction of the code improvement tests is similar to that of the tests for language features. Each test consists of a pair of subprograms for Ada and the HOL. The test version provides the compiler with the opportunity for optimization. The control version is specifically written to prohibit optimization. The only functional difference between the two subprograms is whether or not the optimization technique is applicable. Some code improvement techniques are applied to save storage space, while others are used to reduce execution time requirements. Use of the optimization technique is indicated by a difference between the measured space and/or time values for the two versions.

Example 2 provides a compiler with an opportunity to perform a local value propagation optimization that may lead to the elimination of a load operation. New values are computed and stored in Global_1 and Global_2. In the test version those values are reused immediately in the subsequent assignment statements, offering a compiler the opportunity to retain the values in separate registers and thereby eliminating the need to reload them prior to expression evaluation. The opportunity is removed in the control version by inserting a call to procedure Break_Basic_Block.

Three additional support procedures have been introduced to support construction of the code improvement tests. The call to Init_Globals guarantees that the global variables have initial values. Update_Globals guarantees that the assignments to Global_4 and Global_5 are not dead in the control version. Break_Basic_Block is declared by renaming Update_Globals. Its alternative name is introduced to clarify the usage of the procedure call in the control version. The call to Break_Basic_Block immediately preceding Update_Globals in the test version is required so that execution time and storage space requirements for the two versions will be equivalent except for the possible application of the code improvement technique.

Example 2:

```
procedure Load_Elimination is
begin
  Init_Globals:
  Global_1 := Global_4 + Global_5;
  Global_2 := Global_4 - Global_5;
--Break_Basic_Block;
  Global_4 := Global_1 - Global_3;
  Global_5 := Global_2 - Global_3;
  Break_Basic_Block;          -- comment out in control version
  Update_Globals;
end Load_Elimination;

procedure Load_Elimination_Control is
begin
  Init_Globals;
  Global_1 := Global_4 + Global_5;
  Global_2 := Global_4 - Global_5;
  Break_Basic_Block;          -- comment out in test version
  Global_4 := Global_1 - Global_3;
  Global_5 := Global_2 + Global_3;
--Break_Basic_Block;
  Update_Globals:
end Load_Elimination_Control;
```

TEST COMPILATION AND EXECUTION

Compilation of the performance evaluation tests is a host-dependent activity. Similarly, test execution is target-dependent. Although this paper makes no formal recommendations for a standard approach to compiling and executing the tests, future work to refine this part of the methodology is anticipated.

All of the tests developed to date have been successfully compiled by at least one validated Ada compiler. At the time of this writing, not all of the tests had been processed by the partial Ada compiler that was the subject of the initial application study. To be completely successful, the approach requires a stable, validated compiler.

The following data are collected:

1. Space utilized by test version (ST_{Ada}, ST_{HOL}, ST_{ASM})
2. Space utilized by control version (SC_{Ada}, SC_{HOL}, SC_{ASM})
3. Time utilized by test version (TT_{Ada}, TT_{HOL}, TT_{ASM})
4. Time utilized by control version (TC_{Ada}, TC_{HOL}, TC_{ASM})

For each of the language features tests, the following results are analyzed:

1. Memory space usage (S_{Ada}, S_{HOL}, S_{ASM})
2. Execution time usage (T_{Ada}, T_{HOL}, T_{ASM})
3. Ada space efficiency (S_{Ada}/S_{ASM})

4. HOL space efficiency (S_{HOL}/S_{ASM})
5. Ada time efficiency (T_{Ada}/T_{ASM})
6. HOL time efficiency (T_{HOL}/T_{ASM})

The memory space usage for an Ada language feature, S_{Ada}, is computed as the space required for the object code of the test version minus that required for the control version:

$$S_{Ada} = ST_{Ada} - SC_{Ada}$$

Only the difference, which gives the space cost of using the language feature, is significant. The raw data include the overhead of the code used to inhibit unwanted optimizations. Other time and space usage results are derived similarly.

Since the purpose of the code improvement tests is to determine whether or not the optimization techniques are used, the following results are analyzed:

1. Space improvement measure (Ada) ($SC_{Ada} - ST_{Ada} > 0$)
2. Space improvement measure (HOL) ($SC_{HOL} - ST_{HOL} > 0$)
3. Time improvement measure (Ada) ($TC_{Ada} - TT_{Ada} > 0$)
4. Time improvement measure (HOL) ($TC_{HOL} - TT_{HOL} > 0$)

Data for the analysis of compiler usability are collected during test compilation and execution. Examples of quantitative host resource utilization measures are the following:

1. Compilation time
2. Disk space utilization
3. Main memory utilization.

A qualitative assessment is provided for the following factors:

1. Command usage
2. Diagnostics
3. Documentation
4. Listings.

SUMMARY OF RESULTS

The results from the initial use of this approach are incomplete and are presented only to establish concept validation to guide and refine future work. Although compilation and execution experience has been useful in reporting upon the performance efficiency characteristics of an Ada and a Pascal compiler, insufficient quantitative data are currently available to publish an accurate comparison. Furthermore, the available Ada compiler had not reached a level of maturity at which such a comparison would be constructive.

While the test/control pairs were designed to evaluate the quality of compiler-generated code, compilation efficiency measures were also collected in the expectation that useful results might be derived.

Experience with the language feature tests and code improvement tests have indicated that the results of their executions will provide useful information in understanding the execution results of the application benchmarks without resorting to an intensive study of the generated code for the application.

Concept Validation

The approach is valid only if the test/control pairs can be constructed in such a way as to nullify undesirable side effects from both language specific characteristics and the interactions of the enclosing language constructs. Examination of the code generated for the tests compiled using an Ada and a Pascal compiler has shown that the pertinent code was successfully isolated so that the performance efficiency of language features can be measured and code improvement techniques detected.

An objective in designing the tests was to prevent unwanted optimizations. Although the camouflaging techniques might have unnecessarily complicated the tests by introducing extraneous functionality, analysis of preliminary results has reduced that concern. It is premature, however, to claim that all unwanted optimizations were successfully prevented until the tests have been compiled using a larger sample of compilers.

Use of Generics

The use of Ada generics was an important decision of the construction methodology. The underlying assumption was that the performance efficiency measures would not be compromised by any side effect of using a generic instantiation rather than its nongeneric counterpart. Since there is limited experience in projecting the efficiency of generic instantiations, especially in the presence of shared bodies that may produce adverse effects on code efficiency (Bray 1984), a straightforward experiment was performed to investigate the assumption. The test/control pairs for the loop control language feature tests were modified to reference objects of an INTEGER subtype. The results of compiling and executing those tests were compared with those obtained from compiling and executing the equivalent test/control pairs created by generic instantiation. This comparison revealed that there was no difference in the data that would be used for performance efficiency measures.

At least one validated Ada compiler (Verdix Corporation 1985) supports an option to control the sharing of generic bodies when optimal code is required. It is expected that future compilers will provide a similar option (Digital Equipment Corporation 1984) so that there is minimal risk of invalidating performance measures by the use of generics in the construction methodology.

Language Features

Test execution data from versions of the language features tests written in Ada, Pascal, and MC68000 assembly language have been collected and analyzed. The results have confirmed the expected efficiency of assembly language for very small programming exercises and the value of using it as a baseline when evaluating an achievable objective for HOL compilers.

Code Improvement

Test compilation and execution data for Ada and Pascal code improvement tests have identified differences between the two compilers in detecting opportunities for optimizations. In some instances only partial optimization was performed when there was the potential for further code improvement after the initial optimization was detected, e.g., additional expression simplification and dead code elimination.

Inspection of the generated code has confirmed that all test/control pairs are sufficiently sensitive for the code improvement opportunities to be offered to the Ada and Pascal compilers.

Problems Encountered

Although no serious flaws in the approach have been encountered, distorted measurements were computed for some of the tests. These invalid measurements occurred because the test and control subprograms were enclosed in the same compilation unit and occupied a contiguous address space when loaded for execution. A consequence of this is that, depending upon the target ISA, references to the same global object from within the two subprograms may cause a displacement addressing scheme to force generation of different length instructions since the relative displacements are different from the test and control subprograms. This problem can be eliminated by ensuring that the test and control subprograms are loaded identically for execution.

CONCLUSIONS

This paper has suggested an approach for evaluating the performance efficiency of code generated by Ada compilers. The approach can be used either to compare the efficiency of Ada and other HOL compilers or the relative efficiency of multiple Ada language compilers for the same target. Experience with this approach has been limited to one particular application and the use of two Ada compilers and one Pascal compiler. Although the approach appears to be sound, it is premature to report conclusive results until more extensive experience has been acquired and the data assimilated from using additional compilers. It is anticipated that all existing language features and code improvement tests will be compiled and executed using at least two production quality Ada compilers in the near future.

Current results indicate that the approach achieves a modest and systematic advance over some commonly used, less formal benchmarking approaches. This conclusion is based upon the observation that the separate classes of tests have provided complementary information and assessments of the compilers that have been under evaluation. The language features and code improvement tests fulfilled the expectation that they would provide both quantitative measures of the generated code and insight into the results from the application program test.

There is a need for further results from diverse Ada and HOL compilers. The analysis of these results would assist in refining the tests and perhaps identifying potential flaws in the approach. One possible criticism of the approach is that the simplicity, or feature trivialization, of the tests may not yield sufficient insight into overall compiler performance efficiency since language feature interactions are artificially controlled by the tests. For Ada, in particular, the complexities of these interactions may have significant ramifications on code generation, requiring that this approach incorporate a less trivial testing methodology in order to increase the sensitivity of the tests to these interactions.

ACKNOWLEDGMENTS

The authors wish to acknowledge the contribution of Charles H. Sampson (CSC, San Diego, CA) in the development of the test approach.

REFERENCES

Aho, A. and Ullman, J. (1978). Principles of Compiler Design. Addison-Wesley, Reading, Massachusetts.

Bassman, M.J. et al. (1985). Evaluating the Performance Efficiency of Ada Compilers. In Proceedings of the Washington Ada Symposium, ed. J. Johnson. ACM.

Bray, G. (1984). Sharing Code among Generic Instances of Ada Generics. In Proceedings of the SIGPLAN '84 Symposium on Compiler Construction. SIGPLAN Notices, 19, 6, pp. 276-284.

Davis, M. et al. (1978). Optimization Panel Report, USAF Standard Compiler Workshop.

Digital Equipment Corporation (1984). VAX Ada Technical Summary (Preliminary).

Goos, G. et al. (1983). An Optimizing Ada Compiler. University of Karlsruhe.

Harbaugh, S. and Forakis, J. (1984). Timing Studies using a Synthetic Whetstone Benchmark, Ada Letters, 4, 2, pp. 23-34.

Language Resources, Inc. (1982). Pascal Programming Language Specification, #DP002.

MacLaren, M. et al. (1982). Engineering a Compiler, VAX-11 Code Generation and Optimization. Digital Press.

Motorola (1984) MC68000 16/32-Bit Micro-processor Programmer's Reference Manual. Prentice-Hall, Inc., Englewood Cliffs, New Jersey.

Rosenberg, M. (1984). Comparison of Ada Code Efficiency with Other Languages, AdaTEC National Meeting, February.

Ruane, M. (1984). An Empirical Approach to the Evaluation of Run-Time Environments, SIGAda National Meeting, July.

U.S. Department of Defense (1983). Reference Manual for the Ada Programming Language, ANSI/MIL-STD-1815A.

Verdix Corporation (1985). Private Communication, January.

Weicker, R. (1984). Dhrystone: A Synthetic Systems Programming Benchmark, Commun. ACM, 21, 6, pp. 1013-1030.

THE EFFICIENCY OF STORAGE MANAGEMENT SCHEMES FOR ADA PROGRAMS

Rajiv Gupta
Department of Computer Science, University of Pittsburgh, Pittsburgh, Pa. 15260

Mary Lou Soffa
Department of Computer Science, University of Pittsburgh, Pittsburgh, Pa. 15260

Abstract - The efficient implementation of high level languages which support concurrency is imperative, particularly in such application areas as embedded real-time systems. Various storage management schemes have been proposed for the implementation concurrency. In this work, a methodology is presented for evaluating the performance of these schemes including the standard heap, Berry-heap, cactus stack and quantized heap when used for Ada programs. The methodology involves the generation of workload traces from an executing program and the use of simulators of the alternative storage management schemes to produce measures of the performances of the schemes. The performance evaluation metrics used are space, time and the space-time product.

1. INTRODUCTION

The efficient implementation of high level languages such as Ada which support concurrency as an intrinsic control form is imperative, especially in embedded real-time systems. The correct execution of such systems in either meeting real-time constraints or executing in a constrained memory environment may depend to a large extent on the storage management scheme which is provided by the run-time support system.

Not only is efficiency for concurrent programs an issue but, as Ada is a general purpose programming language, it is also important that the user not have to pay for unused generality; that is, if a program does not have tasks, the user should not be penalized with excessive storage management overhead due to the availability of tasking facilities. Thus, an ideal storage management scheme is one which "contracts" to best fit the control forms actually used in a program. Traditionally, for all programs written in a particular language, the same storage management scheme is employed, regardless of the control constructs actually used.

In a concurrent control regime, there are numerous storage management schemes which can be used to effect the concurrent control semantics. The particular scheme chosen is usually selected by an implementor without much direction as to how well the scheme will perform compared to alternative schemes. Sometimes schemes are selected which restrict or burden the users. For example, the designers of Ada [4] proposed a cactus stack as an efficient storage structure for tasking. However, the use of a cactus stack requires either a user supplied PRAGMA which specifies for each task the maximum storage demand for its data as well as any subprogram that it calls (including recursive subprograms) or a system defined maximum bound, in which case overflow of the cactus stack is possible. At least one certified Ada implementation [9] does use the cactus stack.

In this work, we approach the problem of storage management selection by developing a methodology and defining metrics which permit the performances of storage management schemes to be experimentally evaluated and compared before they are actually used in an implementation. We apply this methodology to Ada programs in order to evaluate several viable retentive storage management schemes.

The methodology, discussed in Section 2, involves the generation of workload traces, resulting from executing Ada programs, which are then fed into simulations of alternative storage management schemes to produce performance measures. The schemes, described in Section 3, include the heap, cactus stack, Berry-heap [1], stack-heap [5], quantized heap [7] and a new scheme which analyzes the text of a program at compile time and determines certain control characteristics that permit the allocation of static storage [8]. In Section 4, the performances of these schemes for a set of Ada programs are compared using the performance metrics of space, time and the space-time product.

2. PERFORMANCE EVALUATION METHODOLOGY

Central to this work is the development of a methodology which is general enough to experimentally evaluate the performance of storage management schemes for any high level language. In this paper, we use the methodology in order to provide guidelines for the selection of a storage management scheme in the implementation of Ada.

An important component of this methodology is a technique for the specification of the workload placed upon the control implementation by an executing program. This specification is approached by viewing the execution of a program as consisting of two kind of operations: (1) the operations related to control events performed during the execution of the program and (2) those that are independent of the control actions. The operations related to control events are those whose execution speed depends upon the choice of control implementation and thus include all operations involving storage management, such as allocation and deallocation. Some of the events that fall in this category are:

--module creation (e.g., procedure call, task activation) and termination,

--task communication activities (e.g., an entry call), and

--creation and reclamation of temporaries.

All other operations whose execution speed is independent of the storage management scheme being used are grouped under the category of data-related events. We call the time spent on performing these operations **virtual time**. Operations that fall in this category include:

--arithmetic and logical operations,

--simple memory accesses, and

--input and output operations.

Using this view of an executing program, the **workload trace** is defined to be a (virtual) time-stamped sequence of control events performed during the execution of a program. The workload traces are used to drive simulations of alternative control implementation schemes in order to determine the relative costs of using those schemes. During the simulation of a scheme, the virtual times are added to the time to execute the control events (control time) in order to compute a comparison figure for the execution time of the program. The control time includes the time spent on performing operations such as incrementing stack pointers and searching for heap elements of appropriate size.

To measure the cost of executing a program managed by a particular storage management scheme, the performance metrics used are the total cpu **time** spent in the execution of the program, the maximum **space** demand of the program and the **space-time** product for the program. Employing only the metric of the maximum amount of space used by the program can be misleading, especially in a situation where the program requires the use of a large amount of memory for only a short period of time. In this situation, the space-time product is a better indicator of performance as it is computed by multiplying the space with the time interval over which that space is required by the program. The total execution time, the sum of the virtual time and control time, does not represent true machine execution time but is based on a time scale where various operations require a certain relative number of time units. Although the execution time computed by the simulators is not expressed as a measure of real time units, the metric is useful because the aim of this study is to compare the performances of the schemes and not to determine the absolute cost of using a specific scheme.

The language vehicle used in this study is an interpreter for Ada which takes as its input an intermediate code representation of an Ada program. As the execution of the Ada program is dependent on the scheduling scheme being used by the run-time support, the scheduler is implemented as part of the interpreter. In this study, two scheduling schemes are used: a non-preemptive first-come first-serve scheduler and a preemptive round-robin scheduler using a fixed time-slice. The interpreter in this study implements those features of Ada which relate to control as well as a subset of the data-related features. This subset includes tasking events, procedures, various forms of the select statement, delay statement, and packages.

Figure 1 summarizes the steps involved in the methodology to experimental evaluate control implementations. The source program written in Ada is first converted to an intermediate representation. The intermediate code is then executed by the instrumented interpreter which generates the workload trace as well as the results of the source program. The workload trace is then used as input to drive the simulations of alternative control implementations, which provides measures of the cost of executing the program under the simulated schemes. One of the attractive features of this methodology is that the implementation of the interpreter does

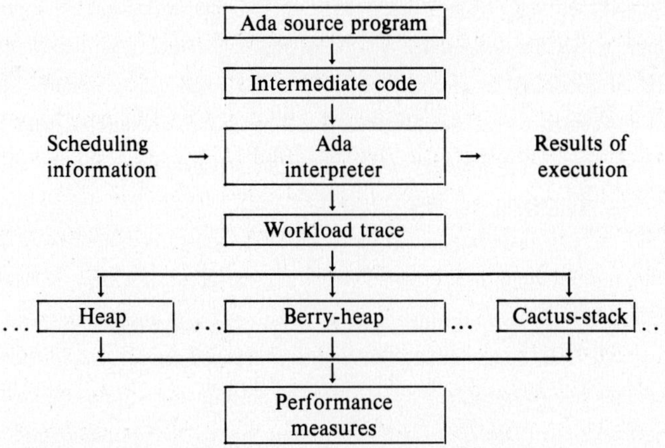

Figure 1. Overview of the system used in the study

not in any way depend on the storage management schemes to be studied.

3. STORAGE MANAGEMENT SCHEMES

In this study, several storage management schemes that are capable of handling the retentive control forms of Ada are considered. Simulations of the following storage management schemes are used in the study.

(a) *Heap:* The standard heap with a first-fit allocation strategy is used as the base storage management technique. In this scheme the storage needed for temporaries of a program module is preallocated in the activation record of the module. It should be noted that whenever any other storage management scheme requires a heap, it is implemented using a first-fit allocation scheme.

(b) *Cactus stack:* In the cactus stack, each activation of a task is allocated a heap element which is then managed as a stack to store the activation record of the task, its temporaries, and the activation records of any procedures in the task's call chain. In order for this scheme to work, the user must either specify the maximum number of recursive calls each procedure in the program can ever make or accept a system defined bound with the possibility of overflow. In this study, the cactus stack simulator is provided with the actual maximum number of recursive calls made by each procedure during execution. Thus the results obtained reflect the best possible performance of the cactus stack for the sample of programs used in the study.

(c) *Berry-heap [1]:* In order to eliminate preallocation of space and excessive copying, this scheme utilizes both a stack and a heap. The storage for a module instance is allocated from the heap. This does not include the storage needed for the temporaries. Storage for temporaries is allocated on the stack. In addition, a "copy-heap" is also used. If at the time of suspension, a task has live temporaries on the stack, then these are copied into the copy-heap. The idea behind this scheme is to save space by not preallocating the maximum space required for the temporaries. A combination of a stack and copy-heap is used to handle temporaries instead. If a non-preemptive scheduling scheme is used for scheduling Ada tasks, the only temporaries that would be live on suspension are those generated by an expression containing a still active function call (i.e., function call has not terminated before the suspension). When a non-preemptive scheduling scheme is used, temporaries involved in function-less expressions and parameter passing could be live at suspension, and thus will need to be copied.

(d) *Stack-heap [5]:* As the name suggests, this scheme also uses a combination of a stack and a heap. By analyzing the call graph of a program which is constructed by a static analysis of the program, we determine at compile time which program modules could possible suspend at execution time (e.g., entry call) and thus require the retentive heap structure. All the others module instances will basically behave in a stack-like fashion at run-time and will be allocated space in the stack. A desirable feature of this contractable scheme is that if a program does not use any tasking features, only a stack is employed.

The nodes of a **call graph** represent the different modules in the program and the directed edges depict the interrelationships among them. A directed edge is drawn from node X to node Y if an instance of module X can create an instance of module Y or if Y is textually dependent on X. In Ada this can occur as result of any one of the following actions:

--module Y is a procedure or block and is called explicitly or implicitly by module X.

--Y is a task or task type and is nested within X.

After the call graph is constructed, a **marking algorithm** marks the modules in the call graph that require retention. The steps involved in this algorithm are as follows:

(i) mark each module that makes an entry call or has any one of accept, delay or select statements,

(ii) mark each module which has a directed edge to another marked module, and continue to mark until no more modules can be marked.

If we follow the above algorithm, all modules that have the potential of being suspended will be marked. A module may suspend by either executing an action causing suspension directly, or indirectly by the suspension of another module. In the former case, the module will be marked in step (i) of the algorithm. In the latter case, there should be a path from the module under question to the module causing the suspension and therefore it will be marked in step (ii) of the algorithm. A similar marking algorithm to identify program components which are potentially retentive can also be found in [6].

(e) *Quantized heap [7]:* Storage is continually organized as a group of permanent heap elements of varying sizes. Whenever storage is needed, a frame is allocated from the quantized heap using a best-fit allocation scheme. This scheme relies on the speed up obtained in the space allocation and deallocation processes by maintaining the initial heap configuration.

In this study, the heap is initially configured so that it has the correct number of frames of only those sizes that are actually needed by the program. Thus the quantized heap scheme cannot perform any better than it did in this study.

(f) *Static allocation scheme:* In [8] a combination of static and dynamic storage schemes for Algol-like languages is presented. An attempt is made through this combination to reduce the overhead involved in the allocation of storage of procedure activation records at run-time. If a procedure is non-recursive then the storage for its activation record is allocated statically in the stack just as is done for the main program. This eliminates the overhead that would incur if the storage is allocated at run-time. A call graph for the program is constructed, and the longest non-recursive intervals in the graph are then determined using an algorithm described in [8]. A non-recursive interval is a sequence of calls which are relatively non-recursive. During execution of the program, the space for the entire interval is allocated at the beginning of the interval.

The above scheme was modified to be applicable for Ada programs. The original scheme was developed for block structured, recursive languages, and thus the space for the activation records of modules is allocated in a stack. In the modified scheme, a simple heap is used as the basic storage structure. Also, the static analysis of the Ada program is performed, but instead of constructing one call graph for the entire program as was done in the original scheme, a separate call graph for each task in the program and a call graph for the main program are constructed. The algorithm to determine the non-recursive intervals in a call graph, which is the same as that described in [8], is then applied to each of the call graphs independently.

In this scheme the overhead involved in allocating storage at run-time is reduced, as compared to the simple heap, because storage is allocated less often. However, it might happen that more storage is used in this scheme than the simple heap. This occurs when a number of non-recursive intervals share a common header node in the call graph. When allocating storage we allocate the amount of space which is the maximum of that required by each of the intervals sharing that header.

4. EFFICIENCY OF THE SCHEMES EXECUTING ADA PROGRAMS

The methodology was used to compare the performances of these schemes for a set of Ada programs. The programs were executed assuming the availability of a single processor. The results of the experiments are based on a sample of 28 Ada programs gleaned from the literature and include programs with combinations of tasks, non-recursive and recursive procedures. Programs without tasks were included in order to test how well the schemes contract when retention is not needed. Programs with tasks include the producer consumer problem, the readers-writers problem, and resource sharing and allocation. The programs without tasks include various sorting algorithms, tree traversal algorithms, Simpson's algorithm to carry out integration,

Newton's method to find the root of a equation, the eight queens problem and the towers of Hanoi problem.

All the programs were executed using the non-preemptive first-come-first-serve scheduler. However, only programs with tasks were executed using the preemptive round-robin scheduler, for a preemptive scheduler cannot cause any rescheduling in a program without tasks and hence the program will execute exactly the same way as it did when a non-preemptive first-come-first-serve scheduler was used. Thus, there would be no change in the behavior and the performance of the storage management scheme for the program.

The results presented in this section give the performance of each scheme relative to the performance of the simple heap. The results of the experiments using the non-preemptive first-come-first-serve scheduler are as follows:

-- The cactus stack did not provide any significant improvement over the heap. Savings of up to 2% in both space and time were achieved for programs with tasks. For programs without tasks, savings of 5% in time were achieved by the cactus stack over the heap but the space-time product was 5% more than the heap. Savings in time can be expected when a cactus stack is used because heap storage has to be allocated less often, and this reduces the overhead involved in searching for heap elements during allocation. One can expect the space-time product to increase, as observed in this study, because the storage needed for procedures called directly or indirectly by a task remains allocated for a longer period of time. However, the space required by the program using a cactus stack can sometimes be more than that required for a heap and sometimes less for the program under question. The space for the procedures called by a task is preallocated at the time the space for the task is allocated. This space may not be actually used, in which case the cactus stack will require more space than a simple heap. However, since heap allocation is done less often in a cactus stack, fragmentation of the heap is reduced.

-- The Berry-heap used 9% less space than the heap for programs without tasks and 4% less space for programs with tasks. It achieved a 9-14% savings in space-time over the heap. In this scheme instead of preallocating the maximum amount of space needed for temporaries, a combination of a run-time stack and a copy-heap is used. This resulted in a savings in space and space-time. When the test programs were executed, the copy-heap was rarely used, and thus in effect only a stack, the most efficient storage structure to handle temporaries, was used. The copy-heap was seldom needed because the tasks were suspended at statement level, and there were usually no live temporaries due to function calls. This resulted in a savings in space. Moreover, when the space for temporaries is preallocated in a heap, it remains allocated for a longer period of time, as compared to when a stack is used, and this explains the savings obtained in space-time.

-- When the programs without tasks were run using a stack-heap, a significant improvement in performance over a heap was observed, including a savings of 10% in space, 7% in time and 17% in space-time. However, the scheme's performance for programs with tasks did not improve over the heap. This is because the space for all program modules that can be suspended directly or indirectly is allocated in a heap, and most modules in the programs were involved in suspension. The stack-heap contracts to a stack for programs without tasks which explains the improvement in the performance of the scheme, which is observed in this study.

-- The quantized heap did not provide any significant improvement over the heap. The allocation in this scheme is faster so some time is saved but the savings were found to be less than 2%.

-- For the static space allocation scheme, savings of up to 5% in time and 3% in space-time were achieved over the heap. The savings in time are obtained because space is allocated less often in this scheme. Savings in time also caused the space-time product for the programs to decrease.

From the results presented above it is clear that the Berry-heap is the only scheme considered which provides significant improvement over a standard heap for programs written in Ada. The stack-heap did provide a significant improvement over simple heap for programs without tasks, but it did not provide any improvement for programs with tasks. Thus on the whole, the Berry-heap performed the best. Basically, the same results were also found in studies on storage management schemes for coroutines [3].

The above results were obtained by executing the programs using a non-preemptive first-come-first-serve scheduler. Under these circumstances the copy-heap in the Berry-heap is seldom used because at time of suspension, the tasks usually do not have any live temporaries. However, if a preemptive scheduling scheme is used, then this will no longer be true. Therefore another experiment to measure the extent of deterioration in the performance of the Berry-heap was conducted. A preemptive round-robin scheduler was implemented, and a set of programs with tasks were run using both of the schedulers. The cost of executing these programs using the Berry-heap under the scheduling schemes was then determined. As expected the cost of executing the programs using the preemptive round-robin scheduler was found to be more than the cost of executing the programs using a non-preemptive first-come-first-serve scheduler. It was found that the savings in space relative to the heap decreased from 4% using the non-preemptive scheduler to 2% when the preemptive scheduler was used. The time used increased by 2% and savings in space-time product fell from 8.5% to 5%. The increase in the performance measures can be attributed to the copying of temporaries from the stack to the copy-heap. From the results obtained one can say that the deterioration in the performance of the Berry-heap is not significant, and it is the best of the schemes evaluated in this study.

5. SUMMARY

The methodology applied in carrying out this study is general and can be applied to study the performance of any storage management scheme for a high level programming language. The implementation of the interpreter developed does not in any way depend on the storage management schemes being studied. Thus, once the workload traces for the sample programs have been generated, the performances of new storage management schemes can be easily studied.

From the data obtained as a result of the experiments conducted, one can conclude that the overall performance of the Berry-heap is significantly superior to all of the other schemes investigated in this study. However, it was observed that each storage management scheme performed better under certain conditions. In particular the results indicate that the stack-heap performs very well for programs without tasks. The cactus stack performs better for programs with tasks having non-recursive procedures. Based on the results obtained we can see that an attempt to design compilers which base their decisions on the program to be executed rather than on the most general features available in the language should be made.

Acknowledgement: We wish to acknowledge the support of this work by the National Science Foundation under Grant DCR-8119341.

REFERENCES

[1] D. Berry, L. Chirica, J. Johnston, D. Martin, and A. Sorkin, "Time required for reference count management in retention block-structured languages, part 1," *Int. J. Comput. Inform. Sci.*, 7(1), pp.91-119 (1978).

[2] P. Brinch-Hansen, *The Architecture of Concurrent Programs*, Englewood Cliffs, NJ: Prentice-Hall, 1977.

[3] L. Coon, John P. Kearns and Mary Lou Soffa, "The Contraction of Control Implementations," *Computer Languages*, 8(1), pp.15-25 (1983).

[4] J.D. Ichbiah, J.G.P. Barnes, J.C. Heliard, B. Krieg Brueckner, O. Roubine, and B.A. Wichmann, "Rationale for the design of the Ada Programming Language," *ACM Sigplan Notices*, 14(6) (1979).

[5] John P. Kearns and Mary Lou Soffa, "Implementation of Retention in a Coroutine Environment," *ACTA Informatica*, 19, pp. 221-233 (1983).

[6] J.P. Kearns and D. Quammen, "An Efficient Evaluation Stack for Ada Tasking Programs," *Proc. IEEE Computer Society Conference on Ada Applications and Environments*, pp.33-40 (1984).

[7] Butler W. Lampson, "Fast Procedure Calls," *Proc. Symp. on Architectural Support of Programming Languages and Operating Systems*, pp.66-76 (1982).

[8] Thomas P. Murtagh, "A Less Dynamic Memory Allocation Scheme for Algol-like Languages," *Eleventh ACM Symposium on Principles of Programming Languages*, pp.283-289 (1983).

[9] *Reference manual for the Ada Programming Language*, Western Digital Corp. (1983).

An Overview and Example of Application of CAEDE: A New, Experimental Design Environment for Ada

R. J. A. Buhr, G. M. Karam, C. M. Woodside

Department of Systems and Computer Engineering,
Carleton University, Ottawa, Ontario, CANADA

ABSTRACT

CAEDE is an experimental, integrated, iconic design environment which supports (1) a structured design methodology based on Buhr's *System Design With Ada* book (2) an iconic design entry system, (3) a design data base, and (4) design tools. The design data base is automatically represented in Prolog and the majority of the design tools are written in Prolog. Tools are currently available for structural and temporal analysis, and for source code generation. This paper describes both the ideas behind CAEDE and an example of a CAEDE tool written in Prolog for representing and analyzing the temporal behaviour of Ada tasking designs, without having to program them in Ada first.

1. INTRODUCTION

CAEDE (CArleton Embedded system Design Environment) is an experimental, integrated, iconic design environment for embedded systems being developed at Carleton University as part of a project on automated aids for protocol system design and implementation. CAEDE is an integrated environment which supports (a) a design methodology (Buhr, 1984; Buhr & Mitchell, 1982; Buhr, 1985), (b) an iconic design entry system (Buhr & Karam, 1984; Hayes, 1984), (c) a design data base, and (d) design tools. The design data base is automatically represented in Prolog and the majority of the design tools are written in Prolog (Buhr et. al., 1985). CAEDE tools are currently available for structure analysis, performance analysis, temporal representation and analysis, and partial Ada source code generation (Ada is a registered trademark of the U.S. Government (Ada Joint Program Office)).

The current experimental version of CAEDE focuses on the structural and temporal aspects of design. Its capabilities in these areas are intended to provide a core to which other capabilities in support of the design methodology, such as preliminary data flow design and detailed functional specification, can be added later.

CAEDE is not itself implemented in Ada. This was a deliberate decision based only partly on the unavailability of a full Ada compiler for our machines at the time the project was started. More importantly, we wanted to use software technologies which would enable rapid prototyping of powerful, experimental versions of CAEDE to a greater extent than would have been possible in Ada. The view that Ada is not the best language for environments for Ada, essentially because the language represents "old technology", has been advanced by Wegner (1984). We decided to develop our experimental environment on a SUN workstation under Berkeley 4.2 Unix using Suncore graphics and C-Prolog. New Prolog work is proceeding using Logicware's M-Prolog on a VAX-11/750 connected to the SUN workstation via Ethernet; this work will move to the SUNs when we acquire an appropriate version of M-Prolog. Prolog provides the new software technology component of our environment.

This paper describes CAEDE from the following points of view: (1) underlying principles, (2) major features, (3) intended role, (4) methodology, (5) current functionality and (6) a design example that demonstrates a Prolog tool for representing and analyzing the temporal behaviour of multitasking designs.

2. UNDERLYING PRINCIPLES

CAEDE is founded on the following principles:

(1) METHODOLOGY: Timely development of reliable, modular, concurrent systems in languages such as Ada requires a design methodology and supporting environment which allows the designer to reason about the system at a high level and to focus the design efforts on critical problems, without becoming bogged down in details. Our view is that the design of embedded systems remains a creative process and that the task of the methodology and environment is to assist this process.

(2) GRAPHICS: A picture is worth a thousand words. Graphical paradigms provide a framework for reasoning about a system under design and for focusing the designer's ability to produce designs that are representable, analyzable and explainable to others in a straightforward fashion. This has always been true for hardware; languages like Ada make it possible for software. Glinert & Tanimoto (1984) provide powerful arguments for a visual approach to program development. The essential point is that human beings can perceive patterns and relationships much better from pictures than from linear text.

(3) CLOSENESS TO PROGRAMMING: The design level should be close enough to the Ada program level that the mapping between designs and programs is straightforward in either direction. This is difficult to achieve with current, widely used languages such as C, which do not support essential design level constructs for modularization and concurrency. However, it is entirely practical for Ada. Not only does this simplify the automated translation of designs into partial programs, it also provides the desirable result that both human beings and automated design extraction tools can read the programs and compare them with the designs.

(4) POSTPONEMENT OF COMMITMENT: The design environment should support postponement of commitment to implementation in hardware or software. Therefore, its major tools should be useable without full software implementation of a design. Furthermore, its paradigms should be accessible to both hardware and software designers. Graphical paradigms are important for this purpose, because they allow hardware designers to use the system without being forced to program in Ada directly.

(5) DESIGN SUPPORT: The design environment should support the three important aspects of design - system structure, temporal behaviour and functional behaviour - with appropriate design tools. It should support incremental design involving all of these aspects. In other words, it should be possible to use design manipulation and analysis tools on a partially completed design.

(6) INCREMENTAL EXTENSIBILITY: The design environment should enable design tools to be easily built in stages, making use of everything that has gone before. It should also enable new tools to be easily added to manipulate and analyze the design data base from different viewpoints for different purposes. This type of extensibility has been one of the important reasons behind the popular success of the UNIX operating system.

(7) BRIDGE BETWEEN REQUIREMENTS AND IMPLEMENTATION: The design environment should provide a bridge between requirements definition on the one hand and implementation on the other, via a design data base which supports the association of data in these two areas with components of the system under design.

3. MAJOR FEATURES OF CAEDE

CAEDE's features are intended to satisfy the principles presented in the previous section in the following manner (the current experimental version of CAEDE does not yet satisfy all of them).

Feature 1: Graphical Design Methodology - this feature satisfies the first four principles and partially, the fifth.

CAEDE supports a graphical design methodology which is an extension of that in Buhr's *System Design With Ada* book (Buhr, 1984). This methodology, used manually, has proved itself useful in practice in both the classroom and in industry (Buhr & Mitchell, 1982). The designer interacts with the system in terms of the graphical paradigms of the methodology.

This feature partially satisfies the fifth principle, by providing support for the structural aspect of design and some support for the temporal and functional aspects, insofar as they are related to structure (e.g., through the temporal properties of the rendezvous mechanism and through the identification of standard types of components in the structure, such as transport tasks, which behave in certain well defined temporal and functional ways).

Feature 2: Graphical Interface - the graphical interface contributes particularly to satisfaction of the fourth, fifth and seventh principles.

As an input medium, the graphics interface supports entry of design structures and associated information, such as performance data and text comments. Text comments may be used for a variety of purposes: (1) the association of requirements with components of the system under design, (2) the entry of Ada program fragments to be included in Ada code produced by the code generator tool and (3) the inclusion of protocol specification language statements (ISO, 1984) or Anna language statements (Luckham & Von Henke, 1984) to describe the intended functionality of components of the system under design. This feature addresses the fifth and seventh principles.

Another potential use of CAEDE's graphics interface as as in input medium would be to create directly some of the information needed for a silicon compiler (Girczyc, 1983). This feature addresses the fourth principle.

As an output medium, CAEDE's graphical interface supports retrieval of the input information. It also allows software implementations to be viewed in terms of the graphical paradigms implicit in them. This feature particularly supports the seventh principle.

Feature 3: Use of Prolog - Prolog completes the satisfication of the fifth and seventh principles and uniquely satisfies the sixth.

CAEDE uses Prolog to act as the design data base and to provide tools to support the design methodology. Both of these functions can be encompassed within a single framework - the Prolog language - because of the uniform way in which Prolog represents both data and operations on data. In the Prolog back end, there is no hard and fast distinction between facts derived from graphics input (e.g., one task calls another's guarded entry), rules about the behaviour of components of the design derived from the properties of Ada (e.g., rendezvous semantics), rules about the behaviour of standard types of design components (e.g., transport tasks) and rules to manipulate and analyze the design. Therefore, new rules may be easily added for different purposes. This feature supports the sixth principle.

Prolog contributes to satisfying the fifth principle in the following ways:

1. The design data base may be searched for unsatisfactory structural features (e.g., a dangling task entry, or a deadlock prone interaction structure).
2. Specifying and reasoning about temporal behaviour is possible, in terms of rules. Rules may be used both to define temporal behaviour of components and to serve as criteria for identifying the possibility of unsatisfactory temporal behaviour of systems (such as deadlock).
3. Textual information relating to function which has been associated with the components of the design through the graphics interface may be processed by Prolog programs.
4. The Prolog representations allow choice of two alternatives for design evaluation: analysis and behavioural prototyping.

The seventh principle is addressed by Prolog's ability to perform translations, given only the translation rules (Buhr et. al., 1985; Warren, 1977). Thus, it can be used to translate design information into partial source programs or complete source programs into extracted design information.

4. INTENDED ROLE OF CAEDE

There is a shortage of experts in designing embedded systems from the software driven, high level language viewpoint required by Ada. To help in addressing this shortage, the CAEDE system aims at fulfilling the following roles:

1. EXPERT'S ASSISTANT: Assist the expert designer, thereby offering the possibility of increasing the productivity of existing experts; provide support for rapid prototyping;

2. TUTOR: Assist in teaching and learning about design, thereby offering the possibility of enlarging the pool of expertise;
3. DESIGN EXPERT: Provide a basis for the incorporation of design expertise in the design environment, thereby offering the possibility of decreasing the need for expertise.

5. CAEDE METHODOLOGY

In CAEDE, designs are entered using menus of primitive icons which may be put together in various ways to form designer-defined icons representing structured system components. Higher level designer-defined icons may be formed from lower level icons (both primitive and designer-defined) in a hierarchical manner to form a complete system design. At each stage, logical properties are associated with the icons automatically. The logical properties serve as the basis for design analysis, code generation and other tools. Thus, the iconic representation is integral to the representation of the design and not just decorative.

In the current, Ada-inspired implementation, there are the following primitive icons: (1) black box icons for packages, tasks, procedures and stored data, (2) socket icons for interface procedures of packages and entries of tasks, (3) plug icons to serve as interface points for outward going actions from designer-defined icons, (4) several different types of action arrow icons to indicate such actions as accesses to stored data, procedure calls, entry calls of various kinds (unconditional, conditional and timed) and dynamic task creation via invocation of "new", (5) channel icons to group sets of action arrow icons between pairs of black boxes, (6) data flow arrow icons and (7) miscellaneous icons to indicate such interface mechanisms as selectively accepted sets of task entries and guarded task entries.

Our philosophy is that the icons in the schematic diagrams should be restricted to those needed to visualize activities and actions of the system under design at run time. As such, they should be as few in number as possible. Therefore, we do not have special icons for task instances created from types or instances of generic objects. Furthermore, we provide no graphical means of indicating the location of type or generic declarations. diagrams more complex without substantial benefit. However, we have allowed that such information can be entered textually in association with icons. In addition, our notation does indicate the context in which tasks execute and terminate.

The iconic design process in CAEDE has its primary focus on structure and on temporal behaviour in association with structure. These are the two aspects of system design in which the visualization of patterns and relationships is most important.

The design process functions in terms of levels and phases of design. Each level of design is characterized by a schematic diagram which is developed in phases. Each schematic diagram has associated with it both physical and logical information. The former enables the picture to be drawn; the latter represents what is depicted in the picture in terms of the semantics of the icons. The rule for design levels is that all compound icons in a schematic diagram have their internal structure defined in a separate schematic diagram. For compound icons this separate diagram represents a nested level of design. Thus, the design is represented as a tree of levels.

Each level of design may be pursued in an incremental fashion in parallel with other levels of design. Moving between levels of design is accomplished by invoking the edit command to edit "up" or "down" Otherwise, icons are manipulated at a particular level by using a mouse in conjunction with icon menus and commands to add, connect, delete, drag, and reshape icons. The logical information underlying the diagram and the topology of the diagram itself are maintained automatically during all of these operations. The designer may also zoom in on a part of the diagram. Text comments may be associated with the icons in such a manner that they are normally hidden, but subject to recall.

The process of incremental design with CAEDE is intended to proceed, for each nested level of design, in the following phases. Each phase may have its own specialized design entry and analysis tools. We first present the phases without reference to how or to what extent they are implemented in the current system. Their implementation status is described later.

Phase 1 - Structure Definition

In this phase, the designer enters schematic diagrams showing black boxes, their interfaces and interconnections. Figures 1 and 2 show examples of Phase 1 CAEDE schematic diagrams which will be explored later in this paper. Further details of this phase are as follows:

1. Black box icons are selected from menus and manipulated on the schematic diagram using a mouse. Compound icons may be selected from a template library or copied from elsewhere in the design.
2. Interface views of compound icons are created by adding plugs, sockets, stub action arrows and associated data flow arrows, as appropriate, to selected icons from Phase 1.
3. The internal structures of these compound icons are defined by following the same phases at a nested level of design. When working on a schematic diagram for a nested level of design, the same interface view seen at the next higher level is displayed as an enclosing box around the diagram.
4. Plug/socket connections are made with action arrows, not only inside the level, but also between the internal components of the level and the plugs and sockets of its interface as seen from the inside.

Phase 2 - Temporal Interface Behaviour

Information entered during this phase specifies the intended external temporal behaviour of task interfaces and task interactions, for design analysis purposes, without having to specify in detail the internal temporal logic of the tasks (to follow in Phase 3).

Phase 3 - Specification of Internal Sequencing Rules

In Phase 3, complete internal temporal sequencing rules are specified, for the level via state machines or other means. These rules define completely the sequences of activation of the action arrows in the schematic diagram for all possible conditions affecting this sequencing. However, they fall short of complete algorithmic definition, because functional details not affecting temporal sequencing are not included. This information could be entered iconically or textually in this phase. In either case, it would be entered and displayed separately from the main schematic diagrams, to avoid graphical clutter.

The information from Phase 2 becomes redundant from a design definition point of view when Phase 3 is completed, although still useful for design checking and testing purposes.

Phase 4 - Program Strip Definition

Program strips are the sequential program fragments which fill in the gaps in the skeleton code produced from the previous phases. Program strips should be entered in text form under control of the iconic interface.

6. FUNCTIONALITY OF THE FIRST CAEDE IMPLEMENTATION

Phase 1 is the only phase implemented iconically in the current version of CAEDE. The current implementation of Phase 1 does not yet support all the structural possibilities of Ada. In future versions of CAEDE we anticipate adding the following Ada structures: the nesting of tasks in procedures, the nesting of accept statements in the critical sections of other accept statements and the propogation of exceptions between icons. Although we have argued elsewhere (Buhr, 1984) that nested rendezvous and exceptions are undesirable, we recognize that there will be cases where they are needed.

The output of Phase 1 in the current implementation is a file of Prolog facts describing the structure of the system under design. The form of the Prolog facts for "task3" of Figure 1 is illustrated in Figure 3. These facts are Prolog representations of lists of components, their properties and their relationships. Ada source code may be generated from these facts by a command to the iconic interface. This code currently includes: specification and body declarations for packages, tasks and procedures, types and modes of procedure and entry parameters and the placement of outgoing calls in the code bodies.

Phase 2 is planned for iconic implementation in the next version of CAEDE, but is currently implemented by non-iconic interaction with a Prolog program which prompts for sequencing information. From this information it generates Prolog rules defining the sequencing behaviour. A more detailed description of the tool is provided in following section.

Future implementations of Phase 2 will provide for characterizing the temporal behaviour of permanent tasks by a predefined role; e.g., transporter, agent and server. We also plan to support the specification of conditional behaviour by associating an interaction state machine with each task to describe its allowed interaction sequence with other tasks.

Phase 3 is not yet implemented. Work has started on a state machine approach.

The integration of Phase 4 with the iconic interface has not yet been accomplished in the experimental system. Currently, program strips may be added to the skeleton Ada code generated from Phase 1 using a standard Unix editor.

7. A PROLOG TOOL FOR TEMPORAL REPRESENTATION AND ANALYSIS (TRAS)

7.1. Introduction

The temporal representation and analysis tool provides the capability to study the temporal aspects of the iconic design. Currently, this tool is used to detect the potential of task deadness; that is, the failure of a task to proceed because of a breakdown in intertask communications (Helmbold & Luckham, 1984). For this analysis we employ an Ada model of multitasking and a detection technique based on temporal logic (Hailpern, 1982; Rescher & Urquhart, 1971). The philosophy of this tool is to *"detect deviations from correct temporal behavior without writing or executing program code"*.

The tool is actually structured as two separate components: (1) a temporal representation generator and (2) a temporal analysis tool. The temporal representation generator uses the facts in the Prolog design data base as a basis for generating the temporal description rules. It acquires the temporal sequencing information from a user through interactive conversation.

The basic organization of the analysis tool includes two components: (1) the temporal logic description of the Ada program components and (2) a theorem prover that determines the temporal correctness of the design by applying the description of the Ada program components against the temporal description of the design. The theorem prover is Prolog itself, with additional rules and facts to support the particular details of the temporal logic proof.

In the temporal description of Ada designs used in the current analysis, all tasks are considered to be endlessly cycling. Although this assumption is valid for many embedded systems, it is not true for all. At the present, the following Ada components have been modelled: tasks, unguarded task entries, packages, package external procedures, procedures, selective accepts, non-critical sections of selectively accepted task entries, procedure calls and task interactions. A short explanation of the underlying theory of the TRAS concept is discussed below.

7.2. Temporal Representation

The execution of a task consists of an endlessly cycling sequence of "interaction" states; that is, states in which the task is engaged in inter-object communications. For the sake of simplicity, let us only consider tasks objects and the following subset of interaction states: "task call", "accept" and "rendezvous". The termination of these states is not guaranteed by the Ada language. The termination of an interaction state implies the execution of non-interaction code until the next occurrence of an interaction state. Non-interaction code is considered to be "temporally safe"; i.e. reaching the next interaction state is guaranteed.

The successful execution of a task is dependent on the termination of interaction states. Thus, using our subset of interaction states, a program is operating "correctly" if the interaction states are described by the following statements: (1) if a task engages in a "task call" then it will "eventually rendezvous" with an acceptor, (2) if a task engages in an "accept" then it will "eventually rendezvous" with a task caller, (3) if a task executes a "rendezvous" then it will "eventually end" the rendezvous, (4) if a task "ends" a rendezvous then it will "eventually return" from the accept and (5) if a task "ends" a rendezvous then it will "eventually return" from the task call. Finally, the temporal statement of the Ada rendezvous mechanism is: "a rendezvous exists if eventually *both* a caller task has called an entry and an acceptor task has accepted the entry". These statements form a simple model of Ada intertask communications program components. Prolog rules specifying some of these statements are shown in Figure 4.

The sequencing of interaction states is described by statements such as: "if eventually return accept, then call". These temporal descriptions represent the guaranteed operation of intervening non-interaction program code. The appropriate Prolog rules are produced by the temporal representation generator tool. An example of the temporal representation rules for the design facts of Figure 3 are presented in Figure 5.

7.3. Temporal Analysis

We demonstrate that a design is functioning correctly (exhibiting no deadness) by proving that each task in the design will always return from its last interaction state, given that it has started and continuously restarts (as is the case of an endless cycle). The theorem prover detects potential deadness by applying the proving mechanism to the temporal descriptions of each task. In the course of this proof, each interaction state transition description is given as a known quantity and the termination of each interaction state must be shown to be true.

Prolog's natural resolution theorem proving capability plus three additional statements are used to implement the theorem prover. The additional statements are: (1) no circular proof is permitted, (2) the proof of a joint eventuality is required and (3) the "start/restart" assumption must be verified. The first statement is required since only the assumption "given that a task starts and continuously restarts" can be used as the terminating fact of a proof. Prolog as a theorem prover, terminates when a "fact", or a contradiction of a fact, has been arrived at in a proof. If neither of these occurs, as is the case of a circular proof, Prolog will not terminate execution. Circular proof implies a failure to prove deadness and therefore must be detected. (Circular proof usually results from deadness due to flaws in program logic). We implement circular proof detection by maintaining a record of interaction states that the theorem prover is currently verifying.

The second statement is required to show that both the calling and accepting states on a given entry can occur given that the program sequencing logic is not in error. Failure due to deadness could still occur because of the blocking characteristics of the Ada rendezvous. For example, Task A may call Task B twice in an endless loop; Task B accepts once in an endless loop with one nested accept on the same entry, thus it executes two accepts; Task A's first call is accepted by Task B, however, because the second accept is nested inside the first, it cannot be accepted for the second call because Task A is already a member of the rendezvous; therefore, although it can be shown that the logic of Task A permits a call on Task B and that the logic of Task B permits it to executes an accept, it cannot be shown that a rendezvous will ever take place, that is, that both interaction states will eventually, jointly occur. Without the joint eventuality test, this proof would succeed. The joint eventuality test is implemented by maintaining a list of tasks which are currently members of a rendezvous that the theorem prover is attempting to verify.

The third statement is required because each task is proven individually and a subsequent proof of failure in one task may falsify a prior proof of success in another task. This is implemented by:

1. maintaining task assumption list facts for each task that is proven to be temporally safe; these lists contain task identifiers of any tasks that were callers or acceptors of the interaction states and,
2. verifying that all tasks specified in task assumption lists were successfully proven.

7.4. Example Analysis

An example of the use of the temporal analysis tool is illustrated in Figure 6. Figure 6 shows an excerpt of the analysis results for the design in Figure 1. For the purposes of this example, the following sequencing of calls and accepts is used:

1. task 'task1' - perform selective accept, call task3.e1 and call task2.e1;
2. task 'task2' - call task3.e2, call task1.e2 and then accept task2.e1;
3. task 'task3' - perform selective accept and then call internal procedure proc_1, which in turn calls task1.e1;
4. task 'task4' - accept task4.e1;

5. task 'task5' - call task4.e1 and call task1.e3;

In this case, a failure to prove deadness due to a circular deadlock is detected in "task3". This is detected by the temporal analysis tool as an attempt to perform a circular proof. The failure traceback indicates the proofs that were pending when the proof failure occurred. Note that the pending proofs are listed in the order of most recent attempt first.

7.5. Discussion

Our implementation experience on the current TRAS tools is as follows: (1) Temporal Representation Generator: 4 weeks of a PhD student's effort resulting in 164 rules over 48 predicates, fully documented; (2) Temporal Analysis Tool: 8 weeks of a PhD student's effort resulting in 109 rules over 57 predicates, fully documented. Design refinement is also included in the quotes on implementation time.

The analysis speed for the illustrated example was approximately 5 seconds wall clock time using interpreted M-Prolog on a VAX-11/750 running BSD 4.2 UNIX with 3MB of main memory, under a moderate system load.

Short term future additions to the TRAS tools include: (1) addition of more Ada models, such as guards, loop structures, conditional structures and dynamic tasking; and (2) integration of an iconic interface for the temporal representation generator. Furthermore, we will be performing analysis on a variety of real-world test examples as a demonstration of the abilities of the TRAS system.

8. CONCLUSIONS

CAEDE is graphics based design environment to support embedded system design with Ada following an extended version of a methodology due to Buhr. Its unique feature is the integration of a front end which supports interactive graphical design paradigms with a Prolog back end which both supports the design data base and provides tools with which to analyze and manipulate the design data base. A skeleton version of CAEDE was demonstrated in September, 1984. A tool for temporal semantics definition and manipulation has been added to the skeleton CAEDE system for use as a designer's assistant to spot potential temporal behavior problems without having to write or run Ada programs.

9. ACKNOWLEDGMENTS

This work is being performed primarily under NSERC strategic grant No. G1136: Computer Aided Design of Computer Systems to Implement Communication Protocols. The local area network and the SUN workstations on which CAEDE runs was funded by a BILD grant from the Ontario government. Many of the ideas in CAEDE emerged from work supported by research grants and contracts from NSERC, DOC, DND and private industry.

Grateful acknowledgment is made to contributions by other members of the CAEDE group: Carol Hayes, Ken Van Der Loo, Brian Mondoux. We also like to thank Herm Fischer, Mark Gerhardt and Ken Bowles for providing encouragement and constructive comments.

10. REFERENCES

Buhr, R.J.A. (1984). *System Design With Ada*. Englewood Cliffs, N.J., USA: Prentice Hall.

Buhr, R.J.A. (1985). "Lessons From Practical Experience Teaching Hands-On, Real-Time, Embedded System Programming With Ada". *Proceedings of the International Ada Conference*. Paris, France.

Buhr, R.J.A. & Karam, G.M. (1984). "An Informal Overview of CAEDE". Invited paper, *Santa Barbara workshop on Future Ada Environments*. Santa Barbara, Ca., USA, (to appear in *Ada Letters*).

Buhr, R.J.A. & Michell, S. (1982). "Object-Oriented Structured Design of Layered Protocol Systems". *Proceedings of the Third International Conference on Distributed Computing*. Ft. Lauderdale, Fla., USA.

Buhr, R.J.A., Woodside, C.M., Karam, G.M., Van Der Loo, K., Lewis, G. (1985). "Experiments With Prolog Design Descriptions and Tools in CAEDE: An Iconic Design Environment for Multitasking, Embedded Systems". *Report SCE 85-1.* Department of Systems and Computer Engineering, Carleton University, Ottawa.

Girczyc, E.F., Buhr, R.J.A., Knight, J.P. (1983). "Analysis of Ada as a High-Level Hardware Description Language". *Canadian Conference on VLSI.* Also, to appear in *IEEE Transactions on Computer-Aided Design of Integrated Circuits and Systems.*

Glinert, E.P. & Tanimoto, S.L. (1984). "PICT: An Interactive Graphical Programming Environment". *IEEE Computer.* Vol. 17, no. 11, November, pp. 7-25.

Hailpern, B.T. (1982). *Verifying Concurrent Processes Using Temporal Logic.* Lecture Notes in Computer Science, No. 129, New York, N.Y., USA: Springer-Verlag.

Hayes, C.J. (1984). "CAEDE User's Guide". *Report SCE-84-24.* Department of Systems and Computer Engineering, Carleton University, Ottawa, Canada.

Helmbold, D. & Luckham, D.C. (1984). "Debugging Ada Tasking Programs". *Conference on Ada Applications and Environments.* St. Paul, Minn., pp. 96-105.

ISO (1984). "A Formal Description Technique Based on an Extended State Transition Model". *Report ISOTC97/SC16/WG1 Nzzzz.* Subgroup B on formal description techniques.

Luckham, D.C. & Von Henke, F.W. (1984). "An Overview of Anna, A Specification Language for Ada". *Conference on Ada Applications and Environments.* St. Paul, Minn., USA, pp. 116-127.

Rescher N., & Urquhart A. (1971). *Temporal Logic.* New York, N.Y., USA: Springer-Verlag.

Warren D.H.D. (1977). "Logic Programming and Compiler Writing", *D.A.I. Research Report No. 44.* Univ. of Edinburgh, Edinburgh.

Wegner, P. (1984). "Capital Intensive Software Technology". *IEEE Software.* Vol. 1, no. 3, July, pp. 7-45.

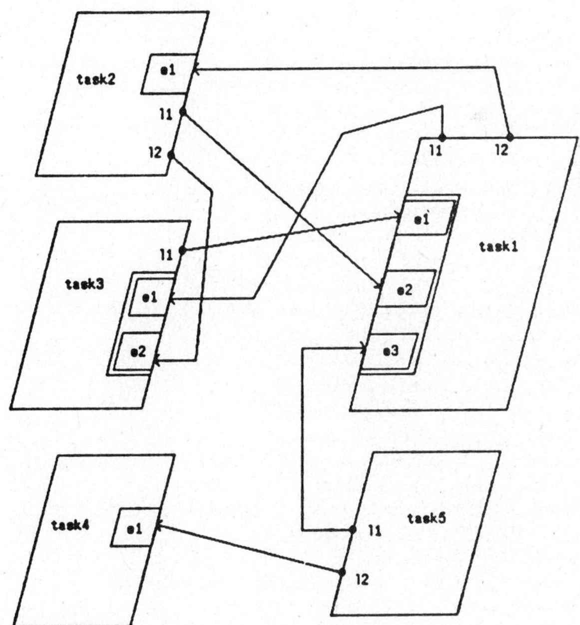

Figure 1: CAEDE Design Example, Level 1 View

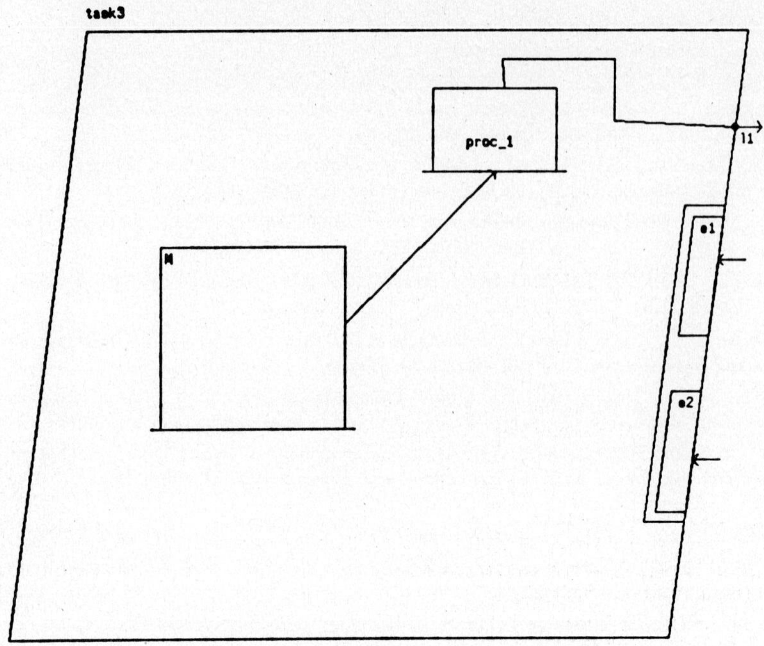

Figure 2: CAEDE Design Example, Level 2 View of Task "task3"

```
object([task,'task3',['main_package']],[]).
abstraction([task_access,'task3',['main_package']],[static,_]).
abstraction([task_externals,'task3',['main_package']],
        [[[select_accept,1,['task3','main_package']],
        [connection_point,'l1',['task3','main_package']]]]]).
abstraction([task_internals,'task3',['main_package']],
        [[[main_line,'task3',['main_package']],
        [procedure,'proc_1',['task3','main_package']]]],[]]).
component([task_entry,'e1',['task3','main_package']],[[]]).
component([task_entry,'e2',['task3','main_package']],[[]]).
component([non_crit_section,'e1',['task3','main_package']],[[]]).
component([select_accept,1,['task3','main_package']],
        [[[task_entry,'e1',['task3','main_package']],
        [task_entry,'e2',['task3','main_package']]]]]).
component([main_line,'task3',['main_package']],[]).
component([procedure,'proc_1',['task3','main_package']],[[]]).
reference([interaction,1,[]],[connection_point,'l1',['task3','main_package']],
        [task_entry,'e1',['task1','main_package']],[wait,static,[]]).
reference([interaction,2,[]],[connection_point,'l1',['task1','main_package']],
        [task_entry,'e1',['task3','main_package']],[wait,static,[]]).
reference([interaction,10,[]],[main_line,'task3',['main_package']],
        [procedure,'proc_1',['task3','main_package']],[wait,static,[]]).
```

Figure 3: Some Prolog Facts Representing Structural Information for "task3" in Figures 1 and 2

```
return_task_call(CALLER_ID,ACCEPTOR_ID) :-
    rendezvous(CALLER_ID,ACCEPTOR_ID),
    end_rendezvous(CALLER_ID,ACCEPTOR_ID).

rendezvous(CALLER_ID,ACCEPTOR_ID) :-
    task_call(CALLER_ID,ACCEPTOR_ID),
    accept_entry(CALLER_ID,ACCEPTOR_ID),
    joint_eventuality(task_call(CALLER_ID,ACCEPTOR_ID),
        accept_entry(CALLER_ID,ACCEPTOR_ID)).

return_accept(CALLER_ID,ACCEPTOR_ID) :-
    rendezvous(CALLER_ID,ACCEPTOR_ID),
    end_rendezvous(CALLER_ID,ACCEPTOR_ID).
```

Figure 4: Prolog Rules Specifying a Subset of Interaction State Descriptions

```
init_task([_V,[<main.task3>]]).
accept([_V,_V,_V],[_V,[<main.task3>],[<task3.e1>]]).
accept([_V,_V,_V],[_V,[<main.task3>],[<task3.e2>]]).
enter_sel_accept(1,[_V,[<main.task3>]]) :-
  init_task([_V,[<main.task3>]]).
proc_call([_V,[<main.task3>],[<task3.main_line>]],[<task3.proc_1>]) :-
  return_sel_accept(1,[_V,[<main.task3>]]).
end_task([0,[<main.task3>]]) :-
  return_proc_call([0,[<main.task3>],[<task3.main_line>]],[<task3.proc_1>]).
task_call([_V,_V,[<task3.proc_1>]],[_V,[<main.task1>],[<task1,e1>]]) :-
  init_proc([_V,_V],[<task3.proc_1>]).
end_proc([_V,_V],[<task3.proc_1>]) :-
  return_task_call([_V,_V,[<task3.proc_1>]],[_V,[<main.task1>],[<task1.e1]]).
end_n_crit_sect([_V,_V],[<task3.e2(non-crit-section)>]) :-
  init_n_crit_sect([_V,_V],[<task3.e2(non-crit-sect)>]).
end_n_crit_sect([_V,_V],[<task3.e1(non-crit-sect)>]) :-
  init_n_crit_sect([_V,_V],[<task3.e1(non-crit-sect)>]).
end_rend([_V,_V,_V],[1,[<main.task3>],[<task3.e1]]) :-
  init_rend([_V,_V,_V],[1,[<main.task3>],[<task3.e1>]]).
end_rend([_V,_V,_V],[1,[<main.task3>],[<task3.e2>]]) :-
  init_rend([_V,_V,_V],[1,[<main.task3>],[<task3.e2>]]).
```

NOTE: "_V" - represents uninstantiated Prolog variables
"<parent.child>" - represents "information" specifying Ada program component "parent.child"
"<aaa.bbb>(non-crit-sect)" - implies the non-critical section of task entry "aaa.bbb"

Figure 5: Prolog Rules for Temporal Representation of "task3" from Figures 1 and 2

```
TESTING TASK --> main_package.task3 <--

*** Failure to prove TASK "main_package.task3" is deadness-free
because of

    cause: circular proof,

==> FAILURE DURING ATTEMPT TO PROVE task "main_package.task3",
origin "task3.proc_1", will EVENTUALLY RENDEZVOUS WITH
task "main_package.task1", entry "task1.e1"

Failure Traceback:

*** Failure in attempting to prove that task "main_package.task3"
  will EVENTUALLY RETURN FROM TASK CALL task3.proc_1
  on accept of task "main_package.task1"
  entry "task1.e1"
*** Failure in attempting to prove that task "unknown",
  origin "unknown", will EVENTUALLY RENDEZVOUS WITH
  task "main_package.task1", entry "task1.e1"
*** Failure in attempting to prove that task "main_package.task1"
  will EVENTUALLY RETURN FROM ACCEPT "task1.e1"
*** Failure in attempting to prove that task "main_package.task1"
  will EVENTUALLY RETURN FROM NON-CRIT. SECTION "task1.e1"
*** Failure in attempting to prove that task "main_package.task1"
  will EVENTUALLY RETURN FROM SELECTIVE ACCEPT 1
*** Failure in attempting to prove that task "main_package.task1",
  origin "main_line.task1", will EVENTUALLY RENDEZVOUS WITH
  task "main_package.task2", entry "task2.e1"
*** Failure in attempting to prove that task "main_package.task1"
  will EVENTUALLY RETURN FROM TASK CALL main_line.task1
  on accept of task "main_package.task2"
  entry "task2.e1"
*** Failure in attempting to prove that task "unknown",
  origin "unknown", will EVENTUALLY RENDEZVOUS WITH
  task "main_package.task3", entry "task3.e1"
*** Failure in attempting to prove that task "main_package.task3"
  will EVENTUALLY RETURN FROM ACCEPT "task3.e1"
*** Failure in attempting to prove that task "main_package.task3"
  will EVENTUALLY RETURN FROM NON-CRIT. SECTION "task3.e1"
*** Failure in attempting to prove that task "main_package.task3"
  will EVENTUALLY RETURN FROM PROC CALL main_line.task3
  on procedure "task3.proc_1"
```

Figure 6: Excerpt from TRAS Analysis of Design
in Figure 1

Semantic Specification of Ada[1] Packages

Friedrich W. von Henke[2]
David Luckham[3]
Bernd Krieg-Brueckner[4]
Olaf Owe[5]

1. INTRODUCTION

Ada packages are the basic building blocks of Ada programs. The separation in Ada into package visible part and body is intended to support a programming style that employs modularization, encapsulation and information hiding. Unfortunately, the visible part provides only the syntactic interface to the package; it does not convey any information about the meaning of, e.g., visible subprograms. Instead, when the user of an Ada package wants to understand what services it provides he needs to study the package body. Thus, the purpose of the separation into visible part and body is somewhat subverted if the body is the only place where semantic information can be found.

More generally, modern software technology advocates giving precise specifications for the various sub-modules of a system, as part of a systematic design process. The specification could be given in a separate specification language that is designed especially for that purpose. Such a language, however, would necessarily replicate various features already provided by the programming language. Thus, the idea of defining the specification language as a variant of the programming language suggests itself.

In the case of Ada, extending packages by constructs that convey semantic information leads to a suitable candidate for a specification language; this approach has been taken in the design of ANNA (ANNotated Ada). ANNA extends Ada text by formal comments, which are lexically distinguished from ordinary comments by special indicators. In this way, extra information is added to a program without disturbing the syntax of the programming language. ANNA includes many specification constructs; besides those useful for specifying packages it provides constructs for lower-level annotation, which will not be discussed here. A full account of the language can be found in [3]; an overview is given in [4].

This paper focusses on specifying Ada packages, more specifically, on what needs to be specified in a package visible part and how those specifications can be expressed. The

---

[1] Ada is a registered trademark of the U. S. Government, Ada Joint Program Office

[2] Current affiliations: [2] SRI International, 333 Ravenswood Avenue, Menlo Park CA 94025; [3] Stanford University; [4] University of Bremen, W-Germany; [5] University of Oslo, Norway.

remainder of the paper is organized as follows. The next section clarifies the sense in which the notion of specification is used here and surveys potential uses of formal specifications. Section 3 presents the basic specification techniques for packages. The particulars of specifying generic packages are discussed in Section 4. A comprehensive example is developed in Section 5; the full text of the specified package is given in the appendix.

2. SEMANTIC SPECIFICATIONS

Ada uses the term "specification" to refer to certain parts of declarations, i.e. *syntactic* entities. In fact, an Ada specification contains primarily syntactic information. In contrast, the specifications this paper talks about are statements about the *semantics* of entities. To disambiguate usage, we will follow the convention that "specification part" of a package or subprogram means (package or subprogram) specification in the Ada sense, and "specification" refers to semantic specification.

Specification of the semantics of a package involves, first of all, description of the *behavior* of the package, i.e. the effects observable by executing it (or its components). This paper addresses specification of *functional* behavior; other aspects of behavior, like those pertaining to performance are not considered. Specifications are *abstractions* from the behavior as implemented in the body; they describe package behavior in terms of visible concepts, from the point of view of the user.

Another aspect of program specification is the description of *structure*, the identification of building blocks of a program and how they are linked together. The basic structural information about an Ada program is already given by the package and context structure. ANNA provides for more detailed specification of access to globals; further facilities are needed if aspects of package interconnections other than those given by Ada visibility rules are to be specified. This paper is concerned with specifying individual packages rather than links between them and will not discuss structural specifications further.

Finally, we are only interested in *formal* specifications, i.e. in specifications given in a language that is as formal as a programming language. Formal specifications tend to be more precise than informal ones; more importantly, they permits the use of mechanized tools for parsing, analysis and processing in general.

2.1 Uses of Specifications

Before discussing specification techniques we briefly review some potential uses and benefits of formal specifications that have been taken into account in the design of ANNA.

Documentation: Specifications describe the services provided by a package more precisely then English text. Their usefulness for documentation depends, however, on their understandability; they are best regarded as complementing informal comments, rather than replacing them.

Requirements Analysis: Writing and analyzing formal specifications of the service to be provided by a package often leads to detection of omissions or inconsistencies. This process can be carried out even without the aid of formal reasoning.

Implementation Guidelines: Specifications written before the implementation define conditions to be satisfied by the body, thus constraining possible implementations.

Reusability and Retrieval from Libraries: Specifications make precise the conditions under which a package can be used. They thus assist in determining whether an existing package can be reused in a new context. For a generic package each instantiation constitutes a reuse; specifications of the generic parameters make explicit the potential and range of (semantically meaningful) adaptation of the package to different situations. Formal specifications are probably not suitable for driving the initial search in a package library, but once a candidate package has been identified by other means they will help in determining whether the package satisfies the requirement.

Prototyping: Formal specifications may be used to simulate the behavior of a package, in effect providing a "prototype" of it. This requires that specifications be, in some sense, "executable". Often, specifications can be executed only symbolically; for instance, rewrite-rule based techniques may be used to execute algebraic axioms.

Formal Consistency Analysis: Formal specifications are the basis for analyzing consistency between implementation and uses of a package, i.e. formal verification. Formal verification of Ada programs is very much a research issue, given the current lack of a completely defined formal semantics for full Ada or a suitable subset.

3. TECHNIQUES FOR SPECIFYING SEMANTICS OF PACKAGES

3.1 Specification Concepts

Virtual Text. Specifications are often given in terms of concepts that are not required in the computation proper. Such concepts may be declared in ANNA in *virtual text*. Virtual text is Ada text marked as virtual by the formal comment indicator --:.

Declarations of related specification concepts may be grouped in a virtual package just like any other collection of declarations. Such *specification packages* can be entered into specification libraries for future reuse. As with ordinary packages, reusability may be increased by making specification packages generic.

Annotations. Specifications are stated in ANNA as *annotations*, which are formal comments indicated by --|. Annotations must follow the syntactic and semantic rules of ANNA; for details see [3].

Package States. If a package contains local variables, the package behavior (i.e. the behavior associated with the visible subprograms) depends on their values; in other words, the package has a *state* represented by the aggregate of its local variables. Obviously, the specifications cannot refer to any entity that is local to the package body. Furthermore, outside the package the state is an abstract entity; its internal structure is supposed to be hidden. ANNA provides a means of referring to the (abstract) state of a package `P` in form of a new attribute, `P'STATE` (abbreviated, if unambiguous, to `P`). This attribute denotes the (value of) the *current* state; the *initial* state of the package (reached after elaboration) is denoted by the attribute `P'INITIAL`. ANNA also provides a notation for package state values that are not readily available as part of the computation. For instance, the term `Q'INITIAL[ENQ(X); ENQ(Y)]` denotes the state of a queue package after entering two items.

3.2 Specification of Subprograms

The behavior of a subprogram may be specified by indicating:

(1) for what set of input values the subprogram is expected to behave "normally";

(2) how the output values (returned in out parameters or as results) depend on the input values;

(3) how the the state of the package and global variables are affected;

(4) under what condition the subprogram may propagate exceptions.

In ANNA, (semantic) subprogram specifications are expressed in a *subprogram annotation* linked to the Ada specification part. A subprogram annotation may include several kinds of annotations. An *in annotation* (an expression prefixed by **in**) expresses a condition on input values. An *out annotation* (an expression prefixed by **out**) is used to express (2) and (3). The reserved words **in** and **out** used as prefixes refer to the entry and exit states, respectively; **in** may also occur inside an out annotation, thus permitting to express input-output relationships. Specifications of kind (4) are dealt with in the following section.

Example of a subprogram annotation (`Q` *is the package name, denoting the package state*):

```
    procedure ENQ(NEW : Q_ITEM);
--|     where out (Q.length = in Q.length + 1),   -- an in/out relationship
--|           out (Q.member(NEW));   -- the new item becomes a member of Q
```

3.3 Exceptions

The propagation of exceptions is an important part of the semantics of a subprogram. In Ada it is, however, not possible to describe the exceptional situation signaled by an exception, nor to link subprogram specifications and exceptions. The standard package `DIRECT_IO` [5], for instance, declares seven exceptions, and the intended semantics of the exported subprograms is intimately connected with them, but the link from the subprograms to the exceptions is only made in explanations in English.

ANNA provides *propagation annotations* for formally specifying links between a subprogram and exceptions propagated from its body; these annotations are included in the subprogram annotation. There are annotations corresponding to three kinds of situations to be specified:

1. the simple fact that an exception E may be propagated:

```
raise E;
```

2. If a condition C_IN is satisfied by the input values, exception E will be propagated:

```
C_IN => raise E;
```

3. An exception E may be propagated; if it is propagated, a condition C_OUT describing the state in which the calling environment is left will be true:

```
raise E => C_OUT;
```

Type (2) is the most common kind needed in translating the informal explanations of DIRECT IO into specifications (see Appendix); they are called *strong* propagation annotations since they express when raising an exception is required. Annotations of type (3) are *weak* propagation annotations; they are needed to specify the program state so as to make meaningful further exception handling in situations where the Ada rules do not specify the value of all state components.

Examples:

```
      procedure ENQ(NEW : Q_ITEM);
--|     where
--|       Q.length = MAXSIZE => raise Q_FULL,
--|       raise Q_FULL => Q = in Q;        -- The package state Q is not changed.

      procedure WRITE(FILE : in FILE_TYPE; ITEM : in ELEMENT_TYPE);
--|     where
--|       raise USE_ERROR,
--|       not IS_OPEN(FILE) => raise STATUS_ERROR,
--|       MODE(FILE) = IN_FILE => raise MODE_ERROR, ...;
```

3.4 Package Axioms

Not all properties of subprograms can be expressed as input/output or propagation specifications. It is, for example, often necessary to state *relationships* between subprograms, which is commonly done in the form of *algebraic specifications*. The ANNA device for expressing algebraic relationships is an *axiomatic annotation* or *package axiom*. With package axioms, full specifications of abstract data types can be given. Axioms are also used to specify properties of the initial package state (denoted by the attribute INITIAL) and visible invariants, i.e. properties of *all* states observable outside the package.

Example:

```
--| axiom for all S : DIRECT_IO'STATE;  F : FILE_TYPE;
--|           I, J : POSITIVE_COUNT;  ITEM, E : ELEMENT_TYPE  =>
--|     S[WRITE(F,E,I)].READ'OUT(F,ITEM,I).ITEM = E,
```

```
        -- Reading deposits into ITEM the value written into that
        -- file position.
--|     I /= J ->
--|       S[WRITE(F,E,I); READ(F,ITEM,J)] = S[READ(F,ITEM,J); WRITE(F,E,I)];
        -- In all states, reading in one position commutes with writing
        -- into another position of the same file.
```

3.5 Specification of Packages

The collection of all forms of annotations in a package visible part constitute the semantic specification of the package. The specification constructs provide a degree of choice of expression; for example, it is often merely a matter of style whether a particular specification item is expressed in an axiom or a subprogram annotation. In any case, all annotations have to be seen in conjunction as there are semantic interactions among the various kinds of specification. Two kinds of connections are particularly important:

(1) In/out-annotations and propagation annotations in subprogram specifications are complementary. An out-annotations is required to be satisfied only for parameter values that satisfy any in-annotation and for calls that terminate normally without propagating an exception. Thus when considering out-annotations one can assume that all in-annotations are true and all conditions in strong propagation annotations are false.

(2) ANNA uses a form of partial quantifiers that make a formula true even if the quantified expression is not always defined. Thus, in contrast to most algebraic specification techniques it is usually not necessary to state axioms in conditional form; the role of the conditions is taken over by in-annotations and propagation annotations of subprograms occurring in the axiom. For instance, the term `S[WRITE(F,E,I)]` is undefined if any of the conditions is true that is part of strong propagation annotation of `WRITE`; in turn, any quantified axiom containing an undefined occurrence of the term is vacuously true. For details see [3]

4. SPECIFICATION OF GENERIC PACKAGES

A generic package may be specified in its visible part just like an ordinary package. The package specifications are templates like the Ada text; they may, of course, refer to the generic formal parameters. The specifications are instantiated together with the Ada text, following the same rules (suitably extended). In this respect there is nothing special about specification of generic packages.

If, however, a generic package has generic formal parameters an additional kind of specifications must be considered. Instantiating a generic unit in Ada is in many respects analogous to calling a subprogram: in both situations, actual parameters are matched to formals and must meet (type) constraints placed on the formals. This analogy carries over to semantic specifications: for instance, a subprogram specification may express a restriction of inputs to a set of values for which the subprogram is intended (or even guarenteed) to work properly; similarly, a generic package may require properties of its parameters that are not expressible in the Ada generic formal part and thus must be stated as additional parameter specifications.

Generic parameters, however, may include types and subprograms; thus the specifications can be much richer. While subprogram annotations specify only relationships among objects and values, annotations of generic parameters may also express constraints on, and relationships among, types and subprograms.

As a simple example, consider a generic sorting package with a type of items and a binary relation as generic parameters. Its intended meaning may depend on the relation being an ordering over the domain of the type. This may be expressed as a constraint on the generic parameters:

```
    generic
        type ITEM is private;
        with function "<=" (X, Y : ITEM) return BOOLEAN is <>;
        type INDEX is (<>);
        type ROW is array (INDEX range <>) of ITEM;
--|     for all X, Y, Z : ITEM  =>
--|         X <= X,
--|         X <= Y and Y <= X   ->  X = Y,
--|         X <= Y and Y <= Z   ->  X <= Z;
    package SORTING is
        ...
        procedure SORT(A : in out ROW);
        ...
    end SORTING;
```

The annotation at the end of the generic part constrains the actual parameters matched to ITEM and "<=" to a partial ordering. Technically, the annotation acts like an assertion that constrains the actuals, similar to an in-annotation of a subprogram. Semantically, it is equivalent to an axiomatic annotation of a package "exporting" the constrained entities; in other words, the aggregate of generic parameters and (semantic) specifications is equivalent to a *(semantic) package specification*. The generic package can be regarded as having a *package parameter*, where the parameter specification states a restriction on any parameter package to make instantiation of the generic package meaningful. Such specifications generalize the notion of generic parameters from a simple list of parameters to *theories* or *views*, as proposed in [1]. The generic parameter annotations in ANNA support specification of such complex parameters; the reader may compare this approach with that proposed in [2].

5. AN EXTENDED EXAMPLE OF FORMAL SPECIFICATION

The package DIRECT_IO is one of the predefined packages for Ada I/O. The service provided by the package and the meaning of the entities it declares are described informally in [5], Chapter 14 (the relevant pieces are spread over several sections). In this section we discuss a translation of the informal description of the package into formal ANNA specifications; this also serves to illustrate the use of many of the specification concepts in a larger context. The section should be read as an introduction to the full specification given in the appendix.

Specification Concepts. A major problem with specifying DIRECT_IO is that the package depends on entities outside the program. In fact, the package encapsulates a substantial part of the file handling system (usually a component of the underlying operating system). The informal description distinguishes between objects of type FILE_TYPE and "external files" and talks about "associations" among them. The specifications have to model these connections with the external world in a sufficently abstract manner. For this purpose we introduce (in virtual declarations) a type of external files and functions from FILE_TYPE and file names (i.e. strings) to external files that express the associations:

```
--:  type EXTERNAL_FILE is limited private;
--:  function FILE_MAP (FILE : FILE_TYPE) return EXTERNAL_FILE;
--:  function NAME_MAP (NAME : STRING) return EXTERNAL_FILE;
```

The two functions are total; their default value is a virtual constant NO_FILE that does not denote a file. The implementation-dependent test function IS_PROPER_NAME expresses whether a string can be interpreted as a file name. All these concepts are collected in a virtual package (with suitable parametrization it could be made a generic library package).

Ordering of Declarations. Before we can begin to write formal specifications for DIRECT_IO we need to reorder the declarations in the Ada specification part. For instance, we have to make the exceptions visible earlier so that their propagation from package operations can be specified. In addition, some functions like IS_OPEN are useful in specifications and thus must be declared so as to be visible in annotations. This is a fairly common situation; since annotations establish more connections among the declared entities the order of declarations is more restricted.

Propagation Annotations. The bulk of the informal description deals with exceptions. Many operations can be meaningfully applied only to open files; thus we have many occurrences of the subprogram annotation

```
--|    where not IS_OPEN(FILE) => raise STATUS_ERROR;
```

The function IS_OPEN simply tests whether its argument is associated with an existing external file:

```
      function IS_OPEN (FILE : in FILE_TYPE) return BOOLEAN;
--|     where return FILE_MAP(FILE) /= NO_FILE;
```

The propagation annotations for MODE_ERROR, NAME_ERROR and END_ERROR are fairly straightforward formalizations of the English text; the conditions for raising USE_ERROR or DATA_ERROR are external to the package.

File Management. The operations for file management affect that part of the package state which is reflected by the functions FILE_MAP and NAME_MAP. The specification of CREATE, for example,

```
--|       out (FILE_MAP(FILE) = NAME_MAP(NAME)  and
--|            (for all F: FILE_TYPE =>
--|               F /= FILE  ->  FILE_MAP(F) /= in FILE_MAP(FILE))  and
--|            (for all N : STRING =>
--|               N /= NAME  ->  NAME_MAP(N) /= in NAME_MAP(NAME)));
```

attempts to capture the concept of "new file": in our model we can only express that a new file is an element of EXTERNAL_FILE that prior to the call to CREATE was not associated with any (open) file or file name. Similarly, the specification of DELETE states that no file name can refer to the deleted file. Note that neither the specifications nor, apparently, the informal description prevent two files being associated with the same external file, so that a deleted external file may still be associated with an open file.

Reading and Writing. The subprogram specifications of READ and WRITE do not express what is being read or written. Instead, the package axioms attempt to state some of the important properties that can be deduced from the English description, which suggests that files have a structure similar to arrays; the axioms are similar to those specifying array operations. The presented list of axioms is certainly incomplete.

Note that though the package is generic, the package does not depend on any properties of the generic parameter; thus there are no specfications in the generic part.

Specifications for all of DIRECT_IO are given in the appendix. The underlying Ada text follows [5, 14.2.5], with the reordering discussed above; in addition, only one version of overloaded functions is displayed as their specifications differ only in minor ways. The specifications are not claimed to be complete (for instance, the parameter FORM has been completely ignored). They certainly do not answer all questions one might have about the package as they do not attempt to formalize more than what is stated in [5].

Readers will notice the considerable increase in size over the pure Ada specification part. But by the time they have collected all the pieces of English text that contribute to describing the meaning of DIRECT_IO they will realize that the formal specifications may actually be shorter; they must judge for themselves whether the gain in clarity and precision is worth the effort.

Acknowledgments. *The work on the design of Anna at Stanford University was supported by the Defense Advanced Research Project Agency under Contract NOO-039-82-C-0250.*

References

[1] J.A. Goguen: Parametrized Programming. *IEEE Trans. on Software Engineering* 10.5, 1984, 528-543.

[2] S.D. Litvintchouk, A.S. Matsumoto: Design of Ada systems yielding reusable components: an approach using structured algebraic specification. *IEEE Trans. on Software Engineering* 10.5, 1984, 544-551.

[3] D.C. Luckham, F.W. von Henke, B. Krieg-Brueckner, O. Owe: *ANNA - A language for annotating Ada programs, Preliminary Reference Manual.* Technical Report No. 84-261, Computer Systems Laboratory, Stanford University, July 1984.

[4] D.C. Luckham, F.W. von Henke: An Overview of ANNA, a specification language for Ada. *IEEE Software* 2.2, March 1985, 9-22. See also: Proc. IEEE 1984 Conference on Ada Applications and Environments, pp. 116-127.

[5] *Reference Manual of the Ada Programming Language*, ANSI/MIL-STD-1815A, US Department of Defense, 1983.

Appendix: Specification of the package DIRECT_IO

```
    with IO_EXCEPTIONS;
    generic
        type ELEMENT_TYPE is private;
    package DIRECT_IO is

        type FILE_TYPE is limited private;

        type FILE_MODE is (IN_FILE, INOUT_FILE, OUT_FILE);
        type COUNT is range 0 .. implementation defined;
        subtype POSITIVE_COUNT is COUNT range 1 .. COUNT'LAST;

--:     package EXTERNAL_FILES is          -- specification concepts
--:       type EXTERNAL_FILE is limited private;
--:       NO_FILE : constant  EXTERNAL_FILE;
--:       function FILE_MAP (FILE : FILE_TYPE) return EXTERNAL_FILE;
--:       function NAME_MAP (NAME : STRING) return EXTERNAL_FILE;
--:       function IS_PROPER_NAME (S : STRING) return BOOLEAN;
--:     end EXTERNAL_FILES;

--:     use EXTERNAL_FILES;

        STATUS_ERROR : exception renames IO_EXCEPTIONS.STATUS_ERROR;
        MODE_ERROR   : exception renames IO_EXCEPTIONS.MODE_ERROR;
        NAME_ERROR   : exception renames IO_EXCEPTIONS.NAME_ERROR;
        USE_ERROR    : exception renames IO_EXCEPTIONS.USE_ERROR;
        DEVICE_ERROR : exception renames IO_EXCEPTIONS.DEVICE_ERROR;
        END_ERROR    : exception renames IO_EXCEPTIONS.END_ERROR;
        DATA_ERROR   : exception renames IO_EXCEPTIONS.DATA_ERROR;

        function IS_OPEN (FILE : in FILE_TYPE) return BOOLEAN;
--|       where return FILE_MAP(FILE) /= NO_FILE;

        function MODE (FILE : in FILE_TYPE) return FILE_MODE;
--|       where not IS_OPEN(FILE) => raise STATUS_ERROR;

        function NAME (FILE : in FILE_TYPE) return STRING;
--|       where
--|         not IS_OPEN(FILE) => raise STATUS_ERROR,
--|         return N: STRING =>  NAME_MAP(N) = FILE_MAP(FILE);
```

```
        function FORM (FILE : in FILE_TYPE) return STRING;
--|         where not IS_OPEN(FILE) => raise STATUS_ERROR;

        function INDEX (FILE : in FILE_TYPE) return POSTIVE_COUNT;
--|       where not IS_OPEN(FILE) => raise STATUS_ERROR;

        function SIZE (FILE : in FILE_TYPE) return COUNT;
--|       where not IS_OPEN(FILE) => raise STATUS_ERROR;

--      -- File management

        procedure CREATE (FILE : in out FILE_TYPE;
                          MODE : in FILE_MODE := INOUT_FILE;
                          NAME : in STRING := "";  FORM : in STRING := "");
--|       where
--|         IS_OPEN(FILE) => raise STATUS_ERROR,
--|         not IS_PROPER_NAME(NAME) => raise NAME_ERROR,
--|         raise USE_ERROR,
--|         out IS_OPEN(FILE),
--|         out (INDEX(FILE) = 1  and  MODE(FILE) = MODE),
--|         out (FILE_MAP(FILE) = NAME_MAP(NAME)  and
--|              (for all F: FILE_TYPE =>
--|                  F /= FILE  ->  FILE_MAP(FILE) /= in FILE_MAP(F))  and
--|              (for all N : STRING =>
--|                  N /= NAME  ->  NAME_MAP(NAME) /= in NAME_MAP(N)));

        procedure OPEN(FILE : in out FILE_TYPE;
                       MODE : in FILE_MODE;
                       NAME : in STRING;  FORM : in STRING);
--|       where
--|         IS_OPEN(FILE) => raise STATUS_ERROR,
--|         not IS_PROPER_NAME(NAME) or NAME_MAP(NAME) = NO_FILE =>
--|             raise NAME_ERROR,
--|         raise USE_ERROR,
--|         out IS_OPEN(FILE),
--|         out (FILE_MAP(FILE) = NAME_MAP(NAME)),
--|         out (INDEX(FILE) = 1  and  MODE(FILE) = MODE);

        procedure CLOSE(FILE : in out FILE_TYPE);
--|       where
--|         not IS_OPEN(FILE) => raise STATUS_ERROR,
--|         out (not IS_OPEN(FILE)),

        procedure DELETE (FILE : in out FILE_TYPE);
--|       where
--|         not IS_OPEN(FILE) => raise STATUS_ERROR,
--|         raise USE_ERROR,
--|         out (not IS_OPEN(FILE)),
--|         out (for all N : STRING =>
--|                 NAME_MAP(N) /= in (FILE_MAP(FILE)));

        procedure RESET (FILE : in out FILE_TYPE; MODE : in FILE_MODE);
--|       where
--|         not IS_OPEN(FILE) => raise STATUS_ERROR,
--|         raise USE_ERROR,
```

```
--|         out (INDEX(FILE) = 1  and  MODE(FILE) = MODE);

        . . .

--      -- Input and output operations

        procedure READ(FILE : in FILE_TYPE; ITEM : out ELEMENT_TYPE;
                       FROM : POSITIVE_COUNT);
--|       where
--|         not IS_OPEN(FILE) => raise STATUS_ERROR,
--|         MODE(FILE) = OUT_FILE => raise MODE_ERROR,
--|         FROM > SIZE(FILE) => raise END_ERROR,
--|         raise DATA_ERROR,
--|         out (INDEX(FILE) = FROM + 1),

        . . .

        procedure WRITE(FILE : in FILE_TYPE; ITEM : in ELEMENT_TYPE;
                        TO : POSITIVE_COUNT);
--|       where
--|         raise USE_ERROR,
--|         not IS_OPEN(FILE) => raise STATUS_ERROR,
--|         MODE(FILE) = IN_FILE => raise MODE_ERROR,
--|         out (INDEX(FILE) = TO + 1);

        . . .

        procedure SET_INDEX(FILE : in FILE_TYPE; TO : in POSTIVE_COUNT);
--|       where
--|         not IS_OPEN(FILE) => raise STATUS_ERROR;
--|         out (INDEX(FILE) = TO);

        function END_OF_FILE(FILE : in FILE_TYPE) return BOOLEAN;
--|       where
--|         not IS_OPEN(FILE) => raise STATUS_ERROR;
--|         MODE(FILE) = OUT_FILE => raise MODE_ERROR,
--|         return (INDEX(FILE) > SIZE(FILE));

--|     axiom for all S : DIRECT_IO'STATE;  F, F1 : FILE_TYPE;
--|            I, J : POSITIVE_COUNT;  ITEM, E : ELEMENT_TYPE  =>
--|         S[WRITE(F,E,I)].READ'OUT(F,ITEM,I).ITEM = E,
--|         I /= J ->
--|           S[WRITE(F,E,I); READ(F,ITEM,J)] = S[READ(F,ITEM,J); WRITE(F,E,I)],
--|         FILE_MAP(F) /= FILE_MAP(F1) ->
--|           S[WRITE(F,E,I); READ(F1,ITEM,J)] =  S[READ(F1,ITEM,J); WRITE(F,E,I)],
--|         FILE_MAP(F) /= FILE_MAP(F1) ->
--|           S[WRITE(F,E,I); WRITE(F1,ITEM,J)] =  S[WRITE(F1,ITEM,J); WRITE(F,E,I)],
--|         . . . ;

    private
        -- Implementation dependent
    end DIRECT_IO;
```

PROGRAMMING LARGE AND FLEXIBLE SYSTEMS IN ADA*

O. Roubine
Informatique Internationale
Centre de Développement de Sophia-Antipolis
06560 Valbonne - FRANCE

Abstract. The parallel processing facilities of Ada are based on the concept of rendezvous, which introduces a tight coupling between two cooperating tasks. Because of the asymmetry of the rendezvous, and of the typing system, these facilities cannot be used directly in a certain number of cases with particularly severe constraints on the system in terms of size, flexibility or extensibility. We indicate some typical such constraints, and investigate possible solutions in Ada. The performance of such solutions is analyzed, leading to an improved solution, which is then shown to be applicable to a large variety of situations.

1 INTRODUCTION

The parallel processing facilities of Ada (DoD 1983) are based on the powerful concept of rendezvous. It is characterized by a tight coupling between two tasks, and by an asymmetric naming scheme, whereby the caller of an entry must name the other task, while the called task generally does not know the identity of its caller.

This paper reports on an investigation performed in order to test the suitability of the language to program large systems upon which a certain number of stringent requirements are imposed, especially in terms of flexibility and extensibility. These constraints are detailed in section 2.

In seeking adequate solutions to our problem, we have been substantially inspired by the ideas of Lauer & Needham (1978), who make a parallel between the so-called message-oriented and procedure-oriented systems (we found it more appropriate, in the context of Ada, to use the term "transaction" instead of "procedure" to refer to the latter approach).

Both approaches are described in section 3, where preliminary solutions are proposed. In section 4, these solutions are examined with respect to the original requirements, and section 5 proposes improved solutions that examplify the use of Ada tasking primitives in what can be viewed as a typical problem.

---

* Ada is a registered trademark of the U.S. Government (Ada Joint Program Office)

2 PROBLEM DESCRIPTION

In order to focus our attention on a concrete example, we will consider the case of a system that can process various requests in order to implement some complex functions. For example, one can think of a telephone switching system, where, for each incoming call, various operations must be performed, such as decoding, routing, transmitting, logging, etc..

We impose a variety of constraints on the system, among which:

- Size and Power: a power increase is essentially translated by a replication of some part of the system. Thus, when a request must be handled, several possible (similar) units could be available. The selection of the appropriate "server" is therefore done dynamically.

- Flexibility: it should be possible to handle a given request in one of several different ways without effect on the behaviour of the system (this kind of requirement is also frequent in systems that implement software redundancy).

- Extensibility: it should be possible to add new kinds of requests, or new ways to handle a request, without incurring recompilation costs if they can be avoided. In some such systems, with no downtime, these changes must be installed while the system remains in operation!

- Efficiency: the intricacies of a solution should not have an adverse effect on the performance of the system.

One should note that each of these constraints is not overly severe when taken in isolation. Most of the difficulties stem from their conjunction.

3 POSSIBLE APPROACHES

The implementation of a complex function is viewed as a sequence of operations that have to be performed. These operations are performed by specialized (software) processors, operating on some input and producing some possible output, which may influence the subsequent operations. For each operation, a request must be made to the appropriate processor.

Two major strategies are distinguished, called respectively the "message approach" and the "transaction approach".

3.1 The message approach

In the message approach, a request is formulated as a "message", i.e., a set of data items that identify both the kind of action to be performed, and the data it is to be performed on. A message is "sent" to a designated server or group of servers (or, in some cases, to any server) in an asynchronous fashion, in that the sender does not wait for any reply.

The message approach involves more than just message communication: because of this form of communication, the application is structured so that each processor decides, once its own processing is finished, which request should be made next, and to whom. One could thus say that each server "passes the task on" to the next.

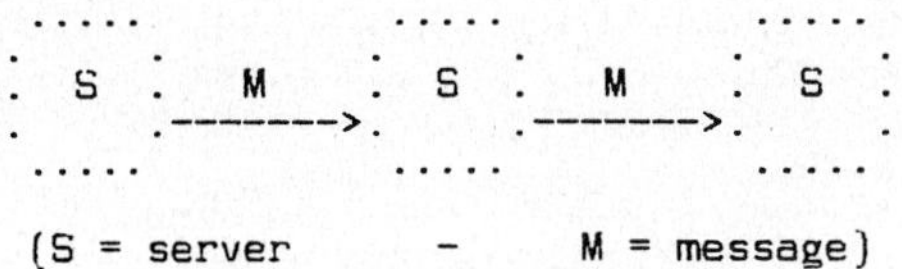

Figure 1: message approach

3.2 The transaction approach

In the transaction approach, each request is implemented as a collaboration between a requester and a server: the requester initiates the request, with appropriate input parameters; the server then performs the request while the requester waits for its completion, at which point results are transferred back. The same requester can then proceed to the next request in the same manner. A request can thus be viewed as a transaction between the requester and the server.

In this case, all the decisions concerning which requests should be made, and to whom, are localized in the requester, leading to a clear separation between the basic functions implemented by the servers, and the high-level ones that are implemented in the requesters.

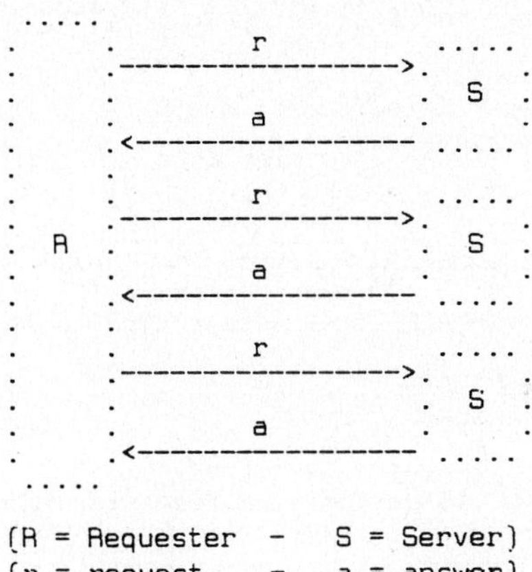

(R = Requester - S = Server)
(r = request - a = answer)

Figure 2: transaction approach

It can be noted that the cooperation paradigm used in the transaction approach is very close to the notion of rendezvous in Ada.

4 INITIAL SOLUTIONS

In either approach, the constraints described in 2 cause two problems that must be addressed: firstly, the appropriate server that will be the destination of a message, or the target of a transaction request will have to be selected dynamically; secondly, it should be possible for servers of different kinds to handle the same request.

Ada offers a certain degree of dynamicity in the way tasks can be created and named, by the use of an access type designating task objects. However, such an access type can only designate tasks of one given type.

As our requirements are somewhat more demanding, we are led to associate a specialized interface task with each server. All interface tasks corresponding to a given kind of transaction (or message) are of a unique type, and they are identified by access values. Each server will have the responsibility of allocating its own interface.

4.1 Solving the dynamic selection problem

The dynamic selection mechanism can now be implemented as follows: for a given kind of request, we will introduce a "dispatch" task that keeps a list of the servers presently available to handle the next request of that kind. When a server is ready to handle a request, it informs the dispatcher, and passes along the identity of its interface task (it is actually the identity of this interface, rather than that of the server itself, that will be saved by the dispatcher). When a request must be issued, the requester obtains from the dispatcher the identity of the next available server interface, and can issue the request directly to that interface. Thus, requesters and servers are isolated from each other as much as possible.

The typical form of a dispatcher is something like:

```
task DISPATCHER is

    -- INTERFACE is an access type to interface tasks

    entry available (I: in INTERFACE);
    -- AVAILABLE is called by a server when ready to accept a
    -- request.

    entry find (I: out INTERFACE);
    -- FIND is called by a requester to  obtain  the identity
    -- of the next available interface.
end DISPATCHER;

task body DISPATCHER is

    -- Here should be some data structures  to  maintain pool
    -- of available interfaces.

    function empty return BOOLEAN;
    -- returns TRUE if there is no available interface.

begin
    loop
        select
            accept available (I: in INTERFACE) do
                -- save I in pool
            end available;
        or  when not empty =>
            accept find (I: out INTERFACE) do
                I := -- some interface taken from pool
            end find;
        end select;
    end loop;
end DISPATCHER;
```

In the following, we will assume the existence of such a dispatcher, operating on interface tasks. We can now attempt at providing solutions for both of the approaches identified.

4.2 Preliminary solution with messages

The basic requirement of a message passing system is that a sender is not required to wait for the receiver when a message is sent. As a consequence, the message must be queued somehow. The canonical Ada solution consists in introducing an auxiliary task to take the message from the sender, and wait until the receiver is ready to accept it. The message will actually be delivered to the interface, whose main purpose is to bring together the messenger and the receiver in a three-party rendezvous, as illustrated below.

```
task type RECEIVER_INTERFACE is
    entry receive (In_Msg: in MESSAGE);
    -- This entry is called by the messenger, which passes the
    -- message along as a parameter.

    entry transmit (Out_Msg: out MESSAGE);
    -- This entry is called by the actual  receiver  to obtain
    -- the message.
end RECEIVER_INTERFACE;

type RECEIVER is access RECEIVER_INTERFACE;

task body RECEIVER_INTERFACE is
begin
    loop
        select
            accept receive (In_Msg: in MESSAGE) do
                accept transmit (Out_Msg: out MESSAGE) do
                    Out_Msg := In_Msg;
                end transmit;
            end receive;
        or
            terminate;
        end select;
    end loop;
end RECEIVER_INTERFACE;
```

A messenger task is equally simple:

```
task type MESSENGER_TASK is
    entry send (M:  in MESSAGE;
                To: in RECEIVER);
end MESSENGER_TASK;

type MESSENGER is access MESSENGER_TASK;

task body MESSENGER_TASK is
    Parcel      : MESSAGE;
    Destination : RECEIVER;
begin
    accept send (M:  in MESSAGE;
                 To: in RECEIVER) do
        -- during the rendezvous,  the  task  merely saves the
        -- message  and  the  identity  of  the   destination.
        Parcel := M;
        Destination := To;
    end send;

    -- The messenger now waits for the message to be accepted,
    -- then dies.
    Destination.receive (Parcel);
end MESSENGER_TASK;
```

4.3 Preliminary solution with transactions

Contrarily to a message system, in the case of transactions, the requester must wait for the result of the transaction, thus reenacting the Ada rendezvous. Unfortunately, the requester does not know the identity of the server, and cannot therefore rendezvous directly with it, having to invoke a given server interface instead. On the other hand, the interface can only accept calls from the server; it cannot call the server directly, for otherwise, the interface type would be dependent on the server type, and would thus defeat the very purpose of interfaces, wiz. to allow requests to be handled by different types of servers.

The transaction must therefore be performed in three distinct steps:

(a) the server obtains the input parameters from its interface (start of transaction);
(b) the actual actions are performed;
(c) the server passes the output parameters back to the interface (end of transaction).

If no transaction has been requested, the server will wait at step a. The requester is blocked until the end of the transaction.

```
task type SERVER_INTERFACE is
    entry request (In_Params  : in  ... ;
                   Out_Params : out ... );
    -- This entry is called by a requester to enter a
    -- transaction

    entry start_transaction (Input : out ... );
    -- This entry is called by the server to obtain the
    -- parameters for the next transaction.

    entry end_transaction (Output : in ... );
    -- This entry is called by the server when the work is
    -- done, to release the requester, and pass the result
    -- parameters.
end SERVER_INTERFACE;

type SERVER is access SERVER_INTERFACE;

task body SERVER_INTERFACE is
begin
    loop
        select
            accept request (In_Params  : in  ...;
                            Out_Params : out ... ) do
                accept start_transaction (Input : out ... ) do
                    Input := In_Params;
                end start_transaction;
                -- The interface waits here while the server
                -- performs the work.
                accept end_transaction (Output : in ... ) do
                    Out_Params := Output;
                end end_transaction;
            end request;

        or
            terminate;
        end select;
    end loop;
end SERVER_INTERFACE;
```

A typical server will contain a sequence such as the one below.

```
          My_Interface : SERVER := new SERVER_INTERFACE;
          ...
     begin
          ...
          loop
               DISPATCHER.available (My_Interface);
               My_Interface.start_transaction (...);
               -- perform the request
               My_Interface.end_transaction (...);
               ...
          end loop;
          ...
     end;
```

5 EXAMINATION OF THE INITIAL SOLUTION

In the preliminary solution, we have addressed two aspects of the initial set of constraints: the dynamic switching requirement, and, to a large extent, the flexibility requirement, since we have made no assumption on the structure of a receiver (resp. server in the transaction approach). These tasks can be programmed in any way that is consistent with the protocol that has been chosen.

We must now consider how these solutions affect the efficiency and extensibility aspects.

In terms of efficiency, the problem may come from the introduction of extra interface tasks, and also, in the message approach, of the creation of an extra task for each message to be transmitted.

Fortunately, owing to the work of Habermann & Nassi (1979), it can be observed that a task that contains only accept statements or selective waits (possibly nested inside loops) can be subjected to a very efficient optimization whereby no separate physical "process" need be created to execute such a task. This is in particular the case of the receiver and server interfaces. However, no such optimization can be performed on a messenger. From an efficiency point of view, the transaction approach is satisfactory, but the message solution should be improved.

With respect to extensibility, one must consider the possibility of adding new kinds of requests, or new kinds of messages. It is possible to add new interface tasks for each kind of request or message that can be handled by a given task. However, a receiver (resp. server) communicates with its interface by issuing an entry call and cannot wait for the first message (resp. request) among different kinds.

One solution would be to encode message (or request) kinds with a certain key. Thus we would not have to extend the existing interfaces, but only the interpretation of keys. Note that this would preclude the use of an enumeration type for the key, since the type would have to be modified whenever a new kind of request is added to the system; hence, the key should be of an integer type. This unfortunately compromises the safety introduced by strong typing.

6 IMPROVEMENTS

We first study the efficiency problem posed by the message approach. We then consider mechanisms to allow multi-way waits in order to increase the flexibility; such mechanisms are presented in the server approach, and can be easily extrapolated for the message approach.

6.1 Efficiency improvement for the message approach

In order to improve the efficiency, a scheme must be devised, where the messenger does not have to initiate the transmission. This can be achieved in two steps: when the sender sends the message, the receiver interface is notified that a message is pending, and is given the identity of the messenger. When the destinee is ready to accept a message, it is given the identity of the messenger, and it can then issue an entry call to obtain the actual message. This solution is feasible only if the receiver interface can respond sufficiently quickly, so as not to unduly delay the sender.

The MESSENGER_INTERFACE task type now becomes:

```
task type MESSENGER_INTERFACE is

    entry send (Msg   : in MESSAGE;
                From  : in MESSENGER;
                To    : in RECEIVER);
    -- This entry is called by a sender, who gives the message
    -- to be sent, indicates the destination (TO), and also
    -- the identity of the messenger_interface itself (i.e.,
    -- FROM should always refer to the task accepting the
    -- call).

    entry transmit (Msg : out MESSAGE);
    -- This entry is called from the receiver when it is ready
    -- to accept the message.

end MESSENGER_INTERFACE;

task body MESSENGER_INTERFACE is
    Saved_Message: MESSAGE;
begin
-- The messenger interface when created, will obtain the
-- message from the sender, and will immediately notify the
-- receiver interface. It then waits for the receiver to ask
-- for the message, delivers it, then terminates.

    accept send (Msg   : in MESSAGE;
                 From  : in MESSENGER;
                 To    : in RECEIVER) do
        Saved_Message := Msg;
        To.waiting_message (From);
    end send;

    accept transmit (Msg : out MESSAGE) do
        Msg := Saved_Message;
    end transmit;
end MESSENGER_INTERFACE;
```

The RECEIVER_INTERFACE is also modified. It is now mostly in charge of keeping track of pending messengers.

```
task type RECEIVER_INTERFACE is

    entry waiting_message (From : in MESSENGER);
    -- This entry is called by a messenger to indicate that
    -- there is a message to be sent. The messenger passes
    -- its identity, which will be recorded so that it can be
    -- called back later for the actual message.

    entry next_messenger (Orig : out MESSENGER);
    -- This entry is called by the actual receiver when it is
    -- ready to service the next request: the identity of one
    -- of the pending messengers will be transmitted, and
    -- deleted from the memory of the receiver interface.

end RECEIVER_INTERFACE;
```

```
task body RECEIVER_INTERFACE is
     ...       -- some data structure to keep a  list  of pending
               -- messengers.
begin
     loop
          select
               accept waiting_message (From : in MESSENGER) do
                    -- record the identity FROM
               end waiting_message;
          or   when waiting_message'COUNT = 0
                         -- This  clause  gives  a priority to  the
                         -- MESSENGERs
                    and is_waiting_message =>
                         -- This clause will block the receiver  if
                         -- there is no message pending.
               accept next_messenger (Orig : out MESSENGER) do
                    Orig := -- some  MESSENGER  selected from  the
                            -- list    kept    by    the    receiver
                            -- interface,    according    to    some
                            -- criterion;
               end next_messenger;
          or
               terminate;
          end select;
     end loop;
end RECEIVER_INTERFACE;
```

A server could obtain the next message by calling the following procedure.

```
procedure get_message (From : in RECEIVER;
                       Msg  : out MESSAGE) is
     Sender: MESSENGER;
begin
     From.next_messenger (Sender);
     Sender.transmit (Msg);
end get_message;
```

The RECEIVER_INTERFACE is coded so that a minimum amount of time is spent inside rendezvous, so as to maximize the availability to a MESSENGER_INTERFACE; this availability is also increased by the priority given to a messenger over a server through the guards. The time spent while the sender is blocked is reduced to a minimum that is commensurate with the time normally spent in a message kernel to register the message.

Note that, in terms of implementation efficiency, each MESSENGER_INTERFACE, and each RECEIVER_INTERFACE as well, is now a passive task in the sense of Habermann and Nassi, so that none of the rendezvous involved requires a context switch (there will of course be a context switch at some point, at least on a monoprocessor system, since the server will eventually take control after the sender). The full message transmission will require four calls that can be implemented as procedure calls. This is to be contrasted with the initial solution, which took only two calls, but with a minimum of three context switches.

6.2 Programming multi-way waits

It is worth examining in more detail what has been achieved by the solution presented in 6.1: a messenger still acts as a message holder, but it will transmit its message on demand directly to the server. The purpose of the RECEIVER_INTERFACE is no longer to achieve a three-way rendezvous between the messenger and the server, but merely to keep track of who is waiting to transmit messages. Messages are no longer queued, but only the identities of messengers are.

This can be exploited, since when the receiver knows there is a message waiting, it does not have to receive it right away. In this way, we can program any selection algorithm among messages of the same type, by passing some extra information concerning the message. This can obviously also apply to transactions. In the remainder, we focus more on the latter approach, chiefly to present a variety of points of view. The reader will easily transpose what is presented to the case of messages.

In order to treat the problem of messages or requests of different types, two strategies are possible: polling techniques, or identification techniques. In the first case, the server would have to interrogate its different interfaces to find out which of them know of pending requests; in the second case, an additional general interface can centralize the list of requests, and tell the server which kind is available.

In both cases, a common necessity appears, namely the need to signal that there is at least one request pending (so that the server can be suspended if there is none). Each server needs a unique "door bell" so that whenever a new message arrives, whatever its kind, the server can be notified. In the solution given below, such a door bell is provided by the task type GATE_INTERFACE.

```
task type GATE_INTERFACE is

     entry signal_request;
     -- This entry is called by the requester to inform the
     -- server that a request has been issued.

     entry request_pending;
     -- This entry will block the server if no request has been
     -- issued.

end GATE_INTERFACE;

type GATE is access GATE_INTERFACE;

task body GATE_INTERFACE is
     N_Requests : INTEGER := 0;   -- indicates the number of
                                  -- pending requests that have
                                  -- not been serviced.
begin
     loop
          select
               accept signal_request do
                    N_Requests := N_Requests + 1;
               end signal_request;
          or   when N_Requests > 0 =>
               accept request_pending do
                    N_Requests := N_Requests - 1;
               end request_pending;
          or
               terminate;
          end select;
     end loop;
end GATE_INTERFACE;
```

The server interface has to be modified slightly to signal the server gate of a newly arrived request (this form of server interface is extrapolated from then one given in 4.3, and from the receiver interface shown in 6.1).

```
task type SERVER_INTERFACE is

     entry initialize (G : in GATE);
     -- This entry is called by the server when a new interface
     -- is allocated, so that the  SERVER_INTERFACE  can inform
     -- the gate of a newly arrived request.

     entry request (In_Params  : in IN_PARAM_TYPE;
                    Out_Params : out OUT_PARAM_TYPE);
     -- This  entry  is  called  by  the requester, who will be
     -- blocked until the transaction is performed.

     entry start_transaction (Input : out IN_PARAM_TYPE);
     -- This entry is called by the server  to  start executing
     -- the request.

     entry end_transaction (Output : in OUT_PARAM_TYPE);
     -- This  entry  is  also  called by the server  after  the
     -- request has been executed.

end SERVER_INTERFACE;

type SERVER is access SERVER_INTERFACE;

task body SERVER_INTERFACE is
     Door_Bell : GATE;          -- The particular gate  associated
                                -- with the server.
begin
     accept initialize (G : in GATE) do
          Door_Bell := G;
     end initialize;
     loop
          select
               accept request (In_Params  : in  IN_PARAM_TYPE;
                               Out_Params : out OUT_PARAM_TYPE) do
                    Door_Bell.signal_request;
                    accept start_transaction (Input : out IN_PARAM_TYPE) do
                         Input := In_Params;
                    end start_transaction;
                    accept end_transaction (Output : in OUT_PARAM_TYPE) do
                         Out_Params := Output;
                    end end_transaction;
               end request;
          or
               terminate;
          end select;
     end loop;
end SERVER_INTERFACE;
```

A server can wait for any request by a call such as:

```
My_Gate.request_pending;
```

but past this point, the server only knows that there is a request pending, without knowing form which source. The particular request must be served by some form of polling, for instance using conditional entry calls:

```
select
     Interface_1.start_transaction (...);
     ...
else
     select
          Interface_2.start_transaction (...);
          ...
     else
          .
          .
          .
     end select;
end select;
```

This polling can be avoided if interfaces are identified by a key that is passed to the gate by the requester, and from the gate to the server. In both cases, it is possible to use different kinds of interfaces, and therefore different types of parameters, since each interface is designated explicitly when the request is serviced.

In terms of efficiency, it can be noted that all the extra tasks introduced (server interfaces and gate) are passive tasks. The number of calls involved to execute a request is five, but with only the minimum number of full context switches possible, namely two.

7 CONCLUSION

The sample system structures that have been considered here are quite typical of a variety of complex software systems. Two apparently different approaches have been dealt with, and it has been shown that satisfactory solutions can be developed in both cases.

One would be tempted to think that the tight coupling of the transaction approach is closer to the Ada concept of rendezvous. However, a look at the full solutions shows that as soon as all the constraints are taken into account, the structure they impose on the overall system prevails over any other consideration, and that the two solutions are strikingly similar.

In terms of efficiency, the feasibility of the solutions relies on known implementation techniques. It is important to stress the desirability of these optimizations. At the time of writing, the author knows of at least two validated Ada compilers where provisions have been made to incorporate such optimizations.

The introduction of small "interface" tasks of reduced complexity, whose identity can be passed back and forth, comes as an elegant solution to a variety of problems. Interfaces can be considered as one example of objects that are implemented as Ada tasks: they are objects in the sense that they represent a rather passive abstraction (e.g., a communication port). The ability to depart from the traditional one-to-one correspondence between tasks and processes seems to be of substantial importance in order to make full use of the Ada tasking facilities. These can then be of substantial use to solve a number of problems that do not have any specific real-time characteristics. A typical application is the use of an object-oriented programming style. Related ideas have been presented by Hilfinger (1982).

On the negative side, one can regret that although an efficient solution can be attained, efficiency should impose a certain style on the program. Furthermore, when examining the solutions, as seen by the implementor of the system, rather than by the user, a certain complexity can be observed, which can be tracked to the fairly static aspect of the naming and typing rules of the language.

REFERENCES

DoD (1983). Reference Manual for the Ada Programming Language. ANSI/MIL-STD 1815A, United States Department of Defense, January 1983.

Habermann, A.N. & Nassi, I.R. (1980). Efficient Implementation of Ada Tasks. Technical report CMU-CS-80-103, Department of Computer Science, Carnegie-Mellon University, January 1980.

Hilfinger, P.N., (1982). Implementation Strategies for Ada Tasking Idioms. Proc. AdaTEC Conference on Ada, Crystal City (Va.), October 1982.

Lauer, H.C., and Needham, R.M. (1978). On the Duality of Operating System Structures. in Proc. Second International Symposium on Operating Systems, IRIA, Rocquencourt (FRANCE), October 1978. (Reprinted in Operating Systems Review, 13, no.2, April 1979.

Lessons From Practical Experience Teaching Hands-On, Real-Time, Embedded System Programming With Ada

R. J. A. Buhr

Department of Systems and Computer Engineering,
Carleton University, Ottawa, Ontario, CANADA

ABSTRACT

This paper analyzes practical experience at Carleton University with a course in hands-on, real time, embedded system programming with Ada, derives lessons from this experience relating to the concerns of the Ada community about teaching/learning Ada in this area, and makes consequential recommendations regarding course content, student preparation and resource requirements.

1. INTRODUCTION

In fall of 1984 an experimental course in hands-on, real time embedded system programming was offered to a group of selected undergraduate and graduate computer systems engineering students at Carleton University. The laboratory for the course supported the development, on an Intellimac system, of real time, interrupt driven, multitasking programs for a Dy4 Motorola 68000 based VME board, using Telesoft software. Although courses in system design with Ada (Ada is a registered trademark of the U.S. Government (Ada Joint Program Office)) had been offered at Carleton for several years before this, using the ideas in Buhr (1984), never before had an Ada programming course been offered, mainly because of the lack of availability at Carleton of Ada compilers on teaching computers. Thus, no one in the course had any Ada programming experience. Furthermore, not all of the students in the real time course had taken the previous Ada-based design courses, although they had all been exposed to similar design concepts for non-Ada environments. The course was therefore somewhat of a leap in the dark, even though we were convinced beforehand that all the correct elements were in place to make it work.

The nature of this course, and the lessons learned from it, are thought to be of wider interest to the Ada community, because of current concerns in this community about teaching embedded system programming in Ada.

We begin by identifying the concerns of the Ada community in this area as we understand them. Then we describe the Carleton experience and the lessons learned therefrom, in relation to these concerns. Finally we present conclusions.

2. CONCERNS OF THE ADA COMMUNITY

The major issues which have arisen on this subject in discussions with members of the Ada community are as follows:

1. While many aspects of Ada are comfortable for recent computer science or computer engineering graduates, few existing embedded system implementors have this kind of background. The problem of converting such existing practitioners is perceived as a significant one.
2. Proper use of Ada for embedded systems requires that the system be designed first, at a higher level than programming. The necessary design expertise is in short supply, both among practitioners in the field and among members of the teaching profession.

3. The idea of designing programs as collections of interconnected, concurrently operating black boxes (important when using Ada for embedded systems) is foreign to many traditional programmers and even to many new computer science graduates.
4. Many existing, traditional programmers find that the features of Ada most important for embedded systems require a new way of thinking, for which they are ill prepared. Such programmers often have built in preconceptions about programs as sequential algorithms. They are likely to have flow charts as the underlying mental model of program organization and execution, even if they actually program in higher level languages such as Pascal. This is because, historically, most first introductions to programming have started with flow charts. They find it difficult to make the mental leap to the design of modular, concurrent programs of the kind required for embedded systems.
5. Embedded systems need what many may think of as advanced features of Ada (packages, tasks, interrupts, representation specs, generics, exceptions). A traditional approach to learning Ada programming would not introduce these features until mastery is achieved of the more "conventional" features of the language. However, this requires too much time and effort, because Ada is very rich in "conventional" features, which take considerable time and effort to master.
6. It is important to take advantage of the familiarity with hardware of existing implementors of embedded systems in devising ways of retraining them in Ada. Such implementors, although they may retain the flow chart model of programs at the assembly language level, are used to dealing with concurrency and real time at the hardware/software interface. For such practitioners, the appropriate mental model of an Ada program may be a set of interconnected, concurrently operating, hardware black boxes.

3. THE CARLETON EXPERIENCE

3.1. Design Courses

Design courses in Ada have been taught at Carleton to graduate and undergraduate students, both full time and part time (from local industry) for a number of years. Several short, intensive courses have also been taught to specialized audiences. Out of the material of these courses emerged the author's book on system design with Ada (Buhr, 1984). Furthermore, several non-Ada courses at Carleton have been taught using the methodology of Buhr (1984), adapted to non-Ada environments.

In the author's personal experience with these courses, the underlying principles behind the use of Ada for embedded systems are relatively easy to teach to young people in undergraduate courses who have not had time to develop a flowchart mind-set about programming. What works best with such students in practice is a combination of design principles with hands on concurrent programming experience. These principles are also relatively easy to teach to electrical/electronics engineers working in chip or board design, not only because such engineers have not had the opportunity to develop the wrong mindset about programming, but also because they are comfortable with the idea of systems as collections of interconnected, concurrently operating black boxes.

These principles can be difficult to teach to hardened practitioners of traditional programming. In this case, what is needed is time, opportunity, and incentive to make the transition to the necessary new mental models. However, even if time and opportunity are present, incentive may be a problem. Hardened practitioners are likely to treat Ada as "yet another programming language" about which they must learn syntactic details to enable them to do the same old things. They may be impatient with attempts to convince them that a new way of thinking is required. The author is aware of some interesting experiments (reported on verbally) where FORTRAN programmers turned loose on Ada produced FORTRAN in Ada syntax, with tasks using large amounts of global data and large numbers of unpackaged global procedures. There is wide agreement in the Ada community that such an approach is unsatisfactory.

3.2. Carleton's Embedded System Course

The course concentrated on two features of real time, embedded system programming: concurrent program organization to achieve control of external devices; and testing and debugging in a stripped-down target environment with limited high level tools.

The course did not attempt to convert the students into expert Ada programmers on a broad front. Therefore it did not cover some topics of undoubted importance to real time embedded systems, such as fixed point arithmetic (or, indeed, arithmetic of any kind), generics, dynamic tasking (except as required to allow main programs to terminate gracefully) and exceptions. Assignments requiring the writing of long or complex program bodies were avoided in the course. Instead any complexity in the course assignments came from the need to coordinate and test the interaction of a number of concurrent components, each of which was quite simple by itself.

The lectures covered the following material:

1. Overview of Ada highlights needed for this course.
2. Review SDWA (Buhr, 1984) graphical shorthand for describing program organization, motivated by the similarity to hardware schematics.
3. Without further ado, or lengthy discussion of the organization of multitasking programs, jump straight into designing and writing interrupt handlers and debuggers in Ada on the Intellimac for the Dy4 (rely on background preparation here). Do it this way to provide a solid foundation for later discussions of design at a higher level.
4. Capabilities and operation of the Telesoft Embedded System Kit.
5. Functionality and control of the target run time system.
6. Communication between interrupt handlers and higher level tasks (shared buffers, rendezvous only at critical points, etc.).
7. Issues in event-driven, multitasking program organization, using graphical paradigms.
8. Testing and debugging, in the context of a thorough review of the testing/debugging facilities in the laboratory.
9. Error handling mechanisms available via the embedded system kit and/or the run time system.
10. Discuss Ada's real time capabilities and shortcomings.

The laboratory projects included interrupt-driven driver packages for timer chip and UART chip support, higher level multitasking programs to use the driver packages, development of test/debug packages written in Ada, and testing and evaluation of error handling mechanisms supported by the target run time system.

We are aware of no adequate text book for such a course. We relied primarily on the Ada Reference Manual, on the supplier's manuals for the laboratory hardware and software, and on a special laboratory manual written during a summer project to develop the laboratory, which provided walkthroughs, guidelines and sample programs. The author's design book (Buhr, 1984) served as a methodology reference.

The course had approximately 30 hours of lectures plus an additional 6 or so hours per project group of student/instructor contact. Independent time spent in the laboratory probably accounted for at least an additional 36 hours for each student and (hopefully) at most 72 hours.

As an intensive short course, the same material would require two weeks of calendar time, including many evenings and weekends of independent effort in the laboratory during this two weeks, or three weeks of calendar time, without the commitment of evenings and weekends.

The students taking this course almost all had the following common elements in their backgrounds (one or two had more experience than this, one had less - the one with less experience found it very time consuming to keep up):

1. some programming experience in Carleton courses in FORTRAN, PL/M, Pascal and assembly language (although in no case assembly language for the M68000);

2. some real time programming experience in a Carleton course using a multitasking operating system environment (RMX86);

3. some practical familiarity with the typical features of a microprocessor board from a programmer's viewpoint, acquired in a variety of Carleton courses, or through practical experience;

4. exposure to the methodology of (Buhr, 1984) or a variant of it;

5. no embedded system development experience;

6. no Ada programming experience.

The students with this background had no problem learning the amount of Ada required for this course; in fact, several commented how easy they found it to get into Ada and how much they liked working with Ada at this level. The author believes that the keys here are two: knowledge of Pascal (which is similar enough to the "traditional" areas of Ada that Ada presents no conceptual hurdles in these areas); and philosophical preparation. They all entered this course with a background in high level languages and in multitasking at both the design principles level and the nuts and bolts experience level. Thus they were ready for Ada as it is presented in this course.

The laboratory used consists of an Intellimac Motorola 68000 system with a Telesoft Ada compiler and Embedded System kit as a development system, capable of preparing real time Ada software for downloading, and a Dy4 DVME multiprocessor system as a target system to which the real time Ada software prepared on the development system can be downloaded. The laboratory supports real time programming through the carefully thought out "fast interrupt" mechanisms of the Telesoft run time system, which are capable of handling interrupts without task context switching. The debugging support for the target environment consists only of a conventional Motorola-type ROM monitor, providing breakpointing and disassembly, among other features.

Although the users of such a laboratory can in principle write all of their programs in Ada, they cannot entirely avoid descending conceptually, and in some cases actually, to the assembly language or machine level. They must know how to control the devices on the target system boards from their Ada programs. This involves reading device documentation intended for assembly language programmers. Even if in principle it is possible to avoid low level debugging through machine level breakpoint and data addresses, the presence of a sufficiently powerful ROM monitor to do these things encourages its use. Furthermore, it is a mistake to try and avoid such low level interactions in an embedded system course, given that one of the purposes of such a course is to give students the opportunity of becoming comfortable with working at the hardware/software boundary.

These considerations all point to a requirement at the very least for the Ada programmer to have knowledge of the physical organization of the program in memory and to have access to low level run time control mechanisms over the processor (such as to enable and disable the processor interrupts). It is also obviously desirable, though difficult to accomplish with commercial products, to have source listings of the run time system, to enable run time problems to be investigated and solved in a timely fashion. Two examples will illustrate these points.

The first example relates to the need for breakpointing. The Telesoft Embedded System Kit fails to produce a symbol table for the Ada program which is to be downloaded. As we understand it, this is because the kit was developed independently of the compiler under the constraint that it not require any changes to the compiler. Because there is no requirement to produce symbol tables in ordinary use of the compiler for non-embedded systems, they are not produced. Therefore, in our laboratory, programmers wishing to use the breakpointing facility of the monitor (which includes everyone) must seed their programs with address attribute statements and arrange to have the addresses displayed after the program is downloaded but before it starts running. Then, using the disassembly feature of the monitor, they can select where to plant the breakpoints.

The second example relates to the need to control the enabling and disabling of processor interrupts. One of the projects of the course was to write interrupt driven Ada programs to support the timer chip on the Dy4 board. A characteristic of Telesoft's Embedded System Kit is that the processor status register priority used for enabling interrupts on startup is set before downloading. When we were using only the USART chip, before attempting to use the timer chip, we had set this startup value so that the relavent processor interrupt levels were enabled when the program started to run, without any problems. However, this strategy led to failures when trying to use the timer chip. One characteristic of the timer is that it is prone to generating unwanted interrupts immediately on power up, before there has been time for the Ada program to make the required run time system calls to bind the timer interrupt task to the timer interrupt vector. Therefore the processor was getting interrupts before a vector had been established for them, resulting in a crash.

What we wanted to do was set the startup priority before downloading to disable all processor interrupts initially and then to enable them from the running Ada program after it had performed interrupt vector binding; however, there is no documented method of doing so in Telesoft's manuals. Discussions of the problem with Telesoft experts revealed that there is a pair of undocumented enable/disable calls in the same run time package that supports interrupt vector binding which are useable for exactly our purpose. However, they had not been provided in the user documentation, because the idea of interrupt enabling and disabling is not supported in the Ada language. There are other ways of handling this problem, but the use of enable and disable calls appeared to the students to be the most natural way.

These two examples illustrate the type of low level interactions required and the need for environment support for such interactions. They also illustrate a further point. A real time embedded system development laboratory is a complex environment requiring interaction by students at many levels. An essential first step before offering a course using such a laboratory is a thorough shakeout of the hardware and software, followed by the preparation of documentation describing walkthroughs of its use, sample programs and important tricks. We have prepared such documentation for the particular laboratory used for this course. It has been an essential component in enabling the students to get started quickly and to keep going effectively.

4. REQUIRED STUDENT BACKGROUND AND AN APPROACH TO PROVIDING IT

The experience recounted earlier indicates that the following background is required before approaching real time embedded system programming with Ada:

Necessary background:

1. Familiarity (including programming experience) with Pascal, to ease the transition to learning the mechanical details of Ada. The important points here are: structured program control; procedures and functions, including the syntax and semantics of parameter passing; arrays, records (including variant records) and pointers; programmer defined types; programming of typical data structures useful in embedded systems, such as stacks, queues and ring buffers. If similar experience has been gained with some other high level programming language, then reading knowledge of Pascal would probably be sufficient.

2. Practical knowledge of the organization of a typical microprocessor board as seen by a programmer, with emphasis on: interrupt control (enabling, disabling, vectoring, priority setting, etc.); device register mapping and access; low level device programming; memory organization. Specific knowledge of the particular processor chip employed (in our case, the M68000) is desirable, but is not necessary. This practical knowledge could have been obtained in a variety of ways: real time assembly language programming courses at university or technical college; experience in the field with embedded system implementation. Experience indicates that reading knowledge alone of this area is not sufficient.

3. An introduction to design principles. A suitable approach is through the author's SDWA book (Buhr, 1984).

Desirable Background:

4. In addition, it is desirable to have some concurrent programming experience. This experience is desirable prior to or in conjunction with Item 3, above. It is not essential that this experience be in Ada. The need for this experience depends on the student's philosophical preparation for a design methodology which treats embedded systems

as collections of interconnected, concurrently operating black boxes. As described earlier, experience suggests that not all individuals are ready for such an approach. Ideally for those requiring it, this item would be combined with Item 3 in a single course. This leads to the idea of a preparatory course for such students.

A Preparatory Course: "An Introduction to System Design and Concurrent Programming With Ada"

This course would be optional for many of the students satisfying the necessary background requirements defined earlier. It would combine Items 3 and 4 of these requirements into a single course providing an introduction to design and concurrent programming in Ada. Students would be required to satisfy Item 3 before coming to the course. The course would require roughly the same time and effort as the embedded system course. Approximately one quarter of the time would be spent on consolidating the major ideas in SDWA and the remainder of the time split between independent programming activity and laboratory sessions covering programming problems and issues. The SDWA material would provide the examples to be implemented as concurrent programs.

The CAEDE system (Buhr & Karam, 1984; Buhr et al., 1985) would be an ideal vehicle for the design principles part of the course and would provide an excellent bridge to the implementation of concurrent programs.

Any Ada compiler can be used for the concurrent programming component of this course, provided it has minimal support for tasks, and supports task timeouts, so that real time events can be simulated without interrupt programming.

Such a course has not been given at Carleton yet, because of the lack of availability of an Ada compiler for the programming laboratories currently used by our computer system engineering students. Instead, we accomplish much the same purpose through a course which covers multitasking design principles and programming practice for an RMX86 operating system environment.

The author's SDWA methodology (Buhr, 1984) occupies a prominent place in these recommendations. Is this methodology appropriate for wide use in the Ada community for this purpose? The author believes so, based on positive feedback not only from students in Carleton courses, but also from members of the Ada community at large (Corr., 1984).

5. CONCLUSIONS

Experience at Carleton with teaching design and embedded system programming with Ada shows how concerns of the Ada community about training methods in these areas can be met.

The students from the embedded system course are comfortable with Ada (although not necessarily expert in all of it) and are confident in working with it at the hardware/software interface level. They are able to design appropriate multitasking organizations for various hardware/software interface purposes, to reason about the temporal behaviour of their designs and to test this behaviour in practice with various software and hardware tools.

Keys to this success are: a design-oriented viewpoint, following the author's SDWA methodology, with some student preparation in this viewpoint first; student background in Pascal, so that the course can concentrate on those aspects of Ada which are crucial for embedded systems, namely packaging, tasking, representation specifications and interrupts, and virtually ignore the rest; student preparation in hardware/software interfacing; and an appropriate laboratory environment supporting real time interrupts vectored to Ada tasks and tools to interact with running programs in the target system in terms of the target hardware, not just the Ada program.

6. ACKNOWLEDGMENTS

Grateful acknowledgment is made of the efforts of numerous Carleton students who took the author's courses and contributed to improving them.

The Canadian Navy provided the equipment for the real time embedded system programming course and funded the development of a suitable laboratory for student use based on this equipment.

Heather Buhr, Cheryl Schramm and Trevor Pearce developed the laboratory to a useable state by writing test programs and case studies and by charting useable paths through a complex hardware/software environment, beset with shortcomings, errors, and undocumented mechanisms.

Thanks are due to Telesoft, who had the conviction to develop and put on the market the embedded system kit and run time support system which made the embedded system course possible; and to Born Rasumussen of Telesoft, who contributed to our knowledge of how to use it effectively.

7. REFERENCES

Buhr, R.J.A. (1984). *System Design With Ada.* Englewood Cliffs, N.J., USA: Prentice Hall.

Buhr, R.J.A. & Karam, G.M. (1985). "An Informal Overview of CAEDE". Invited Paper, *Santa Barbara workshop on Future Ada Environments.* Santa Barbara, Ca., USA, (to appear in *Ada Letters).*

Buhr, R.J.A., Karam, G.M., Woodside, C.M. (1985). "An Overview and Example of Application of CAEDE: A New, Experimental Design Environment for Ada". *Proceedings of the International Ada Conference.* Paris, France.

Comm. (1984). Private communications with: Don Rudisill and D.J. Herkimer, Martin-Marietta, Denver. Col., Gregory McFarland, Grumman Data Systems, Bethpage, N.Y., Reuben Jones, Softech, Waltham, Mass., S. Hirsch, Raytheon Submarine Systems Division., Bob Lent, Amdahl Corp, Sunnyvale. Ca., Ken Bowles, Telesoft, San Diego. Ca., Stephen Franklin, U.C. Irvine, Ca., Herm Fischer, Litton Industries., Tony Brintzenhoff, Syscon, San Diego. Ca., J. D. McGonagle, GE Research, Schenectady, N.Y., Mark Gerhardt, Mitre-Bedford, Bedford, Mass., Joseph Johovich, Natl. Radio Astronomy Observatory, N.M.

IN SEARCH OF "REAL" ADA*

A Software Saga with a Moral or Two

Bryce M. Bardin and Marion F. Moon
Software Engineering Division
Ground Systems Group
Hughes Aircraft Company

A short time ago, in a place nearby, a well-seasoned and battle-scarred software engineer, whose mind had survived veritable waves of horrible languages without ossifying and who had studied the Ada Reference Manual carefully and read the gospels according to Barnes and Booch, set out to try his hand at writing an Ada program. This was one of the first Ada programs he had tried to write so he wanted to keep everything simple; that is why he decided to code a binary search routine. After some thought, what he wrote was (apart from some minor syntax errors) the following:

```
generic
   type Index is (<>);
   type Item is private;
   type Row is array (Index range <>) of Item;
   with function "<" (Left, Right : Item) return Boolean;
   with function "=" (Left, Right : Item) return Boolean;
   with function ">" (Left, Right : Item) return Boolean;
function Bin_Search (R : in Row; K : in Item) return Index;
```

---

* Ada is a registered trademark of the U.S. Government (Ada Joint Program Office)

```
function Bin_Search (R : in Row; K : in Item) return Index is
   L : Integer := Row'Succ(Row'First);
   U : Integer := Row'Last;
   M : Integer;
begin
   loop
      M := (L + U)/2;
      if L > U then
         return Row'First;
      end if;
      if R(Index'Val(M)) < K then
         L := M + 1;
      elsif R(Index'Val(M)) > K then
         U := M - 1;
      elsif R(Index'Val(M)) = K then
         return Index'Val(M);
      end if;
   end loop;
end Bin_Search;
```

As you can see, O Best Beloved, the software engineer was a pretty smart cookie. He had caught on to quite a few of the more sophisticated ideas of Ada right off, and was putting them straight to use. (Although he would have had a few surprises when he tried to compile and execute the code. The Gentle Reader may enjoy guessing what diagnostics his or her favorite compiler will give. (Aha! Missed one, didn't you!))

However, he got a lot of things right. The idea that all you care about the items to be searched is their ordering relations; the idea that you don't care how big the array is; and the idea that it doesn't matter what the index type is -- all these considerations lead to the use of a generic function. The use of attributes is the right idea, although incorrectly carried out. (Not to worry. One or two correct uses in this kind of context will suffice to provide mastery.)

And, of course, returning a conventional value when the search fails is traditional.

At this point, the local Ada fakir looked at the code and saw that it was a nice example of good Ada, except -- well -- it needed just a few small changes and improvements to make it "real" Ada. They talked it over and decided how to fix the usage of attributes (you have to be sure you have integer numbers before you can average them, of course). Then they discussed what value to return when the search failed, and the fakir had this neat idea to allow the user to specify the value he wanted, but even neater was that Ada allowed a default so that if the user was lazy it could be taken care of for him. As an afterthought, since Ada has exceptions, they decided maybe it would be a good idea to let the user decide he would rather have an exception raised when the search fails. And lo, Ada is so flexible that a way could be found to do this!

So the fakir jumped right in and made the changes ("This is so simple that all I need to do is just mark up the original."):

```
generic
   type Index is (<>);
   type Item is limited private;
   type Row is array (Index range <>) of Item;
   Not_Present : in Index := Index'First;
   with function "=" (Left, Right : Item) return Boolean is <>;
   with function "<" (Left, Right : Item) return Boolean is <>;
package Searching is
   function Binary_Search (Table : in Row; Key : in Item)
      return Index;
   Not_Found : exception;
end Searching;
```

```
package body Searching is
   function Binary_Search (Table : in Row; Key : in Item)
      return Index is
      subtype Int is Integer
         range Index'Pos(Index'First) .. Index'Pos(Index'Last);
      Lo  : Int := Index'Pos(Table'First);
      Mid : Int;
      Hi  : Int := Index'Pos(Table'Last);
   begin
      if Not_Present in Table'Range then
         raise Program_Error;
      end if;
      loop
         if Lo > Hi then
            if Not_Present = Index'Last then
               raise Not_Found;
            else
               return Not_Present;
            end if;
         end if;
         Mid := (Lo + Hi)/2;
         if Table(Index'Val(Mid)) = Key then
            return Index'Val(Mid);
         elsif Table(Index'Val(Mid)) < Key then
            Lo := Mid + 1;
         else
            Hi := Mid - 1;
         end if;
      end loop;
   end Binary_Search;
end Searching;
```

Now the fakir had done some good things, O Best Beloved. He had magically changed the function into a package, which is not to be wondered at, since that is the way Ada (largely) is. He had provided convenient default boxes for the generic formal functions; he had eliminated the redundant test and not imported the corresponding relational operator; and he had fixed the algorithm so it might actually work (most of the time). Finally, he had messed around with the names of things to make them nicer to read. But, in spite of everything he had done, he felt it was not real Ada yet.

It bothered him that the way the user specifies that he wants to have Not_Found raised is to set Not_Present to Index'Last, which is ugly; and he felt he really ought to do something about the possibility of overflow.

To fix the first problem he added a declaration to the package specification:

```
Raise_Not_Found : Boolean := False;
-- If Raise_Not_Found is true and the search fails, Not_Found will
-- be raised. If Raise_Not_Found is false and the search fails,
-- Not_Present will be returned, unless Not_Present is within
-- Table'Range (in which case Program_Error will be raised).
```

He also modified the first if_statement to read:

```
if not Raise_Not_Found and then Not_Present in Table'Range then
   raise Program_Error;
end if;
```

and the second if_statement to read:

```
if Lo > Hi then
   if Raise_Not_Found then
      raise Not_Found;
   else
      return Not_Present;
   end if;
end if;
```

To fix the second problem, he changed the value of Mid to:

```
-- This expression cannot overflow:
Mid := Lo/2 + Hi/2 + (Lo rem 2 + Hi rem 2)/2;
```

Now, surely, it was real Ada and he proudly showed the results of a successful test case to the old-timer.

After the pleasurable glow of success wore off, however, he began to realize there were still deficiencies in the program. Firstly, he imagined what would happen to his package if he tried to use it on a machine with 16-bit predefined Integers and an array of more than 32,767 items (perhaps indexed by Long_Integers). Horrors! It would fail to compile!

Well, he thought, that should be easy enough to fix, just redefine Int as:

```
type Int is range System.Min_Int .. System.Max_Int;
```

This seemed to be the best that could be done to extend the range so the chances for overflow would be minimal, but it didn't really leave a good feeling when he put it in.

It wasn't until he showed the code to a distant Ada guru that he got an answer that felt right. The fakir wasn't using attributes the way he should have! It is not necessary to define a new type to perform the averaging; it can be done directly. And what's more, when it is done properly, it also becomes clear how to solve the overflow problem, too.

At the same time, he was not at all happy with how complex the package was getting to be, and (finally!) he began to think about what the "correct" abstraction should be like in Ada.

Returning a conventional value when the search fails, although a convenient solution in many languages, is really not very safe because it provides no semantic help for performing the test against the correct value. In Ada, with its strong typing, it is generally a drag to provide for that extra value (you really need an extra subtype for the index) and you have to carefully check to be sure you never accidentally use it as a key. And returning a boolean status is not much better, since it is easy to forget to test it. The only solution which guarantees that the user of the package will be forced to use it correctly is to raise an exception when the search fails, and this solution both simplifies and clarifies the code.

Finally, he also took a look at how a user would call the function, and this lead him to change some of the names and the order of the parameters.

When the changes were made, the fakir was finally satisfied, "It's real Ada now," he said.

```
--
-- Authors:  Marion Moon and Bryce Bardin
--           Software Engineering Division
--           Ground Systems Group
--           Hughes Aircraft Company
--           Fullerton, CA
--
-- This package implements a generic binary search function.
--
generic

   type Index is (<>);
   type Item is limited private;
   type Table is array (Index range <>) of Item;

   with function "=" (Left, Right : Item) return Boolean is <>;
   with function ">" (Left, Right : Item) return Boolean is <>;
```

```
package Binary_Search is

   function Index_Of (Value : in Item; Within : in Table)
      return Index;
   -- Returns the Index of the Item in Within which matches Value
   -- if there is one, otherwise raises Not_Found.
   -- Precondition:  Within must already be sorted in monotonic
   -- ascending order.

   Not_Found : exception;
   -- Raised if the search fails.

end Binary_Search;


package body Binary_Search is

   function Index_Of (Value : in Item; Within : in Table)
      return Index is

      -- If Value is anywhere in Within, its index is in the range
      -- Within'First .. Within'Last.
      Lo  : Index := Within'First;
      Mid : Index;
      Hi  : Index := Within'Last;

   begin

      loop
      -- Invariant:  if Value is anywhere in Within, it must be
      -- between Within(Lo) and Within(Hi).

         -- If the index range is empty, then Value is not in Within.
         if Lo > Hi then
            raise Not_Found;
         end if;
```

```
      -- Calculate the mean Index value, using an expression
      -- which can never overflow:
      Mid := Index'Val(Index'Pos(Lo)/2 + Index'Pos(Hi)/2 +
               (Index'Pos(Lo) rem 2 + Index'Pos(Hi) rem 2)/2);

      if Within(Mid) = Value then

         -- Value was found, return its index.
         return Mid;

      elsif Within(Mid) > Value then

         -- If Value is anywhere in Within, it must now be
         -- between Within(Lo) and Within(Index'Pred(Mid)).
         -- This statement can raise Constraint_Error, but
         -- in that case the search has failed:
         Hi := Index'Pred(Mid);

      else

         -- If Value is anywhere in Within, it must now be
         -- between Within(Index'Succ(Mid)) and Within(Hi).
         -- This statement can raise Constraint_Error, but
         -- in that case the search has failed:
         Lo := Index'Succ(Mid);

      end if;

   end loop;

exception
   when Constraint_Error => raise Not_Found;
end Index_Of;

end Binary_Search;
```

The resulting package is completely general and portable, the code is easy to read (with the possible exception of the one line where the index averaging is performed), and, what is perhaps amazing to realize, this generality and portability comes at no additional cost in any reasonable implementation.

Attributes take a little getting used to, so an explanation of the calculation of Mid may be in order here. Lo and Hi will be internally represented simply as their corresponding position numbers (that is, Index'Pos(Lo) and Index'Pos(Hi)). (The position numbers of discrete types are just their (integer) internal representation. For enumeration types they begin at zero and increment by one for each succeeding value. For integer types, they are simply the values themselves.)

In the worst case, both position numbers will have the same value and that value will correspond to one of the limits of their base type, either Index'Base'Pos(Index'Base'First) or Index'Base'Pos(Index'Base'Last), and thus both have the same parity, either even or odd. By dividing each position number by 2 before summing the quotients, the magnitude of the sum is bounded so that it can't overflow. If both are even, the sum of their quotients will be the same as their common value; if odd, one less in magnitude. The magnitude of the quotient of the sum of the remainders is either zero or one, depending on whether they are even or odd, respectively, so the final value of Mid is also bounded by their common value. No change of internal representation is ever required and the code is just as efficient for enumeration index types as for integer index types (in fact, it will generally be the same).

An interesting observation is that the only places where Constraint_Error can be raised (and only Constraint_Error is raised by Succ and Pred) correspond exactly to where Not_Found is to be raised. This can happen only in limiting cases:

1) when Mid = Within'First and Within'First > Index'Base'First, assignment of the value of Index'Pred(Mid) to Lo will raise Constraint_Error, and

2) when Mid = Index'Base'First (and thus, of necessity, Mid = Within'First), evaluation of Index'Pred(Mid) will raise Constraint_Error (see ARM 3.5.5/9).

The first case is not uncommon, but the second case would be extremely rare. Two analogous cases exist for the other end of the range of index values.

A common approach in programming search routines in other languages in the past has been to use a dummy item or sentinel to return a value when the search fails. This causes a variety of problems in Ada, however. As Ada is going to do constraint checks anyway, we may as well take advantage of them. Then no explicit checks need to be made to see if we have exhausted all items in the array and, in fact, the loop terminates immediately without doing the now redundant loop termination check. Using exceptions in this manner seems quite natural to Ada and may become idiomatic in use.

An additional statement may optionally be inserted before the loop when large arrays are to be searched and it is desired to minimize the cost of fruitless searches at the expense of some fixed overhead for all searches (in that case, the statements within the loop will never raise Constraint_Error):

```
if Lo > Hi or else
   Within(Lo) > Value or else
   Value > Within(Hi) then
      raise Not_Found;
end if;
```

Whether this statement is desirable depends on the expected usage, so we have left it out for now.

We believe that the final algorithm given here displays the full power of Ada's ability to express abstraction. It will work properly for sorted arrays of any size and any index type which is supported by the implementation, including null (empty) arrays. The arrays may be composed of any type of item, including composite types.

Although it is beyond the scope of this paper to demonstrate it, the user can redefine both "=" and ">" for any type, including non-limited types (in spite of section 6.7/4 of the Ada Reference Manual, which prohibits directly overloading equality for non-limited types). In any case, the names of the generic actual parameters corresponding to "=" and ">" are in fact arbitrary. As long as the parameter and result type profiles match that of the formal parameters, the functions with which the package is instantiated may be defined in any suitable fashion. In particular, the relations may compare only selected parts of the data structure of the type. Thus we assert that the binary search algorithm given here can easily be made to work on every array type that can sensibly be sorted and then searched!

Now for the MORALs (no story about software would be complete without several):

More is not necessarily better. Don't overuse Ada's keen features.

There is no substitute for iteration and critical review.

Many sets of eyes are far better than one set, no matter how experienced and clever they are. (And don't forget the user's view!)

Portability and reusability take considerable extra effort to achieve, although experience undoubtedly will help to make it easier.

When found, the best solution in Ada is often the simplest and at the same time the most elegant solution of all.

DEVELOPING AN AUTOMATED ADA TRAINING PRODUCT

Rene Beretz
Alsys, S.A.; 29, ave. de Versailles
78170 La Celle St.-Cloud
France

Benjamin M. Brosgol
Alsys, Inc.; 1432 Main St.; Waltham, Mass. 02154
U.S.A.

Abstract. The emergence of Ada as a major programming language, and the resulting need for training large numbers of programmers in Ada, has led to the development of a variety of educational products and techniques. These include live courses and seminars, textbooks, videotaped instruction, and Computer-Based Training ("CBT"). In this paper we describe the major technical decisions and Ada educational approach that shaped the design of a particular CBT product developed by Alsys -- LESSONS ON ADA. We present the reasons behind the decisions, give an example from one of the lessons that illustrates the educational approach, and summarize future directions for the product.

BACKGROUND

The LESSONS ON ADA effort began in late 1982, based on a 3-day seminar on the Ada language that had been developed by J. D. Ichbiah, J. G. P. Barnes and R. J. Firth. The intent was to provide a training product that would run on the IBM PC, taking the same educational approach that had been successful in the seminar -- using an example-driven strategy to give students an intuitive grasp of the language constructs -- and adding exercises to reinforce and test students' understanding of the major points.

Additionally, as we shall discuss below, experience from the seminar influenced two decisions on the hardware configuration for the CBT product: the use of color, and the use of two independent displays.

The project comprised the design and implementation of a PC-based authoring system with accompanying tools, and the development of the lessons themselves. A new authoring system was needed because of the requirement to display material on two screens and the sophistication of the response analysis, which we describe later in this paper.

LESSONS ON ADA comprises 27 lessons divided into two volumes. The first volume, "Building Blocks for Modern Programming," comprises fifteen lessons covering program structure, types, subtypes, subprograms, packages, statements and scope/ visibility. The second volume, "Elements for Advanced Programming," comprises twelve lessons covering real arithmetic, tasking, exception handling, generics, separate compilation, input-output, and low-level facilities. The first volume was completed in Spring 1984, and the second volume in Fall 1984.

The product is distributed with a User's Guide, lesson diskettes (four for Volume I, and five for Volume II), and a system diskette. The system diskette contains an interpreter for displaying the encoded lesson text and a configuration program that allows users to specify such information as default disk drives and color schemes.

Lesson preparation effort came to about 50 to 60 person-months. Since the product totals about 50 to 60 hours of instruction, this corresponds to about one person-month of development effort per hour of instruction.

USING A COMPUTER TO TEACH

We see CBT as one vehicle (not the only one) for addressing the training problem that will be with us for the foreseeable future. Among the well-known benefits of CBT are its applicability to training large numbers of students at the same time, its self-paced nature, its ability to provide "hands-on" practice, and its ability to take advantage of techniques such as graphics and animation. On the other hand, a CBT product cannot answer unanticipated student questions, and hardware characteristics (such as screen size or resolution) have direct bearing on the product's effectiveness.

One issue with CBT in general that is not a problem with CBT for Ada is the "fear of computers" syndrome. Since students taking LESSONS ON ADA are assumed to have programming backgrounds, they will not encounter the kinds of problems that other categories of users might have in seeing a computer for the first time during a training session.

On the other hand, we were concerned with possible psychological effects of a CBT product that provides status reporting on student performance. The use of exercises is a necessary part of CBT, but having graded tests as part of the product can be intimidating to the student, has the potential for misuse, and may interfere with the product's educational effectiveness.

Instead, LESSONS ON ADA provides monitoring information on each student's progress -- i.e., how far in each lesson the student has reached. A student may interrupt a lesson at any point, then continue later at the place in the lesson where the interruption occurred. A menu when the student logs on reveals the relevant status: which lessons have been completed, which ones have been started but interrupted, and which ones are recommended next. (Independent of the recommendations shown in the menu, a student may select any lesson at any time.)

The exercises in the lessons are for the student's benefit to assess his or her understanding of the concepts, but were not intended to be used as a measure of programming competence. In fact, at certain points in the lessons we asked "trick" questions to the student -- expecting an incorrect response -- to draw particular attention to important items. We would have been hesitant to use this educational technique if we thought that the student was being graded.

An important element of CBT is the ability of the student to back up (i.e., revisit previously seen material) and to branch (make a selection of next topics). LESSONS ON ADA supports these goals by allowing the student to go forwards or backwards in a lesson on a topic by topic basis (a topic generally comprises about four or five screensful of information), and by allowing the student to select any lesson at any time.

HARDWARE CONFIGURATION

Using Two Displays

Because of its widespread availability, the IBM PC was chosen as the host for the CBT product. However, we recognized that educational effectiveness would be greatly enhanced by using two displays -- similar to using two overhead projectors for in-person Ada seminars. There are frequent occasions when seeing two screensful of information at the same time is preferable to seeing one at a time and switching between them.

Although the two-display configuration is non-standard, we felt that the teaching advantages were worth the cost. Other configurations providing a large amount of simultaneous information were also considered. One of them was to use a single display and provide hard copy as a substitute for the second screen. We rejected this approach because of the problems associated with the student's continuing need to switch his or her eyes from display to hard copy and back.

An alternative to two physical displays is a one-display configuration with an adequate windowing facility driven by the product and controlled by the student. This solution was not selected in the first design, because of the lack of adequate windowing software for the IBM PC back in 1982. We are now considering new versions of LESSONS ON ADA, as well as new CBT products on Ada, that use these techniques.

Using Colors for Emphasis

A monochrome display is used for explanatory text, and a color screen shows program examples and exercises. This choice has several benefits:

- Since the monochrome display typically has higher resolution of characters than a color display, using the monochrome screen for explanation is easier on the eyes.
- Since there may be several portions of an example to which the student's attention should be drawn, using the color screen for examples and exercises can take advantage of the different color combinations that the hardware allows.

Experience at in-person seminars showed the benefits of multiple colors for visual aids, since the color variation helps both to emphasize major items and to avoid what would otherwise be a somewhat monotonous format. Color is all the more useful in a CBT product, where there is no vocal component to stress important points.

The lessons were written with a distinction among foregrounds for normal text, Ada reserved words, emphasized text, incorrect text, and Ada comments; and backgrounds for normal text, emphasized text, incorrect text, and response areas for exercises. For the monochrome screen, emphasis is achieved through highlighting, underlining, and reverse video.

The particular choice of colors can be made by the user. The person who installs the product may choose a default; this can be overridden by the student. In this fashion the color combinations may be selected based on characteristics of the color display that is used -- we have noticed considerable variations from model to model. Moreover, a student who is color blind can choose a combination that maximizes the contrast between foreground and background.

Use of Other Hardware Features

The IBM PC offers facilities for sound, graphics and animation. We were somewhat conservative in taking advantage of these, for two reasons. First, overuse can interfere with teaching. Clever animation or excess use of colors, for example, can be so interesting or distracting that the student pays more attention to the show on the screen than to learning the concepts being taught. Second, in order to increase the portability of the product to other machines, we avoided making unnecessary use of PC-specific facilities.

Sound is used to signal the student to do an exercise, and to warn the student when he or she is attempting to move the cursor outside the editing region on the screen. We do not use sound to signal an incorrect response to a question, since that could be annoying or intimidating.

Semi-graphic characters have been used to draw boxes and arrows, and to compose simple drawings, with modest animation, that illustrate various programming examples. The graphic mode of the computer is not used, since the training function can be adequately fulfilled without it, and since the costs in coding and in the time and space requirements for the product would have been too high considering the large amount of teaching material we were developing.

Summary of Configuration Requirements

LESSONS ON ADA runs on an IBM PC with:

- o At least 150KB memory,
- o Either two 360KB 5 1/4 inch diskette drives, or a hard disk and one (or two) diskette drives,
- o A monochrome display,
- o A color display (requiring a color card on the PC),
- o DOS version 2.0 or higher.

The product also runs on an IBM PC/XT and a PC/AT as well as some PC compatibles.

STUDENT PREREQUISITES

The LESSONS ON ADA product has only the general prerequisite of "previous programming experience." In particular, no previous knowledge of Ada is required, but we assume that the student is familiar with programming concepts such as procedures, functions, types and recursion. We intentionally omitted direct comparisons between Ada and other languages; contrasting enumeration types in Ada and Pascal would not be of much use to a Fortran programmer.

TEACHING ADA

The product covers the complete language -- not every detail in the Reference Manual, of course, but roughly the same degree of detail as would be found in a good Ada textbook such as Barnes (1984).

This level of coverage presented certain challenges and difficulties: how to balance the treatment of _what_ the language rules are, _why_ the language features are the way they are, and _how_ to use particular features effectively. Also, and very importantly, how to treat topics that are unique to Ada or that are significantly different from their equivalents in other languages (notably generics, exceptions and tasking).

We have chosen to present the material principally covering what the Ada rules are. Thus the lessons are organized around specific language topics -- discriminants, access types, parallelism and the rendezvous, etc. Nonetheless, within the discussion of particular topics we have chosen program examples both to illustrate good style and to serve as the focal point for motivating the discussion of the rules. Additionally, we have pointed out rationale for certain design decisions when that would reinforce the student's learning. It is certainly easier to remember a rule knowing why it is in the language, than to be simply presented with it as an isolated fact. For example, in the lesson on generics, it is noted that there is no concept of a formal generic record type. Since the purpose of this restriction might not be immediately obvious, the lesson explains the reason explicitly: the structure of a record type is almost always unique, and so the possibility for matching would be exceedingly rare. It was not worth adding language complexity to handle cases having such little utility.

The depth of coverage did preclude certain techniques that are sometimes found in CBT products. For example, it might be desirable to present a level of detail corresponding to the student's comprehension of the material: shorter explanations, perhaps optional topics for the advanced student, and more tutorial explanations for students with less programming experience. This was not practical in LESSONS ON ADA because of the degrees of variation anticipated for the students. Instead, we make extensive use of exercises to test and reinforce students' learning.

One of the problems in teaching Ada is that it is a highly integrated language and is thus difficult to present on a topic by topic basis. To handle this, we give short descriptions of the necessary aspects of the feature to dispell the mystery, before the full discussion is presented.

CHOOSING EXAMPLES

Constraints and Goals

The most difficult part of writing the lessons was to choose effective examples. First, there are the physical constraints of the hardware to deal with: the example must fit on one screen in an area 25 lines by 80 characters. Moreover, the example should be interesting, illustrative of proper style, and understandable to programmers independent of application background.

Impact of Ada

Ada, with its emphasis on program readability over writability and succinctness, sometimes made the writing of small examples quite challenging. As illustration, a formal parameter declaration in Ada must use a type mark rather than a general subtype indication. Thus it is illegal to write:

```
procedure GO_FOR_IT(SMALL_VAL: INTEGER range 1..10);
```

and instead we must write:

```
subtype SMALL_INT is INTEGER range 1..10;
procedure GO_FOR_IT(SMALL_VAL: SMALL_INT);
```

There are good reasons for the language rule requiring type marks, since it encourages factorization of common information and simplifies the conformance rules for subprogram specifications, but it means that the example requires an extra line.

Here is another case where the language rules affected the choice of examples. We want to illustrate the difference in activation semantics between an allocated task and a declared task. Consider the following program fragment:

```
declare
        task type MESSAGE;
        type MESSAGE_HANDLE is access MESSAGE;
        M: MESSAGE;
        task body MESSAGE is ... end MESSAGE;
        MH: MESSAGE_HANDLE := new MESSAGE;
begin
        ...
end;
```

This would be a nice example to use, since it would show the contrast between M (the declared task, activated at the 'begin') and MH.all (the allocated task, activated as part of the elaboration of the declaration of MH). However, the example is illegal, and attempts to correct it while still showing the allocator in the declarative part result in a bulkier version that obscures rather than clarifies the point being expressed. Therefore, we selected a variation of the example, putting the allocator in the statement part. (Since you may want to test your knowledge of Ada by trying to identify why the above block is illegal, explanation of this is postponed till later in this paper, following the next section.)

Of course there were many more aspects of Ada that made our job of example selection easier. E.g., using stubs and subunits, we could write programs that were complete with respect to compilability but which deferred unnecessary detail. With Ada's exception facility, we could represent succinctly and cleanly the handling of error situations. It would not have been possible in other languages to represent examples with such semantic richness in a similarly concise manner.

AN EXAMPLE FROM A LESSON

Lesson 25 (The Select Statement and Scheduling) covers a number of advanced topics on Ada tasking, and in the concluding part of the lesson it was important to sum up the major points with an intuitively appealing example. The program that we chose was an Ada model of a bank, where arriving customers form a single line and are served first-in first-out by a fixed number of tellers. It is natural for each customer and each teller to be represented by a task object. We define a task type for the customer tasks, and we declare teller tasks individually.

It is frequently necessary in Ada to define an intermediate task to handle communication between two tasks that seem at first glance to be able to rendezvous directly. In teaching Ada tasking, LESSONS ON ADA tries to convey when such an intermediate task must be used. The bank example was designed to illustrate this point.

If a customer were to rendezvous directly with a teller, by calling an entry defined by the teller, this would correspond to multiple queues -- one per teller. (Some real-life banks still have this arrangement, resulting in situations where late-arriving customers lucky enough to choose a fast line may be served before earlier customers waiting in a slower line.) But the example requires a single queue, served by all the tellers, not one queue per teller. Thus, customers do not rendezvous directly with the tellers -- instead, an intermediate task is required with an entry (NEED_TELLER) that corresponds to the desired queue. Customers will call the NEED_TELLER entry in this intermediate "dispatcher" task.

Customers in real life are impatient. If not served within some reasonable time period, they leave (perhaps making appropriately non-complimentary remarks about the bank, which we do not attempt to model in Ada). This leads quite naturally to a timed entry call by the customer tasks.

The example so far looks like this:

```
procedure BANK is
    task type CUSTOMER;
    C1, C2, C3: CUSTOMER;
    task DISPATCHER is
            entry NEED_TELLER(...);
            ...
    end DISPATCHER;
    task body CUSTOMER is
    begin
            ...
            select DISPATCHER.NEED_TELLER( ... );
            or     delay 5.0 * MINUTES;
            end select;
    end CUSTOMER;
    task TELLER1;  task TELLER2;
    ...
begin
    null;
end BANK;
```

The job of the DISPATCHER task is to match an available teller with the next customer in line. We represent this by having the tellers call an entry TELLER_READY declared in DISPATCHER. Thus the task DISPATCHER becomes:

```
task DISPATCHER is
  entry NEED_TELLER(...); -- called by CUSTOMER tasks
  entry TELLER_READY; -- called by TELLER1 and TELLER2
end DISPATCHER;
```

At this point in the lesson, the task bodies for TELLER1 and TELLER2 are presented, further illustrating timed entry calls and features from the CALENDAR package. To save space on the screen, these bodies are replaced by stubs after the explanation of their effect is given.

Next, the body of DISPATCHER is shown; it is interesting since it reveals both a nested accept statement and a select with terminate.

```
task body DISPATCHER is
begin
  loop
    select
      accept TELLER_READY do
        accept NEED_TELLER(...) do ... end NEED_TELLER;
      end TELLER_READY;
    or
      terminate;
    end select;
  end loop;
end DISPATCHER;
```

The nested accept reflects our assumption that tellers have to synchronize with customers in carrying out their transactions. The terminate alternative allows the program to shut down gracefully.

The example in the lesson is concluded with one last change. As it stands, there is a first-in first-out queue that contains waiting tellers, imposed by the TELLER_READY entry in DISPATCHER. In real life, though, the situation is different. If you go into a bank and there are several tellers available to serve you, you don't check which one has been waiting longest to process a customer -- you make an arbitrary choice. How should this be reflected in our Ada program? Each teller should call a different TELLER_READY entry, and DISPATCHER should make an arbitrary choice in case several tellers have called. We need an entry family for TELLER_READY, having one member per teller (thus two in our case). DISPATCHER will perform a selective wait to accept either TELLER_READY(1) or TELLER_READY(2). Each of these in turn consists of an accept of the NEED_TELLER entry, as in the version without entry families.

The characteristics that make this example indicative of the LESSONS ON ADA approach are:

- It is small and self-contained. All the information the student needs at any moment is available on the two screens that he or she is currently viewing: explanation on the monochrome display, and program text on the color screen.
- The example is developed gradually, one point at a time.
- It is intuitively appealing, modeling a real-life situation that will be familiar to the students.
- It demonstrates both the semantics of the language features and their associated stylistic issues.
- It illustrates not just the simple parts of Ada but the aspects that are unique or possibly difficult for new students to learn: using intermediate tasks, select statements, nested accepts, the terminate alternative, and entry families.

<u>SOLUTION TO EARLIER QUESTION</u>

The example shown earlier in this paper (the block declaring task type MESSAGE) is illegal because of the variable declaration (MH) appearing after the task body. Such a restriction makes good sense in large programs, since it avoids various unpleasantries that could result from a small declaration getting lost amidst large bodies, but it did interfere with our attempt to compose this short example. Moreover, reversing the declarations of MH and the task body would not help; it would result in PROGRAM_ERROR being raised during the evaluation of the allocator 'new MESSAGE' since the body for MESSAGE would not yet have been elaborated.

INTERACTIVITY

A difficult part of building a CBT product is to provide the proper amount of interaction and feedback: the author must make effective use of exercises. In most CBT products, exercises are restricted to multiple-choice or fill-in-the-blank questions. Exercises of this type are necessary for drill purposes -- LESSONS ON ADA includes such short-answer questions and its variants (asking the student to move the cursor on the screen to point to a particular program element). However, such exercises are not sufficient in a product that aims to teach a programming language. It is essential to have the student solve problems by writing actual Ada programs.

One technique that we considered was to incorporate an Ada interpreter as part of the course, thus allowing the student to run and test programs immediately. This was beyond the scope of the project, however, and also had certain limitations from an educational perspective that will be described below.

The alternative that we adopted was to develop a response analyzer that processes students' answers. We have used a pattern matching technique based on finite state automata. The fragment of an Ada program written by the student is analyzed piece by piece, according to a sequence of cases anticipated by the author. These cases are compared to the response one by one in sequence until a match is found. If there is no previous match in the sequence, the last case will automatically be matched. The elements that can be included in the cases are:

- o Explicit Ada lexical elements,
- o "Wildcards" (arbitrary Ada lexical elements),
- o Repetition factors,
- o Negation and disjunction.

This technique allows us to make provision for variants in correct responses and to anticipate incorrect responses and thus provide specific diagnostic messages to the student. (Lexical variations such as upper vs. lower case, inclusion of Ada comments, and the number of spaces between lexical elements, are ignored.) When a case is matched, a message unique to the case is displayed. The number of times that a student can match a given case is decided by the author; this is always bounded, so it is impossible for a student to be "blocked" at an exercise. If the student makes the same error several times, the information given becomes more detailed at each try. If a correct response is not given within some author-determined number of attempts, the student will be shown the correct answer and may then proceed with the lesson or go back and review the appropriate material.

The specificity of the diagnostics for incorrect answers can make the response analysis more helpful to the student than having an Ada compiler or interpreter available. Since new students will more often be writing incorrect programs than correct ones, it is better for a training tool to provide detailed diagnostic information based on the particular problem, than an indication of why the program does not conform to the language standard.

Many of the exercises in LESSONS ON ADA display a skeletal version of a program and ask the student to fill in the rest. With this approach we can illustrate good Ada style, free the student from having to memorize extraneous syntactic details, and give the student practice in reading Ada programs.

FUTURE DIRECTIONS

Based on comments from users of LESSONS ON ADA we are currently considering a number of enhancements for future releases of the product. Possibilities include:

- o Rehosting to other machines, including both microcomputers (such as the Zenith 150) and mainframes with appropriate terminals;
- o Providing additional material such as hard copy for program examples and exercises;
- o Providing supplementary quizzes, separate from the product, to benefit organizations requiring a more formalized monitoring of student performance.

CONCLUSIONS

Although CBT products will not replace good human instruction, an effective CBT product can serve a useful function when there is a shortage of qualified training personnel, or where there is there a need to train a large number of students. Both of these situations, present in the Ada environment, motivated the development of LESSONS ON ADA.

To summarize the major points:

- o A student learning Ada via computer needs to have more than a single screenful of information visible at a time. The use of both a monochrome and a color display, though a non-standard configuration, is a highly effective approach pedagogically.
- o Ada is an integrated language. Teaching it topic by topic raises a "chicken/egg" issue: we often want to illustrate a feature before describing it in detail. To handle this, we cover enough of the feature to describe how it is being used, with more complete description occurring later.
- o The authoring system used in writing the lessons was developed especially for the product. The response analysis is quite powerful, allowing students to write program fragments and to get detailed, interactive diagnostic information. From an educational point of view, this can be better than even having a compiler or interpreter available.
- o Examples and exercises were chosen to be illustrative of good programming style, and points of language rationale were introduced where useful. As a result, though the product focuses on _what_ the language is, there is an appropriate treatment of both _why_ the rules are the way they are, and _how_ to use Ada.

ACKNOWLEDGEMENTS

The following persons from Alsys and Cassie -- a French company specializing in CBT who worked with Alsys in developing LESSONS ON ADA -- contributed to the product's design and realization:

- o Rene Beretz, who managed the project, served as lead designer, and participated in the writing and implementation of the lessons;
- o Ben Brosgol, Pascale Carayon, Michael Lott, Eric de Massas, Karen Sather, Suzanne Semiski, and Mike Woodger, who authored lessons;
- o Nico Lomuto, who provided detailed reviews;
- o Yves Egarteler, Daniel Ichbiah, Laurence Kassapian, and Marie-Dominique Liefooghe, who coded the lessons using the Alsys authoring system;
- o Jean-Luc Escudie, Monique Lavige, and Kit Lester who designed the authoring system software and the pedagogical material;
- o Guy Benoliel and Regine Deltombe, who wrote the programs, and Reba Kraus, who served a product support role;

We wish to thank also the many other persons from Alsys, Cassie, Beta Sites, and customers, who have provided useful suggestions on improving the early versions of the product.

REFERENCE

Barnes, J.G.P. (1984). Programming in Ada (Second Edition). London: Addison-Wesley.

Viewing Ada from a Process Model Perspective

Rob Strom and Shaula Yemini

IBM T. J. Watson Research Center
P. O. Box 218
Yorktown Heights, N. Y. 10598

Peter Wegner

Brown University
Providence, RI 02912

Abstract: This paper compares two programming language paradigms for large software systems. The first is based upon nested block structure and static binding, augmented with abstract data types and concurrency, as exemplified by Ada. The second is based upon processes with disjoint data spaces which communicate by passing messages over dynamically bound ports as exemplified by the process model of NIL. We argue that the process model paradigm is simpler, has better support for modularity and programming-in-the-large, and results in more reliable and maintainable programs.

We suggest usage restrictions and language extensions which allow Ada to support a process model with minimal change to the language. We show that our suggested modification of Ada yields a considerably simpler language.

Introduction

Ada and NIL [STR 83b, STR 84] exemplify two alternative paradigms for programming in the large – i.e., for building systems from individual program units. We present the essential features of the Ada and NIL paradigms, and contrast them independently of the languages in which they are embedded. We evaluate the two paradigms with respect to the following requirements for making large, long-lived systems reliable and maintainable:

- **Modularity:** The language should encourage the division of large systems into independent *modules* with low coupling. All of a module's assumptions about how it affects and is affected by other modules should be completely documented in an *interface specification.* It should be possible to proofread and test a module against its interface specification without needing to know the implementation of other modules.
- **Support for Programming-in-the-Large:** To enable supporting module interconnection and system evolution, a module's *bindings* (the set of other modules with which it is permitted to interact) must not be required to be statically predetermined and fixed throughout execution, but instead must be capable of being established and possibly modified under program control. Similarly the set of elaborated module bodies must be allowed to be determined under program control.
- **Detection and Isolation of Errors:** The language should have a strict definition of what is a semantically well-formed program. Semantically ill-formed programs should be detected as early as possible – at compile-time whenever possible. Any remaining

programming errors should result only in incorrect outputs, and should not cause corruption of data of other modules.

The Ada language arose from the Steelman requirements. These requirements were not the broader objectives listed above but instead specific language solutions reflecting the decision to use Pascal as a base language and apply programming language technology as understood in 1975. The resulting language is built on the block structure mechanism of Algol-like languages and the data-abstraction mechanisms of languages like CLU [LIS 79]. Within this framework Ada has added concurrent tasks, exception handling, separate compilation, and generic (parameterized) instantiation.

The language NIL, developed at IBM's T. J. Watson Research Center, was developed to meet the same goals as Ada but builds on a different starting point – distributed, autonomous processes, which we shall refer to as the NIL Process Model.

In this paper, we argue that the NIL process model has significant advantages for reliability, maintainability, and expressive power for large systems. We then show that although Ada was originally designed to support the block-structured model, the NIL process model can be incorporated into Ada by making only a small set of changes to Ada. These changes actually result in a significant simplification of Ada, both in the number of fundamental language constructs and in the number of rules of their interaction.

Definition of A-paradigm and N-paradigm

To emphasize that we are comparing the paradigms for for programming in the large and not the languages themselves, we shall use the terms "A-paradigm" and "N-paradigm" to denote respectively the "Algol-like" paradigm as extended by Ada to include abstraction and concurrency, and the "NIL-like" or process-oriented paradigm.

The main differences between the A-paradigm and the N-paradigm may be characterized in terms of the following three notions:

- *Units of modularity*: units out of which large programs are constructed and maintained.
- *Units of concurrency*: independent threads of execution within modules.
- *Units for name space* region of a program in which a given set of names is known

In the A-paradigm, the interaction between units of modularity, units of concurrency, and units of name space is complex. In particular, a module (e.g. a package) may share data with other modules and be concurrently executed by many tasks. An object may be simultaneously visible to many modules or to many tasks, since nesting, the **with** clause which imports library packages, and the use of access types all result in the non-exclusive ownership of data.

By contrast, in the N-paradigm, the process is at the same time the unit of concurrency, the unit of modularity, and the unit for name spaces.

We are assuming that the reader is familiar enough with Ada and the Algol model that a short summary will suffice. Modules in the A-paradigm may be either functions, procedures, packages or tasks. The system configuration in the A-paradigm is defined by the static nesting of modules within an outermost block -- "the main program". Both the nesting structure and the particular code bodies being nested are predetermined statically. The nesting of modules determines their binding to other modules, their lifetime, their visibility for purposes of invocation, and the accessibility of variables, data types, and other entities defined in a module.

An N-paradigm system is structured as a network of processes connected by communication channels. Each process is an instantiation of an independently compiled module body consisting of a program text and local data declarations. There is neither nesting, nor shared data. Each object in the system is *owned* exclusively, i.e., is local to some process, and is finalized when that process terminates. All object types are first class, and thus may be components of arbitrary structured objects.

Communication channels are formed by connecting an *output port* to an *input port* of matching type. Processes communicate with each other solely by passing messages over the communication channels.

Messages are passed either with (1) a **send** operation sending the message through a local output port and immediately resuming execution. The message eventually arrives at the input port at the other end of the channel. or with (2) a **call** operation sending the message through a local output port and waiting for it to be received by the owner of the input port at the other end of the channel, processed, and then returned.

A receiving process issues **receive** to dequeue a message from a local input port, and **return** to return a message sent using **call**. A process issues a guarded **select** operation to wait for a message on one of a designated set of input ports. A process does not know any external names, i.e., it does not know the names of other process instances, or the names of ports in other processes.

Interface specifications in the N-paradigm consist of port type definitions. Each port type definition specifies (1) the type of messages to be communicated through the port, (in the case of calls, these messages are usually called *parameter lists*), and (2) whether parameters passed in a call will be owned by the caller before and after the call (**in** or **inout**), whether ownership will be passed from the callee to the caller (**out**), or whether ownership will be passed from the caller to the callee (**passed**).

Systems in the N-paradigm evolve dynamically, as a result of the creation and deletion of processes. bound into the system, and other processes terminate. Both the particular code body to be instantiated when a process is created and the bindings, via communication channels, of the newly created process, are selectable under program control. The operands for the process creation operation include (1) the name of the module to be instantiated, and (2) a parameter list for an initial call to the newly created module. By passing and receiving ports on this initial call, the creating process can give the child process access to its necessary "environment", and can receive in return the ability to communicate with input ports in the child process. Further ports may be exchanged during subsequent communication, allowing the system configuration to vary dynamically. Although the value of a port object can vary dynamically, security is preserved, because all ports are strongly typed, and all possible bindings of a port share a common interface.

Processes in a system may have independent lifetimes; some may exist indefinitely, while others may be short-lived. Processes terminate upon reaching the end of their program, or may be cancelled earlier by their owner.

Figure 1 on page 4 shows an example of a miniature operating system structured using the N-paradigm We use this example to illustrate our comparison of the two models. The core of the system consists of an operator module, user manager module and a file manager module. The lifetime of these modules is indefinite.

Users may log on the system, informing the user manager what program (shell) they wish to run. User programs may open files on different devices, by informing the file manager what type of file they want to open, and which input or output device the file should be associated

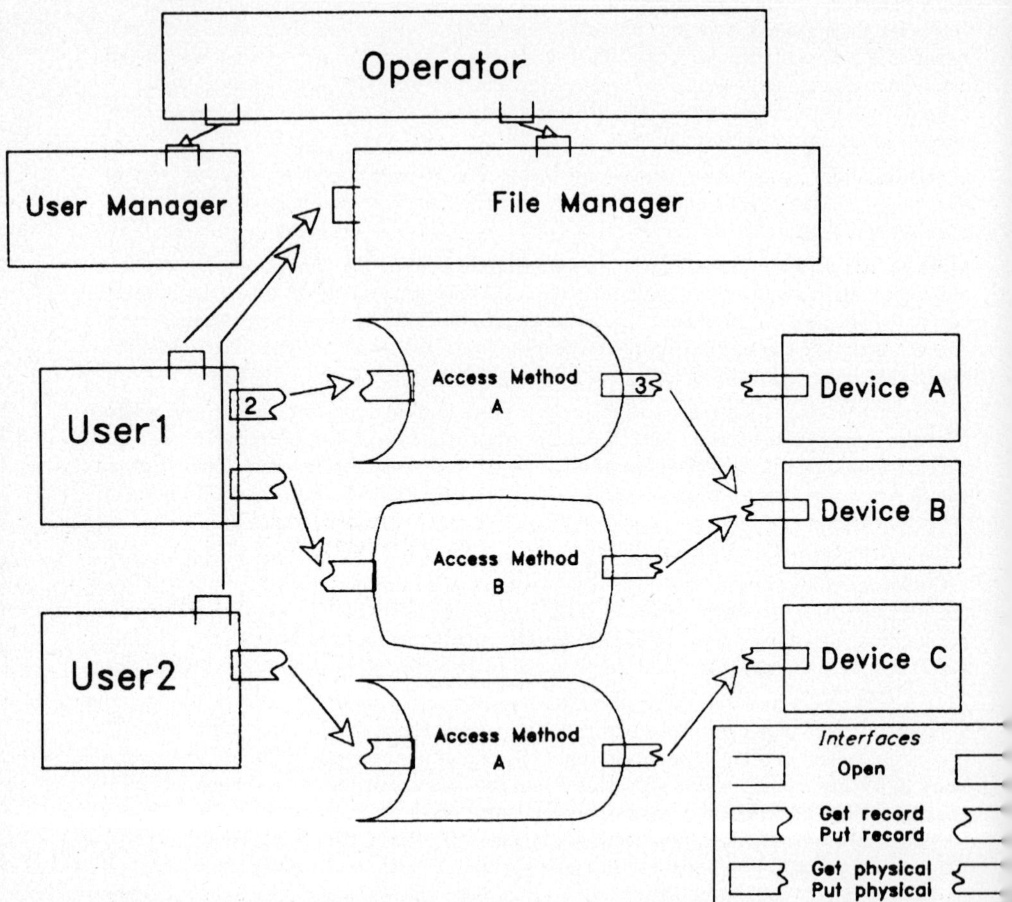

Figure 1. Sample Operating System in the N-paradigm: Boxes denote process modules, and lines denote communication channels between them.

with. The file manager grants a request to open a file by creating a new instance of a *file access method*, and giving the user access to the GET__RECORD and PUT__RECORD ports of the file access method. The access is given by returning output ports bound to the corresponding input ports of the file access method as **out** parameters of the "open" call. Users may then read and write to files via calls to GET__RECORD and PUT__RECORD of the access method process. The operator set of active devices, and the policies for selecting access methods. Boxes denote process modules, and lines denote communication channels between them.

A Comparison of the N-paradigm and the A-paradigm

Localized Ownership vs. Diffuse Ownership

In the A-paradigm, an object does not necessarily have a unique owner, since objects may be shared among several modules through one of several mechanisms (imported global data, nesting, access types).

The lack of a unique owner makes it difficult to enforce the principles that every data object in a system must be first initialized, then possibly updated, and then eventually finalized, and that concurrent shared access to an object is illegal. When these principles are not enforced, execution may result in unpredictable side effects ("erroneous execution" according to Section 1.6 of the Ada LRM). A programmer must manually check all possible interleaved execution sequences of all modules to make sure that all variables are properly initialized and finalized, and that concurrent shared access never occurs. This manual analysis involves the determination of how all modules sharing an object might be scheduled, which in turn may require an analysis of the logic of the entire program. The requirements that systems can be debugged one module at a time, that the effect of programming errors be confined to the module containing the error, and that semantic errors are detected early and automatically, are not met.

In the N-paradigm, each object is owned by a single process module. The owner of an object is the only process which may operate on the object, and has the sole responsibility to finalize the object. It is possible to employ *typestate checking* [STR 83a] on process modules to assure that data is accessed only between initialization and finalization, and that all data is finalized before a process terminates. For example, in Figure 1, the user owns the access method process and the GET and PUT ports for each file he has opened. The user is guaranteed not to be able to issue operations until the file has been opened and the ports have been initialized. The user is also guaranteed not to terminate without closing all files – i.e. finalizing all the access method processes he owns.

The problem of avoiding erroneous concurrent access does not arise, since objects belong to only one module instance at a time, which in turn contain only one thread of control at a time. Therefore, the N-paradigm meets the requirements for modularity and reliability more closely than does the A-paradigm.

Low-Coupled Point-to-point interfaces vs. Overbroad Interfaces

In the A-paradigm, modules may interact in two ways: (1) Explicit communication through operation invocation or entry calls, and (2) Implicit communication through shared global variables and pointers. The explicit communication must be documented via entry specifications, and is "point-to-point", i.e., only the two modules engaged in communication may affect one another. The implicit communication is not documented and is "many-to-many": all modules in a scope may be affected by the modification of a shared variable. Thus, in the A-paradigm, interface specifications are incomplete. One must either examine the code of all modules involved to determine the interfaces, or to assume that all global objects are potentially modified by all modules having visibility to them. Both cases violate modularity. An extreme example of this problem is the "control-block spaghetti" which results when data records are interconnected using pointers. A program which passes any one of these records as a parameter indirectly passes access to most of the data of the system.

In the N-paradigm, there is only one type of inter-module interaction: message passing. All communication is point-to-point over ports whose interface types must explicitly specify how many parameters are being passed, whether they will be modified by the called process, and whether they are initialized prior to and subsequent to the call. Interface documentation is therefore more complete.

Multiple Bodies per Interface vs. Single Bodies

In long-lived programs, reusability of modules is a major concern. Consider for example the user programs in our mini operating system. A typical system might support several kinds of I/O devices, such as e.g. disks, tapes and "windows" on a bit-mapped display. Programs must be able to consider all these devices as the same type, so that they need not be modified whenever they need to use a different kind of file, or whenever the set of supported kinds of files is changed.

The A-paradigm reflects the approach to information hiding used in abstract data types. In this model, each abstract data type corresponds to a particular *implementation* of a type, even though the details of this implementation are hidden from the user. If the programmer desires two different implementations of a type, e.g., a disk file and a window, he must use two different types even when the interfaces are identical. This property is reflected in Ada in the lack of support for multiple package bodies per package specification, and the lack of support for multiple task per task type.

Thus in Ada syntax, the call:

```
X(I).GET_RECORD();
```

where X is an array of tasks and OP1 an entry, or the call:

```
GET_RECORD(Y(I));
```

where Y is an array of objects of some private type and OP2 a procedure defined on that type, always invoke the identical code body independently of the value of I.

In the N-paradigm, abstraction is achieved using processes which hide internal information, and export only ports. The type of an output port defines the interface, while the value defines its binding to a particular input port in a particular process. Nothing prevents input ports within two completely different process bodies from being declared with the same type and hence being alternative values of a single output port. The NIL call analogous to the above Ada call is:

```
GET_RECORD[I] ();
```

The individual ports GET__RECORD[I] have the same type, but they may each be bound to input ports in processes with different code bodies, e.g. Access Method A and Access Method B. The N-paradigm therefore provides a better fit to the requirement that a module depends only on the interfaces it uses and not on other module bodies.

Dynamic System Configuration vs. Static Binding

In large systems, *system configuration* is frequently an important part of the systems function.

Dynamic system configuration is motivated by two considerations:

- The requirement to bind programs to resources, such as binding a user program to a particular file or output device. Since the availability of resources varies dynamically, as do the requirements for resources, resource allocation has to be done dynamically.

- The requirement for an *open-ended* set of resources with a single standardized interface: For example, in our mini operating system above, in addition to standard devices like disks and tapes, new devices may be added later, as well as "virtual devices", i.e., programs which simulate the function of these devices, such as windows. These resource implementations must be loaded and bound dynamically to pre-existing programs expecting the standard interface to the resource.

Dynamic loading and binding is easy to specify within the N-paradigm. The operation for instantiating a process has a parameter which specifies the particular code module to be loaded, and the value of this parameter may be selected dynamically. The initialization rendezvous with the instantiated process includes exchange of bound output ports which serve to dynamically link the new process to the running system.

This mechanism for binding is identical to that used in capability-based operating systems (Ref.) but since the compiler can now assume the burden of assuring that capabilities (ports) are unforgeable, there will be no run-time overhead associated with this mechanism.

In our system example, the initial port given to the user process upon creation is a port for calling the file manager to "open" a new file. Each "open" request will specify a file name (e.g. printout.script), and a preferred device (e.g. bitmap printer). To process the call, the file manager does the following: First, it searches for the file's actual device, if the file already exists. Otherwise it selects an actual device based upon the user's preference and the actual availability of devices. Similarly, it selects a file access method process, based upon the device characteristics and the user's parameters. It then creates an instance of the particular file access method process it has chosen, (e.g. access method A in Figure 1), passing as an initialization parameter an output port bound to the selected physical device, e.g. port 3 in the figure, and receiving in return a pair of ports bound to the GET__RECORD and PUT__RECORD type input ports of the access method, e.g. ports 2 in the figure (shown as a single line). It then returns the pair of ports to the user.

At the completion of the call to "open", an access method process will have been created, bound to the device process, and the user will have acquired ownership of a pair of ports for issuing GET and PUT requests. The access method process itself will be owned by the user, as a result of which, the N-paradigm guarantees that the access method will be finalized, i.e., the file will be "closed", should the user terminate before closing the file.

It is possible to extend the system with new access method processes or new resource processes which had been designed and compiled after the system had begun execution. This is done by giving the operator an output port ADD__FILE, connected to a corresponding input port in the file manager, on which the file manager accepts messages notifying it of the name, characteristics and required initialization parameters of a newly-added file access method in the library. Thus, extensions to the system can be incorporated without having to shut down the entire system and recompile it.

Dynamic loading is not supported at all in the A-paradigm, while dynamic binding can be supported only partially. In our example system, in order to have the same task type, the access method processes must be instances of the *same body*. There is no construct which allows the programmer to specify which of several alternative code bodies of the same type is to be instantiated when a new process instance or package instance is created. The set of alternative access methods would have to have been known and compiled in advance. The common body for an access method process would then be a routing program which examines a parameter and then executes one of the pre-determined programs for the file access method. If a system requires dynamic loading of code, it must invoke an external operating system program. If a system is changed by adding new code, the system must be taken down, recompiled, and then restarted.

Selective Access vs. All-or-nothing access

In the A-paradigm, a data abstraction does not selectively export its operations. If a package is used to implement a private type, *all* operations on objects of that private type are available wherever any are. Similarly, all entries of a task object are available where that task object is visible, as is the right to abort the task. In large systems, the same abstraction may have to be accessed in different ways by different modules. In our example system, we want users to have access only to the "open" port of the file manager, and hide from them ports which are intended to be used only by the operator such as a port for requests to take a device off-line.

In the N-paradigm, a process acquires the ability to perform operations by obtaining a bound output port for each such operation. A process does not acquire access merely as a result of owning another process. Because ports are initialized individually under program control, the granting of access is both selective and dynamic. For instance, in our example, users may make calls on the "open" port of the file manager, but only the operator may make calls on the "start device" port.

Process Abstraction vs. Data Abstraction

One feature of the A-paradigm which is considered valuable for supporting software modularity is the abstract data type, as implemented by packages in Ada.

A data abstraction is straightforwardly implemented by a process. It is merely a process that contains the representation of the abstraction as its local data, and an input port for each of the operations exported by the abstraction. The process contains a loop with a single select statement. The select waits for a call on any of the input ports corresponding to an operation. The guard for all operations is constantly TRUE, since an abstract data type is always prepared to respond to any operation invocation.

This use of processes serves the same purpose as the use of abstract data types. However, the process approach is more flexible and avoids some of the problems of the abstract data type approach:

- It is possible to selectively export individual operations.

- By using Boolean guards on the **select** statement which waits for one of the input ports to be called, the implementation can exert control over when the operations can be scheduled. For instance, a bounded buffer implementation may refuse to accept the insert operation when full, and may refuse to accept the delete operation when empty.

- The N-paradigm approach automatically makes each operation atomic, since the process can only schedule one operation at a time, thus serializing what would have otherwise been uncontrolled shared access.

- The N-paradigm approach allows each instance of a data abstraction to have a different body, including different private data, provided that all such bodies have the same interface. The interface is the collection of initialization parameters and output ports returned when creating the process.

The N-paradigm process, in a single construct, captures the concurrency of Ada tasks, the context-independence of Ada's generics, and the data encapsulation of Ada's packages.

Support for Error Detection

The Ada LRM defines an *erroneous* execution to be one which violates the language rules, but which is not required to be prevented by a compile-time check or a run-time exception. Erroneous executions may cause unpredictable effects including damage to the state of modules that have been proved correct. In Ada, erroneous executions may result from: assignment to a shared variable, use of an undefined value, access to a deallocated object, changing of a discriminant value, dependence on the parameter passing mechanism, suppression of an exception check, unchecked conversion, or other reasons.

A-paradigm languages supporting dynamics and concurrency are unable to avoid erroneous executions. A language which fails to prevent erroneous executions is said to be *insecure* [HOA 81]. In an insecure language, it is necessary to prove that an entire system is free from logic errors before any part of it can be shown to meet its specifications. Thus, a principal advantage of modularity – the ability to test a program one module at a time – is lost.

The N-paradigm permits the avoidance of all erroneous executions, because concurrent access to shared variables cannot occur, and because it is possible to apply typestate checking [STR 83a] within processes to guarantee that otherwise erroneous sequences such as accessing an uninitialized variable or an unbound port cannot occur. The application of this technique in NIL provides an existence proof that erroneous programs are not a necessary feature of procedural languages.

Efficiency

The reader might at this point be questioning the feasibility of efficient implementations of the N-paradigm since every package is a task, all communication is by message passing, and efficient mechanisms such as pointer manipulation and shared data are excluded from the model. While a detailed discussion is beyond the scope of this paper, we mention in passing that the desired efficiency can be achieved *by compilers* which may re-introduce pointers and sharing in implementations of language constructs, as optimizations, either automatically or when directed by *pragmas*. Such optimizations exist in the current implementation of NIL, where message passing is implemented by pointer copying, and where process "swapping" in the most common cases has the same overhead as a procedure call.

The simpler high-level model has its advantages for efficiency as well: Typestate tracking allows the compiler to determine where finalization is need, and allows implementations to avoid garbage collection; since programs are guaranteed not to affect any data but their private data, programs can be compiled into the "protected" regions of an operating system where access to systems services is usually faster; the lack of aliasing facilitates both compiler optimization and the automated synthesis of distributed and parallel implementations.

Evolving Ada to support the N-paradigm

One can simulate a process model in Ada by abandoning block structure and putting all task bodies at the outer level, giving tasks access rights to other tasks by passing pointers to them. This approach is still is inadequate because of (1) the fact that having access to a task gives access to *all* its entries, as well as the right to abort the task and (2) the problem mentioned earlier that multiple task bodies cannot share a common task type. As one attempts to refine the Ada solution to meet these objections using multiple layers of tasks, packages and generics, (see e.g. [LAM 83]) the solution becomes more and more baroque.

We therefore present an alternative approach which involves language modifications. Interestingly enough, even though Ada was designed to support the A-paradigm, surprisingly few changes are required to evolve Ada to support the N-paradigm, and most of these changes involve deleting features and reducing the number of rules of interaction between features, rather than adding.

All the suggested changes derive from the following strategy:

- eliminate constructs which give rise to shared visibility of objects
- replace static binding with dynamic binding

Specifically, we propose the following set of changes to Ada:

1. Additional features
   - type constructors for input and output ports, to replace entries
   - an operation, to bind an output port to an input port
2. Modifications to existing features
   - eliminate nesting of program units
   - all units are type definition packages or program units
   - eliminate access types; allow allocators to create instances of objects instead of pointers to objects
   - eliminate generic formal parameters except for type parameters
   - generalize arrays to maps from arbitrary index sets to arbitrary element sets
   - allocate operation for a task will specify (a) the name of a program body; (b) initialization parameters
   - add a parameter mode: **passed**, to indicate transfer of ownership of parameter from caller to callee, upon a call

Flat Module Structure

Executable modules shall be either tasks or subprograms. Each executable module shall be completely disjoint from any other; there shall be no nesting of tasks or subprograms. There shall be no subunits; all executable modules shall be library units.

Packages shall contain only type definitions, and shall not be nested. Type definitions shall not refer to objects, although they may require discriminants which must be bound to objects by declarations.

The context specification of a module shall be a **with** clause containing names of library packages only. An executable (task or subprogram) module or a non-executable (package) module can be compiled independently of all other modules except the library packages named in its context specification.

The result of these restrictions is a drastic simplification of the visibility rules of Ada. Within each module, only objects declared locally and types defined in packages listed in the context specification are visible. In particular, no executable module can see any object declaration not local to the module.

Single Ownership

Each object shall be local to, i.e., owned by a single module. Port type definitions shall show whenever ownership is transferred between calling program and accepting program. We add a new parameter mode, **passed**, to indicate that data is initialized on entry to the call, but is retained by the acceptor, and therefore shall be uninitialized on return to the caller. The operation **move** shall support such a transfer of ownership from one variable to another of matching type. Unlike assignment, **move** shall leave its source object uninitialized, and passes the value to the target object. The **move** operation shall apply to all types, even limited types.

Elimination of Access Types

There shall be no access type. In Ada, access types provide both dynamic allocation of objects and sharing capability. In our proposed modification, dynamic creation will be supported in other ways, and sharing will be prohibited. (Implementations may still use data sharing, for instance to avoid making multiple copies of constant data, but all such uses of sharing as an optimization will be invisible to the programmer.)

Instead of creating an access type, the operation **new** shall create uninitialized instances of objects. For example, applying **new** to an uninitialized object of a record type will yield an "empty" record structure with uninitialized subcomponents. If the components are themselves records, **new** must be performed again before it is possible to assign to the subcomponents. Record types may be recursive, e.g.

```
TYPE SCase IS (Nil, Atom, Pair);
TYPE SExpr (Kind:  Scase) IS
  RECORD
    CASE Kind IS
      WHEN Nil =>
      WHEN Atom =>
        Printname: Charstring;
      WHEN Pair =>
        Car: SExpr;
        Cdr: SExpr;
    END CASE;
  END RECORD;
```

To create the S-expression (A . (B . NIL)), one might write:

```
X:  SExpr;
 . . .
NEW X (Pair);
NEW X.Car (Atom);
X.Car.Printname := A;
NEW X.Cdr (Pair);
NEW X.Cdr.Car (Atom);
X.Cdr.Car.Printname := B;
NEW X.Cdr.Cdr (Nil);
```

The above allows dynamics without any use of pointers. The compiler may, of course, choose between pre-allocating a fixed size for records, or actually implementing records as pointers to dynamic structures.

An additional requirement for supporting dynamics within Ada is to remove the restriction that arrays have index sets which are contiguous subranges of discrete types, and instead to support flexible arrays which map arbitrary index sets to arbitrary component types, e.g.:

```
TYPE NetworkAddr is NEW integer;
TYPE RoutingTable IS ARRAY (NetworkAddr) OF MessagePort;
```

The replacement of arrays by non-contiguous mappings has several advantages: arrays can grow and shrink dynamically, and there can be no such things as uninitialized values in arrays. Component selection will raise CONSTRAINT_ERROR (a better name would be

DOMAIN__ERROR) if the item does not exist. Assignment cannot be used to extend an array; an explicit **insert** operation shall be used to grow arrays, and **delete** to shrink them.

The elimination of nesting, the elimination of visibility to external objects, and the elimination of access types together result in the disjoint data ownership of the N-paradigm.

Replacement of entries by call- and accept-ports.

In Ada, the program which calls an entry and the program which accepts a call from an entry both name the same entry. In order to use the N-paradigm, it is necessary that the calling program and the accepting program be separate modules, and that they never share names. The name used by the caller shall designate a different object (an output port or *call*-port) from the name used by the acceptor (an input port or *accept*-port). Call-ports and accept-ports shall be declared as regular objects. Since it must be possible to dynamically bind call-ports and accept-ports, and to pass ports from one module to another, these ports shall have the status of first class objects. The interface descriptions which in Ada are called entry declarations or subprogram specifications shall become port type definitions. The only port statically associated with a task object shall be the port used to make the initialization call when the task is first created.

An operation shall be defined in the language to create a call-port bound to a given accept-port. (This operation would be used by the owner of an accept-port to create a call-port so that it can be exported to another module.) Call-ports shall be copyable, since many call-ports may be bound to one accept-port. There is no meaning attached to copying an accept-port; hence accept-ports shall be limited types.

Dynamic creation of processes

The **new** operation shall be the only operation used to create tasks. The operands of **new** shall include the name of the task body from the program library. In addition to the task body name, the operands of **new** shall include the initialization parameters to the task. The task type definition shall specify the number and types of initialization parameters required.

Because tasks, like all other objects, have only a single owner, there is only one task with the right to abort a given task.

Resulting Simplification of Rules

The elimination of nesting, access types, type definitions referring to objects, and shared ownership also results in the elimination of a large number of rules and restrictions in Ada. For example, in current Ada there are a number of rules which combine to enforce the requirement that a task only issue **accept** operations on entries of that task, including a rule forbidding **accept** statements to appear in subprograms. Since accept-ports are first-class objects, and since objects are never shared, it is automatically true that an **accept** operation never applies to another task's accept-port. Therefore rules such as the restriction of **accept** within subprograms can be dropped. Similarly since port types are simply types like any other, all the rules for matching subprogram specifications are already handled by the usual rules of name-equivalence for type resolution.

Conclusions

The N-paradigm provides a rebuttal to Brian Wichmann's contention that Ada is not too big [WICH 1984]. Wichmann argued that Ada was not too big because it could not be significantly improved by removal of language features without substantially impairing its expressive power. His argument that Ada was a local optimum did not preclude the possibility that a new starting point could result in a simpler yet equally expressive language.

The simplicity and power of the N-paradigm for programming in the large derives in large measure from its use of a single modular construct. Identifying the unit of modularity with the unit of concurrency reduces the number of linguistic concepts while making it easier for either a person or a program to analyze modules in isolation. Furthermore, identification of name spaces with modularity and concurrency eliminates troublesome language features like global variables and makes module structure cleaner and more secure than in the A-paradigm. The N-paradigm more directly captures the notion of modularity in hardware design, in which modules are black boxes with plugs and sockets and can be interconnected without an exposure of internal structure.

The N-paradigm has been embodied in the language NIL, designed at IBM T.J. Watson Research Center between 1978 and 1981. Between 1982 and the present, a significant amount of practical systems code has been written in NIL, compiled, and tuned. The results demonstrate significant benefits of the N-paradigm, which we attribute to the greater degree of checking and module isolation supported by NIL. Performance was comparable or even slightly better than that of systems implementing the same function but written in lower-level languages.

The example of NIL illustrates the practicality of using the process model as a starting point for a simpler, more powerful, and more orthogonal language, with better support for large long-lived software systems. We therefore believe that future evolutionary extensions to Ada should be built upon the process model.

References

[CLA 80] Clarke, L., Wileden, J., and Wolf, A., "Nesting in Ada Programs is for the Birds", *Proceedings of the ACM-SIGPLAN Symposium on the Ada Programming Language*, 1980.

[HOA 81] Hoare, C. A. R., "The Emperor's old clothes", reprinted in *Comm. ACM*, vol. 24, pp. 75-83, February 1981.

[LAM 83] Lamb, D. A., Hilfinger, P. N., "Simulation of procedure variables using Ada tasks", *IEEE Trans. Soft. Eng.*, Jan. 1983.

[LIS 79] Liskov, B. et al "CLU Reference Manual", *Laboratory for Computer Science, MIT*, TR-225 October 1979

[NIL 82] NIL Reference Manual, IBM T. J. Watson Research Laboratory, RC 9732.

[SHE 82] Sherman, M., Hisgen, A. and Rosenberg J., "A Methodology for Programming Abstract Data Types in Ada", *Proc. AdaTEC Conference on ADA*, October 1982.

[STR 83a]. R. E. Strom, "Mechanisms for Compile-Time Enforcement of Security," *Tenth ACM Symposium on Principles of Programming Languages*, Austin, TX (January 1983).

[STR 83b]. R. E. Strom and S. Yemini, "NIL: An Integrated Language and System for Distributed Programming," *SIGPLAN '83 Symposium on Programming Language Issues in Software Systems* (June, 1983).

[STR 84] Strom, R., and Halim, N. "A New Programming Methodology for Long-Lived Software Systems"., IBM Journal of Research and Development, January 1984.

[WEG 84] Wegner, P. "Capital-Intensive Software Technology", *Software*, July 1984.

[WICH 84] Wichmann, B. "Is Ada Too Big?", *CACM* February, 1984.

TSL: TASK SEQUENCING LANGUAGE

David Helmbold
David Luckham

Program Analysis and Verification Group
Computer Systems Laboratory
Stanford University
Stanford, California 94305

Abstract TSL is a language for specifying sequences of tasking events in Ada[1] programs. TSL specifications are submitted with an Ada program and are monitored at runtime for consistency with the actual tasking events as they occur. This paper presents a preliminary design for TSL, an informal overview of its capabilities, and an operational semantics.

1. INTRODUCTION

In our earlier studies of the implementation and application of runtime monitoring, it was concluded that the ability to specify the intended tasking interactions would be advantageous in detecting many kinds of tasking errors, and could provide a basis for developing expert systems for task debugging. Design of the Task Sequencing Language, TSL, is based on this earlier work.

TSL is a language for specifying tasking states and, more generally, sequences of tasking states, that either should or should not occur during a computation. These specifications will be monitored by a runtime monitor task of the kind presented in [German 84, Helmbold,Luckham 83, Helmbold,Luckham 84]. TSL is intended for use primarily during testing and debugging of the tasking behavior of an Ada program.

The goal of TSL is somewhat less ambitous than a specification language for concurrent programs in general. It is intended simply to give the programmer an ability to specify some critical kinds of tasking situations that can occur during a computation. Efficient implementation of TSL for runtime monitoring is a primary goal. It is therefore to be expected that the most general kinds of constructs for specifying concurrent computation will not be expressible in TSL -- e.g., unbounded temporal operators such as "it is possible".

This paper gives an overview of TSL and an operational semantics. The operational semantics is intended to provide a method of clarifying questions about the meaning of various constructs, and also to indicate how the language can be implemented. The runtime support for TSL and the uncertainty of the times at which events in a tasking system occur are also discussed.

It must be emphasized that we are presenting a preliminary syntax for TSL which is subject to revision.

---

[1] Ada is a registered trademark of the U.S. Government.

2. OVERVIEW OF TSL

The basic terms of TSL are *events*. Events denote actions taken by the threads of control in an Ada system. Such actions include starting a rendezvous, issuing an entry call, and executing a labeled statement. For example, "the OPERATOR task becomes blocked, accepting entries PRE_PAY and CHARGE" is an event occuring during the execution of a select statement. Sequences of events and tasking states (sets of task statuses, see [Helmbold,Luckham 83]) are TSL's domain of discourse.

The semantics of TSL are based on a model of the computation of a concurrent system (e.g., an Ada tasking program) whereby events occuring during the computation are organized into a linear stream according to time, simultaneous events being ordered arbitrarily. We shall refer to this as the *underlying event stream*. It should be noted, however, that in any implementation of the underlying stream (e.g., by a runtime monitor), only a subset of pairs of events — those that are "connected" — can be guaranteed to occur in the same timewise order in the system and in the stream. We shall discuss connected events in Section 3.

The statements of TSL are called *specifications*. They are built up from the basic events. Specifications are patterns that can match many different sequences of events.

Specifications are placed in any declarative part of the Ada text, and appear as special comments. Essentially, they are a generalization of the concept of assertions. Since they describe sequences of events, they usually cannot be checked immediately like an assertion. Instead, they must be monitored over a period of time. The semantics of TSL specifications informally have the form: "a subsequence of the underlying event stream that matches this pattern must (or must not) occur in any interval between such and such events".

A TSL specification becomes *active* when its declarative region is elaborated and the following **begin** is reached. It remains active until the elaborating thread of control leaves the region. If the declarative region is elaborated more than once, the specification is activated by each elaborating thread of control. A copy of an active specification may be *enabled* by an event in the stream. It will remain enabled until it is either *satisfied* or *violated*. When an elaborating thread of control leaves a declarative region, all TSL specifications declared in that region which were activated by that thread become inactive. Any enabled copies of these specifications are treated as if their "before" event had occurred.

2.1 Types, Basic Events, and Matching

There are seven predefined types in TSL: integers, task names, type names, entry names, family names, variable names, and label names. Values of type task name are the task ids uniquely associated by the runtime monitor with each activated thread of control during a computation. (The domain of task ids depends on the monitor implementation — in many cases it will be integers.) In a TSL specification any task name in the Ada program is a constant (designating its task id value); the constant, **main** always refers to the main program. The sets of values of the types entry name, type name, label name, and so on, are the appropriate identifiers in the Ada program being specified; a standard declaration for each of these types e.g., as an enumeration type, is assumed to be at the beginning of the main declarative part of each Ada program. These identifiers may be used as constants in a TSL specification.

Basic events are built out of these five types of objects. TSL (and the underlying event stream) contains nine classes of events (see syntax summary). We will use the term *event* to refer to events in TSL specifications, and *stream events* to refer to events in the underlying event stream.

There are no explicit type declarations in TSL. Each class of event implies a particular type for each of its constituent values; these types are indicated in the syntax definition of an event class by the italic prefix of the names. For example, the start of rendezvous is an event class. The TSL syntax,

start_rendezvous ::= *task*_name **accepts** *task*_name **at** *entry*_name

indicates the types of the three constituent names. An example of a start rendezvous event is

OPERATOR **accepts** CUSTOMERS(5) **at** PRE_PAY

which specifies an event in which the operator starts a pre-pay rendezvous with the fifth customer task in the array of customers.

The concept of *matching* is fundamental in defining the meaning of TSL events. A TSL event *matches* an event from the underlying stream if the stream event is of the same class and has the same constituent values. The above event would *match* all of the start rendezvous stream events where the OPERATOR has accepted CUSTOMERS(5) at entry PRE_PAY.

We also use the concept of an event matching an interval. An *interval* of the event stream is a contiguous section of the event stream containing one or more stream events. An event matches an interval of the event stream if that interval contains a stream event matching the TSL event.

2.2 Guards

Often, the occurrence of a stream event is important only when certain other conditions are present. TSL provides *guards* to specify context. A guard is a condition on the current tasking state of the program [Helmbold,Luckham 83]. It is bound to a basic event by the reserved word **where** forming a *guarded event*. A guarded event matches only those stream events occurring when the guard condition is true in the current tasking state. There are several kinds of basic guards from which guard conditions are constructed using **not**, **and**, and **or** (see syntax appendix).

Example of a guarded event:

OPERATOR **calls** CUSTOMERS(1) **at** CHANGE **where**
CUSTOMERS(1) **is not terminated**

2.3 Compound Events and Specifications

There are three classes of *compound events*: *one_of*, *all_of* and *sequence* events. They are constructed from finite sets of two or more events joined together by **or**, **and**, and =>. The constituent events of a compound event may be compound events.

A *one_of* compound event matches an interval of the event stream if any of its constituent events matches the interval. An *all_of* compound event matches an interval of the event stream if there is a one — one association between its constituent events and disjoint subintervals of the interval such that each constituent event matches the subinterval associated with it. A *sequence* of N events matches an interval of the event stream if the interval can be partitioned into N disjoint subintervals such that each event matches the corresponding subinterval and the correspondence preserves order (i.e. the first event in the sequence matches the first subinterval, etc.). Note that when matching compound events: (1) non-matching stream events may occur between matching ones, and (2) constituent events must be matched by non-overlapping intervals.

Examples of compound events:

an all_of event:

```
(OPERATOR calls CUSTOMERS(1) at CHANGE and
    CUSTOMERS(1) accepting CHANGE)
```

a sequence event:

```
(CUSTOMERS(1) calls OPERATOR at PRE_PAY        =>
 CUSTOMERS(1) calls PUMPS(1) at START_PUMPING =>
 CUSTOMERS(2) calls PUMPS(1) at START_PUMPING)
```

Matching compound events:

if the event stream is: ..., A, C, B, D, A, E, B, ...

the TSL event, A **and** B *matches intervals:*

[A, C, B], [B, D, A], [A, E, B]

the TSL event, A => B *matches intervals:*

[A, C, B], [A, E, B]

the TSL event: (A **and** D) => (A **and** B) *matches interval:*

[A, C, B, D, A, E, B].

In all cases these intervals are the minimal matching intervals; intervals containing them also match.

The statements of TSL are *specifications*. Each specification consists of three parts: an enabling event, a compound event, and a terminating event. A specification is either *positive* or *negative* depending on the absence or presence of negation, **not**.

Informally, the semantics of a positive specification are:

"whenever the enabling event matches a stream event, then the compound event must match that interval of the event stream starting at the next event in the stream and continuing until (and including) the first stream event which matches the terminating event".

In the case of a negative specification the compound event must not match the interval.

Example of a specification:

```
when OPERATOR accepts CUSTOMERS(1) at PRE_PAY
then not (OPERATOR accepts CUSTOMERS(2) at PRE_PAY        =>
          PUMPS(1) accepts CUSTOMERS(2) at START_PUMPING =>
          PUMPS(1) accepts CUSTOMERS(1) at START_PUMPING )
before PUMPS(1) accepts CUSTOMERS(1) at START_PUMPING
```

2.4 Place Holders

The examples given so far of events and specifications clearly lack generality. The basic events are in fact identical with the matching stream events. What is often required is an ability to specify a set of stream events that differ at their component values, for example, any event in which the OPERATOR accepts a customer at PRE_PAY.

Variable parts of a basic event, guard, compound event or specification are indicated by identifiers beginning with the question mark symbol, "?". They are called *"place holders"* since they indicate a position for any *value* of their type. It should be noted that there is no explicit place holder declaration. The type of a place holder is determined by its position in an event according to the syntax for that class of event. There is also a special wild-card, **any**.

The meaning of place holders is defined by a more general concept of matching. A TSL event or specification may be *instantiated* if there is an association of a unique value with each place holder and with each position of **any**. The instantiation is the event or specification that results when each place holder is replaced by the associated value at all of its positions, and

any is replaced at each of its positions by the value assoiated with that position. An event or specification matches a stream event or interval if there is an instantiation of it which matches that stream event or interval according to the previous matching rules. For example, the TSL event:

```
OPERATOR accepts ?T at ?E
```

matches all stream events where the OPERATOR starts a rendezvous with any calling task at any entry.

The instantiation rules require the same placeholder to be associated with the same value at all positions whereas **any** may have a different value at each position. Thus the stream interval

```
OPERATOR accepts CUSTOMERS(1) at PRE_PAY,
OPERATOR accepts CUSTOMERS(2) at CHANGE
```

does not match

```
OPERATOR accepts ?T at ?E and OPERATOR accepts ?T at ?E
```

but it does match

```
OPERATOR accepts ?T at any and OPERATOR accepts ?T' at any;
```

The previous example of a specification may now be stated in a more useful form.

Example of a more general specification:

```
when OPERATOR accepts ?C1 at PRE_PAY
then not (OPERATOR accepts ?C2 at PRE_PAY   =>
          ?P1 accepts ?C2 at START_PUMPING  =>
          ?P1 accepts ?C1 at START_PUMPING )
before ?P2 accepts ?C1 at START_PUMPING
```

This specification will be enabled each time the OPERATOR accepts a prepayment from any customer. The sequence will match any subsequent stream interval where the OPERATOR accepts a prepayment from a (later) customer who then gets ahead to use the pump to be used by the prior customer. Since the specification is negated it will be satisfied if the prior customer gets to use any pump before the sequence matches.

The event, **now**, matches the next event in the underlying stream. For example,

```
when now then A before B
```

means "after the next event, A must happen before B".

Some parts of basic events can be omitted; the default is **any** (see syntax). Thus

OPERATOR **accepts** ?T *means* OPERATOR **accepts** ?T **at any**.

2.5 Macro Definitions

Macro definitions allow commonly used parts of specifications to be named. This is intended to reduce the amount of repetition in making a set of specifications, and to improve readability. A macro definition has the syntactic form,

define inline identifier parameter-list **is** *compound*_event

where parameters are place holders of the form, #Identifier, and the only place holders allowed in the compound event are the macro parameters (or **any**). If ordinary place holders, ?X say, were allowed, they may clash with place holders in specifications in which the macro is used, since TSL is not block structured.

A macro is used within a specification by binding its formal parameters to actual place holders, rather like a procedure call. Its meaning is in-line expansion, i.e., the actual place holder parameters are substituted for the macro parameters in the macro body, and that text is inserted in place of the macro call.

For example, two tasks are said to be *synchronized* at the start or end of any rendezvous between them. This is expressed by the macro:

```
defined inline SYNCHRONIZED (#S, #T) is
    (#S accepts #T or #T accepts #S
     or #S releases #T or #T releases #S
     or #S activates #T or #T activates #S);
```

This macro can be used to build more complex specifications. Assume, for example, that a variable is shared between tasks and that the operations on this variable are in a block labelled by L. In the specification,

```
when ?A reaches L
    then (SYNCHRONIZED (?A, ?B) => ?B reaches L)
before ?B reaches L (where ?B is not ?A);
```

the macro call, SYNCHRONIZED(?A, ?B), is expanded in-line with ?A replacing #S and ?B replacing #T. Suppose an event occurs in which a task T reaches the label L. A copy of the specification is enabled. This enabled copy will then continue to match events in which tasks start or end rendezvous with T until another task reaches L. At this point, either an instance of the sequence will occur and the specification will be satisfied, or else it will be violated. Thus, this example specifies that if a task accesses the shared variable then it will sychronize with the next task to access that variable.

Macros may contain calls to themselves, in which case they are *recursive.* Recursive macros allow us to express arbitrary repetition of an event. This may be illustrated by constructing a macro to specify a sequence of sychronizing operations connecting two tasks.

```
define recursive SYNC+PATH (#S, #E, #T) is SYNCHRONIZED (#S, #E) or
        (SYNCHRONIZED (#S, #T) => SYNC_PATH(#T, #E, any))
```

A call to this macro, SYNCH_PATH(A, B, **any**), will match any interval containing a sequence of events, each synchronizing the next pair of tasks in a chain, A, T1, ..., Tn, B. When the call is to be matched, it is first replaced by the body. This in turn will match any event that synchronizes A and B; if an event synchronizing A with T occurs, then another call, SYNCH_PATH(T, B, **any**) may be matched to complete the matching. At a point where n calls have been generated, there are n synchronizing sequences, one of length 1, one of length 2, ..., one of length n that will match.

The semantics of recursive macro call, requires some restrictions on where calls may be placed in the body of the macro. We do not want the replacement to get into an infinite loop. Essentially, a call must not be the first event in its own body (see section 5.3).

2.6 The One Match Opeerator

The previous definition of matching requires that a TSL specification searches for all matches of its compound event in the interval between its activating and terminating events. Specifications for some kinds of patterns of events cannot be expressed under this definition of matching. The expressiveness of TSL and its efficiency are increased by allowing the search to be restricted to a single match for a compound event. A natural way to do this is to restrict all matching of constituent basic events to the first possible match.

The **one match** operator on compound events is defined by restricting the previous definition of an event matching an interval of the event stream. A (basic) event *one matches* an interval if it matches the last event and no other event of the interval. A *one_of* compound event *one matches* an interval if one of its constituents *one matches* the interval, and no constituent *one matches* a subinterval. A compound *all_of* or *sequence* event *one matches* an

interval if the previous definition of matching applies with the restriction that all constituent events *one match* the corresponding disjoint subintervals (See section 2.3.
Example of the **one match** *operator:*

```
define recursive BALANCED(#P, #Q, #R) is
    (#R accepts #P or (#P accepts #Q => BALANCED(#P, #Q, #R) => #P accepts #R ) );
```

The specification,

```
when ?T activates A then one match (BALANCED(A, B, C) )
before A terminates;
```

is satisfied by the event stream interval,

```
E activates A, A accepts B, C accepts A, A accepts C, A terminates,
```

but is violated by the interval,

```
E activates A, A accepts B, A accepts B, A accepts C, A accepts C,
A terminates,
```

whereas the specification without **one match** would be satisfied by both intervals.

3. CONNECTED EVENTS

In this section we discuss the implementability of the TSL stream on a multiprocessor network. This requires a model of distributed Ada programs. Unfortunately, ideal stream facilities cannot be implemented on this model. However, we can implement a good approximation to the ideal stream facilities.

In our model, each task executes on its own processor with its own local clock. Each processor is connected with all other processors by communication channels. Messages are delayed somewhat as they pass through the communication channels. The channels pass messages to the destination processor in strict FIFO order, so no message can overtake or pass a previous one. We assume that there is a local monitor at each processor which generates a local stream. Each local stream consists only of events occurring at the local processor.

3.1 Connectedness of the Event Stream

One way to generate the global event stream would be to route each of the local streams to one processor, where they would be merged. Unfortunately, this global stream is unlikely to accurately reflect the real order in which the events occurred. Furthermore, even if the underlying tasking events occurred in the same order on two different runs, the communication delays might cause the resulting event streams to differ. Lamport has shown that, in such a system, many of the events occur *concurrently*, i.e. that their true order can not be determined [Lamport 78]

What we do know about this global event stream is that the events generated by each task occur in the proper order. Although this by itself is not useful, it leads us to the idea that if one event was generated on two processors, then the two local streams could be synchronized by that event. We call an event which is generated on two processors a *dual* event. By using dual events a merging algorithm can generate a better global event stream.

When the merging algorithm encounters a dual event in a local stream then it and further events from that local stream are queued up and not merged into the global stream. Only after the dual event has appeared in both local streams is it passed on to the global stream. Any events queued up by the dual event are also passed on to the global stream. Now both local streams can continue normally. The resulting global stream preserves the proper ordering of each local event stream with the dual event.

We say that two events are *connected* if they appear in the same local event stream. We say that a sequence of events is connected if each adjacent pair of events in the sequence are connected. When dual events occur, a connect sequence may contain events from more than one local stream.

Example:

If one local stream is A_1, D, A_2;
and another is B_1, D, B_2 the
the sequences A_1, D, B_2 and B_1, D, A_2 are connected.

The global event stream generated in the above manner has the property that connected sequences appear in the proper order. Therefore the global event stream is just as good as the actual order of events when evaluating TSL specifications which check for connected sequences of events.

3.2 Connectedness of TSL Specifications

Whether A TSL specification is violated or satisfied should not depend on the delays in the communication channels. We can avoid this problem if all TSL specifications are connected, i.e. their satisfaction or violation does not depend on the order in which unconnected events appear in the stream. We assume that each task constant, task placeholder, and occurrence of **any** appearing in a TSL statement has its own local event stream.

TSL contains three dual events: start_rendezvous, end_rendezvous and activation. Each of these dual events are contained in the local streams for each of their task constituents. It is easy to see that the end_rendezvous and activation events can be generated on the processors of both tasks. It is less clear that the start_rendezvous event can be generated by both the calling and the called tasks. It is not sufficient to simply generate the start_rendezvous event just before the end_rendezvous event because the called task may become deadlocked during the rendezvous. In a timed or conditional entry call, the calling task must be informed when the rendezvous has started. The caller may also need to know when his rendezvous starts because the start of a rendezvous, as well as the other dual events, are synchronization points (Ada LRM section 9.11). Therefore it is reasonable to assume that the calling task's processor is informed when the rendezvous starts and is thus able to generate the start_rendezvous event.

The call, accept, termination, and at_label events are contained in the local stream for the task indicated by the first {task}_name constituent. Some events and guards are influenced by actions on other processors and cannot be considered connected with any other events. These events are:

- the TSL timer, count, and **now** events;
- events with a guard checking the status of a task running on a processor which does not generate the event; and
- events with a guard checking the value of a variable visible to a task running on a processor which does not generate the event.

These definitions allow us to determine if a pair of TSL events are connected at compile time. We say two sets of TSL events are connected if every event in the first set is connected with every event in the second event.

Defining the connectedness of compound events is a little more difficult. We can associate with each compound event two sets of TSL events, the *head* and the *tail* for that compound event. The head and tails of guarded events are simply the guarded event itself. The head (tail) of a sequence is the head (tail) of the first (last) component of the sequence. The head (tail) of a one_of or all_of compound event is the union of the heads (tails) of the compound event's components. A sequence compound event is connected if every component is connected and the head of each component is connected with the tail of the previous component. A one_of or all_of event is connected if all of its components are connected.

A TSL specification is connected if the **when** event is connected to the head of the specifications compound event and the tail of the compound event is connected to the **before** event. It is easy to write a TSL preprocessor which takes an Ada program with specifications and flags those TSL statements which are not connected.

4. EXAMPLE

Simulation of an Automated Gas Station. The full text of this example is given in [Helmbold,Luckham 85]. Here we indicate how TSL specifications can be used at the outer declarative level to specify task interactions.

The gas station contains tasks representing the station operator, the customers, and the pumps. A customer arrives at the station, prepays the operator, pumps gas, receives change from the operator, and leaves. The operator accepts prepayments, computes charges and gives customers their change. The pumps are used by the customers, and report the amount pumped to the operator.

```
with DTTY_IO, PUMP_PACK; use DTTY_IO;
procedure GAS_STATION is
   pragma MAIN;

   NUM_PUMPS     : constant INTEGER := 3;
   NUM_CUSTOMERS : constant INTEGER := 10;

   task OPERATOR is
      entry PRE_PAY(AMOUNT      : in INTEGER;
                    PUMP_ID     : in INTEGER;
                    CUSTOMER_ID : in INTEGER);
      entry CHARGE(AMOUNT  : in INTEGER;
                   PUMP_ID : in INTEGER);
   end OPERATOR;

   task type CUSTOMER is
      entry GET_CUSTOMER_ID(NUMBER : in INTEGER);
      entry CHANGE(AMOUNT : in INTEGER);
   end CUSTOMER;

   task type PUMP is
      entry GET_PUMP_ID(NUMBER : in INTEGER);
      entry ACTIVATE(LIMIT : in INTEGER);
      entry START_PUMPING;
      entry FINISH_PUMPING(AMOUNT_CHARGED : out INTEGER);
   end PUMP;
```

```
-- constraints on the operator.
--+ when OPERATOR accepts ?C at PRE_PAY then
--+        (?P accepts OPERATOR at ACTIVATE =>
--+         ?C calls ?P at START_PUMPING )
--+ before ?C calls ?P at START_PUMPING;

--+ when OPERATOR accepts ?P at CHARGE then
--+        (OPERATOR calls ?C at CHANGE )
--+ before OPERATOR accepting;

-- specification of a customer's protocol.
--+ when OPERATOR accepts ?C at PRE_PAY where ?C is of type CUSTOMER then
--+      (?C calls ?P at START_PUMPING =>
--+       ?C calls ?P at FINISH_PUMPING =>
--+       ?C accepting CHANGE )
--+ before ?C accepts OPERATOR at CHANGE;

-- specification of a pump's protocol.
--+ when ?P accepts OPERATOR at ACTIVATE where ?P is of type PUMP then
--+      (?P accepts ?C at START_PUMPING  =>
--+       ?P accepts ?C at FINISH_PUMPING =>
--+       ?P calls OPERATOR at CHARGE )
--+ before OPERATOR calls ?P at ACTIVATE;

-- Specification guarding against races for a pump.
--+ when OPERATOR accepts ?C1 at PRE_PAY
--+ then not (OPERATOR accepts ?C2 at PRE_PAY    =>
--+             ?P1 accepts ?C2 at START_PUMPING  =>
--+             ?P1 accepts ?C1 at START_PUMPING )
--+ before ?P2 accepts ?C1 at START_PUMPING;
        . . .

end GAS_STATION;
```

5. TSL SEMANTICS

5.1 Introduction

Although the discussion in the previous section describes how TSL works, it is not detailed enough to be used as a language definition. In this chapter we present an operational semantics for TSL in terms of an abstract implementation of a TSL system. First we define several useful semantic concepts and state the static semantic restrictions of TSL. Next we discuss the stream generation and query facilities required by our implementation.

When the abstract implementation is given a TSL statement it converts the statement into a labeled *event graph*. Section 4 contains the definition of event graphs and gives an algorithm for converting TSL statements into event graphs. To record how much of a TSL specification has been matched, we place *tokens* on its event graph. The final sections of this chapter describe the implementation's matching algorithm and what it means for a specification to be *satisfied* or *violated*.

The algorithms described here are **not** intended to be implemented, but rather to define the meaning of TSL statements. A TSL implementation is free to choose any method of determining whether a specification is satisfied, as long as it gives the same results as the implementation described here. The implementation under way at Stanford University is using much more efficient algorithms which require far less copying and runtime overhead.

5.2 Static Semantics

The syntax of TSL reflects some but not all of TSL's semantic information. This section defines TSL's semantic units and base types, as well as describing the semantic restrictions on TSL statements.

As can be seen from the syntax summary, there are two kinds of TSL statements; *definitions* and *specifications*. Both kinds are written as formal comments (prefixed by "-- ") in declarative regions of Ada programs. Specifications are used to check that the event stream is proceeding as the programmer intended. Definitions are used to define macros for use in specifications.

5.2.1 Names and Placeholders

There are two kinds of placeholders. Those placeholders prefixed with a "#" are *formal parameters* of macros. Those placeholders prefixed with "?" are *TSL variables*. Formal parameters can occur only in definitions, and TSL variables can occur only in specifications. Placeholders, whether formal parameters or TSL variables, may only appear where task_names or entry_names are required.

Placeholders are declared and typed implicitly by their use. The scope of a placeholder is the TSL statement where it is used; a placeholder in one statement is not related to placeholders in other TSL statements. We will occasionally use the terms *task placeholder* (or *entry placeholder*) to mean a placeholder used in a position where the syntax requires a task_name (or entry_name). Once a placeholder has been used in a position requiring a task_name it cannot be used as an entry_name in the same statement, and vice versa.

The values that a task placeholder can assume are unique IDs representing the set of task objects in an Ada program, the main program, and an additional value, *"unset"*. The values that an entry placeholder can assume are unique IDs representing the set of task entries in the program as well as the value "unset". It is possible for a specification's placeholders to be bound to tasks or entries that are not visible where the specification appears in the Ada program.

Task_names and entry_names without a leading "#" or "?", family_names, type_names, and label_names are TSL constants and must be a name from the Ada program denoting a task object, entry, entry family, task type, or statement label (respectively), which is visible at the begin following the declarative part containing the TSL statement. Integer constants in TSL must be nonnegative integers. The keyword **main** is a constant, used in place of a task_name, which denotes the main program. Although the main program is not an Ada task, it is convenient to treat it as if it were a task object. The keyword **any** is a constant designating the special value "unset", and may be used in place of a task_name or entry_name. Since the value "unset" is treated as a wildcard in the matching process (see section 7), **any** is an appropriate name for this constant. Constants may appear in both specifications and macro definitions.

5.2.2 Macros

A macro_name is *used* when it occurs as part of a compound event. A macro_name is *defined* when it occurs on the left hand side of the **is** in a definition. Within an Ada program, no macro_name may be defined more than once. Every formal parameter occurring in a definition must also occur in that definition's parameter list.

There are two kinds of macro_names, *recursive macro_names* and *inline macro_names*, depending on whether the keyword **recursive** or **inline** occurs in the definition.

The visibility of an inline macro_name starts following the macro_name's definition and extends throughout the innermost Ada declarative region containing the definition. The visibility of a recursive macro_name is the entire innermost declarative region containing the recursive definition. A macro_name may only be used as part of a compound event within its scope. A recursive macro_name may not be used in an inline macro definition. Furthermore, within a recursive macro definition a recursive macro_name may only be used as (part of) the second or following compound event of a sequence.

The parameter list following a macro_name must *agree* with every other parameter list following that macro_name. Two parameter lists, $p_1, p_2, ..., p_n$ and $q_1, q_2, ..., q_m$ agree if n=m and for all *i*, $1 \leq i \leq n$ either p_i and q_i are both task_names or task placeholders or p_i and q_i are both entry_names or entry placeholders.

5.2.3 Events

Each of the seven classes of basic_events in TSL has a number of constituent values as indicated by the syntax summary. For example, a call event has the calling task, the called task, and the called entry as its constituent values. When an optional task_name or entry_name is omitted, that constituent is given the value "unset". Every event from the stream is a basic_event. No stream event has the value "unset" as one of its constituent values. Guarded_events, counts, timers, and **now** events are abstract events and can only occur in TSL statements.

Within a single basic_event, no placeholder may be repeated. However, placeholders used in the basic_event may appear in the guard.

Example:

Illegal	Legal
?T1 **calls** ?T1	?T1 **calls** ?T2 **where** (?T1 **is task** ?T2)

TSL makes no distinction between upper and lower case, i.e. all TSL statements can be mapped to upper case prior to analysis. The TSL syntax contains a number of keywords. It is assumed that all identifiers in the Ada program are distinguishable from the TSL keywords. Any TSL statement violating either the TSL syntax or the semantic rules stated here is ignored (although a warning should be issued to the programmer).

5.3 Runtime Support for TSL

TSL specifications are intended to be checked at runtime against a stream of events from the program. In addition, most TSL guards cannot be evaluated without examining the program's current state. Therefore the runtime support for TSL must generate the stream of events occurring in the monitored program and must keep a representation of the current tasking state. It is not always possible to generate the event stream so that the events appear in the exact order in which they occurred, but certain pairs of *connected* events can and must appear in their true order. Connected events are discussed in Section 3.

Our abstract implementation of TSL assumes that there is a unique ID for each task, entry, entry family, task type, integer variable, and label in the Ada program. Although the value "unset" is given some sort of unique ID as well, it is convenient to distinguish it from the unique IDs representing actual objects. The constituent values of stream events are unique IDs. Furthermore, when a TSL specification is activated (see section 5), any TSL constants are replaced by the appropriate unique ID.

In order to evaluate some guards, the TSL system must query a *picture* of the program's tasking state. This picture must contain the statuses and types of all the tasks in the program. In addition the picture must contain the values of those integer variables used in guards. We assume that there is some way the TSL system can examine this picture. Since the same program event can cause both a stream event to be generated and the picture to be modified, we insist that the stream event is generated first and the picture is updated only after the TSL runtime system has finished with the stream event. Therefore, guards are always evaluated using the 'old' picture.

The concept of a task runtime monitor has been presented and developed in previous work (i.e. [Helmbold,Luckham 83]); it is straightforward to modify one of these monitors to provide the necessary facilities to TSL. A preprocessing step inserts the monitor into an Ada tasking program. When the modified program is executed, the monitor watches the task interactions and detects several deadness errors (i.e. circular deadlock and global blocking). In order to detect these errors, the monitor establishes a unique ID for each task in the program and maintains a picture of the current tasking state.

The runtime monitor can easily be extended so that entries, labels, task types, and entry families are all given unique IDs. These items can then be incorporated into the monitor's picture so they can be queried by the TSL runtime system. Since the program signals the monitor whenever something important happens, it is no trouble for the monitor to generate the event stream.

It is not conceptually difficult for the monitor to include values of program variables in its picture, although both the difficulty of implementation and the runtime overhead increase dramatically. Restricting the variables to be monitored to one type (integer) eases the problem somewhat. We expect that guard elements such as "*variable*_name relation expression" will be implemented when TSL is interfaced with a good sequential debugger.

5.4 Event Graph Construction

The compound events in TSL specifications and recursive macro definitions are converted into *event graph templates* during the preprocessing step. Each event graph template is a directed graph with labeled arcs reflecting the structure of a compound event. Additional information is associated with the event graph template so that the entire meaning of the original statement is captured.

The first step in creating an event graph from a compound event is to *normalize* the compound event so that it contains no inline macros or all_of constructs. When an inline macro is encountered the compound event in the macro's definition replaces the macro_name and actual parameter list. The actual parameter's are lexicographically substituted for their associated formal parameters. When an all_of compound event, for example "(E_1 and E_2 and ... and E_n)", is encountered, it is replaced by a one_of event whose constituents are sequences reflecting all possible orderings of E_1 through E_n. Now the compound event contains neither inline macro calls nor the all_of construct.

Example: If we have:

```
define inline PUMPING(#C, #P) is
    (#C calls #P at START_PUMPING => #C calls #P at FINISH_PUMPING)
... (?C calls OPERATOR and OPERATOR calls ?P) => PUMPING(?C, ?P) ...
```

then we get

```
... ((?C calls OPERATOR => OPERATOR calls ?P) or (OPERATOR calls ?C =>
        ?C calls OPERATOR)) => (?C calls ?P at START_PUMPING =>
            ?C calls ?P at FINISH_PUMPING)
```

The event graph is initialized to contain distinguished start node, **s**, and a distinguished finish node, **f**. The procedure JOIN(v,v',E) is called with v bound to **s**, v' bound to **f** and E bound to the compound event.

JOIN(v,v',E) is defined informally as follows:

if E is $(E_1 \Rightarrow E_2 \Rightarrow E_3 \Rightarrow ... \Rightarrow E_n)$ then
    add new vertices $v_1, v_2, ... v_{n-1}$
    call JOIN(v, v_1, E_1), JOIN(v_1, v_2, E_2), ..., JOIN(v_{n-1}, v', E_n).
if E is (E_1 or E_2 or ... or E_n) then
    call JOIN(v, v', E_1), JOIN(v, v', E_2), ..., JOIN(v, v', E_n).
if E is a guarded_event or recursive macro call then
    add an arc between vertices v and v' labeled with the guarded_event (or recursive macro call) E.

The event graphs for TSL specifications are modified to include the **before** event. New distinguished nodes, **s'** and **f'**, are added, as is an arc from **s'** to **f'** labeled with the **before** event. The resulting event graph templates have four *distinguished nodes* -- **s**, **f**, **s'**, and **f'**.

Additional information is kept with the event graphs. The event graph for a recursive macro has the macro's formal parameter list and whether the key words **one match** occur in the definition associated with it. The event graph for a TSL specification has: the list of placeholders used in the specification, whether **not** follows the **then**, whether the key words **one match** occur, and the specifications **when** event associated with it.

This section has described how to create event graph templates from specifications. However, in our TSL implementation we do not directly translate specifications to event graphs. During the proprocessing step we replace the TSL specification with Ada code which, when executed, generates the event graph templates. Using this technique we can avoid passing complex data structures from the preprocessor to the run time system.

5.5 Event Graph Life Cycle

During the preprocessing step, a specification is converted into Ada code. At runtime this code creates an event graph template for the specification. Each time the specification's declarative region is elaborated, the event graph template is *activated*. If the **when** event of an activated event graph matches a stream event, then an *enabled copy* is spawned. Each enabled copy will be either *violated* or *satisfied*. When an enabled copy is violated the user is informed that his TSL specification has not been met.

Each time a thread of control passes the **begin** ending a TSL statement's declarative region, an activated event graph is created for that TSL statement. The activated event graph is created from the event graph template by replacing each Ada name in the template with the unique ID for the object denoted by that name (as viewed by the activating thread of control). Since the objects denoted by Ada names can change each time a declarative region is elaborated, each activation of an event graph template may result in a different activated event graph.

An activated event graph for a specification spawns an *enabled copy* whenever that specification's **when** event is seen in the event stream. The spawning process consists of copying the activated event graph and placing tokens on the distinguished s and s' nodes of the copy. The tokens on an enabled event graph propagate through the graph as events from the event stream match events of the enabled copy.

Activated event graphs for recursive macros become enabled when they are *called* (see section 8). Since inline macro definitions never have event graph templates, they are never activated.

An enabled copy is *negative* if the associated specification contains the keyword **not**, otherwise the enabled copy is *positive*. A positive enabled copy is *satisfied* when a token is placed on the distinguished f node, and *violated* if a token is placed on node f' but not node f. A negative enabled copy is *violated* when a token is placed on f and *satisfied* when a token is placed on node f' but not node f. When an enabled copy is violated, the enabled copy is deleted and diagnostic information is produced. When an enabled copy is satisfied, the enabled copy is deleted.

When a thread of control leaves a block containing TSL specifications, all of the event graphs it activated by entering the block are deleted. Any positive enabled copies of these event graphs are violated, and any negative enabled copies are satisfied.

5.6 Matching of Events

The basic operation in TSL is deciding whether a stream event matches a TSL guarded event. Every stream event is a basic event whose constituent values consist of unique IDs. TSL events are always interpreted in the context of some token, so that placeholders can be replaced by unique IDs or the value "unset". To determine whether a particular TSL event matches a particular stream event we must check that they are in the same class (e.g. both are start_rendezvous events). If so, we check that the constituent values of the two events match. Finally we evaluate the guard (if any). The two events match only if they have the same class, their constituent values match, and the guard is evaluated to "true".

At any given time, the implementation attempts to match only certain *relevant* events against the event stream. It always attempts to match the **when** events of activated specifications. It attempts to match a TSL event which labels an event graph arc only if there is a token at the tail of the arc. All other TSL events are (temporarily) irrelevant.

5.6.1 Tokens

Each token contains one component for each of the placeholders used in its event graph. These components always contain either the value "unset" or a unique ID of the appropriate kind. What these components represent are a *binding* of values to placeholders. Once placed on an event graph, the contents of a token's components never change; however, a *candidate token*'s bindings can be modified.

Using a token T, we can *interpret* a TSL event E by replacing E's placeholders with unique IDs (or the value "unset") bound to them in T. We use the notation E_T to indicate the resulting event. Essentially the matching process compares token--TSL event pairs with stream events.

The first step in determining whether a TSL event and a stream event match is to create a *candidate* token. The candidate token will be used to interpret the TSL event. Initially, all of the placeholders are bound to "unset" in the candidate token. If the TSL event is labeling an arc, then there is a *parent* token at the tail of the arc. The bindings of the candidate token are updated to reflect any bindings of placeholders to unique IDs in the parent token. After this happens we say that the candidate token is a *descendant* of the parent. If there is more than one parent token at the tail of the arc or more than one arc from a parent token, then the matching process is repeated (with a different candidate token) for each parent token -- arc pair.

5.6.2 Matching of Basic Events

We say a TSL basic_event E interpreted by the candidate token T (namely E_T), *matches* an event from the stream, S if:

1. S and E_T are in the same class.
2. Each constituent value of E_T
   - is either "unset" or
   - is the same unique ID
   - as the corresponding constituent of S.

If E_T does not match S, then no TSL guarded_event containing the basic event E_T can match S. If E_T does match S then the bindings in token T are updated so that each placeholder in E is now bound to the unique ID which is the corresponding constituent of S. Note that only placeholders originally bound to "unset" will be bound to a new value.

5.6.3 Guard Evaluation

There are four kinds of guard_elements; status, type, membership, and equality. Each kind can either be negative or positive depending on whether the keyword **not** appears in the guard_element. Negative guard_elements are true if and only if their positive counterpart is false.

A positive status guard_element checks if a particular task has the indicated status. If the *task*_name is a placeholder bound to the value "unset" then the guard_element is trivially true. Otherwise, the status guard_element is true if the designated task object has the indicated status in the monitor's picture. Note that if *entry*_names are specified in the accepting status, then all of the indicated entries must be in the set of open entries for the task. If a task or entry is specified with the status calling, then that task and/or entry must be the ones called. Any placeholders following the status in a guard_element which are bound to "unset" are ignored.

A positive type guard_element checks if a given task is of a particular type. If the given task is a placeholder bound to "unset" or the unique ID of a task object which is of the indicated type in the monitor's picture, then the guard_element is true. Otherwise the guard_element is false.

A positive membership guard_element checks if a given entry belongs to the specified entry family. If the entry belongs to the specified family or is a placeholder bound to the value "unset", then the guard_element is true. The guard_element is false otherwise.

A positive equality guard_element checks if two unique IDs or integer values are the same. If both task_placeholders (or entry_placeholders) are bound to the value "unset" then the guard_element is true. If exactly one of the task_placeholder (or entry_placeholder) is bound to "unset", then that placeholder becomes bound to the other unique ID. If both components consist of the same unique ID then the guard_element is true. If the guard_element contains a variable whose current value is the integer constant then the guard_element is true. In all other cases, the guard_element is false.

A guard is true if, when the **or**'s and **and**'s are replaced by the appropriate boolean operators and the guard_elements are evaluated (in the order written), the resulting boolean expression is true.

To determine if a TSL guarded basic_event matches a stream event we first check that the basic_event matches the stream event and then that the guard is true. If either the guard is false or the basic_event does not match then the TSL event does not match the stream event.

5.6.4 Token Placement

If E is the **when** event of an active specification, and E_T matches a stream event then the specification spawns an enabled copy. Copies of T (including binding changes caused by the matching process) are placed on the distinguished **s** and **s'** nodes of the enabled copy.

If E labels an arc of an enabled copy and E_T matches a stream event then the candidate token T is placed on the node which heads the arc. If T is placed on the f or f' finish nodes then that enabled copy will be either satisfied or violated.

Once a candidate token is placed on an event graph, the matching process (for that token--event pair) is over. The candidate token becomes a parent token when the next stream event is generated.

5.6.5 Special TSL Events

Some guarded_events in TSL do not contain basic_events. These guarded events have special rules governing how they match stream events.

The special **now** event matches (only) the first stream event after it becomes relevant. If a **now** event contains a guard, then it matches the stream event only if the guard is true.

When the TSL timer event becomes relevant, a timer is set for the specified number of seconds. The timer event matches the first stream event generated after the timer goes off.

The TSL count event with integer i matches the ith stream event generated after the count event becomes relevant.

The count, timer, and **now** events are included in TSL to aid in debugging real time systems. Unfortunately the semantics of Ada do not allow us to infer any timing properties of programs. Therefore, these events may not have the intended properties in all Ada systems.

The matching of recursive macros are described in section 8.

5.6.6 One match

Normally tokens remain on an enabled copy until the enabled copy is satisfied or violated. However TSL provides the *one match* alternative semantics. Events in TSL statements containing the key phrase **one match** are matched using this alternative semantics.

The one match semantics are the same as the regular matching semantics, except that parent tokens are deleted as soon as one of their descendents has been placed on the event graph. If a parent is on a node containing multiple outgoing arcs, then events on the arc are matched in the order that they appear in the original TSL specification.

5.7 Macros

The inline macros will be textually substituted into the statements during preprocessing. However, recursive macros require special runtime handling. During preprocessing we use the JOIN procedure to create a labeled graph for each recursive macro. Associated with this graph is a token template listing the formal parameters.

When a token is placed on a node with an outgoing arc labeled with a recursive macro call, then:

- the activated event graph for the macro spawns an enabled copy,
- a new token for the macro is created, with each formal parameter in the token initialized to the value of its actual parameter.
- this new token is placed on the distinguished s node of the enabled copy.

In order for the macro call to have an effect on the calling event graph, additional information must be kept. The token whose placement created the macro call is noted, as is the node at the head of the arc labeled with the recursive macro call.

Matching of recursive macro graphs is the same as matching regular event graphs. When a token is placed on the distinguished f node of the enabled copy, then:

- a candidate token is created from the noted token.
- this candidate token is placed on the noted node.
- the macro's enabled copy is deleted.

If the enabled copy which issued the macro call is deleted then the macro's enabled copy is also deleted. Care must be taken that the macro's enabled copy is spawned from the proper activated event graph (the one which was activated at the same time as the calling event graph). When the one match semantics are used, then the macro's enabled copy is deleted when the noted token is deleted.

6. RELATIONSHIP TO OTHER WORK

Many of the concepts used in TSL have appeared in one form or another in earlier papers on concurrent specifications. We mention three important related works. First, sequences and recursive macros in TSL have the same expressive power as path expressions in [Campbell,Habermann 74]. Secondly, TSL has many ideas and features in common with the event description language, EDL, for debugging distributed systems described by Bates and Wileden in [Bates,Wileden 82]. TSL has more general facilities, providing, for example, negation and explicit termination events in specifications. There are also some differences in the semantics of the two languages, TSL being based on matching specifications to subsequences of the event stream that may be separated by irrelevent events. Finally, our event/token graphs used in the operational semantics are clearly related to Petri nets [Peterson 77]. We did not investigate the use of Petri nets in defining TSL semantics.

A. TSL SYNTAX

Names:

name	::= constant | placeholder
constant	::= *ada*_name | **any** | **main** | integer
placeholder	::= # identifier | ? identifier

Guards:

status	::= **running** | **in_rendezvous** | **block_waiting** | **terminated**
	| **select**_terminate)
	| **accepting** [**at** *entry*_name {**and** *entry*_name
	| **calling** [**task** *task*_name [**at** *entry*_name]]
guard_element	::= *task*_name **is** [**not**] status | *task*_name **is** [**not**] **task** *task*_name
	| *task*_name **is** [**not**] of type *type*_name
	| *entry*_name **is** [**not**] **entry** *entry*_name
	| *entry*_name **is** [**not**] **in** *family*_name
	| *variable*_name **is** [**not**] *integer*_constant
guard_list	::= (guard_element {**or** guard_element})
guard_condition	::= (guard_list {**and** guard_list})
guard	::= **where** guard_list | **where** guard_condition

Events:

call	::= *task*_name **calls** *task*_name [**at** *entry*_name]
accept	::= *task*_name **accepting** [*entry*_name {, *entry*_name}]
start_rendezvous	::= *task*_name **accepts** [*task*_}name] [**at** *entry*_name]
end_rendezvous	::= *task*_name **releases** [*task*_name] [**from** *entry*_name]
termination	::= *task*_name **terminates**
at_label	::= *task*_name **reaches** *label*_name
activation	::= *task*_name **activates** [*task*_name]
timer	::= *integer*_constant **seconds**
count	::= *integer*_constant **interactions**
basic_event	::= call | accept | start_rendezvous | end_rendezvous
	| termination | at_label | activation
guarded_event	::= basic_event [guard] | **now** [guard] | timer | count

Compound Events:

compound_event	::= guarded_event | sequence | one_of | all_of | *macro*_name param_list
sequence	::= (compound_event ⇒ compound_event {⇒ compound_event})
one_of	::= (compound_event **or** compound_event {**or** compound_event})
all_of	::= (compound_event **and** compound_event {**and** compound_event})
parameter	::= *task*_name | *entry*_name
param_list	::= ([parameter {, parameter}])

Statements:

specification	::= **when** guarded_event **then** [**not**] [**one match**] compound_event **before** guarded_event
definition	::= **define** [**recursive** | **inline**] *macro*_name param_list **is**

References

[Bates,Wileden 82]
Bates, P.C. and Wileden, J.C.
EDL: A Basis for Distributed System Debugging Tools.
In *Proceedings of Hawaii International Conference on System Sciences,* pages 86-93. Hawaii International Conference on System Sciences, Honolulu, Hawaii, January, 1982.

[Campbell,Habermann 74]
Campbell,R.H. and Habermann, A.N.
The Specification of Process Synchronization by Path-Expressions.
Lecture Notes in Computer Science 16, 1974.

[German 84] German, S.M.
Monitoring for Deadlock and Blocking in Ada Tasking.
IEEE Transactions on Software Engineering SE-10(6):764-777, November, 1984.

[Helmbold,Luckham 83]
Helmbold, D., and Luckham, D.C.
Runtime Detection and Description of Deadness Errors in Ada Tasking.
CSL Technical Report 83-249, Stanford University, November, 1983.
Program Analysis and Verification Group Report 22.

[Helmbold,Luckham 84]
Helmbold, D. and Luckham, D.C.
Debugging Ada Tasking Programs.
Technical Report 84-262, Stanford University, July, 1984.
Program Analysis and Verification Group Report 25. Also: IEEE Computer Society 1984 Conference on Ada Applications and Environments, October 15-18, St. Paul, Minnesota.

[Helmbold,Luckham 85]
Helmbold, D.P. and Luckham, D.C.
Debugging Ada Tasking Programs.
IEEE Software 2(2):47-57, March, 1985.
ISSN 0740-7459.

[Lamport 78] Lamport, L.
Time Clocks and the Ordering of Events in a Distributed System.
Communications of the ACM 21(7), July, 1978.

[Peterson 77] Peterson, J.L.
Petri Nets.
Computing Surveys 9(3), September, 1977.

AUTOMATIC LANGUAGE CONVERSION AND ITS PLACE IN THE TRANSITION TO ADA

P. J. L. Wallis,
School of Mathematics, University of Bath, Claverton Down,
Bath BA2 7AY UK.

Abstract. A number of systems for the automatic conversion to Ada of software written in other languages have been specified or implemented, but such systems are of limited usefulness in planned programmes for the transition to Ada. Managerial and technical implications of the availability of automatic converters for planned transitions to Ada are separately discussed.

INTRODUCTION

In the next few years many organisations currently using other programming languages will be undertaking transitions to Ada. Components of such transitions will typically include conversions of existing software to Ada versions, retraining of programmers experienced in other languages and consequential changes in software development practices. Further, it may be necessary initially to use such bridging technologies as the introduction of mixed-language working or the use of language subsets in writing software that is later to be converted to Ada.

Superficially it might appear that fully automatic conversion to Ada of software written in other languages would be a highly effective component of such a transition programme. If a suitable converter were available, investment in existing software could be preserved across the change in language and transition undertaken relatively painlessly. Further reflection suggests that such hopes may be groundless - for example, the generated Ada software might be extravagant to produce and to run, or so opaque that its use as a basis for subsequent maintenance is out of the question. However, even the specification of a converter can be valuable in planning a transition programme; it might identify subsets of the current language that are particularly easy to translate, or parts of the language whose effective translation presents particular difficulties. Such information can be useful in planning a transition programme as guidance in specifying necessary retraining of programmers or the effective use of suitable bridging technologies.

The purpose of this paper is to draw on experience with automatic language converters involving Ada that have already been specified or implemented for the purpose of explaining their potential relevance to plans for the transition to Ada. Examples of existing converters are the PascAda system (Albrecht et al. 1980) which offers conversions in either direction between Ada and Pascal subsets, and the IBIS system (Slape & Wallis 1983) which features conversion of Fortran to Ada. Studies of conversions involving RTL/2 (Barnes 1976) and Ada (SPL International 1982 a,b) and involving Pascal and Ada (SPL Interntional 1983) have also been undertaken for the Commission of the European Communities. A group of software houses in the UK and the USA is currently developing Cobol to Ada and Fortran to Ada converters for the Institute for Defense Analyses (Washington) for use in the automatic conversion of large volumes of existing source; the design of the Cobol converter for this project is outlined in (Dobbing 1985) and that of the Fortran converter is similar. Technical and other details from many of these sources are to be republished in (Wallis & Thwaites 1985).

Subsequent sections of this paper deal separately with managerial implications of the availability of automatic converters for planned transitions to Ada, and with technical aspects of the converters themselves.

MANAGERIAL IMPLICATIONS

The managerial issues involved in a high-level language conversion on a small scale (such as moving a single software product to a new language environment) are often reasonably straightforward but managerial decisions involving changes in working practices for large numbers of programmers must naturally be considered far more carefully. The conversion of an organisation to Ada from another high-level language involves much broader issues than the availability of a suitable automatic converter. However the mere specification of a feasible converter may be of great vaue in planning a transition; this may provide guidance, for example, in identifying particular training needs or potential problem areas. Further, it may suggest suitable bridging technologies such as the temporary use of the converter, of language subsets or of mixed-language working. To put such possibilites into the overall perspective of a transition strategy, we briefly consider changes in software development practices that should accompany a transition to Ada, and the training needs that they imply. The question of the conversion of existing code to Ada, and possible alternatives to this, are then considered at greater length.

CHANGES IN WORKING PRACTICES

When considering a change in working practices to Ada from another programming language, it must be understood that far more is involved than the simple substitution of one language for another at the most detailed working level. A change of language implies a change in ways of thought suggested by the constructs of the language; transition to Ada makes no sense unless there is a major retraining effort to make sure that the capabilities of the language will be properly used. Substantial retraining is required; it is especially true of transitions to Ada that in changing from one language to another "the most vital conversion required is in the mind of the programmer" (SPL International 1982a).

The necessay change in attitudes does not only concern the programmers' use of the language; it is likely to involve the whole software development process as well. This is particularly likely to be the case in conversions to the use of Ada, both because of the constructs in Ada (such as packages) that encourage well-engineered development of programs and because of the projected development of elaborate APSEs, embracing an integrated management view of the whole software life-cycle (McDermid & Ripken 1984). So conversions to Ada are likely to require associated changes in software development practices, both by programmers and by their managers. Sometimes it is possible to apply bridging techniques to this change, for example, by moving software development support tools between one language environment and the other so that changes in software development practices need not coincide with the change of language.

Clearly, the training requirements for a successful transition to Ada go far beyond a simple quick "conversion" of the programmers involved; software development practices and the necessary retraining of programming managers must also be addressed. In addition to the obvious training aids, specifications of common subsets and of automatic language converters may be useful here. Provision of necessary retraining in software development practices requires careful planning too. One interesting idea that has been proposed, in connection with a conversion to Ada, is training in the software engineering practices encouraged by the use of Ada prior to the change of working language. This could be achieved by using Ada as a design language for the specifications of the packages in a new piece of software, followed by coding of the package bodies in the language previously used. Clearly, the specification of a converter (for example, an Ada-to-Pascal converter if the package bodies are to be developed in Pascal) is extremely useful as a training aid for such an exercise.

CODE CONVERSION

While the availability of suitable automatic converters, or at least of their specifications, may be valuable in the general areas just mentioned, they are most likely to be of direct use in the conversion to Ada of existing code. In assessing this possiblity, the value of the currently existing code that must be evaluated; it may turn out that it has become desirable to rewrite much of it anyway, either to enhance its functionality or to make better use of the features of Ada than would be possible with a code conversion. Alternatively, it might be possible to obtain suitable substitute Ada software from elsewhere or to introduce mixed-language working. Mixed-language working may not be feasible, but it is certainly a possiblity in some cases (van der Laan 1984). Vouk (1984) offers a discussion of costs associated with mixed-language programming in which he concludes that this way of working can be very cost-effective.

If conversion of some existing code is contemplated, it is important to note that this is bound to entail long-term costs, regardless of whether it is manual, partially automatic or fully automatic. These costs may be partly manifested in increased code size, memory occupancy and execution time, although in some cases converted code may actually perform better than idiomatic Ada code since only straightforward Ada constructs are used. The most significant long-term cost, however, is likely to be incurred through the reduced maintainability of the resulting code. Serious code conversion has frequently been considered a non-starter for just this reason; typical experience is that, even where the performance of the generated code is acceptable, the code produced is not suficiently idiomatic in its use of the target language to make subsequent maintenance of the converted software an economic proposition.

If fully automatic code conversion is contemplated, it is naturally necessary to specify conversion rules in detail, both to explore the feasibility of the proposed conversion and to draw attention to likely problem areas. Some potential areas of technical difficulty in such conversions are discussed later. We have seen that even if no code conversion or some limited manual conversion is planned, the projected specification of a hypothetical language converter is still a valuable exercise.

Maintainability

The argument that automatic language conversion results in unmaintainable Ada loses its force in those cases where subsequent maintenance on the generated Ada is not required, for example as a bridging technology applied to well-tried existing software. It should be noted that the generated Ada in such cases may be more efficient in execution than 'idiomatic' versions of the same software later developed in Ada - such experience was reported with conversions from Fortran to Algol 68 (Prudom 1980).

If language conversion is to be used in this way, the converter used should be fully automatic to the greatest possible extent. This contrasts with the situation where a converter specification is to be used for another purpose such as the retraining of programmers; here the specification of a converter that does an adequate job on most of the language may be more helpful than that of a converter that goes to elaborate lengths to accept as much of the source language as is technically feasible under any circumstances. As an example of the major effect on conversion strategy that a decision to convert as much of the language as possible could have, consider the discussion of Fortran COMMON and EQUIVALENCE statements below.

TECHNICAL ISSUES

We have seen that the specification of a possible automatic converter can be a most valuable document even if, in the event, automatic conversion is not actually used in a transition to Ada. Some technical issues related to the design of such converters are now discussed.

Problems with Specific Language Constructs

In general, specifying suitable converter actions for individual language constructs is reasonably straightforward. However, extreme care is necessary to ensure that the translations of language constructs reflect all relevant semantic differences between Ada and the source language. Two examples of the need for such care are Fortran DO-loops and Pascal records; further examples may be found in the references.

Fortran DO-loops. The conversion of Fortran DO-loops into Ada for-loops is discussed in (Slape & Wallis 1983). Two differences between the Fortran and Ada constructs cause particular difficulty. First, a calculation of the appropriate number of traversals for the for-loop is necessary; in the system discussed this calculation is performed using a call to a runtime library function in the generated Ada, and different versions of the function are appropriate to conversions from Fortran 66 or Fortran 77. Secondly, since the scope of the loop parameter in an Ada for-loop is restricted to the loop body, it is necessary in general to increment a variable of larger scope each time the loop is traversed because the scope of a Fortran 77 DO-loop control variable is not restricted to the body of the loop.

Pascal Records. Although the record types provided in Pascal and in Ada are superficially similar, it is explained in some detail in (SPL International 1983) that there are many minor differences that make the task of their mutual conversion extremely difficult. The difficulties can roughly be characterised as being due to differences between Ada and Pascal concerned with the handling on initialisation, default values and discriminants. While these can be overcome in most cases, completely generalised translation between Ada and Pascal record constructs is not possible.

Global Language Issues

The most interesting and difficult part of designing a converter is often that related to the global differences in the organisation of programs in Ada and in the other language. Some examples of these differences follow.

Subprogram Parameters. The use of subprogram parameters is relatively common in Fortran numerical work; the same effect is gained in Ada by using generics. It is explained in (Slape & Wallis 1983) that it is in genral feasible to perform this conversion automatically with one minor reservation but in complicated cases the Ada generated might prove very opaque.

Type Security. Since Ada has a very secure typing system, difficulties may arise when converting to Ada a language with less secure typing. Examples of this difficulty are the use of REF variables in RTL/2 (SPL International 1982a) and the use of structural (rather than name) equivalence in Cobol. In such cases, as proposed in (Dobbing 1985), the only way of handling the problem in general is to model the source-language data store within a vector in the generated Ada. A similar problem with certain Fortran COMMON and EQUIVALENCE statements was handled in (Slape & Wallis 1983) by declaring irregular cases untranslatable so that this kind of store modelling became unnecessary.

Program Structure. Difficulties may arise in deciding how the overall structure of source programs should be mapped onto Ada constructs. For example, Slape and Wallis (1983) explain a decision to convert each subprogram of a Fortran program into a separate package, while (Dobbing 1985) explains why all Ada programs generated from Cobol require a standard artificially-generated main program. A structural difficulty of a different kind is encountered when trying to convert RTL/2 programs with tasks into Ada programs with tasks; this is not possible save in some special cases because of differing storage management strategies for tasks in the two languages (SPL International 1982a).

General Technical Comments

Taken together, the technical comments just given (which have been selected from a mass of similar material) should convince the reader of the need to be cautious about fully automatic conversion - the Ada generated may well be potentially too slow to execute and unreadably opaque,minimising its usefulness as a basis for subsequent program maintenance. It may be possible to improve the situation somewhat by developing suitable program transformers; interactive transformers are planned for the IBIS system, and a toolset for the interactive improvement of the package structure of Ada programs generated from Fortran has been proposed (Wallis 1983a). Further improvements in the quality of the generated Ada may be obtainable from systems that perform some source-code analysis to identify special cases before embarking on the conversion to an intermediate form based on Ada; such source-code analysis is not a feature of the IBIS system, but will be offered in production Cobol and Fortran converters currently under development (Dobbing 1985).

A more serious reason for being skeptical of the lasting value of automatic conversions to Ada is that the generated programs will necessarily be unidiomatic in their use of Ada constructs, so automatic conversion is unlikely to produce software of acceptable quality. For example, Wichmann & Meijerink (1984) argue convincingly by means of an extended example that "there is a substantial difference between a naive transliteration of a subroutine and an ideal Ada package".

This is only one example of the kind of consideration that leads members of the Ada-Europe Numerics Working Group (an informal gathering of interested parties, of which the author is a member) to conclude that, although extensive numerical libraries already exist in other languages, automatic conversion is a non-starter as far as production of an equivalent Ada library is concerned. For instance, the whole structure of a suggested Ada scientific library is governed by the desire for effective use of such features of Ada as exceptions, generics and packages (Symm & Kok 1984). Even the use of Ada numerics appropriate for portable numerical software (Wallis 1983b) is so peculiar to Ada that it is hard to imagine that a portable Ada library making this use of numerics could ever be automatically generated from a numerical library written in another language.

CONCLUSIONS

For both managerial and technical reasons, automatic language conversion cannot provide an easy route to a complete conversion to Ada. However, it may be usable in special cases as a bridging technology, and in any case the detailed design of a projected automatic converter can form a useful reference in its own right. Many daunting problems will be encountered in transitions to Ada; the most we may hope is that the study of automatic language conversion might help find solutions to a few of them.

Acknowledgments

Useful comments were provided by the referees and by members of the Ada-Europe Numerics Working Group, whose meetings are partially supported by the Commission of the European Communities. My thanks also to Brian Maher and John Slape, whose work on IBIS has been supported by the UK Science and Engineering Research Council. Mike Rogers of the Commission of the European Comunities kindly made available various reports cited in the references; he also suggested the production both of this paper and of the forthcoming book on the subject in the Ada Companion Series.

REFERENCES

Albrecht, P.F., Garrison, P.E., Graham, S.L., Hyerle, R.H., Ip, P., and Kreig-Brückner, B. (1980) Source-to-source translation: Ada to Pascal and Pascal to Ada. In Proceedings of the ACM SIGPLAN Symposium on the Ada Programming Language, Boston. ACM SIGPLAN Notices 15(12), 183-193 (1980).

Barnes, J.G.P.(1972). RTL/2 Design and Philosophy. London:Heyden

Dobbing, B.J.(1985). Everything is Possible - Even COBOL to Ada Translation. Ada UK News, to appear.

van der Laan, C.G.(1984). Interfacing Ada to Fortran. In Proceedings of the Third Joint Ada Europe/AdaTEC Conference, Brussels, 26-28 June 1984, ed. J.Teller, pp.179-89. Cambridge: Cambridge University Press.

McDermid, J. & Ripken, K.(1984). Life Cycle Support in the Ada Environment. Cambridge: Cambridge University Press.

Prudom, A. (1980) Run Time Comparison of Fortran and Aglol 68 Routines. In Production and Assessment of Numerical Software ed. M.A.Hennell and L.M.Delves, pp 97-102. London: Academic Press.

SPL International (1982a). A Feasibility Study of the Conversion of RTL/2 to Ada: Technical Guide (September 1982).

SPL International (1982b). A Feasibility Study of the Conversion of RTL/2 to Ada: Managerial Report (October 1982).

SPL International (1983). Feasibility Study of Software Tools for Converting Pascal Programs into Ada and Vice-Versa, Final Report, September 1983.

Slape, J.K. & Wallis,P.J.L (1983). Conversion of Fortran to Ada Using an Intermediate Tree Representation, Computer Journal 26(3), 344-53.

Symm, G.T. & Kok, J. (1984). Guidelines for the Design of Large Modular Scientific Libraries in Ada. In Proceedings of the Third Joint Ada Europe/AdaTEC Conference,Brussels. 26 - 28 June 1984, ed. J. Teller, pp 153-64. Cambridge: Cambridge University Press.

Vouk, M.A.(1984). On the Cost of Mixed Language Programming. ACM SIGPLAN Notices 19(12), 54-60 (1984).

Wallis, P.J.L. (1983a). Towards the Design of a Toolset for Manipulating Ada Packages. In: Proceedings of the Ada-Europe/AdaTEC Joint Conference on Ada, Brussels, March 1983 pp 18-1 - 18-8.

Wallis. P.J.L. (1983b). Ada Floating-point Arithmetic as a Basis for Portable Numerical Software. In: Proceedings of the 6th IEEE Symposium on Computer Arithmetic, Aarhus, pp 79 -81. Silver Spring: IEEE Computer Society Press.

Wallis, P.J.L. & Thwaites, G.K. (Editors) (1985). Ada and High-Level Language Conversion. Cambridge: Cambridge University Press, to appear.

Wichmann, B.A. & Meijerink, J.G.J.(1984). Converting to Ada Packages. In Proceedings of the Third Joint Ada-Europe/AdaTEC Conference, Brussels, 26 - 28 June 1984, ed. J. Teller, pp 131-9. Cambridge: Cambridge University Press.

AN IMPLEMENTATION OF ANNA

Sriram Sankar
David Rosenblum
Randall Neff

Program Analysis and Verification Group
Computer Systems Laboratory
Stanford University
Stanford, California 94305

Abstract. Anna is a language extension of Ada to include facilities for formally specifying the intended behavior of Ada programs. It augments Ada with precise machine-processable annotations so that well established formal methods of specification and documentation can be applied to Ada programs.
This paper describes an implementation of a subset of Anna. The implementation is a transformer that accepts as input an Anna parse tree and produces as output an equivalent Ada parse tree that contains the necessary executable runtime checks for the Anna specifications. An approach called the *Checking Function Approach* is used. This involves the generation of a function for each annotation and generating calls to these functions at appropriate places. The transformer has to take care of various details like hiding, overloading, nesting, etc.
It is hoped that the transformer will eventually cover most of Anna and have various features like a good user interface, interaction with a symbolic debugger, and optimization of runtime checks for permanent inclusion.

1. INTRODUCTION

Anna [Anna 84, Luckham 84] is a language extension of Ada[1] [Ada 83] to include facilities for formally specifying the intended behavior of Ada programs. It augments Ada with computer processable annotations so that formal methods of specification and documentation can be applied to Ada programs. These annotations appear as formal comments within the Ada source text. Anna defines two kinds of formal comments, which are introduced by special comment indicators in order to distinguish them from informal comments. These are: *Virtual Ada text*, which start with the indicator "--:"; and *Annotations* which start with the indicator "--|". The purpose of virtual text is to define concepts used in annotations. Virtual text is Ada text, but has to conform to various restrictions imposed by Anna. Annotations are constraints on the underlying Ada program, their precise meaning depending on their location and syntactic form. Examples of formal comments are given in Appendix A.

The semantics of Anna have been defined using two different approaches—Axiomatic Semantics and Checking Semantics. Axiomatic Semantics provide a basis for a mathematical proof of consistency between the formal specifications written in Anna and the underlying Ada program [Krieg 83]. Checking Semantics is a set of transformations that convert Anna annotations into executable Ada text. The Ada text checks the consistency of the underlying Ada program against the (original) annotations at runtime. Inconsistencies are reported by the propagation of various exceptions together with diagnostic information.

---

[1] Ada is a registered trademark of the U.S. Government

This paper deals with an implementation of the Checking Semantics. Various applications of the Anna checking semantics are possible. Some applications are:

- **Formal Documentation:** The Anna specifications provide a formal notation for documenting the behavior of the Ada program for human readers. The annotations complement the behavior description provided by the Ada text.
- **Rapid Prototyping:** Anna can be used to provide a quick set of specifications for a particular problem. These specifications would be at a higher level and much more reliable than the actual Ada code that will eventually be written. Though these specifications may have to be implemented more inefficiently than the final code, it can be used to determine the correctness of this final code.
- **Testing and Debugging:** Recognition of inconsistencies between Anna specifications and Ada programs is automated. The transformation therefore produces a self-checking program which could interact with other tools (e.g. a symbolic debugger). When the transformed program is executed on test cases, inconsistencies would cause error messages and interaction with conventional tools.
- **Production Quality Programs:** The Anna runtime checks could be left permanently in the program. A transformation tool with good optimizing capabilities could produce a program that is self-checking and that would report the occurrence of any inconsistencies during program operation, therefore creating an opportunity for automatic error recovery.

In order to develop these applications, it is first necessary to establish the practicality of the runtime checking transformation. This paper describes an implementation of a subset of Anna. The paper gives details of the transformations, how the transformations were verified, and experimental results. Possible optimizations of the checking Ada text are discussed.

2. DEFINITION OF THE SUBSET AND THE TRANSFORMATION METHODOLOGY

A subset of Anna was chosen for implementation. This subset was designed to develop a usable pilot version, and also to make future expansion simple and straightforward.

Types and objects that can be annotated have been restricted to scalars only. Object annotations, subtype annotations, statement annotations and subprogram annotations are included in the subset. Special Anna attributes have been excluded, and the attribute DEFINED is always assumed to be TRUE. All Anna expressions are permitted with the exception of those that include quantified expressions or states. Therefore Anna membership tests and conditional expressions are included in the subset. The subset allows virtual Ada text, but the transformation methodology does not include any checks to ensure the correctness of this text. It is therefore the responsibility of the programmer to ensure that virtual Ada text satisfies the restrictions imposed by Anna. For the syntax summary of the subset, refer to Appendix B.

The transformation methodology is implemented as a transformer that transforms the parse tree of the Anna program to the parse tree of an equivalent Ada program [Rosenblum 84]. The equivalent Ada program is the underlying Ada text and virtual text of the Anna program together with executable checks inserted at appropriate places to check annotations. The Anna parse tree is an extended form of a DIANA tree, while the Ada parse tree is a regular

DIANA tree [Diana 83]. The input tree can be provided by a parser, and the output tree can, among other alternatives, be sent to a pretty-printer to obtain Ada text, or to a compiler back-end to produce self-checking code.

2.1 Checking Functions

The concept of a *Checking Function* has been used extensively in the transformation methodology. A checking function is an Ada function that checks for the validity of annotation(s) and takes an appropriate action. This action could either be to return a BOOLEAN value that specifies the result of the check, or to raise an exception if the check shows that the annotation was violated. At various places where it is possible that annotations can be violated, appropriate checking functions are called. The advantages of implementing checks as checking functions and calls to them as against expanding the checks inline are quite apparent. Most important is the fact that using the Ada pragma INLINE, the checking function methodology reduces to expanding checks inline. It is much simpler to generate checking functions and calls to them since the annotations do not have to be remembered by the transformation program; only the names of the generated checking functions have to be remembered. Since it is usually the case that the same annotation has to be checked for validity at more than one place, the checking function approach lowers space requirements.

Checking functions are defined currently for three types of annotations. These are subtype annotations, object annotations, and result annotations. It has been determined that these three annotations are the most basic, and most other annotations in the subset reduce to one of these. Checking functions that raise an exception if the annotation is found to be false are generated for each of the above types of annotations. These checking functions are used to check validity of annotations at places in the program where it is possible that they can be violated. For subtype annotations there is one more type of checking function defined. This returns TRUE if the annotation is satisfied, and it returns FALSE otherwise. This checking function is used to implement the Anna membership operation **is in**.

Sometimes checking functions have to call other checking functions. This has to be done when there is a nesting of annotations. An example of nesting is when a subtype of another subtype is declared, and both these subtypes are annotated. In this case, the checking function of the new subtype calls the checking function of the parent subtype. This ensures that when this new checking function is called, both annotations are checked.

Examples of checking functions of all types are shown in Appendix C.

The transformation methodology is now described in detail. The description is organized into three subsections:

- Transformation of Anna expressions to Ada expressions
- Transformation of annotations to more basic annotations
- Transformation of basic annotations to checking code

2.2 Transformation of Anna Expressions to Ada Expressions

Conditional expressions can occur only as part of BOOLEAN expressions. This is because conditional expressions can occur only in annotations. The conditional operator is distributed outwards until the value of the conditional expression is BOOLEAN. The conditional expression is then replaced by the equivalent BOOLEAN expression.

Initial names and expressions are replaced by a new variable of the same type.

This new variable is declared and initialized to the value of the initial name/expression. The method of initialization depends on the location of the initial name/expression. To determine the type of this new variable, it is necessary to resolve any overloading within this expression.

Anna operators are transformed as follows: Implication "->" is transformed to "<=" and Equivalence "<->" is transformed to "=". Anna membership tests are transformed to a conjunction of an Ada membership test and a call to an appropriate checking function.

New names and operators are declared and used in the annotations instead of the original names and operators to prevent possible problems due to hiding and overloading.

Examples of such transformations are shown in Appendix D; an example which shows how Anna membership operations are transformed is shown in Appendix C.

2.3 Transformation of Annotations to more Basic Annotations

Subprogram annotations are transformed to object annotations at the beginning of the corresponding declarative parts. Compound statements with compound statement annotations are transformed to a block. The compound statement is placed in the statement part of the block, and the annotation is placed as an object annotation in the declarative part of the block. Examples of such transformations are in Appendix E.

2.4 Transformation of Basic Annotations to Checking Code

Transformation of subtype, object and result annotations are performed with the help of checking functions, and the method of transformation has already been described. However, the transformation methodology of the remaining two types of annotations, **out** annotations and simple statement annotations, must be explained. In both these cases, checks are expanded inline. In the case of **out** annotations, checks are generated at all **exit**, **goto** and **return** statements that might take control out of the scope of the annotation, as well as at the physical end of the block where the scope of the annotation ends. In the case of simple statement annotations, a check is expanded at the point of the annotation. Examples of these inline check generations are shown in Appendix F.

3. CONCLUSIONS AND FUTURE WORK

3.1 Current Status of the Transformer—Validation and Results

Validation of the Anna transformer was carried out by executing the transformer on a suite of Anna test inputs. Each of these test subprograms contained a single type of annotation in one of a variety of contexts (e.g., object annotations specifying a mutual constraint on two objects). The complete suite was designed for testing the transformer on every conceivable Anna construct that would occur in a program using the currently implemented subset of Anna. There are approximately thirty such test subprograms grouped according to the type of annotation being tested (subtype, object, result, simple statement, compound statement and subprogram annotations).

In performing the tests, the test programs are first input to the transformer, and the resulting transformed programs are then compiled by a validated Ada compiler to test for syntactic and semantic correctness; finally, the checking functions that are produced are executed in some cases and visually inspected in other cases to ensure that the transformations are correct. Syntactic errors are found by the Anna parser, while the transformer detects semantic errors within annotations. However, virtual text is assumed to be semantically correct; in particular, virtual text is assumed to produce no side effects on the Ada program within which it is embedded. The current transformer has succeeded every step of this testing procedure on the complete validation suite.

3.2 A User Interface to the Transformer

One project for the near future is to provide the user with a robust interface to the transformer that will help simplify the debugging of annotated programs. This interface will initially consist of a major enhancement of the diagnostic information provided during execution of a transformed program, including the location within the original source text at which a constraint was violated as well as the location of the corresponding annotation(s). In addition, the transformer will be extended with the capability of inserting calls to a symbolic debugger at places in the transformed program where the exception ANNA_ERROR could be raised. This capability will allow the user to query during execution of a transformed program the state of the program that caused an Anna constraint to be violated.

3.3 Optimization of the Transformations

Another future project is the optimization of the checking functions produced by the transformer as well as optimization of the algorithms used by the transformer. These optimizations fall into three broad classes: (1) Check function merging, (2) Static checking of annotations and (3) Parallel checking of annotations.

The simplest of these optimizations is the merging together of checking functions during the transformation process. For example, the checking function for an annotated subtype which is derived from other annotated subtypes can be merged with the other checking functions when there are no declared objects or type conversions naming any of the parent subtypes. The proper merging of checking functions is a simple extension of some of the recognition capabilities already available in the current transformer.

The most difficult of the optimizations is static checking of annotations. That is, the transformer would be extended with the capability of verifying statically (i.e., at "transformation time") that a program does or does not satisfy the constraints specified in (a subset of) the annotations it contains. The statically verified annotations which are satisfied would be ignored rather than transformed. Although static verification theorems and techniques have been studied for several years, it is not clear how easy it will be to apply such ideas to the Ada and Anna semantic framework.

A class of optimizations currently under investigation is the checking of annotations in parallel with the original program. The basic idea of such optimizations is that checking tasks running on different processors are substituted for checking functions. Variables are sent to an appropriate checking task via an entry call, and the task performs the annotation checks *after* ending the rendezvous. There are several problems with this approach. Unlike a regular Ada program, an Anna program would be allowed to proceed with its execution in this model even if it has violated some (Anna) constraint. Some would argue that this allowance defeats the whole purpose of specifying constraints, but often further execution of a program would have a "non-destructive" effect in some sense if an annotation were violated. On the other hand, if it turns out that a constraint were *not* violated at the point of the call to the checking task, then the original program has suffered a negligible slowdown. In either case, the checking function must eventually signal the original program that a constraint was violated, after which the sequential semantics would take over; that is, the checking task will eventually "catch up" with the original program and notify the program of an ANNA_ERROR. Parallel checking of constraints would be of great use in such time-critical applications as real-time embedded software; however, a highly intelligent checking model is needed to ensure that the gains achieved in reducing the slowdown due to checking are not negated by the lack of robustness brought about by latent notification of constraint violations.

3.4 Extending the Transformer to Recognize Full Anna

Although the Anna parser is able to recognize the complete syntax of Anna, a viable set of transformations for some Anna constructs has yet to be determined. The first set of enhancements to the transformer in the near future is the enlargement of the subset of Anna that it can recognize. This enlargement will include annotation of composite types and objects, annotation of access types and objects, array states, record states, collections, quantified expressions, package annotations, context annotations and propagation annotations. To appreciate the difficulty in efficiently transforming some of these features, consider an example involving quantified expressions. A reasonable annotation of a prime number subtype can be accomplished in the following manner:

```
type TWO_POSITIVE is new POSITIVE range 2 .. POSITIVE'LAST;
subtype PRIME is TWO_POSITIVE;
--| where X : PRIME => for all Y,Z : TWO_POSITIVE => (X /= Y * Z);
```

The limited intelligence of the current transformer allows a single option for transforming this annotation, namely the formation of two loops on the range of Y and Z with the inequality checked at every iteration. In this case such a transformation is obviously impractical. Aside from asking the programmer to state such an annotation more succinctly, any other method of transformation would require the transformer to somehow deduce (using a simple set of algebraic axioms) which ordered pairs (Y, Z) actually need to be checked *before* the checking function is produced. This example demonstrates the need for further research in determining how to efficiently check constraints expressed in a language as powerful Anna.

4. ACKNOWLEDGEMENTS

The authors wish to thank D. Luckham for his inspiration and guidance in the Anna implementation project. We are also grateful to F.W.von Henke for his contribution in determining the correctness of the design of the checking transformations. This work was supported by DARPA N00039-84C-0211.

A. EXAMPLES OF ANNOTATIONS

Object annotations:

```
CIRCUMFERENCE, DIAMETER : FLOAT;
--| CIRCUMFERENCE = PI * DIAMETER;
```

Subtype annotations:

```
subtype EVEN is INTEGER;
--| where X : EVEN => X mod 2 = 0;
```

Statement annotations:

```
I := 2;
--| with 1 < I <= N;
  -- Compound statement annotation.
while I <= N loop
   if A(I - 1) > A(I) then
      EXCHANGE(A(I - 1), A(I));
   end if;
   --| A(I) >= A(I - 1);
     -- simple statement annotation
   I := I + 1;
end loop;
```

Subprogram annotations:

```
procedure EXCHANGE(X, Y : in out ELEM);
--| where out(X = in Y), out(Y = in X);
```

Result annotations:

```
function SIN(X : FLOAT) return FLOAT;
--| where return X : FLOAT => abs X <= 1.0;
```

Examples of virtual text:

```
package STACK is
   --: function LENGTH return NATURAL;
   procedure PUSH(X : in ITEM);
   --| where out(LENGTH = in LENGTH + 1);
   procedure POP(X : out ITEM);
end STACK;
```

B. SYNTAX SUMMARY OF THE SUBSET

```
basic_declaration ::=
   ... ada_basic_declaration ...
 | basic_annotation_list

basic_annotation_list ::=
   basic_annotation {, basic_annotation};

basic_annotation ::=
   object_annotation
 | result_annotation

object_annotation ::=
   boolean_compound_expression
 | out boolean_primary

full_type_declaration ::=
   ... ada_full_type_declaration ...
   [subtype_annotation]

subtype_declaration ::=
   ... ada_subtype_declaration ...
   [subtype_annotation]

subtype_annotation ::=
   where identifier : type_mark =>
      boolean_compound_expression;

implication_operator ::=
   -> | <->

conditional_expression ::=
   if condition then
      compound_expression
   {elsif condition then
      compound_expression}
   else
      compound_expression
   end if

condition ::=
   boolean_compound_expression

initial_name ::=
   in simple_name

initial_expression ::=
   in ( compound_expression )

simple_statement ::=
   ... ada_simple_statement ...
 | basic_annotation_list

compound_statement ::=
   [compound_statement_annotation]
   ... ada_compound_statement ...
```

```
name ::=
   ... ada_name ...
 | initial_name

compound_expression ::=
   expression
     [implication_operator expression]

relation ::=
   simple_expression
      {relational_operator simple_expression}
 | simple_expression [is] [not] in range
 | simple_expression [is] [not] in type_mark

primary ::=
   ... ada_primary ...
 | conditional_expression
 | initial_expression
 | ( compound_expression )

compound_statement_annotation ::=
   with
      basic_annotation_list

subprogram_declaration ::=
   ... ada_subprogram_specification ...;
   [subprogram_annotation]

subprogram_specification ::=
   ... ada_subprogram_specification ...
   [subprogram_annotation]

subprogram_annotation ::=
   where
      basic_annotation_list

result_annotation ::=
   return [ identifier : type_mark => ]
     compound_expression
```

C. EXAMPLES OF CHECKING FUNCTIONS AND THEIR USE

1. Checking functions for subtype annotations:

The subtype annotation on EVEN:

```
subtype EVEN is INTEGER;
--| where X : EVEN => X mod 2 = 0;
```

transforms to the following two checking functions:

```
subtype EVEN is INTEGER;

-- This is used to check possible violations of
-- annotations.
function CHECK_EVEN_1(X : EVEN) return EVEN is
begin
   if not (X mod 2 = 0) then error; end if;
   return X;
end CHECK_EVEN_1;

-- This is used in the implementation of Anna
-- membership tests.
function CHECK_EVEN_2(X : EVEN) return BOOLEAN is
begin
   return (X mod 2 = 0);
end CHECK_EVEN_2;
```

2. Checking functions for object annotations:

The object annotations on A and B:

```
A, B : INTEGER;
--| A + B > 0, B >= 0;
```

transforms to a checking function for A and another for B:

```
A, B : INTEGER;

function CHECK_A(A : INTEGER)
return INTEGER is
begin
   if not (A + B > 0) then error; end if;
   return A;
end CHECK_A;

function CHECK_B(B : INTEGER)
return INTEGER is
begin
   if not (A + B > 0) then error; end if;
   if not (B >= 0) then error; end if;
   return B;
end CHECK_B;
```

3. Checking functions for result annotations:

The result annotation on function FOO:

```
function FOO(X : INTEGER)
return INTEGER is
   --| return Z:INTEGER => Z > X;
begin
   ...
end FOO;
```

transforms to include a checking function as shown:

```
function FOO(X : INTEGER)
return INTEGER is
   function CHECK_FOO(Z : INTEGER)
   return INTEGER is
   begin
      if not (Z > X) then error; end if;
      return Z;
   end CHECK_FOO;
begin
   ...
end FOO;
```

4. Use of checking functions:

The assignment statement, where E is of type EVEN:

```
E := exp;
```

transforms to:

```
E := CHECK_EVEN_1(exp);
```

The following expression:

```
exp is in EVEN
```

transforms to:

```
TMP := exp;
(TMP in EVEN) and (CHECK_EVEN_2(TMP))
```

The assignment statement:

```
A := exp;
```

transforms to:

```
A := CHECK_A(exp);
```

This return statement, within function FOO:

```
return exp;
```

transforms to:

```
return CHECK_FOO(exp);
```

D. TRANSFORMATIONS OF ANNA EXPRESSIONS TO ADA EXPRESSIONS.

Transformation of conditional expressions:

The conditional expression:

```
X = if C then Y else Z
```

transforms to:

```
if C then X = Y else X = Z
```

which in turn transforms to:

```
(C and then X = Y) or else (not C and then X = Z)
```

Transformation of initial names/expressions:

The expression:

```
A + in (B * C) - in D
```

transforms to:

```
NEW_1 : T1 := (B * C);
  -- T1 is the type of the expression B * C
NEW_2 : T2 := D;
  -- T2 is the type of D

A + NEW_1 - NEW_2
```

Transformation of implication and equivalence operators:

The expression:

```
((A -> B) and (B -> A)) -> (A <-> B)
```

transforms to:

```
((A <= B) and (B <= A)) <= (A = B)
```

Introduction of new names:

The expression:

```
A + B * C
  -- assume that A, B and C are of
  -- type INTEGER.
```

transforms to:

```
NEW_A : INTEGER renames A;
NEW_B : INTEGER renames B;
NEW_C : INTEGER renames C;
function NEW_PLUS(X, Y : INTEGER)
return INTEGER renames "+";
function NEW_STAR(X, Y : INTEGER)
return INTEGER renames "*";

NEW_PLUS(NEW_A, NEW_STAR(NEW_B, NEW_C))
  -- the transformed expression
```

E. TRANSFORMATION OF ANNOTATIONS TO MORE BASIC ANNOTATIONS

Subprogram annotations:

The subprogram annotation on EXCHANGE:

```
procedure EXCHANGE(X, Y : in out ELEM)
   --| where out (X = in Y),
             out (Y = in X);
is
   T : ELEM;
begin
   T := X; X := Y; Y := T;
end EXCHANGE;
```

transforms to the following object annotation:

```
procedure EXCHANGE(X, Y : in out ELEM) is
   --| out (X = in Y), out (Y = in X);
   T : ELEM;
begin
   T := X; X := Y; Y := T;
end EXCHANGE;
```

Compound statement annotations:

The annotated compound statement:

```
--| with 1 < I <= N;
while I <= N loop
   ...
end loop;
```

transforms to:

```
declare
   --| 1 < I <= N;
begin
   while I <= N loop
      ...
   end loop;
end;
```

F. TRANSFORMATION OF OUT ANNOTATIONS AND SIMPLE STATEMENT ANNOTATIONS

Out annotations:

The Out annotations on procedure exchange:

```
procedure EXCHANGE(X, Y : in out ELEM) is
   --| out(X = in Y), out(Y = in X);
   T : ELEM;
begin
   if X = Y then
      return;
   end if;
   T := X; X := Y; Y := T;
end EXCHANGE;
```

transforms to:

```
procedure EXCHANGE(X, Y : in out ELEM) is
   IN_Y : constant ELEM := Y;
   IN_X : constant ELEM := X;
   T : ELEM;
begin
   if X = Y then
      CHECK (X = IN_Y);
      CHECK (Y = IN_X);
      return;
   end if;
   T := X; X := Y; Y := T;
   CHECK (X = IN_Y);
   CHECK (Y = IN_X);
end EXCHANGE;
```

Simple statement annotations:

The simple statement anotation:	*transforms to:*

```if A(I - 1) > A(I) then```
```   EXCHANGE(A(I - 1), A(I));```
```end if;```
```--| A(I) >= A(I - 1);```
```I := I + 1;```
	```if A(I - 1) > A(I) then```
	``` EXCHANGE(A(I - 1), A(I));```
	```end if;```
	```CHECK (A(I) >= A(I - 1));```
	```I := I + 1;```

References

[Ada 83] *The Ada Programming Language Reference Manual*
US Department of Defence, US Government Printing Office, 1983.
ANSI/MIL-STD-1815A-1983 Document.

[Anna 84] Luckham, D.C., von Henke, F.W., Krieg-Brueckner, B., and Owe, O.
ANNA:A Language for Annotating Ada Programs..
Computer Systems Laboratory Technical Report 84-261, Stanford University, July, 1984.
Program Analysis and Verification Group Report No. 24.

[Diana 83] Evans, A., Butler, K.J., Goos, G., and Wulf, W.A.
DIANA Reference Manual, Revision 3
Tartan Laboratories Incorporated, 1983.

[Krieg 83] Krieg-Brueckner, B.
Consistency Checking in Ada and Anna: A Transformational Approach.
Ada Letters III(2):46-54, September,October, 1983.

[Luckham 84] Luckham, D.C., and von Henke, F.W.
An Overview of Anna - A Specification Language for Ada.
Proceedings of the IEEE Computer Society 1984 Conference on Ada Applications and Environments :116-127, 1984.

[Rosenblum 84] Rosenblum, D.S.
A Methodology for the Design of Ada Transformation Tools in a DIANA Environment.
Proceedings of the IEEE Computer Society 1984 Conference on Ada Applications and Environments :63-70, 1984.

A Tool for Ada Program Manipulations: Mentor-Ada

*V.Donzeau-Gouge *, B.Lang **, B. Me'le'se ***

* CNAM
292 rue Saint Martin
75141 Paris Cedex 03

** INRIA
Domaine de Voluceau, B.P.105
Rocquencourt, 78153 Le Chesnay

1. Introduction

Mentor-Ada is an interactive system for the manipulation of Ada programs. It is automatically generated from Mentor [DON 75, DON 83, DON 84] which is a general system for the structure directed manipulation of formal documents of various kinds (programs, technical reports, etc...).

As in other structure oriented systems (Gandalf [Hab 79, Fei 81], Cornell Program Synthesizer [Teit 81, Reps 82]) program manipulations in Mentor-Ada are based on representation of these programs as trees.

More generally, Mentor-Ada inherits all the properties of Mentor, of which it is only a special instance. The Mentor system has been described in several of the references. Our purpose in this presentation is to show how the general facilities of Mentor have been used to generate an environment for Ada, and thus also to give an idea of how this environment can be extended to satisfy new or more specific needs.

The first part of this presentation is a brief overview of the concepts underlying Mentor and their potential role in an Ada environment. It shows how Ada has been specified to Mentor in order to obtain a minimal Mentor-Ada environment. We then describe the tools available in this minimal environment which is mechanically generated. Finally, we show how more complex tools may be programmed by means of the tree manipulation language Mentol.

(Ada is a trademark of the US DoD Ada Joint program)

2. The generation of Mentor-Ada.

2.1. Constrained tree representations.

Mentor is a manipulation system based on a structured representation of documents as labelled trees. For a given language these labels correspond to the various constructs available to organise the information to be expressed in that language. Generally, the constructs are identified whenever possible on semantic grounds, syntactic variations being ignored as much as is possible without impairing the easy understanding of the system and the correspondance between the concrete text and the abstract tree structure. For example we use the same label "header" for the top node of a subtree representing an Ada procedure header, a function header, or a generic subprogram header. This is necessary to reduce the number of labels used in the tree representation of Ada programs, and to present a more uniform view of the structure of Ada.

These labels, when correctly used, are sufficient to evidence the structure of programs. However in practice, it is necessary that the system assists the user by preventing illegal construction or modifications of programs. Thus a notion of tree syntax is introduced. A tree grammar is provided to specify what labels may be used for the sons of a given labelled node. Formally, labels are considered as operators having a fixed or variable arity. Sets of labels, called phyla, are defined that correspond to abstract concepts of the language. For exemple the phylum STATEMENT corresponds to the abstract notion of an Ada statement, and includes operators for the assignment, conditional, loop, case statement and so on.

For each son position of a given operator, the tree grammar specifies a phylum, i.e. the set of operators allowed as labels for the top node of a son in that position. In the case of variable arity operators (usually called list operators) the same phylum constrains all son positions.

The tree grammar of a language may be seen as a set of constraints a tree must satisfy to represent a legal program. These constraints are known to and enforced by the system in all manipulations. Furthermore, they may be used by the system to assist the user by telling him interactively what constructions are available to create specific parts of his program.

2.2. Overview of Mentor organization.

Mentor manipulates trees characterised by an abstract syntax as defined above. Of course, since users want to see their documents as text, a pretty printer is provided for each language manipulated.

Program editing and manipulation is performed via an interactive command language called Mentol. Mentol contains a collection of basic tree oriented primitives described in section 3. In addition, it has a variety of control structures that may be used to build complex tree manipulation programs. These control structures include loops, recursion, call by name and by value, and a form of exceptions. This programmability of the system is used to extend the environment for a given language by programming new tools reflecting the semantics of the language, based on complex manipulations of the syntactic structured representation. Section 4 contains the description of a basic library of Mentol routines for assisting the edition of Ada programs. More complete libraries, including complex program analysers and transformations have been written for other languages.

Another characteristic of Mentor is that it can manipulate several languages at the same time. All (almost) components of system are driven by tables. The system can load simultaneously the tables corresponding to different languages and then manipulate documents in these different languages. Furthermore, it can even combine different languages in a single document by means of an annotation mechanism [Don 84b]. Thus an Ada program may be commented with text manipulated in structured form.

2.3. Definition of Ada under Mentor.

To generate Mentor-Ada we had to define Ada to the Mentor system. This definition is expressed in a (meta-)language called Metal [Kahn 83].

The Metal definition of Ada (see appendix 1 for the Metal definition of the Ada statement) is hierarchically structured in chapters and subchapters. For example, there is a chapter for the declarations and types, a chapter for expressions, a chapter for statements, and so on. The chapter on statements is itself organized in subchapters corresponding to the different kinds of statements, following the standard structure of a language manual.

In each (sub)chapter one may find different components specifying each a given aspect of this chapter of the language. In the current Metal specification of Ada, these components include:

- the Ada abstract syntax,
- an LALR1 definition of the Ada concrete syntax that is used to generate an Ada parser,
- the tree building functions called by the parser to build the abstract tree corresponding to the parsed text.

The Metal specification of Ada is compiled by the Metal compiler into a collection of tables used by Mentor to assist manipulation of Ada programs. The unparser is not yet table driven, and was separately hand coded.

3. The minimal Ada environment.

The minimal environment is the part of Mentor-Ada that is automatically derived from the Metal definition of Ada. Although lacking any semantics based tool, it is already a friendly system for program creation and edition in full screen mode.

3.1. Screen organization and pretty-printing.

Mentor-Ada is normally used as a full screen editor. The screen is divided into four windows. The largest one contains the program fragment (i.e. the pretty-printed subtree) currently edited. The edition cursor points to a subtree of this displayed fragment rather than to a position in text. The cursor position is indicated by emphasizing the pretty-printing of the pointed subtree with a special font, usually brighter or underlined characters.

A small window indicates the language currently edited (since fragments of other languages may be mixed to Ada code), and the operator label of the cursor subtree. The other two windows are for system messages and diagnostics, and for user input of commands or Ada text.

Since the program fragment being edited is often too large to be displayed fully on the screen, the pretty-printer can display only the main structure, and replace missing details by special symbols ('...' for lists operators, and '#' for others). This method of ellipsis (called holophrasting) is illustrated in the fragment of the Metal definition of Ada given in appendix. The level of ellipsis is user controlled.

3.2. Entering programs.

Programs or program fragments are kept within the system exclusively in tree form. They may be entered either by parsing Ada text input from the terminal or with a menu driven programmer's assistant.

The ability to parse Ada text is essential since it is the only way existing programs may be entered into the system. Parsing may be done incrementally: the parser has entries for each family of Ada constructs (essentially each phylum of the abstract syntax). For example, it can parse a single statement, an expression, or a declaration.

A more friendly input mode is provided by a menu system that assists top-down construction of programs [Mig 85]. It is based on replacement of placeholders (corresponding to yet unwritten program parts) by predefined templates offered by the menu and corresponding to Ada constructs permitted in that context. The user is further assisted by a help system that can comment the role in the concerned context of each construct offered by the menu. Help messages appear upon request in a fifth screen window.

The menu system is automatically derived from the specification of the abstract syntax of Ada. The help messages are specified in the Metal specification of Ada as a fourth component of its (sub)chapters. This part of the specification may be easily modified to tailor messages to the needs of a given user group.

A user can at any time switch between the two modes of input according to his knowledge of Ada. Experience shows that expert users tend to prefer parsing, while beginners need the assistance of the menu mode.

3.3. Program manipulation commands.

The minimal environment provides a variety of commands. They are either language independant or automatically derived from the Metal specification of Ada. All commands may be used interactively or within Mentol program. Commands used frequently in interactive mode may be linked to the available function keys of the user's terminal. This facility is often used for navigation commands, or for visualisation changes such as zooming on the cursor for more details (reduced ellipsis) on the pointed subtree.

The available commands may be classified roughly in four groups:

- basic tree motion commands such as u(p, l(eft, r(ight, s(on. These commands may be used as mentol statements with integer argument, or activated with function keys.

- tree modification commands: c(hange for replacing a subtree by another one, d(elete for deleting a list element (e.g. a statement in a list of statements), i(nsert for inserting a new element in a list, x(change for exchanging two subtrees, etc... The subtrees needed as arguments by some of these commands are actually seen as well structured Ada text fragments by the user. They may either be clipped or copied from the existing program or entered from the terminal.

- tree pattern matching commands:
  A pattern is an incomplete tree i.e. a tree in which some subtrees are replaced by meta-variables. For example the pattern

  while $EXP loop $L_STM end loop;

  stands for a while loop where the condition and the statements have been left unspecified. Elementary patterns are provided by the system, while more complex ones may be built like all other program fragments.

  Several commands are based on pattern matching, for example: f(ind searches the program for the first occurrence of the pattern given as argument; forall<P,C> applies the command C at all cursor positions matching the pattern P; up<P> moves the cursor up the tree until it matches the pattern P or reaches the root and fails. More complex manipulations are based on combination of pattern matching and pattern instantiation.

- file manipulation primitives: load, store, parse, unparse.
  The filer can unparse programs into files, to produce listings or to communicate with Ada processors based on the textual representation. With Mentor however, it is standard practice to store and retrieve programs in tree form to and from permanent storage.

It is indeed necessary to keep programs in tree form at all times, without transitions through textual representation. The tree form generally contains information that cannot always be deduced from the text (or may even be invisible). A trivial example is the precise positionning of comments in the program. Furthermore, the tree representation used in secondary storage is substantially smaller than the usual text representation of programs (on the order of 40 percent).

4. Extension of the environment with programmed tools.

Using the basic commands available in the minimal environment, one may program in Mentol a wide variety of commands and tools. These programmed tools usually incorporate their author's knowledge of the semantics of Ada, and assist the user even more in terms of the language concepts in all programming and maintenance activities.

Much experience has been gained in creating and using such tools in Mentor environments for other languages (Pascal, LTR [Ver 83]). This experience is the basis for the ongoing enrichment of Mentor-Ada. We present below some of the tools already existing in the current environment, and indicate intended developments.

Most used among Ada dependant Mentor-Ada commands are advanced navigation commands:-

- an Ada unit to be accessed may be found easily by supplying its name to one of the Mentol routines Fproc, Fpack, Fgen and Ftask; the chosen routine moves the cursor onto the desired unit.
- the routine called Next is used to explore successive constituents of a compound construct such as a record type definition, a compound statement, the parameter list of a subprogram, or the choices in an aggregate, a case statement or the exception part of a block.
- the Cond routine moves the cursor to the controlling part of a controlled statement, for example to the condition of a while or an if statement, to the guard of a select alternative, or to the determinator of a case.
- the cursor may be moved between the specification and the body of a unit with the Mentol routines Myspecif and Mybody.

Again, it is often convenient to link the most frequently used of these commands to function keys of the user's terminal. For exemple one may define a key that moves the cursor successively to the declarative part, the executable part and the exception part of the current unit each time that key is depressed.

Several tree transformation routines assist frequently recurring program modifications. For example one may

- move a declaration between the public and the private part of a package,
- change a type declaration into a private type declaration (automatically moving the full type declaration to the private part of the package),
- transform a package or a subprogram into a generic one,
- sort the choices of a case according to the declaration order or the enumeration type used,
- switch between named and positional association of the parameters of a subprogram or entry call.

One of the most useful transformations changes all occurrences of an identifier to a new name. This transformation is very simple with a structured editor, but is most delicate with a text editor.

A variety of interactive documentation tools is under development. An example is the Mentol routine that lists the overloaded identifiers of the program. A cleaning routine is also intended for (semi-)automatic detection and removal of unnecessary program components such as null statements or unused declarations.

Other tools will concern global analysis of program structure (data flow, side-effects, aliasing), and will mechanically document programs.

5. The multi-lingual facilities.

Mentor-Ada is only a part of the multi-lingual Mentor environment. We believe this to be an essential quality. Indeed the programming activity requires the use of an often large variety of languages and formalisms for such tasks as specification, user and maintenance documentation, program proofs, in addition to the use of Ada for the programming task itself. The availability of an environment that can deal uniformly with the different formalisms needed is then a considerable simplification to the users.

Mentor environments have already been developed for several programming languages, for a technical report language and for specification languages.

The possibility of handling several languages at the same time may also be exploited in the construction of program translators for a faster availability in Ada of software components already developed in other languages.

A last and essential aspect concerns the use of annotations and the development of multi-lingual documents [Don 84b]. Mentor possess an annotation facility which allows precise linking of informations to the nodes of the tree representing a program. The annotations may be seen and used as attributes as in Diana [Goos 81]. They may also be used as an advanced commenting facility to attach to an Ada program specific informations written in another formalism: assertions, specifications, or maintenance comments, for example. This should permit the realization of a rich environment integrating all the document manipulation aspects of software development.

6. Conclusion.

The Mentor-Ada environment has been built after the model of several Mentor environments for other languages (Pascal, Metal, LTR, Flip, ...). Although the availability of Ada compilers is too recent for this environment to have been thoroughly experienced, the success of the other Mentor environments proves the fruitfulness of this approach.

Extensions to this environment may be expected from two directions:

- new developments of the Mentor system such as the specification of the static semantics in a high-level formalism called Typol [Des 83] based on abstract data types and transition systems [Moss 82, Plot 81]. This language extends Metal and has been already used to mechanically derive type-checkers from a specification of the type structure of several languages.

- enrichment of the library of tools programmed in Mentol which is expected from the community of academic and industrial users of Mentor-Ada.

Acknowledgements: We are very grateful to E. Morcos who participated to the elaboration of a first version of the Metal definition of Ada, and to Pr. I. Pyle for his intensive checking of Mentor-Ada and his insightful comments.

Bibliography

Ada 83 U.S. Department of Defense, *Reference Manual for the Ada Programming Language*, ANSI/MIL-STD-1815 A, January 1983.

Des 83 T.Despeyroux, *Introduction de spe'cifications se'mantiques dans Mentor*, The'se de 3ie'me cycle Universite' de Paris 11, Oct. 1983.

Don 75 V.Donzeau-Gouge, G.Kahn, G.Huet, B.Lang, J.J.Levy, *A structure oriented program editor:a first step toward computer assisted programming*, Proc. International Computing Symposium, North_Holland, 1975.

Don 82 V.Donzeau-Gouge, J.C.Heliard, G.Kahn, B.Krieg-Bruckner, B.Lang, *Formal definition of the Ada programming language*, reprinted by CEC, Sept. 1982.

Don 83 V.Donzeau-Gouge, G.Kahn, B.Lang, B.Me'le'se, E.Morcos, *Outline of a tool for document manipulation*, IFIP congress, Paris, Sept. 1983.

Don 84a V.Donzeau-Gouge, B.Lang, B.Me'le'se, *Practical Applications of a Syntax Directed Program Manipulation Environment*, 7th Conference on Software Engineering , Orlando, March 1984.

Don 84b V.Donzeau-Gouge, G. Kahn, B.Lang, B.Me'le'se, *Document Structure and Modularity in Mentor*, ACM SIGSOFT/SIGPLAN Soft. Eng. Symp. on Practical Software Development Environments, Pittsburgh, April 1984.

Goos 81 G.Goos, W.Wulf, *Diana: Reference Manual*, Universitat Karlsruhe Institut Informatik II, report 1/81, March 1981.

Kahn 83 G.Kahn, B.Lang, B.Me'le'se, E.Morcos, *Metal: a formalism to specify formalisms*, Science of Computer Programming, North Holland, 1983.

Mig 85 V.Migot, *A new User Interface in Mentor: the Menu Mode*, Rapport INRIA (to appear).

Moss 82 P.Mosses, *Abstract semantics algebras*, Proceedings of the IFIP TC2 working conference on formal description of programming concepts, June 1982.

Plo 81 G.D.Plotkin, *A structural approach to operational semantics*, DAIMI FN-19, Aarhus University, Denmark, sept. 1981.

Reis 84 S.P.Reiss, *Graphical Program Development with PECAN Program Development Systems*, ACM SIGSOFT/SIGPLAN Soft. Eng. Symp. on Practical Software Development Environments, Pittsburgh, April 1984.

Reps 82 T.Reps, *Generating Language Based Environments*, Tech. Report 82-514, Cornell University ,Ithaca, NY, August 1982.

Reps 84 T.Reps, T.Teiltelbaum, *The Synthesizer Generator*, ACM SIGSOFT/ SIGPLAN Soft. Eng. Symp. on Practical Software Development Environments, Pittsburgh, April 1984.

Stan 84 T.A.Standish, R.N.Taylor, *Arcturus: A Prototype Advanced Ada Programming Environment*, ACM SIGSOFT/SIGPLAN Soft. Eng. Symp. on Practical Software Development Environments, Pittsburgh, April 1984.

Teit 81 T.Teiltelbaum, T.Reps, *The Cornell Program Synthesizer: A syntax directed programming environment*, CACM, vol. 24, no. 9, Sept. 1981.

Ver 83 D.Verove, *Mentor-LTR: Syste'me de manipulation de programmes LTR-V3*, Rapport technique interne DRET-SEMA, March 1983.

Appendix 1

An holophrasted unparsing of a chapter of the Metal definition of Ada.

```
chapter ' 5 :  STATEMENTS '
    rules
        <statement_option_list>::= ... ;
            stm_s-#
        <statement_option_list>::= ... ;
            <statement_list>
        <statement_list>  ::= ... ;
            stm_s-#
        <statement_list>  ::= ... ;
            stm_s-#
        <statement>       ::= ... ;
            labeled ...
        <statement>       ::= ... ;
            <unlabeled_statement>
        <statement>       ::= ... ;
            <pragma>
        <unlabeled_statement>::= ... ;
            <simple_statement>
        <unlabeled_statement>::= ... ;
            <compound_statement>
        <simple_statement> ::= ... ;
            <assignment_statement>
        <simple_statement> ::= ... ;
            <ambig_entry_subprogram_call_statement>
        <simple_statement> ::= ... ;
            <exit_statement>
        <simple_statement> ::= ... ;
            <return_statement>
        <simple_statement> ::= ... ;
            <goto_statement>
        <simple_statement> ::= ... ;
            <raise_statement>
        <simple_statement> ::= ... ;
            <abort_statement>
        <simple_statement> ::= ... ;
            <delay_statement>
        <simple_statement> ::= ... ;
            <code_statement>
        <simple_statement> ::= ... ;
            null_stm ...
        <compound_statement>::= ... ;
            <if_statement>
        <compound_statement>::= ... ;
            <case_statement>
        <compound_statement>::= ... ;
            <loop_statement>
        <compound_statement>::= ... ;
            <accept_statement>
        <compound_statement>::= ... ;
            <select_statement>
        <compound_statement>::= ... ;
            <block_statement>
```

```
chapter ' 5.2 ASSIGNMENT STATEMENTS '
    rules
        #
end chapter;

chapter ' 5.3  IF STATEMENTS '
    rules
        ########
end chapter;

chapter '        5.4 CASE STATEMENTS '
    rules
        ####
end chapter;

chapter '        5.5 LOOP STATEMENTS '
    rules
        #########
end chapter;

chapter ' 5.6  BLOCK STATEMENTS '
    rules
        ########
end chapter;

chapter ' 5.7 EXIT STATEMENTS '
    rules
        #####
end chapter;

chapter ' 5.8  RETURN STATEMENTS '
    rules
        #
end chapter;

chapter ' 5.9  GOTO STATEMENTS '
    rules
        #
end chapter;

chapter ENTRY_POINTS
    rules
        ###############################
end chapter;


abstract syntax
    null_stm        -> implemented as SINGLETON;
    terminate       -> implemented as SINGLETON;
    void            -> implemented as SINGLETON;

*     unary constructs*
    goto            -> NAME;
    return          -> EXP_VOID;
    while           -> EXP;

*     binary constructs*
    alternative     -> L_CHOICE L_STM;
    assign          -> NAME EXP;
    case            -> EXP L_ALTERNATIVE;
    cond_clause     -> EXP_VOID L_STM;
    exit            -> NAME_VOID EXP_VOID;
    for             -> ID DSCRT_RANGE;
    labeled         -> ID STM;
```

```
      loop          -> ITERATION L_STM;
      named_stm        -> ID STM;
      reverse        -> ID DSCRT_RANGE;

*      ternary constructs*
      block          -> L_ITEM L_STM L_ALTERNATIVE;

*      list constructs
            alternative_s    -> ALTERNATIVE * ... ;
      if           -> COND_CLAUSE * ... ;
      item_s         -> ITEM * ... ;
      stm_s          -> STM * ... ;
      comment_s        -> comment * ... ;

*      phyla

      ALTERNATIVE    ::=alternative;
      L_ALTERNATIVE  ::=alternative_s meta;
      BLOCK_STUB     ::=block stub;
      COMMENT       ::=comment;
      COND_CLAUSE    ::=cond_clause;
      DSCRT_RANGE    ::=constrained index range NAME;
      EXP          ::=aggregate all allocator apply attribute binary char
                        conversion function_call id indexed membership
                        null_access numeric_literal qualified selected
                        slice string unary;
      EXP_S         ::=exp_s;
      EXP_VOID       ::=EXP void;
      ID          ::=id;
      ID_S          ::=id_s;
      ITEM          ::=DECL REP package_body subprogram_body task_body;
      L_ITEM         ::=item_s meta;
      ITERATION       ::=for reverse void while;
      NAME          ::=DESIGNATOR all apply attribute function_call indexed
                            selected slice;
      NAME_S         ::=name_s;
      NAME_VOID       ::=NAME void;
      RANGE         ::=range;
      RANGE_VOID      ::=range void;
      STM          ::=abort accept apply assign block call case code
                        cond_entry delay exit goto if labeled loop
                        named_stm null_stm raise return select terminate
                        timed_entry;
      L_STM         ::=stm_s meta;
end chapter;
```

METAL

Unparsing of a subchapter of the Ada Metal definition.

```
chapter '      5.5 LOOP STATEMENTS '
     rules
          <loop_statement>  ::= <named_loop_statement> ;
               <named_loop_statement>
          <loop_statement>  ::= <unnamed_loop_statement> ;
               <unnamed_loop_statement>
          <named_loop_statement>::= <identifier> #: <unnamed_loop_statement>
                                        <identifier_option> ;
                named_stm(<identifier>,<unnamed_loop_statement>)
          <unnamed_loop_statement>::= <iteration_sheme> <basic_loop> ;
                loop(<iteration_sheme>,<basic_loop>)
          <basic_loop>       ::= loop <statement_list> #end loop ;
                <statement_list>
          <iteration_sheme> ::=  ;
               void()
          <iteration_sheme> ::= for <identifier> #in <discrete_range> ;
               for(<identifier>,<discrete_range>)
          <iteration_sheme> ::= for <identifier> #in reverse <discrete_range> ;
               reverse(<identifier>,<discrete_range>)
          <iteration_sheme> ::= while <condition> ;
               while(<condition>)
end chapter;
```

ADA IN THE ECLIPSE PROJECT SUPPORT ENVIRONMENT

R.H. Pierce
Software Sciences Ltd, London and Manchester House, Park Street, Macclesfield, Cheshire, SK11 6SR, U.K.

Abstract. This paper outlines the object management system provided in the ECLIPSE project support environment and describes how Ada compilers are supported by this system. The structure of a common Ada program library is described and the support tools provided with it.

1 BACKGROUND

Eclipse is an integrated project support environment (IPSE), which is being developed by a consortium led by Software Sciences Ltd (SSL) and supported by the UK Alvey programme. The other members of the consortium are CAP (UK) Ltd., Learmonth and Burchett Management Systems, the Universities of Lancaster and Strathclyde, and the University College of Wales, Aberystwyth.

Eclipse is built upon SDS-2, a database management system developed and marketed by SSL and designed specifically to support software development by large teams (Software Sciences Ltd 1985a). SDS-2 employs an entity relationship data model with bi-directional links, which is formally equivalent to the network model. Data fields are inherently variable length and a wide variety of data types is supported including user defined types, and sets of links and subrecords. It is these, together with the experimental update capability and the support for very long transactions, which justify the statement that SDS-2 is designed specifically to support software development.

As in SDS-2, a basic database schema will be provided which must be used if the Eclipse kernel is to run. This schema can be extended to meet the needs of specific tools (e.g. tools based on specific methodologies) or the needs of a specific project.

2 THE OBJECT MANAGEMENT SYSTEM

An object in Eclipse terminology is the smallest unit of information (in any representation - source code, display file, natural language text, etc.) which can be handled by the Eclipse naming scheme. Objects normally consist of control attributes, which are SDS-2 database fields, and a body, which contains the user's information. A minimal set of control attributes for items is included in the basic schema; it can and normally will be extended to meet the needs of a project and of specific tools. The body of an object may be a host filestore file.

The naming scheme is hierarchical; nodes on the tree are catalogues and the leaves are items and synonym tables. Objects normally belong to precisely one item and are named by naming the item to which they belong and then specifying a control attribute which serves to identify the object from among the set of objects belonging to that item. The intended interpretation of objects and items is that an item represents a component of a software system and an object represents a version of that component. The control attribute used to select an object might be the creation time and date or might be a project defined version name or number or some other attribute, at the user's choice.

Synonym tables allow a user to set up his own names to identify objects, items and catalogues. A search path containing catalogues and synonym tables is used to find the appropriate interpretation of a name.

Objects are produced by executing transformation procedures (themselves stored as objects), which are procedures defined in a parameterised form of the host operating system command language; they are the means by which existing software tools are incorporated into Eclipse. Such tools are known as "foreign" tools since they are written without knowledge of the database. For example, a compiler would be executed as a transformation taking as input a source text object and producing object code and listing file objects. The writing of transformation procedures is regarded as a privileged activity to be undertaken by system programming staff, since such procedures must not compromise the integrity of the database. The ordinary user may define <u>derivation procedures</u> which consist of invocations of transformation procedures together with flow of control statements.

When an object is created, all the details of the procedures which created it are recorded in its derivation history. This allows the object's body to be recreated at any time by the automatic rebuild system.

3 OBJECT MANAGEMENT AND ADA COMPILATION

The operation of an Ada compiler is more complex in Eclipse terms than that of a compiler for a conventional language, due to the presence of the program library and separate compilation concepts. While a compiler for a language such as RTL/2 or Fortran takes a source file as input and produces, say, an object file and a listing file, an Ada compiler typically takes a program library and a source file and generates an updated version of the program library. Depending on the implementation of the compiler and possibly on the nature of the source text, the compiler may produce a number of outputs such as object code, DIANA tree, symbol table, debugger table and a host of others. These outputs will usually exist for each compilation unit in the source text, but may not. It seems unreasonable to require the user of an Ada compiler to decide in advance exactly which outputs will be produced by any given compilation, and to create Eclipse objects to represent these outputs. The problems are exemplified by considering two obvious cases. A library subprogram being compiled for the first time into a particular library may create compilation units representing both the specification and the body of the subprogram, while a subsequent compilation of the same text would be treated as generating only a body, leaving the specification unchanged. A particular compiler may decline to produce an intermediate code tree for a secondary unit unless it contains a generic body which may be needed in a later instantiation.

The user however is not interested in these subtleties; moreover, we wish to be able to incorporate more than one Ada compiler into Eclipse (rather than just one compiler with more than one back-end), and each compiler will have its own particular set of outputs.

The approach taken to overcome the difficulties mentioned above is to regard the program library as the only user-visible output from an Ada compilation, apart from a possible compilation listing. The Ada compiler is thus run as a transformation taking as its inputs the source text and initial program library (which are Eclipse objects) and producing an updated program library as its output. In Eclipse, no object can be updated, so in practice the compilation produces a new object representing the updated program library. This leads naturally to the idea that a program library is an Eclipse item, with each compilation of some source text object into the program library producing an object which is a version of the item.

The various outputs of the compiler, which logically form part of the program library object, are created by the compiler rather than by the user. The Ada compiler is thus an "integrated" tool rather than a foreign tool, in that it has direct access to the Eclipse object management system. It is still useful to run the compiler as a transformation since this provides automatic derivation history recording for the output program library. Note that there is in this scheme no concept of a version of a compilation unit within a given library; this is replaced by the concept of versioning the program library itself.

4 THE COMMON PROGRAM LIBRARY

The Ada program library structure in ECLIPSE is intended to support (at least potentially) compilers produced by more than one supplier. Use of a common library system has a number of advantages. It enables a common set of program library management functions and other tools to operate across a range of compilers (the common tools are described in section 6 below), this making it easier for users to migrate from compiler to compiler as the project (or target computer) on which they are working changes. Moreover, in an integrated PSE other tools may wish to invoke an Ada compiler directly, and although the parameters which must be supplied for a compilation will vary in detail from compiler to compiler, the invoking tool can be assured that the effect of the compilation on the library will not depend on the particular compiler in use. The disadvantage is that each compiler to be incorporated into the Eclipse environment will have to be rehosted to conform to the Eclipse program library conventions. This can be done either by modifying the implementation of those parts of the compiler which interface to the program library structure, or by converting the program library structure produced by the compiler to the Eclipse form by a post-processing phase (a pre-processing step to convert from Eclipse to compiler form would also be necessary prior to executing the compiler). If it is possible, modifying the compiler is by far the best solution, and may be the only practicable one. A compiler rehosted under Eclipse in this way would have to be separately validated.

True integration of an Ada compiler into Eclipse (or indeed into any IPSE) demands that the database be used to represent the inputs and outputs of the compiler, which inevitably demands that an existing compiler be modified in some way.

The advantages of representing the Ada program library in the Eclipse database will emerge in the following sections.

5 REPRESENTATION OF THE PROGRAM LIBRARY

The database structure representing an Ada program library is shown in Fig. 1. The program library itself exists in a number of versions, resulting from successive compilations into it. Each compilation unit produced by a compilation is also represented by an Eclipse database object. The dependencies between compilation units are recorded in a dependency map, which is stored in the body of the program library object. One compilation unit may participate in many program library objects, and there is a database link between the compilation unit object and each program library object in which it appears (this may not be true for the predefined Ada units such as STANDARD or SYSTEM, to avoid an excessively large number of links from these units). All links in the database are bi-directional, so that given a compilation unit all the libraries

Figure 1a - Program library versions and derivations

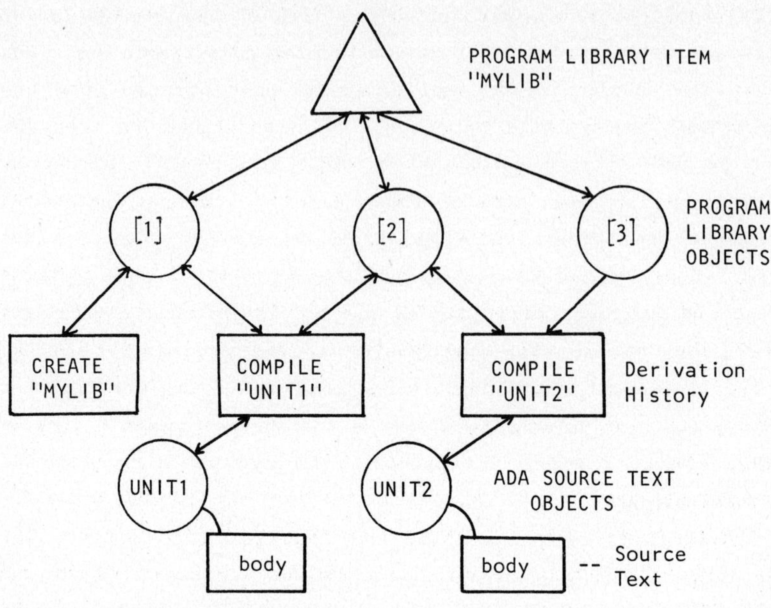

Figure 1b - Program library structure

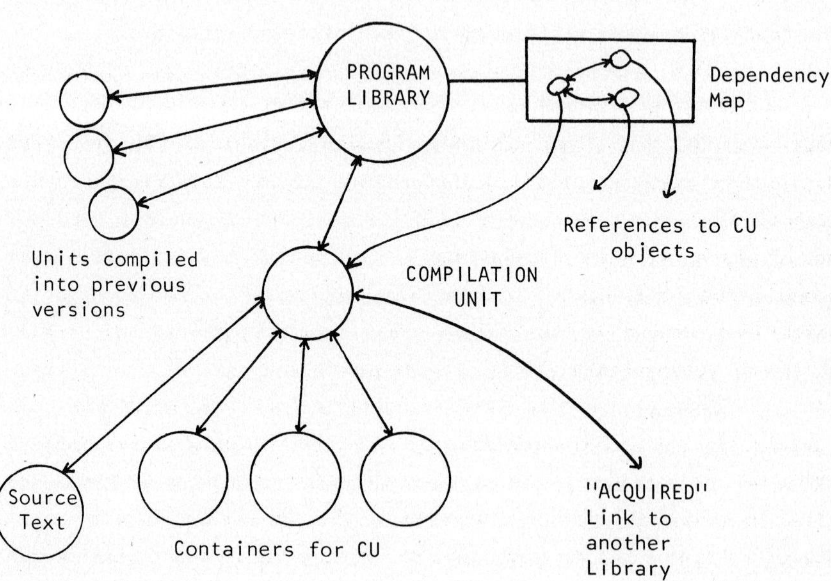

in which it appears can be found; conversely, all units in a given library can be located. There is in addition a link between an Ada source text object and the compilation units which have been compiled from it; these units may be in different program libraries or different versions of one library. A source object can also give rise to a number of compilation unit objects in one library, since the source may contain or generate more than one Ada compilation unit.

The compilation unit object itself exists to enable these links to be set up (their use for "impact analysis" is described below). The compiler will also require to store bulk output such as the object code and symbol table for a compilation unit. These bulk outputs can be represented as further database objects ("containers") linked to the compilation unit object, the bulk information being stored in the bodies of the containers. Bodies in this scheme are just host filestore files and once created by the ECLIPSE object management system can be accessed as such by the compiler. An alternative implementation being considered is to make the body of the compilation unit object a UNIX directory. This directory would then contain all the bulk output files produced by the compiler for the given compilation unit.

The dependency map is a directed graph containing nodes representing the compilation units in the program library and arcs representing their dependencies. Both forward and backward dependencies are recorded, that is if A names B and C in its with-clause, then there is a "with" relationship between A from B and C and a "withed-by" relationship from B and C to A. This allows compilation units made obsolete by compilations of the things on which they depend to be marked, and to be brought to the users' notice or automatically recompiled as required.

The nodes in the dependency map representing the compilation contain references to the corresponding compilation unit objects. The use of a separate map rather than direct dependency links between compilation objects allows the same object to be shared by many program libraries; the dependencies between units may differ from library to library. A compilation unit object can appear in many libraries for two reasons. Firstly, a compilation unit (CU) object is generated by compiling some Ada source into a new version of a program library. Subsequently, this same CU object will appear in all subsequent versions of the library until it is deleted or recompiled, either because of a unit on which it depends being changed or because its source text has been changed. Secondly, the user may acquire the unit into another library. In both these cases, CU objects on which a given CU depends do not change, but the units depending on it may change, in which case its reverse links will differ from library to library.

From the above discussion, it is clear that creating a new version of the program library for each run of the Ada compiler is not very expensive. All that is required is to create a new program library object (in the database) and the corresponding new dependency map, which is a relatively short binary file (the body of the object). The choice of storing the dependency map in the body rather than as a set of linked database nodes is made largely on efficiency grounds; there is a greater overhead expected in creating database nodes than in copying and amending a file. The two structures are logically identical and a change to an all database representation could easily be made.

Multiple compilations

Despite the low cost of producing a new version of the program library for each compilation, there are some cases where this is clearly wasteful. For example, if several compilation units have to be recompiled after a unit on which they depend has been modified, it would be desirable to recompile all the units in one transformation so that only one new version of the program library is created. In another example, it might be necessary to release a complete Ada system consisting of many units in source text form, for example from a development team to an integration team; the receiving team would probably wish to compile all of the source text as one transformation since the release is of no use unless it all compiles. The conclusion is that the "Ada compile" transformation must be prepared to accept as input a list of source text items to be compiled; the new program library generated by such a transformation (if it succeeds) contains all the output objects produced by the compilation.

6 THE COMMON ADA TOOLSET

The Ada support tools in Eclipse which are common to all compilers are described in the following sections. They comprise an Ada linker, an Ada program library enquiry tool, and a program library update tool. The program library enquiry tool cannot make changes to a library, whereas the update tool can, and consequently has to be run as an Eclipse transformation. A particular compiler may offer tools other than the standard ones described below.

6.1 The Ada linker

The Ada linker takes a program library as input and performs the language defined operations necessary to produce an executable program. This tool is the first component of the cross-development system described in section 7 below.

6.2 The program library enquiry tool

This tool enables the compilation units in a given version of a program library to be examined. The library unit-subunit structure can be displayed, together with the dependencies of various kinds between units. In general, information can be requested about a single unit, a named collection of units, or the entire library. There is also a facility to survey the history of a given compilation unit or units across many versions of the program library. These facilities are fairly standard, and do not make any special use of the Eclipse database. These are however used by the "impact analysis" function. Given a named source text object, it is possible to trace the potential effect of a change to this object on other source text objects and program libraries. Using the database link from the source object to the compilation unit objects compiled from it, and the links from the compilation units to the program library objects containing them, all versions of all program libraries affected by the change can be discovered. Then by using the dependency graphs of these program libraries, all the other compilation units made obsolete by the potential change can be determined, and this in turn allows the source text objects corresponding to the affected units to be displayed. This gives a very useful mechanism for project management. It is up to human intelligence to determine from the proposed change whether there is an actual interface change (e.g. an altered subprogram specification) which will require corresponding changes in the affected source objects, or whether these can simply be recompiled without change to their text.

In addition to the standard impact analysis function provided by the program library enquiry tool, the user also has the possibility of writing ad-hoc enquiries about the program library system using the DML (data manipulation language) provided by the database. These enquiries can make use of standard or tailored management information stored in the Eclipse database. For example, a source text object could contain a link to an implementor or team leader record in the project management part of the database; this would allow the persons responsible for each source object to be notified of potential changes revealed by impact analysis.

6.3 The program library update tool

This tool provides the facilities to create a new program library, delete compilation units from a library, acquire units from other libraries and recompile units made obsolete by changes to units on which they depend. This tool is always run as a transformation which produces a new version of the program library.

Recompilation is possible since when a unit is made obsolete it is not deleted from the program library but merely marked as being "invalid". The link to the source text object from which the unit was compiled is used to find the source for the recompilation (if the user has put more than one unit in the source file, there is no way of stopping the other units from being compiled also; this is a good argument for having only one unit per source object).

Acquisition is the process of making compilation units compiled into one library available in others. In Eclipse this is very easy. All that is necessary is to make an entry for the compilation unit in the dependency map of the receiving program library, and make a database link from this library to the compilation unit object(s) being acquired. Once created, a compilation unit object is never changed, so sharing units in this way is safe. The tool allows one or more units to be acquired, and provides the option of acquiring either just a library specifiction, or the specification plus its body and subunit tree. When a unit is acquired, all the units on which it depends (and their bodies) are acquired, unless they have already been acquired previously. Acquisition is not allowed to replace a pre-existing unit.

The program library update tool can perform as many deletion, acquisition and recompilation steps as necessary within one transformation.

7 THE CROSS DEVELOPMENT SYSTEM

The Eclipse PSE contains a complete cross-development system. In addition to the standard Ada compilation environment described above, there is a target-dependent builder, which can combine the output of the Ada linker with modules written in other languages and produce an executable image. This can be down-line loaded into a remote target machine and the Ada program run under the control of a test controller in the host. Initially, Eclipse will offer the Telesoft Ada compiler cross-compiling to the Intel 80286 microprocessor. The work on the cross-development system is being done by CAP(UK) Ltd. In the first version of the system machine-level debugging will be offered. It is anticipated that full Ada symbolic debugging will be introduced later.

8 CONCLUSION

The Eclipse project support environment will offer a complete Ada compilation system integrated into the database and configuration control mechanisms. It is thus an APSE in the sense of STONEMAN (USDOD 80).

9 ACKNOWLEDGEMENTS

The authors would like to thank the Alvey directorate for their financial support for the project, Software Sciences Ltd for permission to present this paper, and their many colleagues who have contributed to the work described. Much of the Eclipse kernel is based on a product called Foundation (Software Sciences Ltd 1985b); this has been supported financially by the National Computing Centre under the Software Products Scheme and this support also is gratefully acknowledged.

REFERENCE LIST

Software Sciences Ltd (1985a). SDS-2 User-Reference Manual.
Software Sciences Ltd (1985b). Foundation Functional Specification.
USDOD(1980). Requirements for Ada programming support environments, "Stoneman", Washington DC.

THE DEVELOPMENT OF AN ADA FRONT END FOR SMALL COMPUTERS

J. Bundgaard
Dansk Datamatik Center
Lundtoftevej 1C, DK-2800 Lyngby, Denmark

Abstract. This paper concerns the design of an Ada front end that was required to be hosted on small computers. The paper discusses the special problems to be solved when implementing a compiler for a large language, like Ada, on machines with limited resources and capabilities, such as 16 bits for storage addressing. We also outline various possible solutions to these problems and describe in some detail the actual solutions applied in the Ada front end developed by Dansk Datamatik Center (DDC) as part of the Portable Ada Programming System.

Introduction

The DDC Ada front end was required to be portable to a wide range of computers, 16-bit mini-computers in particular. The major problem is that the code of an Ada compiler is evidently too large to fit into the usual maximum of 64K of 16-bit words program area.

Likewise, the internal data structures of an Ada compiler, such as intermediate program forms and symbol table, will soon use up the usual maximum of 64K words data area, unless severe restrictions are placed on the programs to be compiled. On the other hand, it was evident that the front end should be able to use the extra addressing space on larger, say 32-bit, machines effectively.

In order to achive maximum portability of the product, the front end should be as target independent as possible. This is particularly interesting in a cross-compilation environment where preferably the <u>same</u> front end should be used with a range of back ends, generating code for a range of targets.

The paper addresses these problems and their solutions in the following sections. Furthermore, a section elaborates on the implementation of Ada semantic analysis, in the framework of the actual structure of the DDC Ada front end.

The entire compiler development, as described by Clemmensen & Oest (1984), was carried out using the Vienna Development Method (VDM), and a compiler was successfully validated for the 32-bit DEC VAX-11/750 running VAX/VMS in September 1984. For the sake of rehostability, the compiler was written in (a subset of) Ada.

A Multi-pass Compilation Scheme

Several possible methods exist for running large programs in small logical storage, but since portability is a must, the method cannot rely on the facilities of a particular operating system. Partitioning the code into segments, for instance, is possible on the 16-bit mini-computer, the Christian Rovsing CR80D, which was chosen as the initial host and target, but the solution is not portable. Also, it requires a large physical storage; otherwise, the system will swap code segments all the time.

A multi-pass compilation technique with several consecutive passes over the program text seems more attractive. Each pass may perform a well-defined logical operation, e.g. lexical, syntactical, or semantic analysis. On a small machine the passes may execute one after the other as separate physical (small) programs.

The multi-pass scheme has some drawbacks: On small machines the "global" data, such as intermediate texts and symbol table information, must be stored on secondary storage between the passes. This, of course, requires some extra code to be managed. Also, all passes must contain (identical) code to store and retrieve these data. But worst of all, the compilation process will be heavily IO-bound.

It is possible to avoid major parts of the identical code in the passes if a separate process administers the global data. Most operating systems allow interprocess communication.

Running the symbol table administrator as a separate process was considered on the CR80D, but we feared that the system was not capable of exchanging messages fast enough to achieve a resonable compilation speed, knowing that the symbol table would be accessed very often. The Program Library manager was, however, successfully implemented as a separate process, since fewer messages are exchanged per compilation.

The DDC Ada front end has six passes which give a realtime usage of about three times the CPU time usage on the CR80D.

Returning to the issue of portability, one may ask how good the multipass scheme suits a larger machine, and how the drawbacks are handled.

On a larger machine several passes may be integrated into a single physical program. This does not require changes in the functionality of the passes. Only the relatively small code used to store and retrieve global data from secondary storage must be rewritten in order to keep the global data entirely in the virtual storage of the larger machine.

Intermediate Text Processing

Since data storage is a critical resource on a small machine, great care must be taken when handling the intermediate program texts. They may grow in size proportionally to the size of the source text of a compilation unit. Therefore, the complete text cannot be held in the internal storage, except for small compilation units.

Tree-structured intermediate texts are generally preferable. This is a well-established fact within compiler construction. Ideally, all passes work on the same tree structure, and the tree is extended and trimmed a little by each pass. But how should tree structures be implemented ?

It is possible to use a paged memory system administered by the compiler itself. This allows for the selection of a data structure with explicit links to subtrees and freedom to visit the nodes of the tree at random. However, it takes some code to handle, and also internal data storage must be reserved for this purpose.

Another possibilty is to use so-called linearized trees, stored in files. In such a tree each record is either the root node of a subtree or a leaf:

```
Tree:          A              Linearized tree:
              /
             B   C              A B D C E F G
             |  /|\
             D E F G
```

The subtrees belonging to a certain root node are placed immediately after the root node, corresponding to a top-down, left-to-right tree traversal.

Linearized trees are space efficient because the links to subtrees are implicit. Each pass can scan its input sequentially, and at the same time produce its output sequentially, using one of the following schemes:

```
procedure TRAVERSE_1 is
  N : NODE;
begin
  GET( N );
  for I in 1 .. N.ARITY loop
    TRAVERSE_1;
  end loop;
  PUT( TRANSFORM_1( N ) );
end;
```

```
procedure TRAVERSE_2 is
  N : NODE;
begin
  GET( N );
  PUT( TRANSFORM_2( N ) );
  for I in 1 .. N.ARITY loop
    TRAVERSE_2;
  end loop;
end;
```

Traversal of the linearized tree above, reading the nodes left-to-right from the file, produces new files which also containins linearized trees:

Input	Implicitly known arities
A B D C E F G	2 1 3 1 1 1

Output from traverse_1	Output from traverse_2
D B E F G C A	A B D C E F G

<- reading order ->

(following pass)

Both files can be read sequentially by the following pass corresponding to top-down, right-to-left and left-to-right tree traversals , respectively. Note that attributes can be inherited and synthesized, and carried from left-to-right and right-to-left, respectively.

The advantages of using such schemes are, that the trees require very little internal storage, and that it is extremely well suited for recursive descent compiling algorithms. The drawback is the inability of peeking into distant parts of the tree at random, without re-positioning the input file.

The best solution for a large machine is probably to keep the entire tree in the heap, using explicit pointers to subtrees. This method allows for a typed interface to the tree, and it leaves the storage management to the operating system. An extra paging system would be overkill.

On the smaller machines the heap is not large enough, so the linearized trees are believed to be the best representation of the intermediate texts because it is the most space efficient representation.

The DDC Ada front end uses such a linearized tree representation, and the six intermediate program forms are all different. In practice we experienced that the linearized tree structure was very flexible to work with. Adding an extra subtree to a node of one of the intermediate texts required only extra PUT-node and GET-node calls in the compiling algorithms for the producing and consuming passes. No large recompilations were required. On the other hand, the compiling algorithms had to be programmed very carefully because it was easy to forget one or two subtrees.

Symbol Table

In an early stage of the development of the front end it became evident that none of the passes are capable of building the entire symbol table or performing all the checks that require symbol table information. Therefore, the symbol table must survive between passes.

The amount of symbol table information is also likely to depend on the size of the compilation units, and hence cannot be held in internal storage, except for small compilation units and units with small contexts. Schemes, similar to those applicable to the intermediate texts, must be provided.

Linearized trees have been used to implement "intermediate" symbol tables, for example in the TFL/DDC CHILL compiler (Haff & Prehn 1982). However, symbol tables will more often be general graphs than trees, and random access is the rule rather than the exception. Hence, the best choice must be an implementation of the symbol table data structure on top of a software paging system.

Also, Ada offers a separate compilation facility which allows types, objects, etc. declared in one library unit to be used in other units with full support of visibility, strong typing, etc. Therefore symbol table information must either be stored (survive) between compilations or reconstructed when needed.

Reconstruction seems attractive because it can be made on the basis of one of the existing intermediate texts (the first one) provided that it is stored in, say, a Program Library which holds the results of all compilations. This method places no particular restriction on how links in the symbol table graph can be implemented. However, for large contexts, the reconstruction scheme may prove very time consuming.

Symbol table information for compiled units can also be stored in a Program Library in a form where the links contain both the identification of a unit, and a local address within a so-called symbol table "container" for the unit. This allows for links directly into symbol tables for units named in with clauses (transitively).

This, however, means that if the links are not restructured when the contents of a container is read into the paging system storage, then following a link becomes a two-level operation.

One could also choose a one-level addressing for links, but then the links must be restructured when a symbol table for a unit is placed in a container, and when it is read into the storage of the paging system. One-level addressing is faster, but requires extra code to do the restructuring of links.

The DDC Ada front end uses two-level addressing in order to save code space. However, no bad performance figures seem to be caused by this design decision.

An idea of using the containers as secondary storage for the paging system did not work in general, however. The CR80D operating system placed a limit on the number of simultaneously open files for a process, and this leads to repeated file open/close operations which "killed" the system performance. A single (paging) file, to which the contents of containers was copied in block mode when referenced the first time, solved the problem.

Static Analysis of Ada Programs

Having decided upon a multi-pass compilation scheme, one must determine how to distribute the various tasks of the static analysis performed by a front end, among the passes.

Ideally, each pass should perform a logically well defined part of the analysis. This is a widely accepted principle in compiler design, and with good reason. It highlights the functionalities of a compiler and it makes the code for the individual functionalities less complex. A typical scheme is to let pass 1 do lexical and syntactical analysis and pass 2 do semantic analysis. This does not work in the case of Ada on small hosts because the semantic analysis part is simply too comprehensive to fit into the code space available for a single pass. We found the lexical and syntactical analysis small enough to fit into pass 1 of the DDC Ada front end, whereas the rest of the semantic analysis was distributed over the following five passes.

This distribution was guided by observations of the Ada language itself, and the possible linearized tree-traversal schemes. This is not a straight-forward task, and much effort was devoted to achieve a complete understanding of the Ada language. For instance, a formal static semantic description using VDM (Bruun et al. 1982) was written as part of the PAPS project, before the front end was designed.

Some examples of the Ada aspects that influence "pass-splitting" of a front end are: Overload resolution is logically a two-pass problem, where the first part (pass) requires knowledge of what names may denote, hence, some symbol table information must be present. Static expressions must be evaluated after the second part of overload resolution is accomplished, because this determines whether operators in expressions are predefined or not. Some tasks, e.g. visibility analysis, are best suited for passes that receive the leaves of the tree from left-to-right (corresponding to a forward scan over the source text).

A Target Independent Front End

An Ada front end depends on the target machine characteristics in various ways. For instance, an integer type declaration is illegal if it defines a range that exceeds any integer type supported by the target system. The correctness of a program may also depend on the (static) value of INTEGER'LAST, or the existence of SHORT_INTEGER, etc.

A simple solution is to have a single package containing all the target dependent constants used by the entire compiler. The drawback is that such a front end must be changed whenever a new back end is integrated into a cross-compilation environment.

A more sophisticated solution is to store the target dependent constants in the symbol table information for the predefined packages STANDARD and SYSTEM. The front end can then look up the range of e.g. type INTEGER. However, if one wants a 100 per cent target independent front end, one must either refrain from any target dependent pragmas and attributes, or leave to the back end to check their correctness.

Conclusion

The first goal was to develop an Ada front end without limitations that could run on a small machine. This is about to been demonstrated. At the present time a reduced version of the (entire) compiler is running on the CR80D. The code generated by our boot-strap compiler on the CR80D is not sufficiently space efficient to squeeze the largest pass into 64K word program area. In order to achieve this, the compiler is currently being self-compiled into the so-called A-code (similar to P-code) which is extremely space efficient. On the CR80D, the front end processes about 50 lines of Ada text per CPU minute.

The second goal was a highly portable front end that was capable of utilizing the potentials of larger machines. This has been achieved. Only a very few modules were rewritten for the VAX version of the front end in order to benefit from both larger addressing space and larger internal storage: The symbol table must not be swapped out to secondary storage after each pass because all the passes are linked together into one single program. The symbol table paging area may be much larger and resides, together with the linearized trees, in the the virtual storage rather than on secondary storage. This has reduced both the CPU load and IO load. On the VAX 11/750 the front end processes from 300 to 500 lines of Ada text per CPU minute. This demonstrates that the design allows the front end to take advantage of large storage, when available.

The portability of the front end has definitely been proven. It has been rehosted on the Honeywell DPS6 mainframe on which a compiler was validated in November 1984. Futhermore, the front end has been rehosted on the Finish NOKIA MPS 10 computer and is currently being ported to the Honeywell DPS8 computer. VAX hosted cross-compilers are being developed for the Intel 8086 and the MIL-STD 1750A.

References

Bruun, H. et al. (1982). Portable Ada Programming System, Ada Static Semantics: Dansk Datamatik Center, March 1982

Clemmensen, G.B. & Oest, O.N. (1984). Formal Specification and Development of an Ada Compiler - A VDM Case Study: Proceedings of the 7'th International Conference on Software Engineering, IEEE March 1984

Haff, P.L. & Prehn, S. (1982). CHILL Compiler Front end Intermediate Texts: Teleteknisk Forsknings Laboratorium and Dansk Datamatik Center, 1982

A RUNTIME SUPERVISOR TO SUPPORT ADA TASKING: RENDEZVOUS AND DELAYS

G. A. Riccardi
Department of Computer Science, Florida State University, Tallahassee, Florida 32306

T. P. Baker
Department of Computer Science, Florida State University, Tallahassee, Florida 32306

This paper describes a simple and efficient approach to implementing the Ada operations of entry calls, conditional and timed entry calls, accept statements, selective wait statements and delay statements. This is accomplished by describing the tasking supervisor -- a collection of programs which control the tasking operations. Ada definitions of the data structures and the supervisor procedures are given. The semantics of the Ada tasking operations are related to the supervisor by following the description of tasking in Chapter 9 of the Reference Manual for the Ada Programming Language (1983). The structure of the object code for various Ada source language constructs is given. The interaction between the Ada object code and the run-time supervisor is described in detail. The remaining tasking operations are described in Part 1 of this report (Riccardi and Baker 1984).

1 Introduction

In order for the Ada programming language to be useful for implementing real time systems on microcomputers, the tasking operations must be implemented efficiently. This paper presents a run-time supervisor to support the rendezvous and delays of Ada tasks, which has been designed to be both simple to implement and efficient to execute. A detailed explanation of the data structures and supervisor operations is given, as well as a description of how these operations are invoked from the Ada object code.

This run-time supervisor is a part of the Florida State University Ada Compiler Project, which is supported by a contract from the USAF Armament Laboratory at Eglin AFB. The initial target machine of the project is the Zilog Z8002, a sixteen bit micro-processor. The host computer is a CDC Cyber 760.

The Ada Reference Manual (1983) gives the standard semantic description of the Ada language. However, the manual is intended to serve as an aid to understanding Ada rather than as a guide to implementation.

In particular, no representation is specified for control or data structures. An implementer's task is to give another semantic description of Ada -- one which uses a specific target machine and gives machine representations for all data structures and operations. This implementation must be faithful to the Ada manual, but might not agree with other implementations in all of its details. The shortcomings of the Ada reference manual as a guide to implementation have led to the development of other semantic models, using various formal techniques, which are documented in the literature (see below).

It is important to note that since the preliminary definition of Ada (1979), the language has been changed in ways significant to the implementation of tasking. Major changes to tasking, including the elimination of the initiate statement and the addition of terminate alternatives for selective wait statements, were made in the first proposed standard (Ada 1980). The revised proposed standard (Ada 1982) introduced the notion of the completion of a declarative unit (see Section 4) and made changes in the activation and termination of tasks. The most current definition (Ada 1983) made less significant changes in tasking, but included a different strategy for shared variables and for aborted tasks. Due to the extent of the changes in the Ada language, any reports which reference neither the 1982 nor the 1983 manuals should be carefully compared with the current manual to determine which parts are still valid.

An operational semantic definition for Ada using the Semanol language is given in Belz, et al. (1980). Lovengreen and Bjorner (1980) use the Vienna Definition Language to present a formal model of tasking. Clemmensen (1982) uses a more denotational approach and also considers a distributed, or multi-processor, environment for tasking. Falis (1982) gives a description of the interface between a tasking supervisor and Ada programs, including descriptions of all necessary supervisor operations. Hartig et al. (1981) give a description of the states of a task and the changes in state induced by various tasking operations.

The efficiency of various implementation strategies, as well as the semantics of the tasking operations are addressed in Stevenson (1980), Haberman and Nassi (1980), Hilfinger (1981) and Jones and Ardo (1982). Stevenson considers a variety of translations of tasking operations into a lower-level language. An implementation of Ada tasking on a specific machine model is given by Haberman and Nassi. Hilfinger considers certain special case tasks which allow for an efficient programs, and which are not expressible in Ada, except perhaps through machine code insertions. For example, when a supervisor call has been completed, control does not necessarily return to the calling task. Rather, the highest priority task which is ready is allowed to continue its execution. In addition, our description depends for its correctness on the assumption that the supervisor "package" be treated as a monitor. Its code is not reentrant, and therefore is all considered a "critical region." Concurrent executions of the supervisor are thus not permitted.

It is possible, and may be desirable for efficient use of processor resources in a distributed or symmetric multiprocessor implementation, to relax this condition slightly, permitting concurrent execution of copies of the supervisor on different processors. Further discussion of this subject is beyond the scope of the present document, since it requires consideration of the specific interconnections and communication capabilities of the processing units. **In the implementation which we describe, the tasking supervisor shares a single processor and memory address space with the tasks that it supervises.**

A task specification provides information which is used to construct and initialize the task control blocks of task objects. This data structure is used by the supervisor in task scheduling and intertask communication. The information from the specification is also used to generate the proper code for other Ada constructs, including task bodies and entry calls.

A task body calls for generation of code, which is shared by all the tasks of that type. The code for a task body is structured much like that of block statements, package bodies, and subprogram bodies. These units, which we shall call declarative units, have two things in common: Each has a declarative part, a sequence of statements, and may have exception handlers. The code for a declarative unit may be viewed as having several parts: (1) code for elaboration of the declarative part; (2) code for the sequence of statements; (3) code for exception handling; (4) code for deallocation of heap storage allocated for objects and access types declared in the declarative part; (5) code for completion of a master of tasks, including code for insuring that all dependent tasks are terminated; (6) code to transfer control from the unit. A more detailed description of the code for a declarative unit is given in Appendix C and in Baker and Riccardi (1983).

2 Task Types and Task Objects

The tasking supervisor must maintain information about each task object, for use in task scheduling and inter-task communication. This information is stored in the task control block (TCB) within the workspace of the task. Creation of a task entails allocation of a workspace and initialization of a TCB. This is discussed in detail in Riccardi and Baker (1984).

A task may be created by the elaboration of a task object declaration in a declarative part, or by an allocator. In both cases, the workspace allocated for the task is not taken from the workspace of the parent task (the one that causes it to be created), but is instead taken from a global pool. In order that the created task may be accessed from the parent task, a task pointer is allocated within the workspace of the parent task and set to the address of the child task's TCB. All references to a task are thus implicitly indirect, through this task pointer.

Ada declarations which describe the fields of the TCB which are relevant to this paper, as well as the other data structures and target system-dependent declarations used by the tasking supervisor, are included in Baker and Riccardi (1983). In order to simplify the supervisor, all list data structures are implemented using the package RINGS. A ring is a doubly linked circular list. One of the useful properties of a ring is that any node may be deleted from its ring without specifying which ring is involved. In fact, an attempt to delete an empty node (one which is not in a ring) does not change the node or any ring.

3 Task Execution

Execution of Ada tasks proceeds in parallel. Whenever more than one task is active on a single processor, that processor must be shared among the tasks. This implementation uses a time-slicing strategy to allocate the processor. The supervisor procedure DISPATCHER (see Riccardi and Baker 1984, Section 2) chooses a task to be the resident task and allocates a period of processor time to that task. Execution of the resident task continues until a call to the supervisor is made, either by the task itself or as a result of a hardware interrupt. At the conclusion of the supervisor call, the dispatcher is invoked. The resident task will be allowed to continue to the end of its time period unless a higher priority task has become ready for execution as a result of the supervisor call.

In order to implement time slicing and delays, we require a virtual interval timer and real time clock. The interval timer must be capable of interrupting an executing Ada task (but not necessarily the tasking supervisor). The timer and clock may be available directly in hardware or emulated by a host operating system. We also allow for the possibility of other interrupts, which may need to be treated as calls to entries in Ada tasks. These, too, may be hardware interrupts or virtual interrupts passed on from a host operating system.

The supervisor executes on the processor in a privileged mode called _supervisor mode_. While it may be interrupted, it must be allowed to complete its execution before any further execution of Ada tasks. If an interrupt occurs during the execution of a supervisor call, the interrupt handler may release an Ada task for execution. However, the execution of that task, no matter how high its priority, is delayed until the completion of the supervisor call. At this time, the dispatcher will be invoked and a highest priority task executed.

In order to simplify the supervisor, the processing of delays and the termination of time slices will be suspended while the processor is in supervisor mode. At the completion of the supervisor call, the dispatcher checks to see if the current time is later than the wake-up time of the first task in the delay queue. If so, the TIMER procedure is executed (see Section 5). It then checks to see if there is time left in the period of the resident task. In this way, if a timer interrupt was posted during the execution of the supervisor, it will be handled before the resident task is allowed to continue its execution.

4 Entries, Entry Calls, and Accept Statements

4.1 Entries

In our implementation, each entry of a task is represented by a variable that stores the address of the currently open accept statement for the entry (if any), and a queue of all the tasks that are waiting for the task to accept calls that have been made on the entry. For an entry family, there is an array of these accept statement addresses, known as the accept vector, and an array of queues, known as the entry queue vector, with an element of each array corresponding to each entry of the family. Since the index range of these arrays may be dynamic, they are allocated space in a variable-length part of the TCB of the task to which the entry family belongs, and addressed indirectly, via the entry family vector. In order that the same addressing mechanism can be used for both simple entries and entries that are members of families, each simple entry is treated as a member of an entry family with a single member. The implementation of selective waits requires that the accept vectors of all entry families of a task be zeroed out frequently. The accept vectors of all entry families are stored contiguously so that this operation may be done efficiently.

Each entry queue is either empty, indicating that there are no tasks waiting for calls on this entry to be accepted, or it is a ring of the tasks waiting for calls on the entry. The representation of entry queues as rings allows for efficient deletion from the queue,for example when a timed entry call is cancelled due to expiration of the delay. The tasks in this ring are linked via the field Q of each TCB.

4.2 Entry Calls

Consider the entry call "T.F(I)(arguments);" An entry call is similar to a procedure call in the way arguments are handled. The arguments of the entry call are evaluated in the same manner as those of a procedure call. If the type of T is an access to a task, the TCB_pointer is the value of T. If T is a task object, the TCB_pointer is found in the workspace of its parent task. This TCB_pointer, together with the family name F and the index expression I are passed as parameters to the supervisor procedure ENTRY_CALL (see Section 6.2). The CALL_STATUS parameter is passed the value SIMPLE. The calling task is suspended until the call has been accepted and the corresponding accept statement has been executed. When the calling task resumes execution, it restores the values of the arguments, as necesary.

4.3 Accept Statements

The execution of an accept statement for an entry begins by setting the accept vector element for the entry to the address of the code to perform the rendezvous. A supervisor call to SELECTIVE_WAIT will suspend the task until an entry call on the entry can be accepted. When a call is accepted, the supervisor will copy the arguments of the entry call and the TCB_pointer of the calling task into the local storage of the accept statement and release the accepting task. The sequence of statements of the accept statement will be executed. The parameters are referenced in the same way as parameters of a procedure. At the conclusion of the accept statement, the supervisor procedure END_RENDEZVOUS is called. It copies the parameters back to the workspace of the calling task and releases the calling task. (This procedure also completes either task participating in the rendezvous if it has become abnormal - see Section 7 of Riccardi and Baker 1984.)

An accept statement is treated like a declarative unit in that it has local declarations for the parameters of the entry and a sequence of statements. However, it can have no declarative part and no exception handler.

5 Delay Statements, Duration and Time

Delays, whether from delay statements or delay alternatives, are implemented by means of a single priority queue, ordered by increasing wake up times.Each task is represented at most once on this queue. (When there is more than one open delay alternative for a selective wait, an alternative with the minimum delay is chosen.) In our implementation, this queue is reresented as a doubly linked circular list, or ring. It is doubly linked so that deletions can be done efficiently from the middle, as when the delay for a timed entry call is cancelled because the call is accepted. The header of this queue is stored at address DELAY_Q in the supervisor's own memory.

The delay statement is implemented as the evaluation of the delay duration followed by a supervisor call to the procedure DELAY. The delay duration is passed as a parameter. Procedure DELAY is also used for selected wait statements and timed entry calls (see Section 6). The supervisor procedure TIMER is invoked from the DISPATCHER when the wake-up time for the head task on the delay queue has passed.

```
procedure DELAY(T: TCB_pointer; DELAY_DURATION: integer);
-- Arrange for task T to be delayed for the specified duration.
P,L: LINK;
```

```
begin
     T.WAKE_UP_TIME := CLOCK + DELAY_DURATION;
     T.DELAYED := true;
     T.READY := false;
     P := NEXT(DELAY_Q);
     L := PREV(P);
     while P /= L loop
          exit when TCB(P,D_offset).WAKEUP_TIME >
                    T.WAKE_UP_TIME;
          P := next(P);
     end loop;
     INSERT(T.D,P);
     DELAY_EXPIRATION :=
                    TCB(NEXT(DELAY_Q),D_offset).WAKE_UP_TIME;
end;
procedure TIMER;
-- Release all delayed tasks whose delays have expired.
T: TCB_pointer;
begin
     While not EMPTY(DELAY_Q) loop
          T := TCB(DELAY_Q.NXT,D_offset);
          exit when T.WAKE_UP_TIME < CLOCK;
          RELEASE(T); -- T is deleted from DELAY_Q.
     end loop;
     if EMPTY(DELAY_Q) then DELAY_EXPIRATION := ETERNITY;
     else DELAY_EXPIRATION :=
                    TCB(DELAY_Q.NXT,D_offset).WAKE_UP_TIME;
     end if;
end;
```

As mentioned earlier, we assume that there is a real-time clock available. The value, which is of type TIME, is denoted by CLOCK. We presently intend to represent CLOCK with a 32 bit integer. Description of the implementation of the package CALENDAR is omitted, since it is not relevant to tasking.

6 Select Statements

6.1 Selective Waits

The execution of a selective wait statement begins with the evaluation of the alternative conditions. For each open accept alternative, the entry index, if any, is evaluated and the corresponding ACCEPT_VECTOR element is assigned the address of the code for the accept statement, as already described in Section 3. For each open delay alternative, the delay duration is evaluated, and the minimum of these values is computed.

After all of the alternative conditions have been evaluated, and the minimum delay has been computed, the supervisor procedure SELECTIVE_WAIT is called. The minimum delay duration is passed as the parameter DELAY_DURATION and the address of the sequence of statements for the corresponding open delay alternative is passed as the parameter DELAY_LOCATION. The parameter SELECT_STATUS is passed the value:

DELAY,	if there is an open delay alternative;
TERMINATE,	if there is an open terminate alternative;
ELSE,	if there is an else part;
SIMPLE,	otherwise.

The supervisor call to SELECTIVE_WAIT is followed by the code for the sequence of statements of the else part, if there is one. Execution of the task will resume at the instruction following the supervisor call only if the else part is selected by the supervisor. Otherwise, execution of the task will resume at the beginning of the code for the alternative selected by the supervisor. Before resuming execution at an accept alternative, the supervisor will invoke procedure BEGIN_RENDEZVOUS, which engages the calling and accepting tasks, and copies the arguments of the entry call into local storage of the accepting task.

If there is an open delay alternative and no entry call can be accepted immediately, SELECTIVE_WAIT will invoke supervisor procedure DELAY to place the task on the delay queue. If no entry call is accepted within the specified duration, the supervisor procedure TIMER will zero the ACCEPT_VECTOR of the task, to ensure that no entry call will be subsequently accepted, and release the task (see Section 3 of Riccardi and Baker 1984). Execution of the task will resume at address T.STATE.BASE.PC, which has been set to the address of the code for the selected delay alternative. If an entry call is accepted within the specified duration, the task is removed from the delay queue.

If there is an open terminate alternative and no entry call can be accepted immediately, the supervisor procedure MAKE_PASSIVE is called to set the field PASSIVE of the task to true and report that the task is asleep (see Section 4 of Riccardi and Baker 1984). If an entry call is subsequently accepted, supervisor procedure WAKE_UP is called when the accepting task is released for execution of the rendezvous (see procedure RELEASE in Section 3 of Riccardi and Baker 1984). This procedure sets PASSIVE to false and reports that the task has been awakened.

The code for an accept alternative consists of (1) the code

for the sequence of statements of the accept statement, (2) a call to the supervisor procedure END_RENDEZVOUS, which copies the arguments of the entry call back into the workspace of the calling task and releases the calling task, (3) the code for the optional sequence of statements, and (4) a branch to the end of the selective wait statement. In the code for the sequence of statements, the parameters of the entry are addressed in the same way as parameters of procedures and functions.

An accept statement in Ada may contain accept or entry call statements. Hence, the fields IN_RENDEZVOUS and DISPATCHING_PRIORITY of the TCB must be saved as local values of the accept or entry call statement before the nested rendezvous may be begun, and restored at its end. This is accomplished in supervisor procedures BEGIN_RENDEZVOUS and END_RENDEZVOUS. The details of the method used to save and restore values from stacks are omitted. In addition, END_RENDEZVOUS participates in the aborting of tasks by completing abnormal tasks as required. (For a discussion of aborting tasks, see Section 6 of Riccardi and Baker 1984.)

```
procedure SELECTIVE_WAIT(SELECT_STATUS : STATUS_RANGE;
          DELAY_DURATION : TIME; ALTERNATIVE : ADDRESS) is
-- DELAY_LOCATION is the code address of the delay
-- alternative. The return address of the SVC is the address
-- of the code for the else part.
T: TCB_pointer renames RESIDENT_TASK;
C: TCB_POINTER := null; -- used when calling END_RENDEZVOUS
   open_accept:  boolean := false;
begin
     for I in 1 .. T.NUMBER_OF_ENTRIES loop
          if T.ACCEPT_VECTOR(I) /= 0 then
               OPEN_ACCEPT := true;
               if not EMPTY(T.ENTRY_QUEUE_VECTOR(I)) then
                    CALLED := true;
                    C :=

                       TCB(T.ENTRY_QUEUE_VECTOR(I).NXT,Q_offset)
                    T.STATE.BASE.PC := T.ACCEPT_VECTOR(I);
                    DELETE(C.Q);
                    DELETE(C,D);
                    BEGIN_RENDEZVOUS(T,C);
                    return;
               end if;
          end if;
     end loop;
     if SELECT_STATUS = ELSE then
          T.STATE.BASE.PC := ALTERNATIVE;
          T.ACCEPT_VECTOR(I) := (others => 0);
     else T.READY := false;
          if SELECT_STATUS = TERMINATE then
               MAKE_PASSIVE(T);
               T.WAITING_FOR_ACCEPT := true;
```

```
          elsif SELECT_STATUS = DELAY then
               T.STATE.PC := ALTERNATIVE;
               T.WAITING_FOR_ACCEPT := true;
               DELAY(T,DELAY_DURATION);
          elsif OPEN_ACCEPT then T.WAITING_FOR_ACCEPT := true;
          else raise(tasking_error,t);
          end if;
     end if;
end SELECTIVE_WAIT;

procedure BEGIN_RENDEZVOUS(A,C : TCB_POINTER) is
-- Sets the states of accepting task A and calling task C to
-- IN_RENDEZVOUS, places a pointer to C on the top of A's
-- stack, and zeroes out the elements of the ACCEPT_VECTOR of
-- task A.
begin
     push(A.IN_RENDEZVOUS,A);
     push (A.DISPATCHING_PRIORITY,A);
     push C.IN_RENDEZVOUS,C);
     push (C,A);
     A.IN_RENDEZVOUS := true;
     C.IN_RENDEZVOUS := true;
     A.WAITING_FOR_ACCEPT := false;
     A.ACCEPT_VECTOR := (others => 0);
     MOVE_PARAMS(C,A);
     A.DISPATCHING_PRIORITY := max(A.DISPATCHING_PRIORITY,
                                   C.DISPATCHING_PRIORITY);
     RELEASE(A);
end BEGIN_RENDEZVOUS;

procedure END_RENDEZVOUS(A : TCB_pointer) is
-- Terminates the rendezvous and restores the parameters to
-- task C. A is the accepting task and C is the calling task.
C: TCB_pointer; -- The calling task.
begin
C := pop(A);
A.IN_RENDEZVOUS := pop(A);
A.DISPATCHING_PRIORITY := pop(A);
C.IN_RENDEZVOUS := pop(C);
     C.STATE.BASE.PC := C.CALL_ADDRESS;
     MOVE_PARAMS(A,C);
     if A.ABNORMAL then
          if not A.IN_RENDEZVOUS then
               COMPLETE(A); TERMINATE(A);
          end if;
          RAISE(TASKING_ERROR,C);
     end if;
     if C.ABNORMAL and not C.IN_RENDEZVOUS then
          COMPLETE(C); TERMINATE(C);
     else RELEASE(C);
     end if;
end;

procedure MOVE_PARAMS(SOURCE,TARGET: TCB_pointer);
-- Moves the parameter list which is on the top of the stack
-- of task SOURCE to the top of the stack of task TARGET.
-- The body of MOVE_PARAMS is omitted.
```

6.2 Conditional Entry Calls

The evaluation of a conditional entry call begins with the evaluation of the arguments of the call. Two implicit parameters are added, the TCB_pointer of the task and the size of the parameter list. The TCB_pointer for the called task and the entry index are evaluated as in Section 3. The supervisor procedure ENTRY_CALL is called with the value ELSE for parameter CALL_STATUS. If the called task is waiting to accept an entry call to this entry and the corresponding ENTRY_QUEUE is empty, procedure BEGIN_RENDEZVOUS is called to engage the tasks and release the accepting (or called) task.

The parameter CONTINUATION supplies the location to return control after the the rendezvous is complete. If the entry call cannot be made immediately the task resumes its execution at the beginning of the code for the else part. In both the conditional entry call and the timed entry call (see Section 5.3), the statement after the SVC ENTRY_CALL is the beginning of the code to be executed if the entry call is not made, either because it cannot be made immediately, or in the case of a timed entry call, because the delay has expired.

```
procedure ENTRY_CALL(CALL_STATUS : CALLING_MODES;
                      A : TCB_POINTER;
                     F,I: integer; DELAY_DURATION : TIME;
           ALTERNATIVE : ADDRESS) is
-- Checks to see if an entry call to A.F(I) can be made. If
-- so, the rendezvous is begun. Otherwise, the appropriate
-- alternative action is taken, depending on CALL_STATUS.
-- ALTERNATIVE is the address of the sequence of statements
-- following the entry call for conditional and timed entry
-- calls.
T: TCB_pointer renames RESIDENT_TASK;
QUEUE : RING renames
        A.ENTRY_QUEUE_VECTOR(A.ENTRY_FAMILY_VECTOR(F) + I);
ENTRY_address : INTEGER :=
        A.ACCEPT_VECTOR(A.ENTRY_FAMILY_VECTOR(F) + I);
begin
    if not A.callable then RAISE(TASKING_ERROR,C);
    elsif ENTRY_address /= 0 and C.WAITING_FOR_ACCEPT then
      -- accept call.
        C.READY := false;
        C.CALL ADDRESS := C.STATE.BASE.PC;
        A.STATE.BASE.PC := ENTRY_address;
        BEGIN_RENDEZVOUS(A,C);
        RELEASE(A);
    else
        if CALL_STATUS = ELSE then
```

```
                    T.STATE.BASE.PC := ALTERNATIVE;
                    return;
                else -- Unconditional or timed entry call.
                    C.READY := false;
                    C.CALL_ADDRESS := ALTERNATIVE;
                    INSERT(C.Q,QUEUE);
                    if CALL_STATUS = TIMED  then
                        C.CALL_ADDRESS := C.STATE.BASE.PC;
                        C.STATE.BASE.PC := ALTERNATIVE;
                        DELAY(C,DELAY_DURATION);
                    end if;
                end if;
            end if;
        end ENTRY_CALL;
```

Note that the use of CONTINUATION here is the complement of the use of DELAY_LOCATION for select statements. That is, here CONTINUATION tells where to go if the rendezvous is made before the delay expires. For select statements, the DELAY_LOCATION tells where to continue if the rendezvous is *not* made before the delay expires.

6.3 Timed Entry Calls

Timed entry calls are executed similarly to conditional entry calls, above. The delay duration is evaluated and passed as an argument to ENTRY_CALL, and CALL_STATUS is passed the value TIMED. If no entry call can be made immediately, ENTRY_CALL calls DELAY to place the task into the delay queue for the specified duration. If an entry call is accepted during the specified duration, the task is removed from the delay queue. If no rendezvous is started within the given delay, procedure TIMER will remove the task from the entry queue, thereby cancelling the entry call, and release the task. Execution of the task will resume at the beginning of the code for the delay alternative, which immediately follows the supervisor call to ENTRY_CALL.

References

Ada (1979). Preliminary Ada Reference Manual, SIGPLAN Notices, v. *14*, no. 6.

Ada (1980). Reference Manual for the Ada Programming Language, Proposed Standard Document, United States Department of Defense.

Ada (1982). Reference Manual for the Ada Programming Language, Draft Revised MIL-STD 1815, Draft Proposed ANSI Standard Document. United States Department of Defense.

Ada (1983). Reference Manual for the Ada Programming Language, ANSI/Military Standard MIL-STD-1815A. United States Department of Defense.

Baker, T.P. & Riccardi, G.A. (1983). A Runtime Supervisor to Support Ada Tasking: Part 2 Rendezvous and Delays. FSU Ada Project Report 83-7.

Belz, F.C., Blum, E.K., & Heimbigner, D. (1980). A Multiprocessing Implementation-Oriented Formal Definition of Ada in SEMANOL. Proceedings of the ACM-SIGPLAN Conference on Ada, Boston, 202-212.

Clemmensen, G.B. (1982). A Formal Model of Distributed Ada Tasking. AdaTEC Conference on Ada, Arlington, Virginia, 224-237.

Falis, E. (1982). Design and Implementation in Ada of a Runtime Task Supervisor. AdaTEC Conference on Ada, Arlington, Virginia, 1-9.

Haberman, A.N. and Nassi, I.R. (1980). Efficient Implementation of Ada Tasks. Technical Report, Department of Computer Science, Carnegie-Melon University.

Hartig, H., Pfitzmann, A. & Treff, L. (1981). Task State Transitions in Ada. Ada Letters, v. 1, no. 1, 31-42.

Hilfinger, P.N. (1982). Implementation Strategies for Ada Tasking Idioms, AdaTEC Conference on Ada, Arlington, Virginia, 26-30.

Jones, A. & Ardo, A. (1982). Comparative Efficiency of Different Implementations of the Ada Rendezvous. AdaTEC Conference on Ada, Arlington, Virginia, 212-223.

Lovengreen, H.H. & Bjorner, D. (1980). On a Formal Model of the Tasking Concept in Ada, Proceedings of the ACM-SIGPLAN Symposium on Ada, Boston, 213-222.

Riccardi, G.A. & Baker, T.P. (1984). A Runtime Supervisor to Support Ada Tasking, Part 1, Activation, Execution and Termination. Proceedings of the Conference on Ada Applications and Environments, St. Paul, Minnesota.

Stevenson, D.R. (1980). Algorithms for translating Ada Multitasking, Proceedings of the ACM-SIGPLAN Symposium on Ada, Boston, 166-175.

THE ADA+ FRONT END AND CODE GENERATOR

M.R. Barbacci
Dept. of Computer Science, Carnegie-Mellon Univ., Pittsburgh, PA 15213

W.H. Maddox,
Dept. of Computer Science, Carnegie-Mellon Univ., Pittsburgh, PA 15213

T.D. Newton,
Dept. of Computer Science, Carnegie-Mellon Univ., Pittsburgh, PA 15213

R.G. Stockton,
Dept. of Computer Science, Carnegie-Mellon Univ., Pittsburgh, PA 15213

INTRODUCTION TO THE COMPILER

The Ada+ compiler is being written as a part of the SPICE project at Carnegie-Mellon University, and is intended eventually to be a full implementation of the Ada programming language. *(Ada is a registered trademark of the U.S. Government, Ada Joint Program Office.)* A preliminary version has been released within the university and runs on both the PERQ workstation and the Digital Equipment Corporation VAX, producing code for the PERQ under the Accent operating system (Rashid & Robertson, 1981). The goals of the Ada+ project are briefly described in (Barbacci et al., 1984); this paper deals with compilation issues alone.

The current version of the Ada+ compiler compiles a large subset of Ada. The major omissions are fixed point types and tasking. Also, as permitted by the language, the compiler disallows representation specifications and ignores most pragmas. With the exceptions mentioned above, the compiler implements all Ada data types, as well as generic units and most features of the separate compilation facility.

The compiler executes in four distinct phases: syntactic analysis, semantic analysis, post-semantic analysis, and code generation. These phases communicate through an internal representation of the source program which will be referred to as the *database*, and are fully separable. Each phase will be described in its own section, along with a description of the utilities upon which it depends.

The compiler consists of three programs: the Front End (syntactic and semantic analysis), the Middle End (post-semantic analysis), and the Back End (code generation). This allows the use of multiple code generators with a common Front End. The Middle End provides generic expansion services for any code generator which cares to take advantage of them.

The design of the Ada+ syntactic, semantic, and post-semantic phases was influenced by a desire for ease of implementation and maintainability. Ada is a very large language and thus affords plenty of opportunities for bugs to creep into a compiler. Factoring out the Ada features of overloading and generics into separate modules made the rest of the semantic analyzer easier to understand and to debug. In addition, it is fairly easy to locate the procedure(s) responsible for a particular section of the Language Reference Manual.

The design of the Ada+ code generator was influenced by a desire for simplicity and ease of implementation, as the implementors wished to begin coding exclusively in Ada as soon as possible. Furthermore, it was decided that a high-quality code generator would best be built after gaining some experience with Ada implementation. After studies of the Charrette compiler (Lamb et al., 1980) and the Ada BreadBoard (Wetherell, 1982), it was determined that the complex runtime descriptor schemes used by these compilers could be greatly simplified without unduly complicating other parts of the implementation. The resulting design borrows heavily from Charrette, but avoids retaining most type information at runtime.

THE DATABASE

The Ada+ database consists of the source program's syntax tree and collections of structures that describe various components of the program. It serves primarily as a communications medium; each phase of the compiler acts upon the database, modifies it, and passes it on to the next phase. The syntax phase reads the source program and produces the syntax tree. The semantic phase examines the syntax tree (completely ignoring the source code) and annotates it with information about the various types and objects which occur in the program. The post-semantic phase instantiates generic bodies and places the resulting instance bodies into the database. The code generator uses the database associated with a compilation unit to produce PERQ code files. The database also serves as an external communications medium for passing information to various tools in the Ada+ programming environment.

The database has three major components: nodes, symbol blocks, and type blocks. *Nodes* are the basic components of the syntax tree. Each node contains basic information about one production in the user's program, as well as references to the productions above and below it in the tree. *Symbol blocks* store general information about any Ada entity which may have an identifier, and are used as tokens to refer to the entity. For the sake of consistency, all anonymous types also have symbol blocks associated with them. Each identifier in the user program has a corresponding symbol block. *Type blocks* describe all Ada types as well as any Ada entity which may have a separate scope associated with it. These entities include subprograms, packages, and tasks as well as record and enumeration types. Each type block serves as a repository for information about the corresponding entity, as a root for the symbol table associated with the scope of the entity, and as a token to represent the entity.

The database utilities include facilities to create, modify, and manipulate all of the basic database structures, and to read and write the database from and to an external file.

THE FRONT END

Syntactic issues

Lexical analysis is an operation which is common to all compilers. Considerations of simplicity and flexibility influenced the choice of the scheme used in the Ada+ compiler. For each lexeme, a value and a lexical token are produced. If the lexeme is a numeric literal, the numeric value is computed and the token is assigned based on the type of the literal. If it is a special symbol, no value is computed and the token is assigned by case. If it is an identifier, the lexeme is entered in a hash table which yields (as a value) a pointer to the textual representation. Since each identifier occurs only once in the table, this pointer may also be used as a unique token representing the identifier. In addition, each slot in the hash table contains the value of the token which should correspond to the identifier. When the table is initialized, the slots containing reserved words are assigned corresponding tokens, and all others are assigned a special token which denotes simple identifiers. The token-value pair which this scheme produces provides all of the information required by the syntactic phase.

Syntactic analysis in Ada+ is done by recursive descent. Each production in the language is parsed by a different function which returns the corresponding syntax tree. Whenever an error is detected, lexemes are discarded until some member of a 'recovery' set is found. The recovery set, which is passed as a parameter to the function, is dynamically constructed such that the next routine will be in a reasonable place to continue. In addition, erroneous sections of the code are pruned from the syntax tree so that it always corresponds to a syntactically correct program which may safely be run through the semantic phase.

Symbol table utilities

The symbol table is organized as a set of *contexts*, each of which corresponds to a single scope in the user program. Each context consists of a ternary tree of symbol blocks. The key for this search tree is an arbitrary hash value which is computed by the lexical analyzer the first time a given identifier occurs. The key is used to direct the search down the left or right subtree. When multiple entities are declared with the same identifier (e.g. overloading), the corresponding symbol blocks are stored in the context as a linear list of symbols (the middle subtree). The contexts are organized in two different stacks. The first of these stores all contexts which are directly visible, and the second stores all contexts which are visible through **use** clauses.

The symbol table utilities provide the capability to enter symbols in the topmost (i.e. current) context, and to search either a single context or all visible contexts for either the first or all occurrences of a given identifier. When searching for multiple occurrences, these utilities dynamically determine which symbols are hidden and remove them from consideration.

Semantics

The semantics phase does an ordered walk over the tree created by the syntactic phase, annotating it with semantic information. Each production is handled by a specialized routine which takes the corresponding node as a parameter. The tree walk generally proceeds in a top-down, left-to-right fashion, although there are some exceptions. Scattered throughout the semantics code are calls to the overload resolution and generics modules, which are described in further detail below. As the compiler walks the tree, it creates type and symbol blocks to represent various Ada entities and leaves pointers to these blocks in the parse tree nodes.

If the compiler discovers a semantic error in the tree, it marks the offending node and all of its ancestors as being erroneous. Depending on which semantic routine discovered the error, the compiler may either attempt to continue semantic analysis (to try to find other errors) or simply give up on that branch of the tree. In either case, the compiler will never attempt to generate code for an erroneous compilation unit or attempt to enter it into the program library (by writing a database file).

Overload resolution

One challenging area of semantic analysis is overload resolution. Since all occurences of numeric or string literals, as well as aggregates and standard operators, are overloaded, most basic expressions will involve overloaded entities. Therefore, the compiler should be able to handle overloading efficiently in the typical case. In addition, it must be able to deal with such features as default and named parameters in subprogram calls, and the syntactic ambiguity between array references and function calls.

In the Ada+ compiler, the overload resolution facility consists of a library of subprograms which are called as necessary by the semantic phase, and a set of rules which determine the proper calling sequence. In all cases, overload resolution proceeds from the bottom up (i.e. returning to the root of the tree), with one of these routines being called for each node in the expression. The routine will first generate descriptions of all possible interpretations for the given identifier, and then examine each to determine whether it is consistent with any interpretations that exist in a lower level. If so, it stores descriptions of these lower level interpretations for later use. If not, it eliminates the given interpretation.

After all inconsistent interpretations have been eliminated, the routine will either store information about a single unique interpretation in the node, store descriptions of several valid interpretations, or signal an error if there are no valid interpretations. It can be shown that, at the top level, this scheme yields every valid interpretation and no invalid interpretations. A proof of this can be found in (Stockton, 1985), which describes the overload resolution facility in more detail.

Certain types of expressions, such as aggregates, allow a large enough set of interpretations that it becomes infeasible to generate all possible interpretations. In these cases, an empty list of interpretations is entered in the node, and routines from the next level are allowed to fill out this list. When this higher level routine wishes to interpret the node in a given way, this interpretation is then checked against the actual constraints on the expression type and is entered if they are satisfied. In the situations where this scheme is used, the constraints tend to be simple enough to make this feasible.

The ambiguity between array references and subprogram calls is resolved by the simple expedient of finding all valid interpretations under both assumptions. These sets of interpretations are then merged to produce one complete set of interpretations for the overall construct.

Generic units

Another challenging area of semantic analysis concerns generic units and their instantiations. Ada generics are safer to use than macros, but they are also harder to implement. Correctly binding names in generic units requires extra work during semantic analysis. The semantic analyzer must also enforce various special restrictions on the use of generic formal objects and types.

The Ada+ compiler performs semantic analysis on generic templates and propagates the results to their instantiations. At the heart of the generics facility in Ada+ is the idea that one can copy the attributed syntax trees representing a generic unit and customize the copies to produce the specification and body for each instance. Some analysis must be performed upon the resulting instances, but this scheme has definite advantages over ignoring the template and performing full semantic analysis upon each instance.

During the semantics phase, the compiler analyzes generic templates, matches generic formal and actual parameters, and copies specifications from generic templates to create specifications for their instances. The semantics phase only uses generic expansion to make instances visible; it leaves the choice of how to generate code for each instance up to later phases.

To detect circular instantiations and contract violations, the compiler keeps track of generic templates and their instantiations in the program library. Note that it may not be possible to detect an error in a compilation unit while compiling that unit -- in the following example, it is impossible for the compiler to detect the error in package BAR until it compiles the body of FOO.

```
generic
    type T is limited private;
package FOO is
    A : INTEGER;
end FOO;

package BAR is
    type UNCREC(DISC: INTEGER) is
        record
            Y : STRING(1..DISC);
        end record;
    --
    -- the contract violation is here
    package BAR is new FOO(UNCREC);
end BAR;

package body FOO is
    --
    -- can't detect error until we see this
    B : T;
begin
    null;
end;
```

A more complete description of the Ada+ generics facility can be found in (Newton, 1985).

Other semantic issues

There are other features of Ada that present special challenges for the implementor. These include aggregates, renaming, and private types.

Aggregates provide a convenient way of writing record and array values. Since the type of an aggregate must be determined purely from context, the semantic routine for aggregates may not be able to determine the aggregate's type. In this case, it returns without doing any work, and semantic analysis on the aggregate is deferred until the overload resolution routines determine the type of the aggregate. Once the compiler determines the type of the aggregate, the semantic analyzer determines the aggregate's subtype based on a large number of rules in the Language Reference Manual.

Renaming declarations allow programs to declare new names for any object, exception, package, or subprogram. This can be a problem when a renamed object is something like an array component which normally does not have a well-defined access path (as represented by an entry in the symbol table). In order to keep track of the semantic properties of a renamed object, the compiler sometimes needs to create symbol blocks that represent the operations of selecting record components, indexing arrays, slicing arrays, and dereferencing access values.

In order to support data encapsulation, Ada introduces the concept of limited and private types. Certain common operations are only available for non-private or non-limited types. The Ada+ compiler deals with these operations by making them visible at all times and checking the status (i.e. private/non-private, limited/non-limited) of the types during overload resolution. If the status is such that the given operation is unavailable, the corresponding interpretation is eliminated in the same manner as any other invalid interpretation. This scheme requires that the status of the type be checked frequently, so these checks should be made as efficient as possible. Ada+ achieves this by performing calculations at declaration time to determine exactly what tests will need to be performed for the type. With sufficient information about the type, it becomes possible to determine the status very easily in the most common case, even though the general case is fairly hard.

THE MIDDLE END

The post-semantic phase does an ordered walk over the annotated tree, looking for subtrees that represent generic instantiations. It copies the bodies of generic templates to create bodies for their instances, using many of the techniques and procedures that the semantics phase uses to copy specifications.

The main reason that generic bodies are not expanded in the Front End is that Ada allows the instantiation of generic units whose bodies have not yet been compiled. The hidden dependency between generic bodies and their instances is not allowed in any way to affect compilation order. Fortunately, the Ada definition of compilation (entering a unit into the program library) allows us to say that "compiling" a unit means running it through the Front End and that invoking the Middle End and Back End are "link-time" activities.

THE BACK END

The code generator operates in one left-to-right, top-to-bottom pass over the annotated parse tree produced by the first two phases, deferring examination of nested subprograms until code has been generated for the parent.

This section of the paper begins with a brief overview of the Ada+ runtime environment, then explores the representations chosen for the Ada data types and the effect of these choices on code generation. A more detailed discussion of these topics may be found in (Maddox, 1985).

Runtime organization

The PERQ instruction set (PERQ, 1984) is a stack-oriented architecture similar to UCSD P-Code (Sites & Perkins, 1979), but with extensions to support the extended PERQ Pascal language. In particular, exception-handling facilities suitable for implementing Ada exceptions are provided at the instruction-set level.

The Ada+ virtual machine is a superset of the PERQ Pascal virtual machine. The runtime environment of a PERQ Pascal program consists of a code segment for each separately compiled program unit, a stack segment, a global data area (allocated at the base of the stack segment), and a heap segment. To this Ada+ adds a second stack, referred to as the AStack, which provides storage for stack-allocated data objects of sizes unknown at compile-time. In addition, the AStack provides a convenient place to return the results of array- and record-valued functions. The pointer to the top of the AStack is held in a pseudo-register in memory, and is normally saved and restored on subprogram entry and exit.

The current Ada+ implementation does not retain most type information at runtime; it implicitly encoding it in the generated object code instead. Subtype (constraint) information must, however, be manipulated at runtime in the general case. Relieved of the need to interpret type descriptors, the runtime support library is reduced to a collection of short, independent routines implementing an extended instruction set.

Data representations

The representations chosen for the scalar and access types are conventional. The size of an object of any of these types is determined by the type, and is known at compile time. Only index constraints and discriminant constraints may depend on a discriminant or appear in an allocator. Thus every scalar subtype indication is uniquely associated with the actual constraint values over an activation of the containing block or subprogram. Scalar subtype constraints are implicitly declared as constants, which are statically associated with the objects they govern.

In general, the size of an array or record is not known at compile time. The required storage may vary widely with the values of the index or discriminant constraints. To allow efficient access to variables and record components, however, it is desirable to assign static displacements to the objects within a stack frame or within a record. Hence, the compiler uses an indirect representation, with a fixed-size *static part* serving as a placeholder, pointing to a dynamically-sized *dynamic part* elsewhere in memory. The pointer is actually an offset relative to the base of the static part, making it permissible to move such objects in memory, provided that both parts are displaced equally.

Like those of Charrette and the Ada BreadBoard, Ada+ objects are always represented in the same way independent of the context in which they appear. Thus code generation for the operations on an object need not be concerned whether the object is allocated on the stack, as a component of another object, or on the heap. This uniformity avoids much tedious case analysis, but often at the expense of some efficiency. In practice, a clever compiler could often determine that the constraints on a given array or record were static, in which case it could use a direct representation. The current Ada+ implementation forgoes this optimization in the interest of simplicity.

In addition to the pointer to the dynamic part, the static part of an array contains the dimensionality and, for each dimension, the bounds and multiplier. The components of the array are stored contiguously in the dynamic part, as shown in figure 1. The static part of a record contains the maximum dynamic part size, the actual size required by the current variant, the *layout number* for the current variant, and a flag indicating whether the record object is constrained. (The layout number indicates which components are valid given the current discriminants. A component selection may be checked in at most two comparisons, regardless of the number of nested variant parts in the record. Reference (Katwijk & Someren, 1984) explains this mechanism in detail.) The dynamic part of a record contains the static parts of all the components followed by their dynamic parts, as shown in figure 2. Discriminants are treated as ordinary components, and appear at the beginning of the dynamic part. The total storage allocated to the dynamic part of an unconstrained record is the largest required by any permissible set of discriminant values, as determined by the bounds on the discriminant subtype. A constrained record can never require more space than that required for its initial discriminants; thus its maximum size and allocated size are the same.

Operations on arrays and records

The equality and inequality tests on composite objects use a block comparison, after checking for compatible subtypes. Note that embedded constraint information, including array bounds and discriminants of subcomponents, must be equal for equal parent objects in a legal Ada program.

On assignment of a composite object, the dynamic part of the source object is copied into the dynamic part of the destination object, after the necessary constraint checks are performed. Additionally, an unconstrained record assignment requires that the actual size and layout number fields from the static part also be copied. If the new actual size of the destination is smaller than its previous size, the assignment code clears the remaining space within the destination, preserving the invariant that all unallocated words within an object contain a canonical value. This prevents block-comparisons of composite objects from being misled by invalid data at the tail of some unconstrained record subcomponent. (See (Lamb et al., 1980) for further discussion of this issue.)

Array and record parameters are always passed by reference. The presence of complete constraint information in every object makes handling unconstrained array and record parameters no more difficult than any other case. Returning the results of functions declared with an unconstrained result type is a well-known trouble spot in Ada implementation. In Ada+, the caller passes a pointer to a temporary location containing space for the static part of the result as an implicit **out** parameter. The called function fills in the static part with constraint information and a relative pointer to the dynamic part of the object which appears as the argument to the **return** statement. The function does not pop the AStack in the usual fashion; rather the caller does this after using the returned value.

Figure 1: Array object format

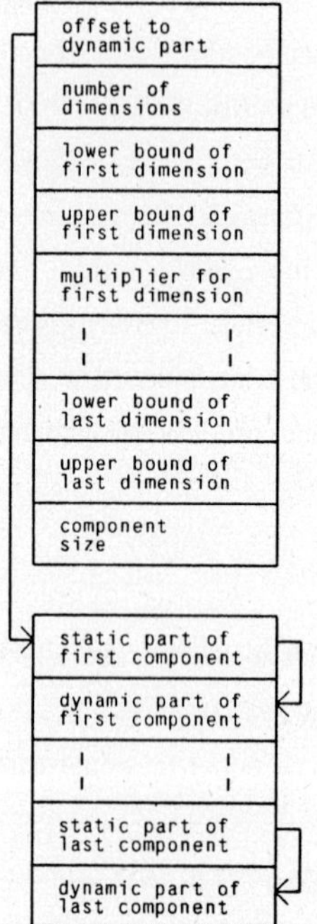

Figure 2: Record object format

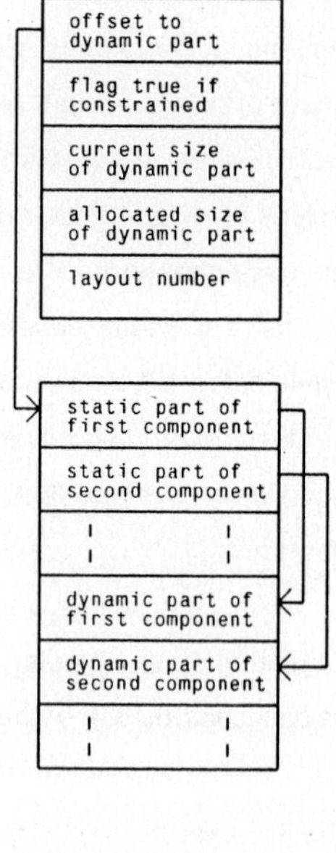

Object creation

Declared scalar and access objects are assigned static stack frame offsets in the conventional manner. The static parts of declared arrays and records are allocated in the same fashion. The dynamic parts are allocated on the AStack. The static parts of heap variables are allocated directly in the heap. The dynamic parts of heap records and arrays are created first on the AStack, and then copied to the heap after the size of the object has been determined. Initial values are assigned in exactly the same manner as an assignment statement, using the same code generation routines. (Array and record constants, initialized by aggregates, are treated somewhat differently.)

A novel feature of the Ada+ representations is the treatment of composite object creation. The dynamic part of a composite object is created as an implicit initialization. Elaboration of array declarations is performed by a combination of in-line code and calls to the runtime system routines *InitArray*, *AllocArray*, and *AllocIArray*.

Elaboration of a record declaration is performed by the initialization procedure for its type. The parameters to this procedure are the address of the static part, a flag indicating whether the record object is to be constrained (*IsConstrained*), a flag indicating whether default component initializations should be performed (*DoInit*), and the discriminant values, which are the default discriminants if the record is unconstrained.

Note that the size of all dynamically-allocated objects is computed as a side-effect of instantiating those objects. This makes it straightforward to express initialization of composite objects as a composition of their respective initialization code.

CONCLUSION

It may be seen from the descriptions above that the general design of the Ada+ system has been kept as simple and straightforward as possible. This has proven immensely useful in that it provides a simple framework for dealing with many of the difficult details involved in Ada semantics. The semantic areas mentioned above would have been much harder to implement if the compiler had attempted to use a more efficient or restrictive scheme. In addition, the separation of facilities tended to minimize interaction between various features and made it easier to produce correct code.

We have described a simplified runtime represention for Ada programs, as implemented by the Ada+ compiler. We believe that our experience may be of assistance to others undertaking the development of an Ada compiler with limited resources.

REFERENCES

Ball, J.E. et al. (1981). The Spice Project. In Computer Science Research Review 1980-1981, pp: 5-36. Department of Computer Science, Carnegie-Mellon University.

Barbacci, M.R. et al. (1984). The Spice Ada Compiler. Spice Document S162. Department of

Computer Science, Carnegie-Mellon University.

van Katwijk, J. & van Someren, J (1984). The Doublet Model. SIGPLAN Notices, 19, no. 1, 78-92.

Lamb, D.A et al. (1980). The Charrette Ada Compiler. Technical Report CMU-CS-80-148, Department of Computer Science, Carnegie-Mellon University.

Maddox, W.H. (1985). The Ada+ Code Generator. Spice Document. Department of Computer Science, Carnegie-Mellon University.

Newton, T.D. (1985). Generics Facilities in the Ada+ Compiler. Spice Document. Department of Computer Science, Carnegie-Mellon University.

PERQ Systems Corporation (1984). Pasal/C Machine Reference. 2600 Liberty Ave., Pittsburgh, PA 15230: PERQ Systems Corporation.

Rashid, R.F. & Robertson, G.G. (1981). Accent: A communication oriented network operating system kernel. In Proceedings of the Eighth Symposium on Operating System Principles, 64-75.

Sites, R.L. & Perkins, D.R. (1979). Universal P-Code Definition, Version [0.2]. Technical Report UCSD/CS-78/029. Department of Applied Physics and Information Science, University of California at San Diego.

Stockton, R.G. (1985). OverLoad Resolution in Ada+. Spice Document. Department of Computer Science, Carnegie-Mellon University.

Wetherell, C.S. (1982). The Ada BreadBoard Compiler: An Overview. Technical Memorandum TM 82-45412-13. AT&T Bell Laboratories.

THE ALS ADA COMPILER GLOBAL OPTIMIZER

D. A. Taffs
SofTech Inc., Middletown RI, USA

M. W. Taffs
SofTech Inc., Middletown RI, USA

J. C. Rienzo
SofTech Inc., Middletown RI, USA

T. R. Hampson
SofTech Inc., Middletown RI, USA

INTRODUCTION

The Ada™ language was designed to allow programs to be optimized in order to improve their efficiency. For this reason the language definition specifically allows implementations freedom to choose from a range of alternative semantic effects of a program. Programmers should be aware of these possibilities in order to avoid erroneous or incorrect programs. This paper presents the design of the Global Optimizer in the Ada compiler component of the SofTech Ada Language System (ALS), and discusses the optimizations performed and how the optimizer design deals with the language issues involved. Programming guidelines are provided for best use of the optimizer.

OVERVIEW OF THE COMPILER

The ALS compiler consists of a Front End, the TR1 phase, the Global Optimizer, and the Back End. The Front End converts an Ada compilation unit into DIANA and performs static semantic checking. The TR1 phase next translates the DIANA into a lower-level tree representation called the Translated Tree, which makes the dynamic semantics of the program explicit. The Translated Tree is then optionally passed through the Global Optimizer, which performs optimizations by modifying the tree structure and adding additional information. The output of the Global Optimizer (or TR1 if the optimizer is not requested) is finally passed through the Back End of the compiler, which allocates storage and generates machine instructions.

The Front End of the compiler is target independent, with the exception of two TR1 packages that deal with implementation-

This work was supported by US Army CECOM Contract No. DAAK80-80-C-0507.

predefined types. TR1 is basically target independent, with a few specific and isolated target dependencies. These include SYSTEM.ADDRESS and SYSTEM.STORAGE_UNIT, predefined numeric types, representation clauses, implementation-defined PRAGMAs and attributes, and the algorithm for aligning record and array components. In addition, different targets may choose to alter the strategy used by TR1 for elaboration checks or for filling in addressing expressions (called chainbacks) on storage references (for example, using a hardware display instead of individual static links, or providing a base expression if needed to address literals or global static data). Since the Translated Tree represents target-dependent information in a target-independent format, these changes have minimal impact on the Global Optimizer. Although target dependent, the Back End of the compiler can be readily adapted to other target machines.

The Global Optimizer is target independent except for three well isolated exceptions. In order to perform correct bounds analysis, the optimizer must be able to round floating point values to model numbers, and so attributes of the predefined floating point types (not currently available from TR1) are required. Since the optimizer creates references to objects, the optimizer must use the same chainback scheme as TR1 to provide addressing. (It is planned to eliminate these target dependencies in the future by adding the needed information to the Translated Tree.) The third target dependency is the setting of a four-state architecture model parameter used to adapt the optimizer to the target's indexing hardware (if any). This parameter influences the specific tradeoff point for deciding which addressing expressions are complex enough to be worth making into common subexpressions or loop invariants.

The Translated Tree is an explicit, low level representation of the dynamic semantics of the Ada program. Complex Ada constructs are broken down into smaller "basic operations" which can be optimized independently. Each node of the Translated Tree corresponds to a machine instruction for a virtual Ada target machine with a conventional stack architecure. The order of evaluation of each operation is fully determined, but may be changed by later phases if they can determine that the effect is the same. TR1 expands tasking constructs and delay statements into target-independent Runtime Support Library (RSL) calls. The optimizer must understand the RSL conventions in order to process entry parameters, ACCEPT statements, and various task descriptors correctly. An interface with the ALS debugger is defined such that users may be warned when assignment to a variable by the debugger might violate an assumption made by the optimizer. Similarly, users may be warned when displaying a variable whose value might not be correct because of dead assignment elimination.

ALLOWABLE OPTIMIZATIONS

The Ada language specifically allows a compiler to perform certain optimizations that the programmer must consider. For example, if the optimizer decides that the result of a predefined operation is not needed (it might be multiplied by zero or part of a dead assignment), Ada allows the operation to be removed (even if it raises an exception, such as a qualified expression or division by zero). The programmer must be careful to not depend on exceptions from such operations. If the optimizer changes a program in an unanticipated way, the programmer's analysis is thwarted and the program may not do what was intended. Programmers must be especially careful of the assumptions made by the optimizer when interfacing with machine language code or microcode.

Ada allows the optimizer to reorder actions involving predefined operators and basic operations except assignment, as long as the operation would always be invoked in the absence of predefined exceptions propagated by predefined operations. Extraction of loop invariants is therefore prohibited after a subprogram call that might propagate an exception, after an EXIT statement, or inside an IF or CASE statement. The optimizer is not required to prove termination of intervening loops and subprogram calls. Additional optimizations may be performed if they don't change the "effect" of non-erroneous programs, other than the allowed reordering, removal, or introduction of predefined exceptions. The optimizer may change an erroneous program arbitrarily, including raising PROGRAM_ERROR or performing unsafe optimizations.

Ada defines two parameter mechanisms, "by copy" and "by reference". A programmer must assume that any composite parameter may be passed either way, or else the program is erroneous. Since the compiler assumes that the program is not erroneous, it can assume that the programmer does not rely in any way upon aliasing effects of reference parameters. The programmer must be aware that the compiler assumes that the program is not erroneous. This allows the optimizer to treat all parameters as if they are passed by copy, even if they are actually passed by reference. The optimizer can thus perform full optimizations on uses and assignments of reference parameters, just as if they were copy parameters (which are treated like local variables). Any problems caused by reference parameter aliasing are the programmer's, not the optimizer's.

OPTIMIZATIONS PERFORMED

The Global Optimizer performs the following optimizations whenever it can, except for common subexpressions and loop invariants that are deemed too simple to benefit from the optimization. The contents of the database (discussed in the next section) determine whether an optimization is applicable in any given situation. Since one of the major benefits of performing an optimization is to enable subsequent optimizations, the optimizer is careful to systematically apply every optimization possible. It should be noted that the TR1 phase also performs significant local optimizations, particularly constant propagation and folding. Since TR1 is always executed and the optimizer is optional, TR1 can perform certain optimizations that the Global Optimizer cannot (such as removal of constant declarations visible outside the current compilation unit).

The optimizer performs constant propagation by replacing a reference to an object by a literal representing the value of the object. It keeps a database of objects with known values, which is updated at each assignment. At each reference to an object, it looks in the database to see if the object has a known value. If so, it replaces the reference with the value. As defined here, constant propagation deals only with objects, as distinguished from general and special case folding, which deal only with operations.

General case folding involves evaluating expressions all of whose operands are known at compile time. The optimizer replaces the operation with its result (or a predefined exception). This optimization is uniformly applied to addition, subtraction, multiplication, division, exponentiation, ABS, MOD, REM, the relational operators, and scalar AND, OR, XOR, and NOT.

In some cases, only one operand of a binary operator is needed to optimize the expression. This is called special case folding, and involves replacing the expression with one of its operands, a literal value, or a predefined exception. This optimization is applied to all scalar boolean operations with a literal operand (except XOR by TRUE, but including AND THEN and OR ELSE). It is also applied if an operand is zero for addition or subtraction, or if an operand is zero or one for multiplication, division, exponentiation, MOD, and REM.

Subsumption is the replacement of a reference to an object by a reference to another object with the same value. This may allow simpler addressing, or complete removal of the declaration and initialization of the unused object.

Bounds analysis is performed for objects, values, and expressions. Bounds for objects are computed using the declared subtype of the object, the bounds of expressions assigned to the object, and relational assertions maintained in the database (see below). Separate mechanisms are used to keep track of the current bounds of an object and bounds that apply over the object's entire lifetime. Lifetime bounds are maintained to allow better storage allocation by the Back End (for example, putting a 16-bit object in an 8-bit register). Rounding up and down to model numbers is required for floating point bounds calculations. Floating point literals are rounded to the nearest number implemented by the target, so that the value assumed by bounds analysis will be consistent with the number actually used by the code generator. Floating point bounds are not calculated unless explicit constraints apply.

Bounds for expressions are stored directly in the Translated Tree, in order to allow the code generator to generate better code (for example, doing 16-bit arithmetic on 32-bit objects). In general, they are computed by applying the operator to the bounds of the operands. This is straightforward for addition, subtraction, ABS, and numeric conversions. Bounds calculations for the MOD operator use only the bounds of the divisor. Other operators are more complex. For multiplication, division, and REM, the bounds of the operands are used to determine which of a number of cases applies. There are 21 separate cases to calculate the bounds for the division operator. As a typical example, in the expression X / Y where X and Y are integers that may be positive or negative, and X has bounds available, then the expression is bounded by plus or minus the absolute value of the larger bound of X (unless it is a fixed point division, which can round the result differently). Multiplication and REM each have 9 different cases. Exponentiation is particularly complex with 30 cases. In the (very infrequent) worst case for floating point exponentiation, the optimizer performs 16 exponentiations, each of which is performed by repeated multiplications, rounding to model numbers at each step. To conserve compile time, the optimizer does not calculate exponentiation bounds if the exponent is outside the range -200 .. 200.

Relation analysis is used along with bounds analysis to determine the results of relational operators and eliminate constraint checks and unreachable case alternatives. Relation analysis is also used to help determine the bounds of objects. To do this, assertions are added to the database at constraint checks, allowing removal of subsequent redundant checks. Assertions are added to the database for simple IF conditions, which are known to be true in the THEN part and false in the ELSE part. Relation analysis applies to equality also, allowing removal of checks for null pointers.

IF and CASE statements are optimized away if the control path is known at compile time. Unreachable code is removed by the optimizer after RETURN, EXIT, GOTO, RAISE, LOOP, IF, and CASE statements that do not flow through.

Common subexpressions are eliminated when the optimizer recognizes that an adequately complex expression is recomputed where the resulting value is already available. They often occur for addressing calculations which are invisible at the source code level and as a result of INLINE subprograms, in addition to redundant source language expressions. Common subexpression elimination may occur for objects with non-trivial addressing (such as A(I) and P.all) as well as for expressions. A value numbering scheme is used to determine the commonality of subexpressions. Commutativity rules are used to recognize simple reordering of expressions. For common subexpression elimination, the optimizer declares an object to hold the value of a scalar or access expression that is used more than once, and initializes the object at the first computation of the expression. Subsequent computations of the expression are replaced by references to the object. Lifetime and object usage analysis (see below) can be used to reduce the incremental performance cost of declaring the additional object.

Loop invariants are extracted if no referenced object is modified directly or indirectly anywhere inside the loop, and if the expression is invoked every time through the loop. An assignment statement to a compiler-declared object is placed just before the loop, and the expression is replaced by a reference to the object. Loop invariants are processed in the context of their parent expressions, such that only the largest invariant expressions are moved out of a loop, without requiring object declarations for the subexpressions. Ada disallows extraction of assignment statements from loops.

Dead assignments, which assign to a local variable whose value is not used later, are deleted. Any object declaration that is not used is removed.

WHAT THE OPTIMIZER DOES

The Global Optimizer consists of four sequential phases. The Data Collection Phase first collects side-effect information, so that the direct effects of subprogram calls and loops will be known to later optimization phases. The Interprocedural Analysis Phase next calculates the indirect side effects of subprogram calls and loops, so that their entire effect is known. The Forward Optimization Phase then performs optimizations using information propagated in the forward direction in the tree. Finally the Backward Optimization Phase performs optimizations propagating information in the backward direction.

TR1 restructures WHILE loops so that the termination check occurs at the bottom, surrounding the loop with an IF statement and duplicating the WHILE condition. This provides the optimizer with a place to move loop invariants, and allows removal of the unconditional branch instruction at the bottom of each WHILE loop. This also limits the "loop-connectedness" parameter of the flow graph of structured Ada programs (i.e. those without backward GOTOs) to one, allowing information propagation problems to completely converge with two passes [Hecht 1977]. Thus, ignoring interactions among optimizations, the phase structure of the optimizer is optimal for such programs. For performance reasons, the information needed by the Backwards Optimization Phase is collected during Data Collection, rather than being recomputed during the forward optimizations (which would require another transitive closure). Because of the optimizations performed by the TR1 phase, the penalty for this is small.

The Data Collection Phase walks the Translated Tree, creating imports lists of nonlocal objects used or modified directly within each subprogram body and loop. A sparse matrix representing the subprogram call graph is also constructed, including a list of subprograms called from within each loop. The maximum (innermost) scope level of any external subprogram called is also maintained. An external subprogram (whose body is separately compiled) is assumed to use every object and alter every variable within whose scope it occurs. A given imports list (or call subgraph) only contains items whose scope is between that of any external subprogram called directly or indirectly and that of the subprogram or loop itself. The Data Collection Phase performs additonal minor bookkeeping, such as classifying GOTOs and labels.

The Interprocedural Analysis Phase performs a transitive closure on the call graph, and then propagates the used and modified information from each called subprogram to its caller. At the end of Interprocedural Analysis, the worst possible side effects of every subprogram body and loop are available, including the effects of indirect subprogram calls. The transitive closure algorithm keeps track of the outermost scope level on each call path, which is used to limit the side effects propagated along that path. Objects imported directly into a task body or imported into a subprogram directly or indirectly called by a non-enclosing task body are marked as shared.

The Forward Optimization Phase performs an execution order walk on the Translated Tree, keeping a layered database representing the current state of program execution for each object seen so far. As the tree is walked, the database is updated and referenced as needed. The optimizations performed during this forward pass are constant propagation, general and special case folding, subsumption, relation and bounds analysis, unreachable code deletion, common subexpression elimination, and loop invariant extraction. These optimizations are reflected directly as structural modifications of the Translated Tree. The database keeps track of value numbers, available expressions, object bindings and bounds, and true assertions. At a structured control fork (such as an IF or CASE), the current database is frozen and a new layer is pushed on top to represent changes inside the fork. At the end of a branch (e.g. at the ELSE), the topmost layer is saved, and the database is restored to what it was at the fork. At the control join point (the

END IF) the information from the alternatives is merged. At the top of a LOOP the worst-case side effects of the loop are reflected in the database. Side effect information from EXIT statements is collected, and reflected when the tree traversal gets to the bottom of the loop. Forward GOTOs and labels are handled by keeping lists of side effects and propagating them appropriately. Backward GOTOs are handled by reflecting a worst-case situation in the database at the label. At an external subprogram call, where the body is not available for analysis, every variable whose scope extends outside the current compilation unit or that has been marked shared is assumed to be modified. Since any call to the RSL is an external call, this mechanism works for synchronization points as well. At a call where the subprogram body is available, its side effects are reflected in the database. At an exception handler, the database is first restored to its state at the BEGIN, and then all possible side effects from the statement part are reflected.

The Backward Optimization Phase is the conceptual dual of the Forward Optimization Phase. The Translated Tree is traversed in exactly the reverse order, but everything else is fundamentally the same except for implementation details. The database keeps track of modifications and uses of objects. Dead assignments and unused declarations are deleted, and usage information is collected about each object to help the Back End generate efficient code. At each use and assignment of an object, the distance to the next use of the object and a use count are stored. The use count is the number of subsequent uses of the value, weighted heavily by loop nesting level if TIME is specified by the OPTIMIZE pragma (or a maintenance flag). Use count, weighted if time is being optimized, and next use information is also provided at the top of each loop, allowing initial register allocation for the entire loop to be performed at the top. At each assignment, a "Zombie" bit indicates whether or not the object's canonical location needs to be updated. If set, the Zombie bit indicates that the object (i.e. its canonical location) is dead, but the value of the object is live. This allows the store instruction to be omitted if the code generator can remember the value in a register. (Zombies should not be live across calls if the target machine does not save registers. This may become an additional architecture parameter.)

The Backward Optimization Phase also stores lifetime information for objects, so that the Back End can allocate multiple objects to the same memory location or register if their lifetimes do not overlap. Separate use counts and weighted use counts are also collected on object declarations to indicate how often each object is used (and used in deeply nested loops). An Always_Zombie bit tells whether an object may always float among registers and local temporary locations, as opposed to requiring a canonical location, which it does if there are up-level references to it, or if a subcomponent of it is referenced.

HINTS FOR USING THE OPTIMIZER

The optimizer makes certain assumptions, primarily dealing with scope rules. Unchecked conversion to an access type must not create aliases for other objects known to the compiler, and the designated object must obey the Ada scope rules for the collection (e.g. if the access type is declared local to a subprogram, the designated object will be considered local to the subprogram, and therefore dead at the return). Subprograms are assumed to not use or modify any object (except parameters) whose scope does not include the subprogram body. If an object is shared between tasks but PRAGMA SHARED does not apply, the optimizer assumes that it is local to the current task except at synchronization points. No optimizations are performed on objects with either PRAGMA SHARED or address representation clauses. Machine code insertions are assumed to have no effect whatsoever, and so programmers must be careful that assignment statements and objects needed by the machine code are not optimized away.

The optimizer performs optimizations based on the information available to it and the restrictions that the Ada language imposes on it. More optimizations may be made possible by judicious use of Ada features. A few ways to do this are described below.

Declare objects as constants wherever possible, especially in a library package specification or body, and use IN parameters instead of IN OUT parameters. Constrain discriminated objects where possible. Use scalar constraints judiciously to exploit bounds analysis. Local objects can be optimized better than global objects. The optimizer assumes that variables declared in a package body obey the same scope rules as those in the package specification, because subprograms in the package body may modify the variables independently.

Avoid separate compilation. Since other compilation units are not available for analysis by the compiler, the optimizer must assume that they contain tasks and modify every possible variable. Programmers may want to replace stubs with the subunit bodies to achieve maximum possible compiler optimization, although this may reduce opportunities for optimizations performed by the linker or by an overlay mechanism.

Use WHILE LOOPs instead of LOOPs with EXITs. Do not put loop invariant expressions inside IF or CASE statements, or after EXITs. Put subprogram calls at the bottom of a LOOP, rather than at the top.

Avoid the use of GOTO statements whenever possible. The presence of GOTOs, especially those that branch backwards, cause fewer optimizations to be performed. The presence of unreferenced labels does not affect optimization.

PERFORMANCE RESULTS

The areas of interest when evaluating the performance of an optimizer are the decrease in execution time of an optimized program, the decrease in its object code size, and the increase in compile time when the optimizer is run. Each of these depends somewhat on the nature of the program being optimized. In general, the larger the program, the better the optimizer's performance. Typically, using the optimizer increases compile time by 15-20%. Object code size savings tend to be in the 10-20% range, although one quicksort procedure had its object code reduced by 46%. Currently, few realistic execution time statistics are available. The optimizer did, however, decrease execution time by 38% on a matrix multiplication program.

CONCLUSION

This optimizer design shows how a high-performance target-independent optimizer can be constructed for the Ada language. Ada programmers need to be aware of the kinds of optimizations which may be performed in order to take full advantage of the optimizer. The ALS Global Optimizer provides a wide variety of space and time optimizations in a cost effective manner, making it an effective tool for use in the development of military and commercial applications.

REFERENCES

Cocke, J. and Schwartz, J. T. (1970). Programming Languages and Their Compilers. New York: Courant Institute of Mathematical Sciences.

Evans, Arthur, Jr. and Butler, Kenneth J. (1983). DIANA Reference Manual. Pittsburgh: Tartan Laboratories, Inc.

Freiburghouse, R. A. (1974). Register Allocation Via Usage Counts. Communications of the ACM, 17, no. 11, pp. 638-642.

Gries, David (1971). Compiler Construction for Digital Computers. New York: John Wiley and Sons.

Hecht, Mathew S. (1977). Flow Analysis of Computer Programs. New York: North-Holland.

Ichbiah, Jean et al. (1983). Reference Manual for the Ada Programming Language. United States Department of Defense.

Wulf, William et al. (1975). The Design of an Optimizing Compiler. New York: Elsevier North-Holland.